Date Due

FE 16 '98			

Southern Strategies

Southern Women and the Woman Suffrage Question

Southern Strategies

Elna C. Green

The University of North Carolina Press

Chapel Hill & London

Strategies

Manufactured in the United States of America

The paper in this book meets the guidelines for permanence and durability of the Committee on Production Guidelines for Book Longevity of the Council on Library Resources.

Library of Congress Cataloging-in-Publication Data
Green, Elna C.
Southern strategies : southern women and the woman suffrage question / by Elna C. Green.
p. cm.
Includes bibliographical references and index.
ISBN 0-8078-2332-5 (cloth : alk. paper). — ISBN 0-8078-4641-4 (pbk. : alk. paper)
1. Women—Suffrage—Southern States—History—Public opinion.
2. Public opinion—Southern States—History. I. Title.
JK1896.G66 1997
324.6'23'0975—dc21 96-36992
CIP

01 00 99 98 97 5 4 3 2 1

Portions of this work appeared earlier in somewhat different form in "Those Opposed: Antisuffragists in North Carolina, 1900–1920," *North Carolina Historical Review* 67, no. 3 (July 1990): 315–33; "The Rest of the Story: Kate Gordon and the Opposition to the Nineteenth Amendment in the South," *Louisiana History* 33, no. 2 (Spring 1992): 171–89; and "'Ideals of Government, of Home, and of Women'; The Ideology of Southern White Antisuffragism," in *Hidden Histories of Women in the New South*, ed. Virginia Bernhard et al. (Columbia: University of Missouri Press, 1994), 96–113, and are reproduced here by permission of the publishers.

To the memory of my father,

GILMER G. GREEN JR.,

who bought me my first history book

CONTENTS

ILLUSTRATIONS

PREFACE

Before another century has elapsed, the suffragist and her friend the anti, will have passed into history; the struggle for sex equality will have been won and the new generation will have new problems to confront it.

But when some historian writes of the present age of the women who helped lift humanity one step higher by lifting womanhood to a level of human equality, let the services of the antis, who furnished the antagonism on which all progress thrives, be fittingly commemorated.

—Pattie Ruffner Jacobs, 1916

As an undergraduate doing a research paper on the suffrage movement in North Carolina, I was surprised to find that a woman surfaced as the most prominent leader of the antisuffragists in my home state. I had assumed that all women would naturally desire their own enfranchisement, and it had never occurred to me that women might actually organize to prevent the adoption of such a reform. (The obvious parallel, that Phyllis Schafley appeared almost nightly on the evening news as the most prominent opponent of the ERA, under consideration at the same time I wrote that seminar paper, seemed not to have occurred to me then.)

I remained intrigued by the paradox of female antifeminists and pursued that interest as a dissertation. I began with some very simple questions: who were these women who opposed their own enfranchisement, and why did they do so? But the search for answers led instead to more complicated questions: What social and economic class in the New South opposed the enfranchisement of women? What did the various interest groups that made up the antisuffrage coalition believe they had to fear from woman suffrage? Why did some educated middle-class white women organize against the Nineteenth Amendment while other educated middle-class white women organized in its behalf?

Having become convinced that antisuffragists in fact were not the same "educated middle-class white women" as the suffragists, I chose to use a comparative prosopography in order to identify and describe the economic and political interests involved in the antisuffrage movement. By comparing antisuffrage activists to their suffrage opponents, I hoped to highlight the differences between the two groups. This methodology, however, meant that the suffragists themselves became an important part of this analysis. Originally envisioned as nothing more than a "control group" providing a base for comparison, the suffragists soon moved to the center of the story as I concluded that the two movements must be interpreted together. Suffragists and antisuffragists were locked in something resembling an organizational ping-pong game, with each action of one group requiring a response by the other. To understand completely the strategies and activities of the antisuffragists, one must look simultaneously at the activities of their opponents. Likewise I contend that one cannot understand suffrage ideology and its evolution over the years without considering that suffragists often acted in response to new initiatives of the "antis."

Moreover, as the suffragists kept pushing themselves into my vision, I felt compelled to consider more carefully the varieties of southern suffragism, including those suffragists who demanded a states' rights approach to enfranchisement as well as those who aligned with the "militants," the Congressional Union/National Woman's Party. In short, although I had not intended to do so, I found myself writing a larger history of southern women and their varied responses to the woman suffrage question. I have come to conclude that the range of southern suffragism is an important observation in and of itself. Historians have generally neglected to recognize the rich variety of opinions that the New South could propagate.

I am not, of course, the only historian interested in southern suffragism; recent years have seen a small explosion of literature in this field. One of the principal concerns of these historians has been the role of race and racism in shaping the suffrage movement in the South. Central to the following interpretation of the southern suffrage movement is the rejection of racism as the major impetus for southern suffragism. I contend that southern white women did not band together and work for ten or twenty (or more) years to obtain the ballot in order to outvote their black neighbors.[1] Instead, southern white women came to the suffrage movement in much the same way northern women did. Suffragism moved south of the Mason-Dixon line only after the New South had generated a critical mass of industrial and urban problems around which reform-minded southern women could organize, and had produced urban centers with sufficient numbers of middle-class women willing to join reform movements. After years of higher education, paid work, voluntary associations, and participation in reform movements that pitted them against the powerful forces of industrial capitalism, southern middle-class white women came to demand the vote for themselves and for working-class women as both a means to an end and an end in itself. Like their northeastern counterparts, southern suffragists were both a product of and a response to the urbanization and industrialization of the American economy and society.[2]

As Jacquelyn Hall wrote nearly twenty years ago, southern suffragists responded to issues of race and gender with a range of beliefs.[3] From the virulent racism of Kate Gordon, to the more genteel racism of Laura Clay, to the racial moderation of Gertrude Weil, to the racial liberalism of Mary Johnston, southern suffragists shared no uniformity of opinion on race relations. While some suffragists saw no contradiction in advocating both woman suffrage and white supremacy, others squirmed uncomfortably at the racist language of their coworkers.[4] Nor were southern suffragists any more monolithic in their views about gender. While Lila Meade Valentine issued denunciations of militancy, her fellow Virginians Pauline Adams and Maud Jamison were picketing the White House.

With this interpretive background in mind, I will then turn to focus more intensively on the antisuffragists. Three chapters will examine the constituency, the rhetoric and ideology, and the organizational activity of the southern antisuffrage movement. Understanding exactly who opposed woman suffrage helps to explain why they took the position they did. Similarly, knowing the social/economic characteristics of the participants helps to explain their approach to organizing a small, but powerful, countermovement.

Next, this account of southern women and the suffrage question considers the "states' rights" faction of the southern suffrage movement. The states' rights suffragists have caused much difficulty in past efforts to analyze the southern suffrage movement as a whole, as scholars have grappled with a movement that contained such contrary elements as Kate Gordon and Mary Johnston. The states' rights faction will be presented here as a completely separate movement from the mainstream suffrage effort: I contend that the states' rights suffragists were a minority group that ultimately failed to win over the majority of southern suffragists. As a separate movement, the states' rights faction created a three-way contest in the South, which meant that success would go to which ever end of the spectrum (the "ratificationists" versus the antisuffragists) won the allegiance of the states' rights group in the middle. As opponents of the federal woman suffrage amendment, the states' rights suffragists effectively became allies of the antisuffragists at certain critical points in the suffrage contests.

Finally, a state case study will put the preceding pieces together and tell the story of the suffrage contest in Virginia. Moderates, militants, states' rights suffragists, and antisuffragists will all defend their positions and will appeal to the public for support. They will lobby their legislators and will maneuver behind the scenes in the excitement of a state ratification campaign. Virginia makes for a good drama, for it had a large suffrage organization, smaller dissenting factions of suffragists, and an antisuffrage movement that was unusually large and well organized.

From the outset, it should be made clear that individual women, both pro- and antisuffrage, are considered here to be members of social classes, the boundaries of which are generally defined by position in the economic structure. The prominence of women in the antisuffrage camp is difficult to explain if class is not a category of analysis. My understanding of class formation and class relations in the New South has been greatly informed by Janette Greenwood's recent monograph on race and class in Charlotte, North Carolina. Greenwood carefully distinguishes between the urban middle class and the manufacturing elites, who all too often find themselves lumped together in one big group by historians less skillful in handling class politics. In her rendering, and I hope in mine, the term "middle class" means something quite specific: the middle class was composed of small businessmen, teachers, physicians, and other professionals who resided in small towns and cities, made their livelihoods by providing goods and services to the growing urban populations, and held a unifying set of values. In particular, the "reforming activities of members of the middle class . . . defined them as a cohesive class and set them apart from both the elite and poorer members of the community." As leading reformers, women played an especially important role in defining the middle class and providing the glue that held it together.[5]

The industrial elite, on the other hand, created by the New South's cotton mills and other industries, distinguished itself not only by its wealth and power, but also by its values. The profits from textiles, railroads, and steel increased the economic distance between the manufacturing elite and the urban middle class and contributed to the growing distance in their interests and mores. Although one usually thinks of middle-class reformers concentrating their efforts on the poor and working class only, in fact much of the middle-class reform impulse also stemmed from its critique of elite culture. Much like the "evangelical revolt" of the 1760s,[6] the Progressive Era middle class condemned the values and lifestyles of the elites and created an alternative set of values for themselves.

The manufacturing elites and their wives and daughters were an important component in the antisuffrage coalition. Men and women worked together on both sides of the suffrage contest, as should be expected from movements so representative of class interests. But, while the sexes worked together for a common goal, gender did inform the basic organizational strategies, most importantly for the antisuffragists. Roles within the antisuffrage movement conformed more rigidly to the nineteenth century's prescribed gender roles. By determining the division of labor within the antisuffrage movement, gender can be seen as determining both the scope and the content of the antisuffrage movement.[7]

This study also finds a direct relationship between the black disfranchisement movement at the turn of the twentieth century and the antisuffrage movement that followed it. A large number of prominent male antisuffragists had also spearheaded the earlier black disfranchisement effort. They saw the enfranchisement of women as a threat to the edifice of white supremacy, which black disfranchisement had recently served to buttress. So the disfranchisers, or their relatives and business associates, then organized and funded the antisuffrage forces in an effort to shore up their earlier victory. The two movements must be seen as having one common goal: the "protection of white supremacy," which meant in practical terms the continued supremacy of the Democratic Party.

This study will also include, where appropriate, accounts of the ideas and activities of black southerners, both pro- and antisuffrage, both male and female. Living in a period of rising segregationism and racial violence, African Americans in the South responded cautiously to the woman suffrage question, fearful perhaps of drawing too much attention to their interest in the issue. Their understandable caution has made the historian's job more difficult: there are relatively few records to examine. The available materials do suggest that black middle-class southerners generally supported woman suffrage, and many African American women attempted to register and vote when given the opportunity, but they may have considered suffrage a secondary goal to those of ending lynching and segregation.

Another major argument of this study is the difference in social/economic backgrounds between southern suffragists and their opposition. Most historical accounts have lumped the opposing forces together in the "middle and upper-middle classes," leaving one to wonder why people with the same class interests nevertheless differed on this important question. This study finds subtle but demonstrable differences between the social and economic backgrounds of the southern suffragists and antisuffragists. Briefly stated, antisuffragists were most often the product of the South's traditional ruling elite, whose political and social positions were based upon plantation agriculture, closely related commercial enterprises such as textile manufacturing, and leadership in the Democratic Party. Suffragists were more often part of the emerging national urban economy, whose families made their livelihoods by serving the needs of the growing urban workforce and the urban middle classes. Male and female alike, suffragists often were white collar workers in what might now be called the service sector, or a more "middling" middle class. While they were also likely to vote for the Democratic Party, suffragists' families were less often at the helm of power within that party.

Clearly, residence in a city did not automatically produce suffragism. The relationship between "urbanization" and suffragism is more subtle than that. But a relationship between the two remains, nevertheless. Likewise, a college education did not uniformly convert southern women to suffragism. Yet, again, there is still a relationship between higher education and support for woman suffrage. I hope that the chapters that follow will help to explain the complexity of those relationships.

This study employs several different methodologies, dictated by the needs of the subject and the sources available. Unlike researchers of the prosuffrage side, who have an embarrassment of documentary riches, the historian of the opposition to woman suffrage must be more creative in finding source material on the "antis."[8] To uncover the ideology of the southern antisuffragists, I examined the printed words of those who served as spokespersons for the movement. This area of inquiry lent itself to a traditional intellectual history approach. To discover the activities of the antisuffragists, I surveyed the small amount of private correspondence extant, which was supplemented with newspaper accounts of the public activities of the antis. My chapter on the antisuffrage ideology takes more the form of a gendered analysis of a social movement. In order to determine who filled the ranks of the antisuffragists, I compiled membership lists (generally obtained from newspaper accounts and from organizational letterhead stationery) and collected information on education, profession, religion, family background, political offices, economic investments, business associations, and any other data that seemed pertinent to the question of class membership. I quantified this data, which was obtained from a large body of biographical dictionaries produced in the years between 1880 and 1940, from city directories, and from the federal census, and it appears in the Appendix. The data provides the basis for the profiles of the southern suffragists and their antisuffrage opponents. More than 800 women were included in this investigation, making it the largest, most extensive effort of its kind.[9] Enabling the reader to see beyond the leadership of both the suffrage and the antisuffrage movements, this examination delves deeply into the rank and file of both movements, extending not only to local leaders, but including local followers as well.

The statistical profile drawn from that collected data points out the historian's error of using leaders as typical representatives of a movement. I will demonstrate that women such as Belle Kearney and Lila Meade Valentine were not representative of the southern suffrage movement, in spite of the historical treatment accorded them.[10] Historians' nearly exclusive attention on the state and regional leadership of the southern suffrage movement has given one a distorted picture of suffragism in the region. The leaders of the various state organizations were often better educated, wealthier, and somewhat younger than their rank-and-file supporters. Yet their philosophy of "noblesse oblige" could not apply to the vast majority of southern suffragists who did not come from the same privileged background. Rather than focusing on leadership, future studies should focus on women such as Lura Craighead of Mobile, Alabama (a club woman who was also a local leader in the suffrage movement), or Marin Fenwick of San Antonio (a reporter for the San Antonio *Express* who was president of the local suffrage association), or Lillie O'Daniel of Nashville (a teacher and WCTU organizer who also joined her local suffrage society). These women, and their coworkers in small towns and cities across the South, are the more typical southern suffragists. Once the profile of the typical southern suffragist is revealed, one will find it somewhat easier to distinguish between the "suffs" and the "antis."

Although this is an examination of the South as a whole, the reader will notice that several states figure more prominently than others. This is by design. In order to narrow the statistical material down to a more manageable size, six states were chosen upon which to focus more closely. To obtain the most representative cross section possible, a combination of states was chosen (from both upper and lower South, states with strong suffrage movements and those with weaker efforts, and states with strong antisuffrage organizations and those with a weaker movement).[11] Because of the topical arrangement of the material, each chapter stands as a discrete essay; there is consequently some necessary repetition of certain critical information.

Finally, I have attempted to avoid the public/private, male/female dichotomy that has dominated the study of women's history for a generation. Much recent work suggests that those rigid categories have hindered our understanding of politics and what could be considered "political." In this discussion, I have placed southern suffragists in the middle of an industrial reconstruction; I have placed southern antisuffragists in the inner sanctum of political power; I have linked women's organizations to their male counterparts; and I have shown the overtly political actions of allegedly nonpartisan women.[12]

Although political, it was not often "high politics." Party politics did not play a central role in the woman suffrage contest in the South. During the first wave of suffragism at the end of the nineteenth century, while many states still engaged in something resembling viable two-party politics, southern suffragists did seem to be attracted to the "reform" party, which was effectively the Republicans. But by the final maturity of the suffrage movement in the South in the twentieth century, the southern Republican parties had generally been weakened. Reform sentiment, thanks partly to the rise of Woodrow Wilson, had drifted into the Democratic Party, making it easier for reform-minded women to work within the Democratic machinery. Thus the majority of southern white suffragists appeared to be Democrats; and those who entered partisan politics after enfranchisement nearly always did so through the Democratic Party. African American women, however, tended to remain loyal to the Republican Party.

ACKNOWLEDGMENTS

I gratefully acknowledge the support and assistance of the many people and institutions that have contributed to the completion of this book and the dissertation upon which it was based. Sylvia Frey, Lawrence Powell, Patrick Maney, Clarence Mohr, Anastatia Sims, Marjorie Spruill Wheeler, Elizabeth Hayes Turner, Wayne Flynt, Paul Fuller, Jane Sherron De Hart, and Suzanne Lebsock have read all or parts of the manuscript. Special mention should be made of the late A. Elizabeth Taylor, who agreed to read a chapter in spite of her retirement from such duties. In addition, readers who have critiqued portions of the book for conference presentations included Martha Swain, Patricia Meador, Sidney Bland, Eileen Boris, and Wanda Hendricks. I cannot say that I actually enjoyed taking criticism, but the spirit in which all of the above readers offered their comments made the ordeal much easier.

Several people shared research, unpublished papers, and ideas with me. At a time when this project was barely underway, Mary Martha Thomas generously shared with me her research on the Alabama suffrage movement. Sandra G. Treadway, editor of the forthcoming multivolume *Dictionary of Virginia Biography*, graciously allowed me to use the extensive research files of the Publications Division of the Virginia State Library. The biographical data obtained from those files helped to speed up the time-consuming chore of identifying pertinent information on less well known women. Glenda Gilmore and Anastatia Sims shared their unpublished conference papers. Marjorie Spruill Wheeler allowed me to use an advance copy of her then-unpublished *New Women of the New South*. And although he still has yet to read the manuscript in its entirety, Michael Powelson's influence on my thinking permeates every page.

Funding has come from several sources: the Newcomb College Center for Research on Women, the Department of History and the Graduate School of Tulane University, the U.S. Department of Education (in the form of a Patricia Roberts Harris Dissertation Fellowship), and the Mellon Research Fellowship of the Virginia Historical Society. All of these funds are gratefully acknowledged.

As a former reference archivist myself, I take great pleasure in thanking the numerous librarians and archivists who have helped facilitate the research for this book. The bibliography lists the various repositories consulted; I thank the helpful staffs at each. A special word of appreciation goes to George Stevenson of the North Carolina Division of Archives and History. During my brief "apprenticeship" there, George taught me more about the art of historical research than I ever learned in grad school.

Southern Strategies

I

Origins of the Southern Suffrage Movement

As a law abiding citizen; as a tax payer; as a graduate of a Kentucky High School where I took honors above every boy in my classes . . . as still the wife of one man (for thirty-two years); as a worker in the church all my life; as a worker in charitable and other civic organizations for the betterment of the community; as one who finds at fifty-two years of age, more time, leisure, money, brains, health and strength to study and handle the questions of the day . . . I beg and implore you to vote favorably on the Woman Suffrage question now.

Jessie E. Townsend
to Edwin J. Webb, 1914

Even before the twentieth century opened, the middle-class daughters of the New South, with time and resources at their disposal, looked at the cities their fathers had built and found much they disliked. Joining together in reform movements to soften the iniquities of industrial capitalism and assist the needy, southern women forged ahead of their menfolk in joining the progressive reform movements already underway elsewhere in the country. And as they worked on behalf of others by joining reform movements to help children, the poor, working women, and southern blacks, southern white women increasingly found themselves demanding something on their own behalf: the vote.

The southern suffrage movement, lagging a generation behind its northeastern counterpart, arose when it did because southern women trailed a generation behind their northeastern sisters in the critical experiences that produced support for woman suffrage. Those critical experiences were the products of an industrializing economy and urban living conditions, developments that were reshaping the region at the time southern women made their first halting steps toward organizing a suffrage movement at the end of the nineteenth century. As the builders of the New South attempted to remake the region in the image of the North, they unwittingly created the conditions that spurred suffragism: a growing middle class willing to endow colleges and send their daughters to them; an industrial working class plagued by poverty and in need of services that the state did not yet provide; and urban centers where those two classes lived in close proximity to one another. Reprising the experiences of their northeastern counterparts, middle-class women in the South embraced the suffrage movement after years of activism in other women's organizations.

The National Movement

The history of the woman suffrage movement in the United States is usually dated from 1848, with the call for the enfranchisement of women at the Seneca Falls woman's rights convention.[1] But the ballot for women constituted a small plank in a much larger platform, as the women of Seneca Falls demanded equality for women in all areas of civil, political, economic, and private life. Much more pertinent (or so it seemed in the context of the mid-nineteenth century) were women's rights to control their own property, their rights to guardianship of their own children, their need for equal wages and access to higher paying professional jobs, and their desire to limit the size of their families. Suffrage remained a secondary demand at best and one with which not all women activists of the nineteenth century agreed.

Although suffrage remained controversial, the suffrage movement continued to gain support and respectability throughout the remainder of the century for a number of reasons. As women involved in the temperance crusade or in other reform efforts recognized their inability to influence legislators without the leverage of voting power, they learned to appreciate more the need for political clout. As women from other reform movements swelled the suffrage ranks, it ultimately became one of the largest mass movements of women in American history.[2] Moreover, "votes for women" served as a focal point, a source of unity among diverse groups with different agendas. A "clear, easily understood goal" that tapped the "strain of natural rights doctrine in American thought," suffrage united a coalition of organizations behind a common goal. What originally had seemed the least viable demand of Seneca Falls eventually became the one demand upon which nearly all the major women's organizations agreed.[3]

The nineteenth-century movement struggled through a series of internal troubles that threatened to undermine its effectiveness and perhaps destroy it altogether. As the Civil War ended, leading suffragists such as Elizabeth Cady Stanton and Susan B. Anthony, who had been loyal foot soldiers in the abolition movement, now asked that they be rewarded for their work on behalf of the slaves and in support of the Union war effort. They asked that the Fourteenth and Fifteenth Amendments make women, not just black males, citizens and voters. Not all their suffrage colleagues agreed with this position, however, and the disagreement splintered the movement in two.[4]

Personality clashes and internal rivalries compounded the fundamental differences over tactics and philosophy as the suffrage movement tore itself apart. The issues at stake included how best to use chronically limited funds; whether men should be welcomed as allies; whether the Fourteenth and Fifteenth Amendments should receive suffragists' support; and whether the focus of their subsequent efforts should be on federal or state amendments.[5] A formal split, occurring in 1869, produced two competing organizations: the American Woman Suffrage Association (AWSA) and the National Woman Suffrage Association (NWSA). Although it has been argued that the split arose from personal frictions generated by a struggle for power within the leadership,[6] such an analysis only belittles the participants by dismissing the validity of their disagreements. More was at stake than personality. The question of federal or state suffrage amendments remained unsolved and would continue to cause the movement difficulty all the way through 1920. The tactical question took on even greater significance in the final decades of the suffrage movement when it entered the southern states.

Following the split of 1869, the suffrage movement fell into a predictable pattern of activity. The two sets of suffragists, working separately, held annual conventions, petition drives, lecture tours, and above all, endless travel by a dedicated cadre of suffrage workers. Furthermore, the same set of leaders continued to dominate the movement: Stone, Stanton, Anthony, Mott, and a handful of others led the movement for thirty years with very little change of leadership at the top.[7]

In the late 1880s, however, a new generation of suffragists began to rise to national prominence, waiting impatiently for the "old guard" to retire. As the first generation of suffragists now reached their seventies and eighties, the "New Women," such as Carrie Chapman Catt, Nettie Rogers Shuler, Harriet Taylor Upton, and Anna Howard Shaw, assumed the highest national offices. Having had little to do with the experiences of abolitionism or the split of 1869, this second generation of suffragists saw no reason to continue operating two competing national organizations. In 1890, after several years of negotiations, the two associations finally merged to form the National American Woman Suffrage Association (NAWSA).[8]

The unification of the suffrage organizations came at a time when the movement itself was experiencing declining enthusiasm and limited successes. Usually called "the doldrums," the period from 1896 to 1910 was sluggish and unexciting. The union of the two organizations into a single, streamlined unit did little to halt the decline.[9] Several factors contributed to the waning interest in the movement. First, after several relatively easy successes in the western states, the suffrage movement encountered its first organized opposition in the late 1890s. Antisuffrage associations and saloon protective leagues pumped money and political influence into the opposition, and state legislators responded to the pressure by refusing to experiment further with woman suffrage. Second, the overall mood of the American public had changed in the post-Reconstruction years. The earlier popular support for radical Republicanism and social reforms in general eroded in the face of rising conservatism in the Gilded Age. Americans had grown apprehensive of potential changes in family, gender, and race relations. The rising tide of foreign immigration and the growing influence of Social Darwinism helped to make the natural rights and liberal egalitarian philosophies of the past less persuasive. The new generation of suffrage leaders responded to the changing temperament of the times by concentrating on the suffrage issue alone rather than on a general critique of women's role in society.[10]

The newly united organization chose Anna Howard Shaw as its president in 1904. Shaw's lackluster presidency did nothing to help boost the movement out of its period of sluggish monotony. The emergence of two dissenting groups (the Congressional Union and the Southern States Conference) was at least partly an expression of dissatisfaction with Shaw's leadership.[11] By 1915, the restlessness of the rank-and-file membership of NAWSA under Shaw's direction had reached dangerous levels, and she agreed to step down.[12]

Shaw's successor, Carrie Chapman Catt, was no match for Shaw on the lecture platform, but she was better suited for the generalship of this massive army of women. Catt possessed a talent for organization. She had demonstrated her expertise in the New York state suffrage campaign, and now, as president of NAWSA, she promulgated her "Winning Plan." Assigning every state organization a specific duty, Catt's winning plan rejected state campaigns, and focused instead upon the federal amendment as the quickest, most efficient way to enfranchise American women; the winning plan also tried to coordinate campaigns in such a way that the NAWSA could concentrate its resources and its staff in one or two states at a time.[13]

Partly because of the suffragists' war work, partly because of the passage of the Prohibition amendment, partly because of the rising political clout of women voters in several states, and partly because of the successful lobbying effort mounted by the several suffrage organizations, Congress finally adopted the Nineteenth Amendment in June 1919 and sent it to the states for consideration. The effort to win ratification from thirty-six legislatures caused bitter fights in many states but nevertheless proceeded rapidly.

Opponents of woman suffrage across the country hoped that the "solid South" would remain true to its reputation and vote solidly against the amendment. Only thirteen states were required to block ratification of an amendment to the federal constitution, and "the South" contained thirteen states. But the South did not hold solidly together. It gave way around the fringes, as Texas, Arkansas, Kentucky, and finally Tennessee ratified the Anthony Amendment. Seventy-two years after Elizabeth Cady Stanton had insisted that woman suffrage be included in the Seneca Falls Declaration of Sentiments, American women finally won their enfranchisement, and southern border states had provided the critical margin of votes.

The Southern Suffrage Movement

The story of the woman suffrage movement has been told several times now, and the outlines of the story as given above are generally familiar. In the southern states however, suffragism had an often different history, one that is not so well known. Suffrage sentiment, although present in individual southern women as early as the 1850s,[14] never coalesced into a "movement" until the late 1890s. Even as late as 1900, Belle Kearney could write that "very slight effort has been made there to secure the ballot for women, and the thought is somewhat a new one to the masses."[15] The southern suffrage movement therefore matured more than a generation later than elsewhere in the country, and scholars have only just begun to scrutinize that delay.[16]

Southern white women of the upper and middle classes of the late nineteenth century, who might be expected to mirror the activities of their northeastern counterparts, remained tightly bound by the same restrictive forces that had limited the lives of their antebellum mothers and grandmothers. Still predominantly living in rural settings, most southern women continued to live in a world where family, church, and neighborhood were dominated by men. Even when women joined together in prayer circles or quilting bees, they were closely supervised by their ministers, husbands, or kin who guarded against the development of "bonds of womanhood" and the dangerous challenges to patriarchy that might spring from this separate women's culture.

Although elite southern women often expressed interest in politics,[17] they nevertheless remained untouched by many of the politically oriented reform movements that had helped to produce suffragism elsewhere in antebellum America. Abolition, the reform that had done the most to move other women into the public arena, was not an issue a majority of southern women could support.[18] The abolitionist crusade taught a small band of women to speak in public, to organize a petition drive, and perhaps most important, to apply the language of natural rights to the question of human rights.[19] Women's missionary societies, another important empowering experience in the antebellum northeastern cities, made little headway in the South until the 1870s.[20] Similarly, the small numbers of women who attended postsecondary institutions in the region were closely supervised and protected from the intrusion of "dangerous" foreign ideas.[21] It was not until urban life and industrial problems began to chip away at the foundations of the "enclosed garden" in the 1870s and 1880s that southern white women had the opportunities for broadening activities and they would begin to experience the same bonds of womanhood as women in the northeastern cities.

Some of the earliest public expressions of support for woman suffrage in the South, appearing in the late 1860s and early 1870s, related to Reconstruction and constitution making rather than feminism or women's activism.[22] In Texas, for example, the constitutional convention of 1868 considered, but rejected, a proposal for the enfranchisement of women in the new order. That same year, North Carolina constitution drafters heard a minority suffrage report that recommended woman suffrage as a natural right. Also in 1868, Arkansas legislators discussed woman suffrage, but too many feared it would promote "revolutions in families."[23]

It was not coincidental that the first suffrage clubs in the South were organized during this same period. Baltimore's Equal Rights Society formed in 1867, although it only lasted until 1874. Virginia's suffragists joined together in Richmond in May 1870 and sent a delegate to that year's NAWSA convention. An interracial suffrage club formed in South Carolina, sending a black woman as its first delegate to a national woman suffrage convention.[24] Whether it was as a result of the constitutional conventions or because woman suffrage was a general topic of debate at the time, southern women organized their first local suffrage societies in the wake of this series of constitutional conventions.[25]

Another round of discussions of the woman suffrage question in the South was generated by Redemption and Democratic constitution making. In Tennessee, the Democratic state convention of 1876 heard a call for woman suffrage by a Mississippi woman who argued that such a reform would help return Tennessee to white supremacy.[26] That same year, Lide Meriwether began to speak publicly for woman suffrage in Memphis. Louisiana lawmakers, having heard Caroline Merrick and Elizabeth Lyle Saxon argue for the enfranchisement of women, debated a suffrage provision in the constitutional convention of 1879.[27]

These debates on the "woman question" preceded the formation of equal suffrage organizations in most southern states. The *History of Woman Suffrage*, an important source for much of our information on the movement, noted that Caroline Merrick and Elizabeth Saxon went to the Louisiana constitutional convention with their plea for enfranchisement "before there had been any general agitation of this question in the state."[28] Indeed, it is entirely possible, given the chronology of events, that the discussions of woman suffrage in the Reconstruction and Redemption conventions actually served as an impetus to organized suffragism. Emily Collins of Louisiana, for example, wrote Susan B. Anthony that, since the legislature would be writing a new constitution that year, "I feel that now if ever is the time to strike for woman's emancipation."[29] Priscilla Holmes Drake, perhaps inspired by the discussions of constitutions and electorates, joined the NAWSA in 1868, as an individual member from Alabama.[30] Laura Clay's sister, Mary Clay, reported that she attended the NAWSA annual conventions beginning in 1879 as the "self-appointed" representative of her state.[31] Likewise, after 1880, Orra

Langhorne "represented" Virginia at the NAWSA meetings.[32] Women who were already converted to suffragism felt that the time was right to acknowledge their beliefs publicly and affiliate with others who shared those beliefs.

But discussing an issue is not the same as organizing a movement. These two series of southern constitutional conventions and the debates on woman suffrage that they precipitated did not immediately produce a woman suffrage movement. The idea of suffragism continued to percolate for more than two decades in the South before a movement finally emerged. The South experienced two waves of suffrage organizing, the first beginning around 1890 and lasting until around the turn of the century, and the second wave beginning around 1910 and culminating in the ratification of the Nineteenth Amendment by four southern states.

The first drive to organize the South, coming after the Redemption and during the disfranchisement period, was prompted partly by internal changes in the national suffrage movement. In 1890, the two national suffrage associations mended their fences and merged, forming the National American Woman Suffrage Association. One of the first decisions of the newly unified movement was to work toward organizing affiliates in every state in the Union. To that end, NAWSA appointed vice presidents in every state, whose assignment was to create as many local suffrage clubs as possible and then form state associations. The 1891 annual convention also decided "to give especial attention to suffrage work in the southern States during the year" to come.[33]

Although local suffrage clubs, such as the Portia Club of New Orleans (1892) and the Equal Rights Association of Memphis (1889), had spontaneously begun to crop up across the South in the late 1880s and early 1890s, very few of these scattered groups had yet begun to affiliate and organize state suffrage associations. As a direct result of the new NAWSA policy, in state after state, new locals formed and then affiliated into state associations. South Carolina, in 1892, Virginia, Texas, Florida, and Alabama in 1893, and North Carolina in 1894 added their names to the roster of NAWSA affiliates. It looked as though the South, long considered impenetrable, might yet join the suffrage cavalcade.[34]

NAWSA followed up this promising start with extensive organizing tours led by some of its most experienced and dedicated workers. Susan B. Anthony and Carrie Chapman Catt crisscrossed the region in 1895, appearing in larger cities like Memphis, Huntsville, and New Orleans. Laura Clay, Elizabeth Meriwether, Belle Kearney, and other pioneer southern suffragists traveled thousands of miles each, speaking for the cause, as did many other workers. Missouri's Ella Harrison spent much of 1897 traveling through the smaller towns and crossroads of Mississippi and Louisiana.

Harrison's letters to her father from that organizing tour testify to the difficulty of her job. For example, she wrote of how, after checking into her hotel in Grenada, Mississippi, Harrison asked her landlady to tell her which local women were interested in temperance "or any other thing." But the landlady claimed that "as for suffrage she said she did not believe that the women knew a thing about it or would even listen to a speaker—there was absolutely no sentiment here in favor of it."[35]

In spite of the entrenched conservatism Harrison encountered in the Deep South, many other southern women did respond to the entreaties of NAWSA. As early as 1894, the *History of Woman Suffrage* paid tribute to the presence of southern women in the annual convention: "The Southern women have distinguished themselves in the national suffrage conventions during the last few years. This year, on 'presidents' evening,' among a number of brilliant addresses[,] that of Mrs. Virginia D. Young of South Carolina fairly brought down the house."[36] Also giving testament to the increasing participation of southern women in the movement was the election of southerners to national office. Laura Clay, selected as first auditor of NAWSA in 1896, became the first southern woman to sit on the board of officers.[37] A handful of other southerners followed Clay into the highest levels of national leadership.

Worth noting is the impact of travel or other extensive experience outside the South in influencing suffrage sentiment in individual women. Many of these early, pioneering suffragists came from outside of the South, or had extensive experiences (such as a college education) outside of the region.[38] North Carolina's Suzanne Bynum remarked that she had long been interested in the question of suffrage, but only after having spent a winter in New York did she decide to organize a suffrage league in her hometown.[39] Lizzie Dorman Fyler, one of Arkansas' earliest suffragists, had moved to the state in 1880 from Massachusetts. As both an attorney and a temperance worker, Fyler was nearly a generation ahead of most southern women in the critical experiences that produced suffragism.[40] Annette Finnigan, a native of Texas, had graduated from Wellesley College and then worked in New York City, where she joined her first suffrage club, before she returned to Texas to start a movement there.[41] Similarly, Ella Chamberlain of Florida first attended a woman suffrage convention in Des Moines, Iowa, and returned to her home state a convert.[42] Historian Nancy Hewitt has recently noted the strong influence of northern experiences on women activists in Tampa, Florida: the founders of the Civic Association, local WCTU, Suffrage League, Children's Home, and Woman's Club were either northern residents who wintered in Florida or local women who visited the north.[43]

NAWSA also attempted to support the fledgling southern suffrage movement by holding several of its annual conventions below the Mason-Dixon line. Atlanta hosted the annual event in 1895, New Orleans in 1903, and Baltimore in 1906. NAWSA's leaders used these conventions, especially the Atlanta meeting, as opportunities to make extensive speaking tours through the South, both before and after the convention. As the *History of Woman Suffrage* reported, "during several weeks" before convening in Atlanta, Anthony and Catt made a tour of major southern cities. And afterward, Anthony lectured in a number of cities "on her way northward."[44]

The 1903 NAWSA meeting in New Orleans stands out in importance for its open discussion of the racial policies of NAWSA. When challenged by a local newspaper to defend its position on the "negro question," NAWSA's board of officers responded that "the doctrine of State's rights is recognized in the national body and each auxiliary State association arranges its own affairs in accordance with its own ideas and in harmony with the customs of its own section."[45] In effect, this statement freed the southern affiliates to ban black women from their leagues and to work exclusively for state amendments if they wished. NAWSA would, at the time, accept any form of association that its affiliates desired. Interracial associations, like the early South Carolina league, began to disappear after the 1903 convention.[46]

However, NAWSA refused to go further and work only for white woman suffrage despite the urging of the emerging southern leaders Laura Clay and Kate Gordon. Gordon and Clay seemed determined to push a "southern" agenda on the national organization, insisting on a whites-only clause to any suffrage proposal. They attempted to coerce the national organization by threatening to cut off financial support from the southern states to the NAWSA. It was a contest they lost; the NAWSA leadership ultimately refused to make the exploitation of racism the cornerstone of suffrage strategy. In Marjorie Spruill Wheeler's words, "the NAWSA had let it be known that there were, after all, limits to the racism in which they would indulge."[47]

Having established associations in each southern state and having begun the work of building up the membership of those organizations, southern suffragists were further encouraged by the public discussions of woman suffrage in yet a third round of constitutional conventions in the southern states. Starting in the late 1880s, southern legislatures, now tenuously in the hands of white Democrats, began to consider methods to dilute the voting power of black men.[48] One of the possibilities discussed in several state constitutional conventions was white woman suffrage. Mississippi considered the possibility in 1890.[49] In 1891, Arkansas lawmakers debated a white woman suffrage provision but opted instead for an election reform act that disfranchised illiterates.[50] South Carolina solons deliberated over woman suffrage in 1895 but under the influence of Ben Tillman rejected woman suffrage as an inadequate guarantee of white supremacy.[51] In Alabama's constitutional convention of 1901, Benjamin Craig of Selma introduced a white woman suffrage clause, which was vigorously debated but ultimately vetoed.[52] In Louisiana, the constitutional convention of 1898 disfranchised the majority of its black voters by a literacy test, after having considered and rejected woman suffrage.[53]

In state after state, as southern legislators considered woman suffrage as a remedy for the "negro problem," the debate over the disfranchisement of blacks generated discussions about the enfranchisement of women.[54] Southern legislators seemed willing to entertain the suggestion, but only if enfranchisement of women would provide a foolproof—and constitutional—guarantee of white supremacy. A few southern suffragists, like Belle Kearney, were willing to advocate suffrage on that very basis.[55] But it is also important to point out that the majority of suffragists appeared more reluctant than male legislators to argue for woman suffrage as a means of guaranteeing white supremacy. In Alabama, for example, Frances Griffin addressed the constitutional convention in favor of woman suffrage for a full half hour, but she based all her arguments on the simple justice of woman suffrage and the good works that enfranchised women might do. She did not mention the race issue, which the male legislators who followed her promptly raised.[56]

Indeed, most southern suffragists tended to avoid the "woman suffrage as white supremacy" argument. Outspoken (and highly quotable) women like Belle Kearney and Kate Gordon were the exceptions. Their efforts in 1906 to create a suffrage organization explicitly advocating the ballot "as a solution to the race problem" met with a lukewarm response, and only "a handful of delegates" met to proclaim themselves the Southern Woman Suffrage Conference.[57] Most southern white suffragists rejected this organization (and a second such effort in 1913), preferring to stick to the NAWSA mainstream.

None of these state disfranchising conventions adopted a woman suffrage plank, however. In spite of the rising expectations of southern suffragists, their legislators concluded that poll taxes, literacy tests, and grandfather clauses provided more protection for white supremacy than woman suffrage could. After the Supreme Court upheld the constitutionality of the literacy qualification in 1898, there was little further discussion of the efficacy of woman suffrage as a solution to the "negro question." Having disfranchised one group of citizens, southern legislators had no desire to open the question of suffrage expansion again. As Marjorie Wheeler has noted, by 1910 it was clear that southern legislators had solved "the negro problem" without the assistance of woman suffrage.[58] At this point the southern suffrage movement entered its own version of "the doldrums."[59]

Rosy predictions about the suffrage potential of the South now gave way to disappointment, as, one by one, the infant state organizations folded. From 1896 to 1910 was a period of waning enthusiasm and defunct suffrage clubs. It was not because of a lack of leadership, however; there were plenty of intelligent, dedicated, capable women present, ready to tackle the obstinate southern legislators. But still missing was a critical mass of middle-class women ready to fill the ranks of a movement, a lack that made young suffrage leagues inordinately dependent on a handful of strong leaders. Time and again, a suffrage society faltered after an important leader moved away or retired from the work. When Ella Chamberlain, founder of the Florida Woman Suffrage Association, left the state in 1897, the WSA disbanded.[60] The fortunes of the Texas suffrage association waxed and waned according to the place of residence of its dominant spirit, Annette Finnigan.[61] Mississippi's movement faded when Nellie Nugent Somerville curtailed her activities for several years.[62] South Carolina's longtime leader, Virginia Durant Young, died in 1906, and the cause there languished as a result.[63] Arkansas had two periods of doldrums, each following the death of a strong state leader.[64]

The suffrage movement needed numbers, but suffrage workers found it extremely difficult to convert southern women in these years. As organizer Ella Harrison wrote during a trip to the interior of Mississippi, "the people here are so easy going and don't seem to have special desire for anything or to be other than let alone. The women are even opposed to literary clubs in some places. They seem to think that the little education they rec'd in school is sufficient for all time. . . . I tell you death and education has much to do to redeem this south-land."[65]

With few southern women advocating the ballot for themselves and most southern legislatures having rejected woman suffrage as an inadequate tool of white supremacy, there was little chance this premature suffrage movement could survive. "The doldrums" in the southern states were a product of southern Redemption politics and the still immature southern industrial economy, and not a reflection of the national trend of the woman suffrage movement at the time. Although the southern doldrums occurred at much the same time as the national suffrage movement's period of lethargy, the two did not stem from the same forces.[66]

Thus, the first wave of suffragism sputtered to an unsuccessful close. But the second wave proved more permanent. Beginning around 1910, new life was breathed into state suffrage associations. One by one, dormant organizations sprang back into action, working vigorously as if to make up for lost time. By 1913, every southern state had a permanent state suffrage organization.[67] The numbers of women involved were impressive: Nashville reported

3,000 members in 1917, and several other cities in Tennessee had more than 1,000 members each.[68] That same year, Alabama's state suffrage convention reported that eighty-one local suffrage clubs were at work and a paid organizer was in the field.[69] Virginia's state association had 13,000 members by 1916, 3,000 of whom were in Richmond. Its members distributed more than 200,000 pieces of literature that same year.[70] Even conservative South Carolina reported twenty-five leagues in 1917, with a combined membership of 3,000.[71] Indeed, NAWSA brought attention to the "marked increase of public opinion in favor of woman suffrage in the southern States" by holding a "Dixie evening" at the 1916 national convention.[72]

Why now? Why could the southern states sustain a movement in the 1910s when a similar effort had failed in the 1890s? There are two reasons usually given for this phenomenon. First, it is argued that since the national movement had accepted states' rights, racial discrimination, educational requirements for voting, etc., southern suffragists felt comfortable in joining NAWSA. In this interpretation, much is made of the complementary racism of nonsoutherners.[73] However, in many places in the South, no suffrage organizations existed more than a decade after the New Orleans convention of 1903. Apparently a good number of southern women still did not feel they had enough in common with their "equally racist" northern counterparts to inspire them to affiliate with NAWSA. Second, it is frequently argued that southern states had disfranchised blacks between 1890 and 1908, which permitted southern suffragists to ask for the vote for themselves while stressing that woman suffrage would not enfranchise black women.[74] But, as demonstrated above, the completion of black disfranchisement contributed to *declining* suffragism, not increasing suffrage activity.

There are two other reasons for the success of the second southern suffrage movement that seem more likely: the revitalization of the national suffrage movement after 1910, and emergence of an army of New Women in the New South.

The burst of enthusiasm for suffrage in 1910, symbolized by the sudden successes in several nonsouthern state campaigns, stimulated the suffrage movement in the United States enough to break it out of its decline for good. Partly inspired by a new approach to publicity first developed by the British "suffragettes," the energized movement built upon the quiet organizational work that had been continuing during the "doldrums."[75] The series of state referenda after 1910 served to excite suffragists everywhere, and suffragists in the South were no exception.

But this rising national interest in woman suffrage would never have had such impact in the South if sufficient numbers of southern women had not been ready to join the movement. In the intervening years since the first wave of suffragism, large numbers of southern women had gained the necessary experiences that tended to galvanize suffrage sentiment. The forces that had long restrained women's activism, that tightly "enclosed garden" of family, community, and religion, had given way under the relentless onslaught of "modernization," industrial capitalism, and bourgeois individualism.[76] Southern women now eagerly followed a path that their northeastern sisters had mapped a generation earlier. Higher education, paid employment, and the need for progressive reform in areas such as child labor, schools, Prohibition, and pure food and drug legislation had provided the impetus for women to take up the cause.[77] But before such reform movements could begin in the South, the region needed something to reform. In other words, the South first needed to build up a level of urban, industrial capitalism before it could generate a homegrown progressive movement.

The South's industrial sector finally began to heat up in the 1880s. Fueled by northern and English funds that began pouring into the region as the country rebounded from the depression of the 1870s, a railroad construction boom, which began in 1879, laid the base for further development. Southern railroad trackage nearly doubled in the 1880s.[78] Other measures of industrial development are also impressive. In Memphis, for example, investments in manufacturing establishments quadrupled between 1880 and 1890.[79]

Population figures, too, give testament to the changing nature of the southern economy as urbanization accompanied industrialization. By 1910, the number of towns and cities in the South was eight times what it had been in 1860.[80] Between 1900 and 1910, Memphis's population increased 28 percent, Atlanta grew by 72 percent, and Birmingham, in the throes of a steel boom, increased a staggering 245 percent.[81] Many residents of these burgeoning cities earned their bread in the new factories and mills that now dotted the southern landscape. In Memphis, the number of wage earners nearly doubled between 1899 and 1919, rising from 6,626 employees to 11,963.[82] Even Montgomery, not usually considered one of the centers of industrialization, was home to 35,500 wage earners in 1920, many of whom worked in one of the city's 165 factories.[83] For the South as a whole, nearly 20 percent of the population lived in urban areas by 1910.[84]

By the mid-1890s, New South industrialization had also generated a new urban class structure. An industrial working class, segregated by race, migrated to cities and small towns to work in textile mills, tobacco factories, and steel plants. An industrial elite grew powerful from the profits of these enterprises. And a middle class learned to make its living by selling goods and services to their urban neighbors.

The propagandizers of the New South Creed had much of which to be proud.[85] In spite of a still overwhelmingly rural population, it seemed that the New South might be on the road to industrialization, which was widely regarded as the only hope for a ravaged economy. City boosters and industry builders tried to rebuild the South in the image of the northeast, in spite of the fact that that region unfortunately had not yet learned to solve the problems that accompanied aggressive industrial capitalism. Urban sanitation nightmares, corrupt political machines, child labor, and poverty-producing wage levels were just a few of problems the New South now had to confront.[86]

The southern progressive movement was the response to these problems.[87] Men and women, mostly urban and middle class, themselves products of the New South, demanded an end to the evils of unrestrained capitalism. While accepting that industrial capitalism was irreversible, progressives insisted that it must be made humane. Mary Johnston, for one, argued that industrialization demanded new responses from those who recognized the need for reform in American society.[88] One of those new responses would be the enfranchisement of women. North Carolina's Mary Cowper believed that woman suffrage would introduce a "great moral force" into politics that would "modify and soften the relentlessly selfish economic forces of trade and industry in their relation to government."[89] As a part of the progressive movement, woman suffrage must be seen as a challenge to the tenets of the New South Creed, a challenge to the new faith in industrialization that had held sway in the South for a generation.[90]

Sources of Suffragism

A decade or more before there was a progressive movement per se, southern women were at the forefront of the various reform efforts that eventually came to be called a movement. (Indeed, if historians of progressivism incorporated more of women's voluntary associational activities into their analysis, they might well date the beginning of the Progressive Era a decade or more earlier than is generally done.) Beginning in the 1870s, their experiences in churches, local communities, and schools were preparing southern women for leadership roles in the progressive movement. Although it might have seemed to contemporary observers as though the New Women appeared spontaneously on the scene, years of critical experiences had been preparing them for new roles as activists and reformers and, later, as suffragists.

One of those critical experiences was higher education. Higher education for southern women is an area that has been relatively neglected by scholars.

There are not even basic statistics available about the numbers of southern women receiving college degrees at this time. A. D. Mayo's compilation of statistics for the year 1888 concluded that nearly 8,000 women were enrolled in collegiate departments in the southern states, nearly 1,000 of whom graduated the following spring.[91] Those figures, however, attest only to the quantity, not the quality, of postsecondary education for southern women. In 1893, for example, the U.S. Commissioner of Education reported that only sixteen of the 166 women's colleges in the country could receive a division A rating. Of that sixteen, only one was in the South. The other eighty-seven women's colleges located in the southern states had B ratings or below.[92] A decade later, in 1903, of the 140 southern institutions bearing the name "college for women," only two offered a full four-year course of study.[93]

Just as women's colleges in general lagged behind men's colleges in the size of endowments, size of libraries, size of faculty salaries, and other such measures of quality, southern women's colleges compared unfavorably with their northern counterparts. Thomas Woody, in his now-classic work on women's education, concluded that "compared with colleges for women in the North, all Southern colleges for women were poor."[94]

Progressive reformers throughout the South called for improved educational facilities for women. Educational leaders such as Duncan McIver and Edwin Alderman believed that women, as teachers, were part of the region's solutions for its poverty and underdevelopment.[95] Another voice calling for the improvement in educational standards in the region's women's colleges was the Southern Association of College Women (SACW). Organized by southern women in 1903 and modeled after the Association of Collegiate Alumnae, the SACW devoted most of its energies to the improvement of standards for higher education for women in the South.[96] Its most important service was publicity, and the SACW devoted a decade to advertising the inferior quality of southern colleges for women.

Although there are no statistics available that would compare the degrees granted to women in various regions, southern women lagged at least a generation behind their northeastern sisters in their opportunities to obtain a college education.[97] The Southern Association of College Women was founded almost exactly twenty years after the Association of Collegiate Alumnae was formed. This two-decade delay accurately reflects the generational differences in regional education. As late as 1910, a woman graduating from a high school in Virginia had to leave the state if she wished to obtain a college education equal to that available to the men in her state.[98]

Just who were these college women? One study of women's education at the turn of the century concluded that southern women who attended college at this time were the "daughters of the New South." Their parents were merchants, professionals, and manufacturers—in short, the makers of the New South. Relatively few came from the planting class, and even fewer were daughters of the working class.[99] The "New Men" who built the New South and sent their daughters to college had come of age after the Civil War, and relatively few of them had fought for the Confederacy or supported secession. Born in or near small country towns, they often had moved to the growing towns and cities of the South before the war to make their fortunes. Many came from small farming backgrounds, but approximately one-third were descended from the small antebellum middle class of merchants, lawyers, doctors, and clergy.[100]

Moreover, progressive reformers in the region had imbued many of the women's colleges with the reform ethos. Women's colleges expected that their students would serve their communities and improve their region. Southern college women during the Progressive Era received heaping doses of progressive idealism: Charles McIver's students, for example, were lectured to "see the real needs of the world and then do something about it."[101] An education received in "progressive institutions" was one steeped in ideals of service and mission. A generation of women was taught that education was a gift that had to be shared with others.

Higher education, particularly when it was of high quality, acted as an incubator for suffragism in some southern women. While college education was still relatively rare for southern women in general, the number of southern suffragists who had attended or graduated from college was remarkably high. As shown in Table A.7, of the southern suffragists for whom educational background is known, more than 50 percent had graduated from college. An additional 28 percent had at least some college experience.

While not all college graduates became suffragists, it seems clear that higher education encouraged women to believe that enfranchisement would either help them, or it would help them to help others. It also appears that college education sped up the "conversion" to suffragism. As demonstrated in Table A.8, the suffragists who were known to have graduated from college were on average five years younger than suffragists as a whole. When the San Antonio branch of the SACW endorsed woman suffrage, it spoke for many college educated women in the South.[102]

Because the numbers of southern women attending college were relatively small, paid work was arguably more important than higher education in contributing to a demand for political equality. Increasing numbers of southern women worked for pay during the Gilded Age and Progressive Era, far more than received college educations. Suffragist Pattie Ruffner Jacobs of Alabama recognized the relationship. As she told the Florida legislature in 1917, "some state that the woman's place is in the home, and yet the war is thrusting them into fields they never occupied before. Economic conditions forced woman to seek her livelihood. It was not from choice but necessity."[103] Belle Kearney had stated much the same idea at the turn of the century: "The women of the South have not sought work because they loved it; they have not gone before the public because it was desirable for themselves; they have not arrived at the wish for political equality with men simply by a process of reasoning; all this has been thrust upon them by a changed social and economic environment. It is the result of the evolution of events which was set in motion by the bombardment of Fort Sumter."[104]

While it is true that women have always worked, the nature of women's work in the United States began to change in the nineteenth century as "work" came to mean work for pay and often meant work performed outside of the home. In the South, the changing nature of women's work, while less noticeable before 1860, accelerated under the continuing impact of the Civil War and postwar economic change. The loss of one-fourth of white adult males to wartime casualties contributed to a postwar labor shortage, a vacuum into which needy women gladly moved to fill. And, as Anne Scott has noted, the inability of many veterans to take the loyalty oath opened further opportunities for paid employment for women of the first postwar generation.[105]

The growing cities of the New South provided new employment opportunities for women, and it was in the cities where employment rates reached their peak. In Atlanta, for example, in 1900, 21.7 percent of adult white women worked for pay; by 1920, the figure had risen to 30.4 percent. Richmond women were only slightly behind, with 21.1 percent of white women working in 1900 and 30.2 percent working by 1920. New Orleans experienced one of the most dramatic jumps in white women's employment: from 17.8 percent in 1900 up to 28.9 percent by 1920. (See Tables A.29–A.31.)

For white women at least, some of these wages were earned in white-collar jobs that had been long monopolized by men but now were being infiltrated by ever-larger numbers of women. By 1920, the percentage of employed women in the southern states working in clerical jobs had reached 9.0 percent, although that remained considerably below the national average of 25.6 percent.[106] Similarly, 13.3 percent of working women in the United States were employed in professional capacities in 1920, compared to only 9.4 percent in the southern states.[107] Another 6.7 percent of gainfully employed women taught school in the South.[108]

The evidence suggests that suffragism was related to these changes in women's work. Professional women in particular led the various state and local suffrage organizations, and the numbers of professional women in the suffrage ranks were extremely high.[109] And while it is true that relatively few working-class women joined southern suffrage societies, it was knowledge of the problems of working-class women that prompted suffrage sentiment in many other middle-class women.[110] Middle-class reformers often saw the ballot as a weapon in their battle against poverty, child labor, alcoholism, and poor working conditions. Alabama suffragists, to give just one example, have been credited with persuading merchants in Birmingham to close their stores early two days a week in order to reduce the work week for women employees.[111]

Although increasing numbers of southern women were working for pay in the early twentieth century, the majority of southern women remained unpaid workers. For them, voluntary associations filled much of their time, particularly for women of the urban middle class. Their activities in women's clubs, civic clubs, and church missionary societies, critical to the formation of a middle class, were also critical to producing reform sentiment. Based on the numbers of women involved, voluntary associations appear to have had more impact on the consciousness of southern women than did higher education or waged work.

Beginning in the 1870s, women in all the southern states and in every denomination organized missionary societies. Originally intended to raise money for the support of foreign missionaries, within a decade the movement had broadened to include support for domestic missions as well. The timing and the location of this change provides clues as to its impetus: the first Methodist home mission was founded by Laura Haygood in 1882 in Atlanta, the premier city of the New South. Mission work could bring women of the middle classes into direct contact with the poverty and related problems of growing industries and growing cities. Missionary societies grew extremely popular with southern women; by 1910, 92,000 Methodist women had joined the movement.[112]

While southern Protestant churches were not known for their participation in the social gospel movement, southern church women frequently spearheaded what limited reform efforts the churches undertook. Lucy Randolph Mason entered the suffrage movement out of her conviction that suffragism was an expression of "social Christianity." "There is in the suffrage movement a religious element," she wrote, "a deep strain of spirituality and altruism, which gives it a peculiar moral significance and fully justifies faith in its ultimate vindication."[113] Many women moved from missionary societies to suffrage advocacy. Among the more prominent were Nellie Nugent Somerville, Belle Bennett, and Tochie MacDonell. Missionary societies contributed to the growing demand for laity rights for women within the churches, and the laity movement and the secular suffrage movement encouraged and supported one another.

Closely related to the development of missionary societies was the national temperance movement, which served as another magnet drawing southern women toward suffragism. Institutionalized in the Woman's Christian Temperance Union (WCTU), temperance activism provided an important vehicle for southern women to develop their skills and talents. As was the case for the club movement and experiences in higher education, the southern WCTU movement matured ten to fifteen years later than that of the northeastern states. Intensely loyal to the WCTU once converted, southern women were again a generation behind in a "consciousness raising" experience that helped to build the later suffrage movement.

Although a powerful institution in some parts of the country by the 1870s, the WCTU made slower headway in the South. In a manner that would be copied by suffrage workers a decade later, the WCTU began the monumental job of organizing southern women. In 1878, the annual convention met in Baltimore, in hopes of spawning temperance sentiment there. Three years later, national president Frances Willard made the first of a series of lecture tours in the South, speaking in over fifty cities in every southern state.[114] But the work was slow to germinate. An early historian of the Texas WCTU reported that an organizing effort in Tyler in 1885 nearly folded, for no woman would consent to chair the local union. A Baptist minister, "not willing to have it fail," accepted the presidency of the new group until a woman brave enough to preside could be found. It took four months.[115]

But slowly, women overcame their fears and formed local unions throughout the region. In Alabama, the WCTU first organized in Gadsden in 1882, and six locals formed a state association in 1884.[116] In Tennessee, the first state local formed in 1882, and the state Union put an organizer in the field as early as 1884. That organizer, Elizabeth Lyle Saxon, a noted suffragist, formed thirty-seven locals in her first year on the job.[117] In 1883, North Carolina and Mississippi organized their state unions, the last two southern states to do so. Twenty years later, North Carolina's union boasted a membership nearing 3,000.[118]

Black women also joined in the temperance movement, although in segregated branches of the WCTU. Generally labeled "Number 2" unions, the WCTU's black unions were numerous and popular. Black women were able to hold prominent offices in the WCTU, like Frances Joseph of Louisiana, who acted as the American representative of the WCTU to the 1900 world's WCTU convention. In locations where the WCTU itself did not have a chapter, local club women could also work for reform through the temperance department of the National Association of Colored Women or other women's clubs. Nationally renowned African American women leaders like Mary Church Terrell and Margaret Murray Washington encouraged support for temperance because of its potential for improving conditions for many in the black community and the good will such activism could elicit from the white community.[119]

Conservatives in the South put up fierce resistance to these challenges to traditional gender roles. One Tennessee woman reported that "the prejudices of the southern people are all against women doing anything in public, and especially opposed to the Woman's Temperance Crusade. Particularly is this true of our ministers. . . . They quote St. Paul, and tell us we are wonderfully out of our places."[120] Reluctant at first to cross the traditional boundaries of female activities, many southern women soon found irresistible the opportunities for personal growth and social enrichment that the WCTU provided. Belle Kearney, in a widely quoted assessment of the WCTU, remembered that "the Woman's Christian Temperance Union was the golden key that unlocked the prison doors of pent-up possibilities. It was the generous liberator," she exclaimed, "the joyous iconoclast, the discoverer, the developer of Southern women."[121]

Although the southern chapters remained a conservative element in the national WCTU, they nonetheless significantly contributed to the nontraditional experiences of a growing body of southern women. Memphis's Lide Meriwether gave testament to the ways in which the WCTU pushed women into unfamiliar roles. In 1884, Meriwether suddenly found herself elected state WCTU president. "At that time," she wrote later, "I had been in the work just four months, had attended the four monthly meetings of our local union, and this was the second time I had ever been within sight or sound of an organized convention of any kind, conducted by either men or women."[122] Historians have given the WCTU much credit for producing experienced platform speakers and for creating a network of women that suffragists would use to their advantage later on.[123]

Although the WCTU concerned itself primarily with drink, its attack on intemperance led it into other areas of reform as well. Through their work with the WCTU, many women became convinced that poverty contributed to alcohol abuse, and they set about to wipe out the causes of poverty. Others found a relationship between alcoholism and ignorance, and they began working for adult literacy or school reforms. An early example of how involvement in temperance activism led to other concerns is found in the establishment of a boys' reformatory in Texas. In 1886, the state WCTU president visited the men's penitentiary to preach temperance to the convicts. She was shocked to find 300 boys housed among the 3,000 "hardened criminals" and returned home to start a statewide petition drive to the legislature, demanding that separate facilities be established for young offenders. A lobbying campaign by the WCTU produced quick results: a boys' reformatory was opened in Gatesville.[124] Similarly, in Houston, the WCTU joined forces with other local women's organizations in 1900 to petition for a police matron to supervise women detained in the local jail. The city council agreed.[125]

A small number of women got their first taste of interracial work through their activism in the WTCU. In North Carolina, for example, white temperance workers made contacts with local black schools and, working in conjunction with black temperance women, helped to organize a movement called "Bands of Hope." Black and white women of the "better classes" in Charlotte who had first worked together on the state Prohibition campaign later cooperated to establish and operate a black hospital in the Queen City.[126]

Although the WTCU is popularly remembered, and derided, for activities such as removing wine from the communion cups throughout the South, that caricature unfairly ignores much of the larger agenda of the organization. Membership in the WTCU frequently encouraged women to see the world beyond the boundaries of their own class and race. Tennessee's state union, for example, worked to raise the age of consent, lobbied for a separate reform school for juvenile offenders, and obtained police matrons for the city court system.[127] The wide range of activities of the WTCU, the product of its "do everything" creed, must be credited for its significant contribution to rising suffragism in the South. Alabama provides one of the clearest examples of how suffragism was spawned directly from temperance work. The state's suffrage movement burst out of the doldrums when a Prohibition vote failed in 1909. Mary Winslow Partridge, a devoted temperance leader, convinced her coworkers that the only way to succeed with the Prohibition campaign would be to vote in the reform themselves. They formed the Selma Woman Suffrage Association in March 1910.[128] The Alabama state WTCU endorsed woman suffrage in November 1914.[129]

In the South, the woman's club movement, another agency of "critical experience," lagged a generation behind that of the northeastern states. On her suffrage organizing mission in Mississippi in 1897, Ella Harrison had written that "these people look upon [woman suffrage] as a sort of 'heresy that has a real devil in it'—They have not thought of it and many, many will not come out to hear about it. Mrs. Bradford [her partner on this trip] has not gotten one new club so far and only 19 members to an old one in Greenville. I told her I did not believe Mrs. Catt would think we were the people for this work—while the truth is they are not ready for it—In many places they have no literary clubs at all, never have had."[130] Harrison's concern with the lack of literary clubs was not unfounded. Suffrage organizers at the time—and historians since—have found a strong correlation between women's clubs and the development of suffragism. Like the WTCU, women's clubs provided a forum for discussing women's issues and a training ground for honing the skills necessary to address those issues.[131]

The first woman's club in the country, Sorosis, was founded in New York in 1868; the earliest women's clubs in the South did not appear until the 1880s. And some southern states lagged even further behind in organizing women's clubs: the first women's clubs in North Carolina, for example, were founded in 1895,[132] and the earliest such organization in Virginia was established in Richmond in 1894 (with a constitution prohibiting the discussion of religion or politics).[133] Not until 1907 did every southern state have a Federation of Women's Clubs.[134]

The women who had the leisure time to join women's clubs and the financial wherewithal to contribute to their civic endeavors were members of the growing urban middle class. Housewives who joined "self-culture" clubs to improve their minds began reading and discussing current events. They found themselves attempting to solve the burning problems of the day, such as child labor abuses or adulterated foods. In their capacities as wives and mothers, club women organized around a particular local grievance, usually related to the home, school, or children. After limited successes outside of politics, they found themselves turning to politicians for redress. And soon women who had originally wished for nothing more than to become better informed mothers found themselves unpaid lobbyists at the state legislature and part of the great swell of middle-class activism called the progressive movement.[135]

The developments in the town of San Antonio, Texas, illustrate this evolution from club activity to suffrage activism. In 1898, eighteen women formed the San Antonio Woman's Club, which grew to include 175 members by 1917. From the outset, this club demonstrated its penchant for political activism. It claimed to be the first woman's club in the state to take an active role in civic life, and its admission into the state's Federation of Women's Clubs made it "necessary to change the state constitution by dropping the word 'literary' from the name 'Federation of Literary Clubs.' "[136]

In addition to forming a "political science department" within the city club to work for woman suffrage, a group of San Antonio club women organized a separate suffrage league, the Equal Franchise Society. Formed in 1912, its relationship to the mother organization was direct: four out of the eight charter members had also been charter members of the San Antonio Woman's Club.

Marin Fenwick, local suffrage leader from San Antonio, undated (Courtesy of Archives Division, Texas State Library, Austin)

The officers were nearly interchangeable at times.[137] More than a decade of club work had produced a body of dedicated suffragists.

Other San Antonio women's organizations felt a similar irresistible pull toward suffragism. The Phoenix Club, born in 1903 as a study group for women who wished to broaden their learning, soon found itself involved in local politics and endorsing woman suffrage. The Sorosis Club, also formed in 1903, while not formally calling for the enfranchisement of women, nevertheless followed that familiar path from study club to civic work.[138] The Texas

Federation of Women's Clubs officially acknowledged this strong relationship between club work and suffragism when its membership endorsed woman suffrage in 1915.[139]

This pattern was repeated in town after town across the South. The Birmingham Equal Suffrage Association grew out of a study club that had been meeting in its leader's living room.[140] Memphis's Nineteenth Century Club, founded in 1890, grew to such numerical strength and political power that it "exerted decisive influence in obtaining reform measures from the city government."[141] The early leaders of the suffrage movement in Houston also had come from positions of leadership in the club world.[142]

Club work could lead women into unexpected activities. Some southern club women, like their counterparts in the WTCU, had opportunities for occasional interracial contacts through their women's clubs. In North Carolina, for example, noted suffragist and physician Delia Dixon-Carroll addressed the black women's club convention of 1915 and then joined in informal discussions about the interracial work open to club women. Club women in Charlotte earned a public reproach from the local newspaper for their efforts at interracial cooperation and understanding.[143] Under the prodding of reformer Mary-Cooke Munford, white club women joined black club women in Virginia to establish and support a home for delinquent girls.[144]

These white club women learned that middle-class black women in their own communities had often been conducting very similar activities to their own. The relative absence of social welfare institutions in the South and the exclusion of blacks from those that existed meant that the urban black community had great, even dire, needs. African American women had organized clubs and associations to fund kindergartens, nursery schools, orphanages, and visiting nurses programs. Often unable to tap into the resources of the white charities, black club women drew upon the meager resources of the black community, with occasional assistance from northern philanthropies like the Slater or Jeanes funds. Like their white neighbors, black women formed local clubs, state federations, and national collectives. They ran charities, built schools, and founded settlement houses. In the process, they gained valuable experience in organization, fund-raising, and public relations.[145]

Many black women reformers argued that woman suffrage could be a vehicle for "racial uplift." In a symposium on the woman suffrage question in 1915 in *The Crisis*, African American leaders like Francis J. Grimke, Oscar De Priest, Mary Talbert, and Coralie Cook all argued that women would do much good with the vote and that women were equal citizens who deserved equal rights. Nannie Helen Burroughs, speaking for black club women, added that the black woman needed the vote "to ransom her race."[146]

It is important to note, however, that black suffragists in the South faced different circumstances than they did elsewhere in the country, and those circumstances made them more cautious in the expression of their support for woman suffrage. While African American women in Chicago, for example, could form the Alpha Suffrage Club and speak openly of their desire to vote, most black women in the South feared to speak too boldly. The response of white conservatives could not be predicted: lynching and other forms of violence were never far from the minds of southern black activists. In the more hostile racial climate of the South, black suffragists had to be wary that their suffragism did not actually hurt the cause.[147] In the famous 1913 suffrage parade in Washington, northern black women like Ida Wells-Barnett and Alice Dunbar Nelson marched, but there were no southern black women present. Southern black suffragists like Adella Logan and Margaret Murray Washington were unusual for their willingness to speak in public on the issue, although Logan occasionally relied on her ability to "pass" for white in order to attend suffrage conventions.[148]

The Second Wave: Competing Organizations

Collectively, these experiences of secular and religious activism, and paid and volunteer work, produced a generation of New Women—both black and white—confident of their abilities and impatient with the shortcomings of the New South. By 1910, these southern middle-class women frequently had had more than a decade of "critical experiences" behind them and had perfected the organizational skills that made the ratification of the Nineteenth Amendment possible.[149] A generation behind in education, club activism, paid work, and reform activities, southern women were not ready to begin a suffrage movement until around 1910. This generational lag explains the failure of the premature first wave of suffrage organization as well as the timing of the more successful second wave.

The second wave of southern suffragism erupted suddenly around 1910, reached every southern state by 1913, and matured rapidly as the seasoned activists who made up its ranks took charge and harnessed the experienced womanpower around them to create a viable movement. Drawing on their organizational experiences in the missionary societies and the women's clubs, capitalizing on their lobbying skills gained in the WTCU and civic leagues, and utilizing the networks founded in women's colleges or professional associations, the second-wave suffragists set out with grim determination to win their enfranchisement and to do it in the shortest time possible.

Thanks in part to increased numbers of supporters and in part to the example set by more creative suffragists in the northeast, the second suffrage wave launched a wider range of activities than its predecessor. The New Women wanted more publicity and faster results. Some state organizations hired professional lobbyists and opened permanent offices for their headquarters.[150] Several state associations, and even a few local societies, published their own suffrage journals.[151] Southern suffragists held parades, set up booths at state fairs, spoke on street corners, organized at women's colleges, conducted essay contests in the schools, put on suffrage plays, and spoke from the back of open cars, tactics that would have been unthinkable to the first-wave suffragists.[152] One South Carolina suff, Eulalie Salley, went so far as to hire an airplane to drop suffrage leaflets over the city of Aiken.[153]

Just as it gained in numbers and vitality, however, the southern suffrage movement was torn asunder over questions of tactics and ideology. Before 1910, the question of state suffrage versus federal suffrage had been discussed by suffragists throughout the country, with the issue remaining unresolved. But several events made it clear that the leadership of NAWSA was moving toward preference for a federal amendment. In 1909, Carrie Chapman Catt conducted the "Great Petition drive," which called on Congress to approve a federal amendment. The following year, Congress agreed to consider a woman suffrage amendment, something it had not done since the 1890s. Also in 1910, the NAWSA formed a new committee called the Congressional Union. The Congressional Union (CU, later renamed the National Woman's Party), led by Alice Paul and other "young turks" of the national movement, was specifically dedicated to work for passage of the federal amendment.

The South was not immune to this trend. New suffrage clubs were formed in several states for the express purpose of working more aggressively for the cause. The Equal Suffrage Party of Georgia, born in 1914, was one such association.[154] In South Carolina, a faction favoring greater activism broke away from the state association and joined the National Woman's Party.[155] Many southern suffragists found the militancy of the CU/NWP distasteful and possibly dangerous, but others were more supportive.

The Congressional Union appointed membership chairmen for most southern states in 1915. In North Carolina, Lilian Exum Clement of Asheville headed the movement to recruit new members. (Clement would later become the first woman elected to the state legislature in North Carolina.)[156] Tennessee's membership chairman was Mrs. C. H. Dyer; and in Florida, Mrs. Newton Allen Strait was in charge of recruitment.[157]

The National Woman's Party stepped up its efforts to organize the South in 1917, sending organizers far and wide. Tennessee's Sue White responded to the entreaties of the NWP because the NAWSA seemed to have given up hope for success in the South.[158] White was not alone in her interest in the NWP. In fact, by the end of the year, the NWP had members in every state in the South, and notably large memberships in Texas, Maryland, and Virginia.[159] Although the NWP remained smaller than the NAWSA, the success of the CU/NWP in recruiting southern members suggested that southern suffragists might have been more eager for the federal amendment and for more aggressive campaigning than NAWSA had (and subsequent historians have) recognized.

The movement away from the state amendment principle did not go unchallenged, however. Kate Gordon, one of the few southern suffragists to reach national office in the NAWSA, resigned her position in protest over Catt's Great Petition and its implications. In 1913, Gordon organized a countermovement, the Southern States Woman Suffrage Conference (SSWSC), to work for state-controlled suffrage.[160] Although Gordon cloaked the SSWSC in the language of cooperation and claimed that its purpose was to assist the NAWSA in its work in the South, it became clear to observers that cooperation was not foremost in Gordon's mind. She soon demanded instead that the NAWSA stay out of the southern states altogether and allow the SSWSC to be *the* woman suffrage organization in the South.[161]

Much like the national movement's "split of 1869," state suffrage associations throughout the South now split into warring factions over the question of state versus federal amendment. Not surprisingly, Gordon's home state was the first to be torn apart. A group of federal suffrage advocates, unwilling to align with Gordon's states' rights philosophy, walked out of the state association and formed a separate organization, the Woman Suffrage Party. Headed by Sake Meehan of New Orleans, the WSP applied for, and was granted, affiliation with NAWSA.[162] Other states suffered similar rifts. For example, after considerable internal debate, the Alabama state association refused to join either the SSWSC or the Congressional Union and in 1914 announced that it would work for "appropriate state *and* national legislation" to obtain women's equal right to vote.[163] While several of Virginia's suffrage leaders joined the SSWSC, many others in the Virginia state association staged a mini-revolt in 1915 and established a chapter of the Congressional Union.[164]

This split over tactics—whether to support state amendments or a federal amendment—proved to be the insurmountable problem within the southern suffrage ranks. Even as late as 1920, the issue remained dangerously divisive, a situation that antisuffragists would use to their advantage. As will be demonstrated in more detail in the following chapters, antisuffragists wooed states' rights suffragists into alliances to defeat the federal amendment.

In spite of the rift, the second wave of suffrage organizing in the South ended far more successfully than the first. By 1913, every southern state had a state association affiliated with NAWSA, and most states had active, enthusiastic local chapters working to raise public support on behalf of woman suffrage. In addition, two alternative suffrage organizations (the Southern States Woman Suffrage Conference and the National Woman's Party) had also established small followings in the region. Together, these organizations represented many thousands of southern women willing to enroll in a suffrage organization, pay dues, and support the cause.

Suffragism seemed to be waxing. As western states slowly increased the total of woman suffrage victories, even southern states began hesitant experiments with limited woman suffrage. In 1894, for example, the legislature of Kentucky granted women in three cities the right to vote in school elections (a right that was later revoked.)[165] In 1898, Louisiana women gained the right to vote on tax questions if they were taxpayers. More than 10,000 of the 70,000 adult white women of New Orleans did so at the first opportunity they were given and were credited with passage of an important sewerage and drainage reform bill in 1899.[166] Florida's legislature began granting municipal suffrage to individual cities that approved it: the city of Felsmere was the first to agree, in 1915.[167]

In response to the growing support for woman suffrage in the South, antisuffragists in the region stirred nervously. The following chapters, which describe the opponents of woman suffrage and their beliefs, will confirm that the antisuffragists perceived suffragism as an attack on their own political and economic hegemony. And an examination of antisuffrage activism will demonstrate the lengths to which they were willing to go in order to protect the region's racial, political, and economic status quo.

2

Origins of the Southern Antisuffrage Movement

The serious opposition to [woman suffrage] has been financed by the Whiskey Interests and the Cotton Mill owners of New England and the South.

The former feared the suppression of the whiskey traffic and the latter the suppression of the exploitation of child labor, and of the competition of insufficiently paid labor of women in their mills.

Chief Justice Walter Clark
to Henry Watterson, 1919

Who were the southern antisuffragists? Mississippi suffragist Belle Kearney thought she knew: "To this class belong the liquor dealers, the wily politicians of the lower stamp, the ultra-conservative ecclesiastics, the superfine 'swells' and men who have risen from the humbler walks of life deprived of early advantages of education and the refinements of elevated home environments."[1] Notably absent from Kearney's assessment was any mention of the role of women in the antisuffrage movement, a surprising (and significant) omission considering the prominence of women on both sides of the public discussion of the woman suffrage question. When suffragists mentioned female antisuffragists at all, they tended to separate them from the rest of their opposition. The chapter on Texas in the *History of Woman Suffrage*, for example, noted the presence and activities of the female antisuffragists and then claimed that "the [1919 state constitutional] amendment failed[,] but not because of their feeble efforts. It was opposed by the strongest political forces in Texas, including the liquor interests."[2]

Historians, relying heavily on records generated by the suffragists, have frequently followed this lead and have focused on the men who worked against woman suffrage while ignoring or minimizing the numerous women's organizations opposed to suffrage.[3] The presence of women in the antisuffrage ranks means that the suffrage debate cannot be interpreted as a struggle between progressive women demanding autonomy and conservative men defending the patriarchy. Women played a pivotal role in the antisuffrage movement, and that fact requires explanation.

Establishing the context within which antisuffrage women operated requires close attention to the social basis of the antisuffrage movement. This foundation of the movement will be revealed through an examination of the biographies of the men and women who acted to prevent the enfranchisement of women. A comparative collective biography of southern antisuffragists and their prosuffrage opponents provides a means of demonstrating the subtle ways in which the social and economic backgrounds of the suffragists and antisuffragists differed. The differences are important clues as to what the participants believed was really at stake in the woman suffrage contest in the South.[4]

One of the most important trends that emerges from the biographical data is the relationship between the planter class and the antisuffrage movement. Members of the planter class, both male and female, were prominent leaders of the opposition to woman suffrage in the southern states, and the bulk of support for the antisuffrage movement was found in the plantation districts of the Black Belt. Large numbers of antisuffragists, both leaders and rank-and-file members, came from planting families or from other families residing in the counties with large black populations.

Many other antisuffragists came from groups that were closely aligned with the planters, among them textile manufacturers. Other economic groups with compatible interests, including the railroads, merchants, and lawyers who provided services for the Black Belt districts, also contributed support to the antisuffrage effort. Together with the planters, these economic groups were part of a small but powerful economic and political elite, united by business, friendship, and kinship ties. Their participation in the antisuffrage movement was their response to the perceived danger that woman suffrage posed to their common economic and political interests.

The discussion of this planting class must begin where the class itself began: on the plantations of the antebellum South. Although slaveowners, and especially slaveowners who qualified as "planters," represented a relatively small percentage of whites in the South before the Civil War, their economic strength, political power, and perhaps even cultural hegemony far outweighed their numbers. Antebellum planters and others closely tied to them dominated state legislatures and local politics, as well as the southern economy. Their interests became the policies of their governments, and their demands served as the foundation of the political economy.[5]

Antebellum Antecedents

Long before the advent of the New South movement and its faith in salvation by industrialization, some antebellum planters had been building or investing in textile mills, lumber mills, foundries, and other industries. The funds for these enterprises came from agriculture, as the planter turned industrialist or became partners with the industrialist. Such a transition was not as contradictory as one might first assume, for planters and industrialists could share many interests (such as the desire for low wage levels and minimal taxation). When they found common ground on these critical issues, planters and industrialists could work together or become one.[6]

Using profits generally produced by cotton, these antebellum planters often established mills to process future cotton crops. Several of North Carolina's textile dynasties, such as the Holt Mills, were founded on agricultural monies.[7] Other southern industrialists, like Daniel Pratt and Allison F. Page, also found seed money in agricultural profits.[8] Warehouses, cotton gins, railroads, banks, merchants, and attorneys provided the critical infrastructure serving the agricultural economy, and the money and personnel for those services often originated in the agricultural sector as well. A handful of examples illustrates the pattern repeated over and again: Tennessee's Edmund Russell came from a farming family, but he himself became the president of the Nashville and Chattanooga Railroad; Alabama legislator Archibald Carmichael, son of an antebellum planter and attorney, moved from a law practice into banking; North Carolina's Bennehan Cameron, son of the richest planter in the state on the eve of the Civil War, continued to farm until his death but also invested in banks, railroads, and textile mills.[9]

Before the Civil War, therefore, the basis had been laid for a marriage of agricultural and industrial interests. After the war, this potentially powerful union of Bourbonism and Whiggery continued to grow but required the cooperation of state governments, which had the power to tax and otherwise control the direction of business and industry, in order to meet its full economic potential. The opportunity for southern white conservatives to regain control of the state legislatures came in the 1870s, when a severe depression and other diversions directed northern attention away from the "southern question." Prodded by economic coercion and physical violence, black Republicans stayed away from the polls, and one by one, the southern states returned to the Democratic fold and were said to be "redeemed."

These Redeemers, or Bourbons, were often the same white conservatives who had held positions of political prominence in the antebellum South, positions usually attained by the profits of plantation agriculture. In South Carolina for example, the Redeemers were antebellum Democrats and planters who had weathered the Civil War and Reconstruction quite comfortably. They still wielded great economic power, which was only dented, not destroyed, by the loss of their slaves. They still held the land, which was the major source of wealth in the South. Many were adding to their wealth by pioneering in southern industry. And planters began to return to positions of political power as well. The genealogies of the postbellum political leadership often included several generations of economic, social, and political elites.[10]

However, all did not return to the status quo antebellum. While the planter class remained economically and politically powerful, the South's traditional leaders now shared power with mercantile and industrial interests.[11] The line between planter and industrialist or between rural and urban grew fuzzy, as planters invested in industry and merchants bought country property.[12] Especially after the dramatic growth of railroads and other industries in the 1880s, men in commerce and manufacturing rose in wealth and social stature and began elbowing their way into politics as well.

Moreover, a burgeoning free labor force presented a new challenge to the planters. A still significant body of black voters remained a possible threat, especially if the federal government ever chose to intervene in southern affairs again. And dissatisfaction among smaller farmers, who had generally kept their grievances to themselves during the slavery regime, surfaced throughout the region in the 1870s and 1880s. These small farmers, now producing for the market economy rather than for their own subsistence, suffered intensely from the falling cotton prices during the post-Reconstruction years. Many thousands of formerly independent farmers found themselves pushed into the ranks of landless tenant farmers, and they were understandably unhappy with the change. As Edward Ayers explains, Redemption had failed to eliminate the opposition the conservatives had faced during Reconstruction. Republicans, Independents, and then Populists received significant electoral support throughout the 1880s.[13]

The planter-dominated political machinery could handle each of the various challengers separately. But if free labor, black voters, and up-country yeoman farmers were to unite, they might pose a more serious threat, as the agrarian revolt of the 1880s and early 1890s would prove. The Populists, occasionally allied with the southern Republican parties, openly solicited black voters for their insurgency. In Arkansas, for example, the People's Party platform condemned lynching in an effort to attract black support.[14] Georgia Populists made several efforts to cross the racial divide, including holding local party conventions open to both races and incorporating black speakers in the programs.[15] North Carolina Populists, in a more formal arrangement with the state Republican Party, created "fusion" tickets, won control of the state legislature in 1894, and immediately reformed the electoral system to assure greater black voting power. The "fusionists" also appointed blacks to local offices, including those of the influential county deputy sheriffs.[16]

The potential union of white yeoman farmers, blacks, and Republicans threatened the ascendancy of the Bourbons. The weapon of the Democratic Party in response to this threat was racism.[17] Increasingly vicious racial rhetoric accompanied rising racial violence, and white conservatives began to devise new methods of racial segregation while reviving old methods of racial intimidation. Lynchings reached an all-time high: in 1891, whites in Alabama lynched twenty-four blacks. In the same year, the state passed its first Jim Crow law.[18] More than 200 southern blacks were lynched between 1900 and 1901.[19]

Southern white conservatives began to discuss the possibilities for the outright disfranchisement of blacks in the 1880s. But a "safe" method, meaning one that the federal government could not contravene, had yet to be found. Legislatures in various states experimented with several possibilities. Alabama's Speaker of the House in 1892, Francis L. Pettus, sponsored a bill for literacy and property qualifications for voting. (Pettus represented Dallas County, a county with a black majority long dominated by the planting class.)[20] Several state legislatures discussed but rejected woman suffrage as a means of obtaining white majority electorates.[21] All the while, legal segregation of public and private facilities proceeded apace.

The Democrats' need for a thorough disfranchisement mechanism became all the more immediate as Populist parties showed increasing strength in each successive election. In North Carolina, the fusion tickets of Populists and Republicans had surprising success at the polls in 1894 and 1896. The response from the Black Belt was to orchestrate the infamous Wilmington race riot in 1898, which killed twenty blacks and provided an excuse for the disfranchisement campaign of 1900. The "chief engineer" of the disfranchising amendment to the state constitution was Francis Winston.[22] Winston had earlier been appointed by the Democratic Party to take charge of the Red Shirt campaign to intimidate black voters.[23] The Wilmington riot was not the spontaneous expression of lower-class racism, but was a carefully organized revolution from above, planned by the economic and political elites of Wilmington.[24]

Georgia's disfranchisement experience occurred a bit later, in 1908, but the chronology of events confirms the view that the disfranchisement of blacks was the Democratic response to the rise of a vigorous two-party political system in the post-Reconstruction South. Dewey Grantham has concluded that there had been no real demand for disfranchisement in Georgia until fierce intraparty factionalism split the Democratic Party in two in 1905, and the effect was a temporary two-party system. Another orchestrated race riot, this time in Atlanta in 1906, provided an excuse for the immediate disfranchisement of blacks and poor whites, a measure taken allegedly to prevent a repetition of the violence.[25]

Populists, suspicious that any disfranchisement scheme would also affect poor whites, had fought the numerous disfranchisement proposals throughout the 1880s and early 1890s. But the disintegration of the Populist Party after 1896 left the advocates of disfranchisement with little real opposition, and black disfranchisement quickly became reality.[26] Poor whites also found themselves struck from the voting rolls, as broadly cast disfranchisement clauses caught many illiterate whites in their nets, in spite of the pledges of many state conventions not to disfranchise white men. The Democratic Party feared the poor white voter as much as the black voter, and reducing the power of this constituency was an important part of the entire disfranchisement movement. The existence of the grandfather clauses (which allowed many whites to vote despite poverty and illiteracy) has tended to obscure this strategy. But the grandfather clauses were drawn with purposely short life spans, which quickly closed off this loophole for poor whites.[27]

With the black voting population down to a nominal level and a great number of poor whites out of the electorate, Democrats from the Black Belt began to tighten their control over local and state political machinery. But they believed they had to remain ever vigilant, reacting swiftly to any possible further attack on their political hegemony. As the Montgomery *Advertiser* warned, "we need not feel too confident that the present laws of Alabama, which keep the negro out of politics, will always be effective."[28] For, as one pamphleteer put it, "each year the negroes of the South will be better able to meet the 'grandfather' and other tests, and pay the poll taxes through which so many of them are now disfranchised."[29]

The Antisuffrage Coalition

Against such a background, what Joel Williamson has termed one of the "hot" periods in race relations, southern white women began to ask for the vote.[30] In the words of Donald Mathews and Jane De Hart, "the politicians to whom suffragists would appeal, therefore, had come to power . . . by killing people, restricting suffrage, and identifying successful politics with arrogant masculinity and terror."[31] Southern conservatives perceived the woman suffrage movement, like the agrarian revolt that preceded it, as a potential threat to the Democratic Party's supremacy. James Gray, wealthy tobacco and textile entrepreneur from Winston-Salem, North Carolina, wrote that he opposed woman suffrage for fear of "the dangers that confront us. . . . This Commonwealth has gotten along so well since 1900, that it does seem a pity to bring back unnecessarily upon us the days of 1896 and 1898."[32] A friend warned Alabama's U.S. Senator Oscar Underwood that he considered woman suffrage "an absolute menace to democratic supremacy. . . . The State would be hopelessly republican and every democratic congressman from Missouri knows it."[33] Virginia's antisuffragists made the connection explicit: "[Woman suffrage] would undo the work of the constitutional convention by throwing the balance of power into the hands of the Negro women instead of the Negro men."[34]

Across the region, former leaders of the movement to disfranchise blacks now rose up to protect their prior handiwork by preventing the enfranchisement of women. In Alabama, Oscar Underwood, who had headed the Democratic campaign committee for ratification of the Alabama disfranchising constitution,[35] was a nationally known opponent of woman suffrage. And in neighboring Mississippi, Colonel Hiram Henry, editor of the Jackson *Clarion-Ledger*, an ardent supporter of the constitutional convention to disfranchise blacks, always "bitterly opposed" any form of woman suffrage.[36] Although unsuccessful, Henry attempted more than once to instigate the formation of an antisuffrage organization for his state. Joe Bailey, "the last Democrat" from the state of Texas, had first made a name for himself in politics by the physical intimidation of Republican voters in Mississippi.[37] His later opposition to woman suffrage was unwavering, and he threw the full weight of his influence as a U.S. senator against the federal amendment. Governor "Jack" Montague of Virginia, an opponent of woman suffrage and a supporter of disfranchisement, came from a long line of tidewater planters who were local and state leaders. His father was an antebellum planter and state legislator who had advocated secession even before Lincoln's call for troops.[38]

Other examples of the continuity between the antisuffrage movement and the disfranchisement movement are numerous.[39] Richard I. Manning, South Carolina's governor during the contest over ratification of the woman suffrage amendment, opposed the Nineteenth Amendment on states' rights grounds. A member of "one of the state's most prominent and aristocratic families," Manning had served in the constitutional convention of 1895, which had disfranchised black men in the state. Manning's own suggestion for electoral reform, the Australian ballot, had as its purpose "weeding out the ignorant voters and allowing intelligent voters to vote independently by secret ballot," which would mean, of course, "weeding out" both poor whites and blacks. Manning's biographer noted that Manning had the support of "the group that a quarter of a century earlier would have supported a Bourbon, or Conservative, candidate."[40]

In Louisiana, Martin Behrman, mayor of New Orleans and head of the powerful Choctaw Club that ran the city, was prominent in the disfranchisement movement of 1898. The Choctaws had supported disfranchisement because of their belief that black votes had been responsible for their defeat in a critical election in 1896. For the next twenty years, "exclusion of the Negro from politics . . . remained a 'commandment' of that organization." During those same twenty years, the Behrman machine also opposed woman suffrage in any form.[41]

Disfranchisers were aided in the antisuffrage campaign by Redeemers. Men who had been active in the Redemption process in the 1870s who then went on to participate in the antisuffrage movement included Judge Samuel F. Wilson of Nashville; Calvin Vance of Batesville, Mississippi; and Joseph Neal Brown of Desoto County, Mississippi. Relatives of the Redeemers were also active in the movement to stop woman suffrage. Mississippi planter and legislator Walter Sillers Sr. was an important leader of the 1875 Redemption campaign. More than forty years later, his son, Walter Sillers Jr., voted against the state suffrage amendment as a representative from Bolivar County. Known members of the Ku Klux Klan who also worked against woman suffrage included W. T. Saxon of Hamilton, Texas, Thomas Heflin of Alabama, and Carroll Kendrick of Kendrick, Mississippi.

Conservative Democrats all, the disfranchisers, Klansmen, and Redeemers were products of, and defenders of, the plantation economy of the southern Black Belt districts. They were often the descendants of families whose political and economic power stretched far back into the antebellum past. The constituency of the southern antisuffrage movement gives testament to the continued strength and prominence of the South's antebellum political leadership in the postbellum years.[42]

Using the membership of the Louisiana Men's Anti–Woman Suffrage League as a typical example, the strength of the agriculture sector in the antisuffrage movement can be quickly demonstrated. Of the fifteen members of the organization, four came from farming or planting families, another four were merchants in rural parishes, four were attorneys in rural parishes, and one was a banker in Acadia Parish.[43]

Roll call voting patterns in the various states provide more evidence of the strength of antisuffragism in the plantation districts. For example, in North Carolina's vote on a state woman suffrage amendment in 1915, legislators from counties with small black populations (under 20 percent of the whole) split their votes down the middle: half approved, half opposed the state amendment. Representatives of counties with larger black populations (40 to 80 percent of the whole) voted against the measure three times as frequently as those who supported the suffrage bill. (See Table A.23.) Five years later, when the North Carolina legislature debated the ratification of Nineteenth Amendment, the outcome was quite similar. As shown in Table A.24, counties with black populations under 20 percent of the whole voted 30 to 21 in favor of the federal amendment. But in counties where the black population was larger (more than 40 percent of the whole) votes *against* the Anthony Amendment were nearly three times the number as those in its favor.

Clearly, the presence of a large black population did not dictate that a county's representatives would automatically vote against woman suffrage. A small number of legislators from the Black Belt in North Carolina and other southern states voted in the affirmative on woman suffrage. But black majorities still made legislators nervous about the possible impact that woman suffrage might have on electoral politics. They made lawmakers even more nervous when a federal amendment was under consideration, as the evidence from Alabama makes clear. As demonstrated in Tables A.20 and A.21, Black Belt legislators voted quite differently on the federal amendment than on a state woman suffrage bill. In the 1915 state amendment contest, Alabama's Black Belt legislators voted surprisingly favorably on the woman suffrage legislation. Remarkably, counties with black majorities supported the bill more often than counties with black minorities. (This unusual outcome may be the product of the long-standing feud between the Black Belt and the up-country counties. Up-country legislators probably feared that woman suffrage, in the wake of the thorough disfranchisement of poor whites in 1901, would work to increase further the electoral power of the Black Belt at the expense of the up-country.)[44]

When the issue was the federal suffrage amendment, however, Alabama legislators' votes were dramatically different. Fearful that a federal amendment meant federal control over elections, Black Belt legislators recoiled in suspicion against the Nineteenth Amendment in 1919. Those same Black Belt counties that had been willing to support state-controlled woman suffrage in 1915 threw their considerable strength against the federal amendment, providing the bulk of the votes against it and only a handful of votes in support of the measure. Only nineteen Alabama counties had black majorities (in the 1920 census count), but they provided thirty-four votes against the amendment. By contrast, those counties with black populations under 20 percent of the whole who had opposed the state-controlled version just four years earlier, now supported federally mandated woman suffrage.[45]

In state after state, the trends were similar: southern whites in areas with large black populations remained fearful of woman suffrage; and their fears increased when woman suffrage was offered in the form of a federal amendment. Alabama's "Steering Committee to Defeat the Susan B. Anthony Amendment" was, not surprisingly, dominated by members from the Black Belt who were planters, farmers, and associated professionals (see Table A.22). The large number of lawyers, merchants, and doctors in the southern state legislatures, many of whom lived in towns and cities throughout the region, might lead some to argue that such legislators were not representatives of the planter class but instead, as urban professionals, were part of an urban middle class with different interests. But even a shallow genealogical dig would demonstrate the shortcomings of that assumption. Even those who did not themselves plant and had moved to the town or city in order to pursue their professions often came from the family plantation where other family members continued to live and work. A small number of examples will illustrate a much more frequently occurring phenomenon: Walter Green, a state representative in Mississippi, was an attorney in Natchez. His father, however, was a cotton planter in Louisiana, and Green voted against the state woman suffrage amendment in 1918. Another Mississippi legislator, Edmund Irby, was a merchant and a college-educated artist. But his father, Richard, was a planter, and his grandfather, Wyatt, was an antebellum legislator. Irby voted against the state suffrage amendment in 1918. In neighboring Louisiana, John R. Perez was a college-educated attorney practicing in New Orleans. His father, however, was a prominent sugar planter, and Perez voted against the Nineteenth Amendment in 1920. W. D. Cowan of Sansaba, Texas, was president of the Pecos Valley Bank and a member of the "Commercial Club" (an early version of the Chamber of Commerce), but he continued to own and run his cattle ranch as well. Cowan joined the Men's Anti–Woman Suffrage Association. Alabama's Martin Lee Calhoun, prolific antisuffrage editorial writer, lived in Selma, where he was the district agent for the Pennsylvania Life Insurance Company. Calhoun's father, a nephew of John C. Calhoun, was a planter and prewar state senator.[46] Planter families held onto their lands when they could, even when the family moved to town; and they held onto the plantation ideal just as fervently.[47]

Southern antisuffragism thrived in cotton soil, and both male and female antisuffragists shared this common background. As the Montgomery *Advertiser* exulted, "the personnel of the Anti-Ratification League of Montgomery is representative of the highest type of Southern womanhood; its members are from Alabama families, which have exemplified the best in Southern life and they grew up and have lived in the atmosphere of the culture and traditions of the South."[48] Molly Elliot Seawell, a leading antisuffragist from Virginia, confirmed that her earliest influences came from "the secluded life I had led in the library of an old Virginia country house, and in a community where conditions more nearly resembled the eighteenth than the nineteenth century."[49] North Carolina's acknowledged female antisuffrage leader, Mary Hilliard Hinton, came from a planting family that had long been prominent in the state's politics. (In fact, her uncle, Elias Carr, had been governor during the 1890s.) Hinton lived on her family's plantation, Midway, in Wake County, named for its location between the family's other two plantations in the Piedmont.[50] Mildred Lewis Rutherford, antisuffrage leader from Georgia, was a niece of Howell Cobb and T. R. R. Cobb and had grown up with her family's slave children for playmates. As an adult, she devoted herself to, among other things, a defense of slavery.[51] As beneficiaries of the privileges of their class, plantation women had a long tradition of defending those privileges.[52]

Reinforcing this line of analysis is considerable evidence that southern suffragists had difficulty reaching and organizing rural women. An Atlanta suf-

Mary Hilliard Hinton, state leader of antisuffrage movement in North Carolina, ca. 1910s (Courtesy of N.C. Division of Archives and History, Raleigh)

frage worker wrote in 1915 that "we are working very hard but it seems almost impossible to reach the rural districts, & this population is such an ignorant & hopeless one."[53] One study of Virginia's suffrage movement concluded that the organization of small town leagues "never repaid the effort the suffragists put into it."[54] Whether they lived on large plantations or in crossroads communities, rural women had little appreciation for the urban-based arguments utilized by southern suffragists. Few rural women, regardless of class, had seen a settlement house, inspected a factory for child labor abuses, or raised money for a free kindergarten. Woman suffrage remained, under their circumstances, a hypothetical idea, not an immediate need.

By contrast, suffragism sprang to life in the 1910s and flourished in the growing towns and cities of the South, especially those most closely tied to the national market economy. The urban boom at the turn of the century was most notable in those towns with populations under 10,000. These places were the former hamlets that had blossomed into cities nearly overnight with the arrival of the railroads, commerce, and factories.[55]

The women from the growing towns and cities who joined the suffrage ranks were often the descendants of the small commercial middle class of the South's antebellum towns. Their fathers and grandfathers were urban doctors, lawyers, merchants, teachers, and newspaper editors. Alabama's Mary McNeill, for example, was the daughter of an architect and the wife of professor of art history. Memphis's Corrinne Beattie, daughter of a local druggist, married an attorney (who was himself the son of a merchant). And Mobile club woman Lura Craighead, the daughter of a merchant, married a journalist and newspaper editor.

Table A.14 summarizes the available information on the livelihoods of suffrage families and contrasts it to the profile of the antisuffragists in Table A.15. While families in both groups were generally middle class and occasionally quite wealthy, there were nevertheless subtle differences in their respective places in the economy. Although suffragists and antisuffragists had similar numbers in commerce, government employment, and manufacturing, they diverged in two telling categories: suffrage families appeared more often in the white-collar professional positions (most significantly in the newer service professions), and antisuffrage families appeared more often in agriculture.

By the twentieth century, these urban suffragists were often married to men in the service sector of the growing urban economy: insurance agents, car salesmen, white collar civil servants, as well as the usual doctors, lawyers, and professors. They or their husbands worked in jobs that provided services to urban residents rather than serving the needs of the plantation economy. In short, their families had often been "townsfolk" for more than a generation, and their economic and cultural ties to the plantation were increasingly remote.

Goldsboro, North Carolina, illustrates this point. A tiny crossroads before the Civil War, Goldsboro had the good fortune of standing at the intersection of both north-south and east-west railroad lines by the 1880s. Growing quickly into a regional marketing center with strong links into the national market economy, Goldsboro was the home of one of the state's first women's clubs and one of the state's first local suffrage leagues. Goldsboro was also the home of the state's foremost suffrage leader, Gertrude Weil. Weil was the daughter of a German Jewish immigrant who had settled in Goldsboro just before the Civil War. With family in New York and Baltimore and with lives and livelihoods that had little dependence on antebellum agriculture, the Weil family was the embodiment of the New South.[56]

Farther south, Zaida Kirby of Scottsboro, Alabama, lived in a small town connected by rail and commerce to a larger urban community. Before her marriage, Zaida Brown had already seen a world outside of rural Alabama. She had graduated from Vassar College, which made her one of the few southern women eligible to join the discriminating Association of College Alumnae. After her marriage to Atticus Kirby, a successful business entrepreneur who sold real estate and owned a gas station, Zaida Kirby settled into the middle class whirl of women's voluntary associations, primarily through her Episcopal church. In 1919, she volunteered to serve on the Ratification Committee of the state suffrage association.

Nashville's Margaret Caldwell is yet another example. The daughter of a doctor, Margaret Winston did not receive a college education but nevertheless took advantage of all the opportunities that a city like Nashville could provide. After her marriage to Alex Caldwell, who owned a car dealership, Margaret became very active in women's clubs. She joined a literary society, an art association, and at one time served as state president of the Federation of Women's Clubs. A talented woman with much business sense of her own, as a widow she ran the family's car dealership while her sons served in World War I.

Like Caldwell, many other suffragists earned their own middle-class status; that is, their own careers (rather than those of their fathers or husbands) placed them in the emerging urban middle class of the New South. As shown in Table A.11 (and discussed in further detail in Chapter 3), suffragists themselves frequently earned a living in the urban service sector. Their ranks were peppered with social workers, journalists, librarians, government agents, and "pink-collar" workers of various sorts. Urban lifestyles and livelihoods did not instantly convert residents to support of woman suffrage, of course. But support for progressive reforms was one way that this new middle class at-

Gertrude Weil, prominent suffrage leader from Goldsboro, North Carolina, ca. 1920s (Courtesy of N.C. Division of Archives and History, Raleigh)

tempted to define itself and its values and set itself apart from the plantation/industrial elites.[57]

It might be argued that the presence of antisuffrage organizations in cities like Nashville disproves the above interpretation of the rural origins of antisuffragism. Quite the contrary. Towns and cities in the Black Belt were usually fully integrated into the plantation economy. Montgomery, in the heart of the Black Belt of Alabama, served as the major cotton entrepôt for the immediate region. In the 1880s, cotton sales constituted one-fifth of the city's entire commercial trade.[58] Not coincidentally, the Montgomery *Advertiser* regularly spoke in opposition to black voters, railroad regulation, and woman suffrage. Likewise, Macon, Georgia, the acknowledged center of that state's antisuffrage activity, lay in the heart of Georgia's plantation belt. Macon's major economic function was the processing of cotton produced in the region. Cotton came in and out of the city on several different railroad lines that were based in Macon. The Macon *Telegraph*, owned by a former cotton mill agent, was an outspoken opponent of the state's railroad commission.[59] Other southern towns and cities that produced antisuffrage organizations had a similar relationship with the plantation economy. Houston, for example, had built its economy on the transportation and processing of cotton. In 1920, it was the home of the largest cotton brokerage firm in the world.[60]

Other southern cities with significant antisuffrage organizations were state capitals. Montgomery, Raleigh, Nashville, and Richmond were the centers for antisuffrage activities in their respective states. These sites were a logical place for antisuffrage activities from an organizational standpoint. The need to lobby legislators and the desire to show antisuffrage strength at critical times meant that capital cities in particular were strategic locations in the antisuffrage campaigns. Like the suffs, the antisuffragists recognized the importance of having strength on the "home ground" when the legislature met.[61] Thus, despite the presence of antisuffrage organizations in some southern towns and cities like Macon and Montgomery, the real heart of southern antisuffragism was rural.

Powerful Interest Groups

Another important source of antisuffragism also had strong ties to the plantation economy. The textile industry in the South was tightly linked with the agricultural elites, and the industry itself was structured in such a way as to complement the agricultural economy rather than compete with it. Textile manufacturers were themselves often heavily involved in plantation agriculture. For example, in the period from 1865 to 1884, over half the textile mills in North Carolina were owned completely or partly by planters. Big agriculture built the textile industry in North Carolina, and the economic and political interests of planters and mill owners frequently overlapped.[62]

Southern textile mill owners were prominent in their opposition to woman suffrage. For example, Nashville's Garnett Andrews, secretary of the Tennessee Constitutional League (which opposed the enfranchisement of women), served as the vice president of a hosiery mill and two knitting mills. North Carolina's William Holt Williamson, president of the States' Rights Defense League (the men's antisuffrage organization in the state), was the president of Pilot Cotton Mills of Raleigh, Hopedale Mills of Burlington, and Harriet Mills of Henderson. Williamson was also the grandson of Edwin M. Holt, a textile industry pioneer in the state. Another grandson of the cotton king, Robert Holt of Burlington, North Carolina, owned cotton mills and banks and served on the executive committee of the States' Rights Defense League. Malcolm A. Graham, antisuffrage legislator from Prattville, Alabama, was secretary-treasurer of the Prattville Cotton Mills. J. Cheshire Webb of Hillsboro, North Carolina, owned two cotton mills and served on the advisory board for the state branch of the Southern Rejection League.[63]

Like their male counterparts, many female antisuffragists had close ties to the textile industry. Mattie C. Elsberry of Montgomery, for example, was married to an officer of the Tallahassee Falls Manufacturing Company, which produced cotton goods. Cornelia Hardaway's husband, James, owned another cotton company in Montgomery. And Minnie Tucker Baker of Raleigh, wife of the president of the Virginia Cotton Mills, Ashby L. Baker, was secretary of the state branch of the Southern Rejection League.

Other antisuffragists effectively bridged the gap between textile manufacturers and cotton planters. A large number of antisuffragists were cotton brokers, including Raleigh's Charles E. Johnson, whose elegant mansion still stands on the capital city's Hillsborough Street. Hails Janney, husband of antisuffragist Margaret Janney, was a cotton broker in Montgomery. William H. Taylor, a member of the Men's Anti–Woman Suffrage Association in Texas, was a cotton buyer in Waco. John Lee Long, antisuffrage legislator from Butler County, Alabama, was a cotton buyer who had also worked to disfranchise black voters in 1901.[64]

Another powerful interest group widely believed to be behind the antisuffrage movement was the liquor industry. In the summer of 1917, for example, Arkansas suffragist Alice Ellington wrote to Minnie Fisher Cunningham for information about who the Texas antisuffragists were and where they got their financial assistance. Cunningham replied:

> The campaign of the Anti-Suffragists in the Texas legislature was waged on the floor of the House, and off, by the leaders of the Liquor machine. Speakers against Suffrage on the day that our bill came up to be voted on were W. T. Bagby, of Hallettsville, floor leader for the liquor interests in the House; Geo. W. Mendell, of Austin, whose name appears as leading Anti-Prohibitionist in the criminal proceedings against the Texas Brewers Association; Barry Miller, of Dallas, a well known Anti-Prohibitionist. . . . There were no outside speakers sent.
>
> The Anti-Suffrage campaign, as far as we can locate it in Texas, is waged by the corrupt political machine of the state, which is the Liquor Machine. The Anti-Suffrage leader is Mrs. Jas. B. Wells, of Brownsville, Texas, wife of the political dictator of that section of the country.[65]

The antisuffragists, however, always denied the charges of their association with the liquor industry. In an undated letter to Josephine Pearson, Virginia Vertrees defended her husband against charges that he was a liquor lawyer: "When Hooper dared to say that Mr Vertrees was att[orney] for the whiskey party, He denounced him in the newspaper and Hooper never opened his mouth, and when his man Will Taylor attempted to back up Hooper, Mr Vertrees took his pistol and went to Taylor's office, denounced him as a l——, so no one has dared to charge him of it since. . . .He has always been Mr Shwabs lawyer in everything, business deeds, wills, settlements, but lawyer for the W Ring *never*, and it is not safe for anyone to charge it."[66] When the Raleigh *News and Observer* ran an editorial cartoon suggesting that whiskey was behind the antisuffrage movement, North Carolina antis reacted with anger. Through their journal *The State's Defense*, antisuffragists denounced the "affront" and demanded "an apology to our ladies."[67] The Southern Rejection League in Alabama went so far as to threaten to sue anyone who claimed that it was financed by or associated with any liquor interest. "Not one cent has come from any other source than among our own people, whose names we will gladly publish if occasion demands," they asserted.[68]

Such protestations notwithstanding, most historians have accepted without much question the assertion that the liquor industry financed the antisuffrage campaign.[69] Evidence from the southern states, where Prohibition came early, suggests that the liquor interests were not the monolithic powerhouse of antisuffragism that the suffragists liked to claim. Undoubtedly, the distillers in Kentucky provided solid opposition to both Prohibition and woman suffrage, as did the brewers and the saloon keepers of southern Louisiana. The same can be said of Memphis, Tennessee, where there were more than five hundred saloons at the turn of the century, all of which were "enmeshed" in politics.

Cartoon depicting coalition of interest groups. Note that the antisuffragist is depicted as female. (Courtesy of Tennessee State Library and Archives, Nashville)

Memphis was also the home of large warehousing facilities for major liquor companies, which distributed liquor to the surrounding region.[70] Likewise, individuals with other interests in the liquor industry participated in the antisuffrage movement. For example, J. O. Martin, Tennessee state representative from Hamilton County, was a liquor wholesaler. He voted against the Susan B. Anthony Amendment in 1920. State representative J. S. Boyd from Davidson County, Tennessee, was a former saloon owner who also voted against the Nineteenth Amendment. Max Mayer, a traveling salesman for a liquor company in San Antonio, joined the Men's Association Opposed to Woman

Suffrage in Texas. John J. Vertrees, prominent Nashville attorney (who, according to historian Paul Isaac, was also an attorney for liquor concerns), was a well-known opponent of woman suffrage, directing organizational activities behind the scenes.[71]

But the financial strength and political omnipotence of the liquor forces in the South must be questioned, since all nine southern states that rejected the Anthony Amendment had voted *for* the Prohibition amendment. The power of the "liquor lobby" must be questioned even further in places such as North Carolina and Georgia, where local option laws had long before dried up most alcohol dispensaries and removed saloon keepers from the equation.[72] It would therefore be more accurate to say that the liquor interests were important only in certain areas in the southern suffrage contests and that suffragists overstated their case by pointing at the liquor lobby bogeyman behind every antisuffrage vote. (It is quite possible that the suffragists knew this themselves, but purposely linked antisuffragism with the liquor interests as a political strategy.)

Perhaps because so much attention has been directed toward the liquor industry, other interest groups that played a role in the antisuffrage movement have received inadequate attention. One of the most important—and overlooked—participants in the antisuffrage coalition was railroads. Railroads were arguably a more important source of antisuffrage strength than the liquor industry. Contemporary observers occasionally mentioned those with interests in the railroads as opponents of woman suffrage. In Tennessee in 1920, for example, Carrie Chapman Catt and Abby Crawford Milton went on a statewide speaking tour on behalf of the federal amendment to convince the public that the forces against them were "the whiskey lobby, the manufacturers' lobby, and the railroad lobby." But historians have tended to focus on the first two while ignoring the last.[73]

Railroad involvement in the antisuffrage movement was discreet: the railroad directors never made official pronouncements against woman suffrage, nor did they lobby openly against the various suffrage bills. But their opposition was nevertheless manifest. Railroad "pocket legislators," such as antisuffragist Alfred M. Tunstall of Alabama, voted under the direction of their patron railway.[74] Alabama's Oscar Underwood had substantial railroad interests through various family members (including his father, who was on the board of directors of the Louisville and Nashville Railroad). Underwood's biographer concluded that "by the time his House career ended, he, on occasion, frankly represented their interests." His closest friends were also railroad lawyers.[75] Underwood's opposition to woman suffrage has already been noted.

Other legislators did the bidding of the railroads as well, such as Seth Walker, Speaker of the House in Tennessee in 1920 and an attorney for the Louisville and Nashville Railroad (L&N) who opposed ratification of the Susan B. Anthony Amendment.[76] An important Alabama antisuffrage legislator, Walter B. Jones, was the son of former governor Thomas Goode Jones, who had once been the chief attorney for the L&N in Alabama. The younger Jones had followed in his father's footsteps, serving as counsel for the railroad.[77] Charles B. Aycock, Black Belt "aristocrat" and disfranchisement manager from North Carolina, was also a railroad attorney.[78] When Furnifold Simmons needed to raise money for North Carolina's "white supremacy" campaign of 1898, he turned to bankers and railroads for funds. They generously contributed,[79] and Simmons's later opposition to woman suffrage was unwavering. North Carolina's governor in 1892, Elias Carr, served the railroad interests to such a degree that he actually leased the state-owned North Carolina Railroad to J. P. Morgan's Southern Railway system for ninety-nine years, against the wishes of most of the states' citizens.[80] Carr's grandniece, Mary Hilliard Hinton, was the state president of the North Carolina antisuffragists.

James B. Wells, a political boss in southeast Texas, personifies the close connections between big agriculture, railroads, and antisuffragism. For many years Wells was counsel for the Rio Grande Railroad.[81] But Wells had further reason to support railroading in Texas: he had collected vast tracts of land in the Rio Grande valley, eventually accumulating more than 44,000 acres. The right railroad connections could make that land infinitely more valuable. One account has noted that "every practical suggestion for a Texas railroad into the lower Rio Grande country was supported by his great influence and open purse."[82] His wife, Pauline Kleber Wells, led the antisuffrage campaign in Texas.

In addition to Pauline Wells and Mary Hilliard Hinton, many other antisuffrage women had close ties to the railroad industry. Annie Brown of Nashville, a member of the Tennessee antisuffrage association, was married to the superintendent of the Nashville Railway and Light Company. Anna Russell Cole, famed beauty of Nashville, was married to the president of the Nashville and Chattanooga Railroad. Alice Hill of Chattanooga, a member of the state antisuffrage association, was married to J. T. Hill, an officer of several Tennessee railroad companies. Mamie Jackson of Nashville, an opponent of woman suffrage, was the wife of an attorney for the Nashville Railway and Light Company. Queenie Woods Washington, vice president of the Tennessee Association Opposed to Woman Suffrage, was married to George A. Washington, one of the directors of the Louisville and Nashville. Roxalee Andrews of Houston, a member of the Texas antisuffrage organization, was married to an attorney for the Gulf Coast Railroad. San Antonio's Carrie Cobbs, another opponent of woman suffrage, was also the wife of a railroad attorney.[83]

However, association with railroads did not necessarily determine one's position on woman suffrage: suffragist Mary-Cooke Branch Munford of Virginia married an attorney for the Richmond and Danville Railroad.[84] Tennessee suffragist Mary Fleming Meek married an employee of the Southern Railway. But in general, railroad officers and attorneys (and their spouses) filled the ranks of the antisuffrage movement, their names appearing far more often on the rosters of antisuffrage organizations than on those of the prosuffrage effort.

Although less numerous than railroads in the South, and certainly less powerful, a handful of political machines were also significant participants in the southern antisuffrage coalition. The work of boss Martin Behrman of New Orleans exemplifies the overlapping of antisuffragism, disfranchisement, big business, the liquor interests, and political machines. His Democratic machine, the Choctaw Club, controlled New Orleans's politics for more than twenty years. Although it was urban in nature, based on the voting strength of a largely ethnic working class, the Behrman machine aligned itself with big business (including the brewers) and big agricultural interests in the state. This combination of voting power and economic clout made the Behrman coalition a formidable force. In order to protect its interests, the machine "regularly interfered with reform movements associated with progressivism."[85] One of those reforms was woman suffrage.

Two political machines in Texas were also especially important in the antisuffrage movement. Pauline Wells, the antisuffragist who "single-handedly" defeated a Texas suffrage proposal in 1915, was the wife of one the most powerful political bosses in the South. Her husband, Jim Wells, ran a South Texas machine well known for corrupt election practices. Likewise, Wells's political ally and fellow machine boss, Archie Parr of Duval County, threw his considerable influence against woman suffrage. As a member of the state Senate, Parr voted against all proposals for woman suffrage. And as a politico in control of other politicians, he delivered their votes to the "nay" column as well. Parr's plundering of public funds is legendary in Texas history, and progressives in that state came to regard him as the "symbol of the worst qualities in Texas politics: corruption, violence, and intransigent opposition to reform."[86]

In sum, antisuffragists in the southern states, both male and female, came from families with economic power and political experience that stretched far back into the antebellum period. Planters (or sons and daughters of planters), textile mill owners (and their kin), railroad builders, and politicians at the local, state, and national level, all felt that woman suffrage held potential danger for them and their interests. Just as they once had worked to redeem their states from Republican rule and then had disfranchised black voters to protect the Redemption, they then worked to prevent women from upsetting the political balance that they had worked to create. Women of the planter class, and the spouses, daughters, cousins, and in-laws of the other antisuffrage interest groups, shared their interests. As sociologist Jeanne Howard has concluded, female opponents of suffrage demonstrated an allegiance to class over gender and a fear of what change might bring when they had so much to lose.[87]

The Question of Motivation

Planters, textile men, railroad magnates, machine bosses, and liquor lawyers: what united these diverse interest groups in their opposition to woman suffrage? Although these groups might not have agreed on every issue of the day and should not be seen as a monolithic unit, when it came to woman suffrage, at least, they were united in their opposition. Simply put, they feared that suffragists would make good on their promises to vote in various reform measures and, in effect, change their world.

Suffrage rhetoric claimed that enfranchised women would outlaw child labor, pass minimum-wage and maximum-hours laws for women workers, and establish health and safety standards for factory workers. Chief Justice Walter Clark believed that the textile interests opposed woman suffrage for fear of "the power of women's votes in preventing the exploitation of child labor, in requiring 'equal pay for equal service' irrespective of sex."[88] (Clark had some reason to know whereof he spoke: his son, David Clark, published the *Southern Textile Bulletin* and was a spokesman for the cotton interests in the South.[89]) If the threatened reforms were enacted, the textile industry in particular would suffer, as it relied so heavily on the cheap labor of women and children. In 1900, for example, 25 percent of the textile mill labor force of Alabama were children under the age of sixteen.[90] Twenty-four percent of North Carolina's textile workers were children that same year.[91] The figure for Mississippi was almost identical: 23.8 percent. The southern textile mills together employed nearly 30,000 children as early as 1900.[92] The textile manufacturers believed they had good reason to fear the enfranchisement of women.

And why would railroads in particular feel they should oppose the enfranchisement of women? The railways feared the possibility that suffragists would make good on the their threat to launch a full-scale assault on the corruption of this particular big business. During the Progressive Era, railroads were widely regarded as one of the most corrupting forces in American society. Their influence in state legislatures nationwide had reached staggering proportions by the 1880s, creating a great deal of popular sentiment for regulation. Prosuffrage rhetoric claimed that women, as an incorruptible moral influence, would help to wipe out the abuses of the system with their ballots.

In the meantime, railroads maintained their power in a number of ways. They generously dispensed free passes to judges, sheriffs, legislators, editors, and other important men. The passes, of course, had strings attached; reciprocity was assumed.[93] The Louisville and Nashville Railroad, for example, gave the entire Alabama legislature a free trip to Mobile for Mardi Gras in 1899. One investigation reported in 1913 that thirty-five members of the Tennessee legislature had received free passes totaling $115,647 in fares. Not coincidentally, the legislators were considering a railroad regulation bill at the time. In 1912 and 1913, the L&N loaned the state of Alabama more than $249,000 to weather some temporary financial difficulties. The expectation was that Alabama would treat the railroad kindly in any future regulatory efforts.[94]

Railroads curried the favor of the press as well, again by the distribution of free passes and cheap loans. The Louisville and Nashville made loans to both the Louisville *Courier-Journal* and the Montgomery *Advertiser* during particularly lean times.[95] Not surprisingly, these papers consistently opposed railroad regulation and wrote positively about the value of railroads to the New South. Railroads also employed large numbers of people in the southern states, from attorneys to ticket agents. As early as 1886, the Louisville and Nashville, for instance, employed five hundred people in the Montgomery-Mobile division alone. And by 1926 (at its peak), the L&N employed more than 53,000 people in the region. And needless to say, continued employment required loyalty.[96]

The cultivation of friendly relations with the press served the railroads well in the woman suffrage contest. For example, Henry Watterson, longtime friend and supporter of the Louisville and Nashville Railroad, used his *Courier-Journal* to preach his Bible-based antisuffragism. From a wealthy planting family himself, Watterson became a major spokesman of the New South movement, and his *Courier-Journal* was second only to Henry Grady's Atlanta *Constitution* in degree of advocacy for industrial and commercial development of the South.[97] Nashville's E. B. Stahlman, editor of the *Banner* and leader of the Tennessee Constitutional League, had been an agent for the L&N for thirty-five years before taking over the newspaper. He continued to work closely with the railroad and to oppose the enfranchisement of women for the rest of his life. Seldom recognized as such in the historical literature, railroads were one of the most powerful and important sources of antisuffragism in the South, and perhaps in the country at large.[98]

Although all railroads had the potential for corruption, the bigger ones had more to offer, as well as more to lose. The biggest of them all was the Louisville and Nashville, which was one of the most powerful corporations in several southern states.[99] By 1902, the L&N owned more than 3,400 miles of track, over which moved 38 million tons of freight and 6.6 million passengers annually.[100] Eventually branching out to touch every southern state, the combined resources of the L&N were more than any single state could handle. Only interstate regulation could begin to tame such a monster, nicknamed the "Long and Nasty" for its size and its reputation.[101]

The Louisville and Nashville had a substantial record of corruption and abuses. When Tennessee began to consider railroad regulation in 1883, the L&N sent E. B. Stahlman, a former railroad official and then editor of the powerful Nashville *Banner*, to work against regulation. Stahlman's assignment was to gain newspaper support for the railroad by the generous distribution of "loans."[102] The very next year, Stahlman led a successful drive to abolish the state's railroad commission.[103] In 1906, when B. B. Comer ran for governor of Alabama on a reform platform and made effective railroad regulation one of the key elements of his campaign, the L&N struck back, secretly spending $50,000 in the unsuccessful effort to defeat Comer.[104]

Just as railroads perceived a threat from ballot-wielding women, so did the machine bosses. As machine politicians, men like Archie Parr and Jim Wells depended on predictable votes. As machine politicians in south Texas, they depended on predictable Mexican votes. Woman suffrage was therefore doubly dangerous. Not only were women an unknown element in politics ("no one on earth can either tell how they are going to vote, to control them" according to Wells), but Mexican women, as Catholics with more traditional views on women's role in society, were generally felt to be averse to voting. As Parr wrote to his friend Wells, "you ought to be able to vote all the Mexican women. Though I know they do not want to go to the polls."[105] If Mexican women refused to vote as Parr feared, the impact of woman suffrage would be to increase the relative strength of the "Anglo" vote in Texas. And that Anglo vote might very well be cast in favor of progressive reforms. Because of its dependence on loyal Hispanic voters, Wells's machine consistently opposed election reforms that might undermine its influence with this constituency. It blocked the passage of the Australian ballot and laws limiting the assistance to illiterate voters, and it solidly opposed woman suffrage.[106]

Other career politicians also perceived a threat to their livelihoods when suffragists promised reform. Politicians who had grown wealthy by government contracts and political contacts became fierce defenders of the status quo. Men like John Bankhead of Alabama, who had made a fortune as state warden (in charge of the convict lease system), opposed progressive reforms in general and woman suffrage in particular.[107]

And finally, why did big agriculture fear woman suffrage? Black Belt political and economic elites looked at woman suffrage and saw an enlargement of the electorate, which they had spent more than a generation trying to reduce. Southern conservatives had gained control over political institutions and covered their coup with a cloak of legitimacy, not by expanding but by contracting the electorate.[108] The planter class seemed convinced that woman suffrage would undermine the hard-fought disfranchisement and segregation campaigns. Black Belt politicians like Cameron Morrison worked hard to defeat woman suffrage by making it a symbol of the opposition to white supremacy.[109]

A coalition of political and economic interest groups created and supported the southern antisuffrage movement. This coalition, representing the combined forces of big agriculture and big business and the Democratic Party, believed it had sufficient reason to fear the enfranchisement of women. The Black Belt aristocrats and their associates had spent the better part of a generation reassembling their former political hegemony and were not about to let millions of untested voters destroy that accomplishment.

It is important to distinguish between the larger, more powerful, antisuffrage movement and the smaller organizational expression of the movement. For the most part, antisuffrage forces in the South preferred to let women's organizations handle the public expression of antisuffrage sentiment. Women in several states founded small antisuffrage organizations to lobby, raise money, and distribute literature. The fact that women were allowed to lead the public movement had important ramifications, for the antisuffrage movement was thereby limited in significant ways by the gender roles to which antisuffrage women subscribed. Gender was at work on many levels in the antisuffrage campaign, including influencing the way members were recruited for the movement, as Chapter 3 will detail.

3

Women of the Causes

In the course of time, I became . . . a householder, a property-owner, a taxpayer, and the regular employer of five persons.

My experience, therefore, has been more varied than that of most women, and I know something of the interests both of the woman who works and of the woman property-owner, the taxpayer, and the employer.

I can say with positiveness that there never was a moment when the possession of a vote would not have been a hindrance and a burden to me.

Molly Elliot Seawell,
from *The Ladies Battle*, 1911

Weary of battling the negative stereotypes that suffrage activists had long faced, in 1914 Anna Howard Shaw ridiculed antisuffragists for their constant appeals to traditional images of women, calling them the "Home, Heaven, and Mother Party." Antisuffragists throughout the country immediately seized upon the slogan as their own, brandishing it proudly as an emotional symbol of great strength.[1] One of many such incidents, this exchange illuminates the issue of image and publicity in the suffrage contests. Women on both sides of the suffrage movement recognized that their arguments had to appeal not only to the heads but also to the hearts of the legislators who ultimately would decide the fate of the woman suffrage question. They crafted rhetoric and imagery with purposefully emotional cores.

In the southern states, the battle over image was especially hard fought, as the "New Women of the New South" squared off against the "True Daughters of the Old South."[2] While the suffragists may have held a stronger position when it came to arguing the issues of "simple justice" or "no taxation without representation," antisuffrage women in the South used the images of sacred motherhood, the Old South, and the Lost Cause to their distinct advantage.[3] Antisuffrage leader Nina Pinckard literally wrapped herself in the "Stars and Bars" and posed beside an ancient Confederate veteran for a photograph that captured succinctly the symbols that southern antisuffragists claimed for themselves.

An analysis of the efforts of activists to influence popular perceptions and to create useful stereotypical images can reveal much about the two sides of the woman suffrage question in the South, especially as images contrasted with reality. While the two preceding chapters have examined men and women together, this chapter focuses more narrowly on the women on both sides of the suffrage contest. A closer look at the separate world of women uncovers some ways in which the experiences of these two groups of women differed. While they may have shared some experiences of voluntary associations and organizational activities with their suffrage counterparts, the women who worked to defeat woman suffrage in the South also had some significantly different life experiences, experiences that were undoubtedly important in drawing women into the antisuffrage ranks. The statistical composites of the two groups of women suggest the need to reevaluate the notions of "women's culture" and the separate "female world of love and ritual" as the seemingly inevitable propagators of feminism.

“Sameness” and “Difference”

In the popular press, the stereotypical images of suffragists and antisuffragists differed dramatically. Antisuffragists successfully established the popular belief that suffrage supporters did not marry, have children, and make homes like “normal” women. A Methodist minister from Texas, for example, claimed that “the leaders of the Suffragette movement, as a rule, are divorced women, women who prefer pug dogs to children, and supernumerary spinsters, bankrupt in sentiment and possessors of worthless assets of faded charm, who, failing to capture a man, propose to remedy this misfortune by turning [into] men themselves.”[4] In a similar vein, Louisiana lawmaker E. L. Simmons portrayed suffragists as “so many disappointed old maids with masculine ambitions, and so many women that [would] rather be away from home than to have cares of their home and their children (when they have any).”[5] An anonymous editorialist from Richmond gave as his “private opinion that all this racket about woman’s suffrage is engineered by a few forward, sour, ugly, old maids, and married women who want their husbands to be ‘submissive without looking so.’ ”[6] Antisuffragists insisted that women who rejected their assigned “separate sphere” must necessarily be something less than complete women.

The attacks on the appearance and personality of suffragists must have stung, for the suffragists spent a great deal of time refuting them. In 1895, the Atlanta *Constitution* interviewed an Ohio suffragist and attorney, Mrs. Albert Holbrook (who was always so identified). Originally from Mississippi, Holbrook had left the South in order to practice law, illegal for a woman to do in her home state at the time. The article, which was clearly sympathetic to woman suffrage, stressed how “slender and graceful” Holbrook appeared and quoted her at length about cooking and housekeeping rather than about suffrage or her nontraditional occupation.[7] When Raleigh’s first suffrage club organized in 1914, it pointedly announced that the majority of the sixty-seven members were married.[8] Virginia suffragists especially favored bake sales as a fund-raising technique, for it allowed them to demonstrate that their advocacy of woman suffrage did not impair their competency in the kitchen.[9] Similarly, during World War I, Birmingham suffragists published a cookbook of wartime recipes to demonstrate that suffrage women were both patriotic and domestic.[10]

In further response to the antisuffrage attacks, southern suffragists felt compelled to prove that they did have happy home lives (even in a few cases when they did not). Tennessee suffragists used a sentimental photograph of Anna Dallas Dudley reading to her children as part of their suffrage literature.[11] Texas suffragists were equally concerned about the image of the happy homemaker: a family portrait of Jessie Daniel Ames, circulated as campaign literature, evoked the proper domestic ethos, in direct contradiction of Ames's actual marital situation.[12] And Birmingham suffragists advertised that they were "No Less Ardent in their Home Life Than in Devotion to the Cause."[13]

In an age when the "Southern Lady" continued to be an integral part of regional iconography, southern suffragists also stressed the compatibility of femininity and suffragism. When Elizabeth Meriwether made her first suffrage speech in Memphis in 1876, she was careful to be "plainly but elegantly dressed." Her stage was likewise carefully prepared, and the local press noted that "the exquisite taste displayed on the platform of furniture, colors, and scenery, demonstrated that the lecturer understands the character in which she appeared."[14] The Raleigh *News and Observer*, a professed prosuffrage paper, described a visit from National American Woman Suffrage Association (NAWSA) organizer Lavinia Engle in 1914. "She came here in nice feminine clothes, with much more manners than the men who didn't like her coming," reported the paper. Engle, it continued, "left the city without hurting it at all. The women who heard her and cheered her address, returned to their homes finding everything there intact."[15] Likewise, Judith Hyams Douglas described her coworkers in the New Orleans Era Club as "physicians, dentists, journalists, attorneys, philanthropists," all of whom presented "a very feminine appearance."[16]

Femininity, by definition, excluded any hint of militancy, a guideline to which the majority of southern suffragists rigorously adhered. A Virginia suffragist noted that "the wise suffrage leaders here have realized . . . that success depends upon showing their cause to be compatible with the essentials of the Virginia traditions [of] womanliness, and both instinct and judgment have prevented the adoption here of the more aggressive forms of campaigning."[17] Even those who actually were "militants" rarely bobbed their hair or dressed daringly.[18]

While antisuffragists never found their femininity under question, southern suffragists always worried about their proper image. Kentucky suffrage leader Madeline McDowell Breckinridge teased her fellow southerners for "trying to get suffrage in the most lady-like manner," an effort Breckinridge described as not "having anybody find out they want it."[19] But despite all efforts at sustaining the most feminine image possible, suffragists still found themselves characterized as aggressive he-women who, as a Tennessee antisuffragist wrote, "thrust out their breasts like pouter pigeons, swish their scanty skirts, stamp the floor with their dainty feet, (I reckon some of them are dainty), and with militant bearing exclaim: 'We come not to ask you for our rights, but we come to *demand* them.'"[20]

In response to such attacks, suffragists sometimes went on the offensive themselves, attempting to wrestle the molding of popular opinion away from the control of the antisuffragist camp. One prosuffrage political cartoon showed an attractive young suffragist sitting safely between the pillars of the Constitution, while the antisuffragist (depicted as a little mouse) shook its powerless fist in frustration.[21] Another cartoon showed a fashionably dressed (although somewhat less attractive) suffragist wooing a male legislator, while the antisuffragist—an antiquated relic still carrying a fan—looked on, scandalized.[22]

On the whole, however, southern suffrage women spent more time working on improving their own image rather than promulgating negative stereotypes of the female antisuffragists.[23] For example, Elizabeth Langhorne Lewis wrote to a Norfolk suffragist to take care of her health: "It will never do for us suffragists to break down: the Antis will swear we have[n't] the stamina needed for politics."[24] And Laura Clay warned her coworkers to keep potentially dangerous affiliated causes, such as bicycling, dress reform, or anything else that might tarnish their image, out of their campaigns .[25] Southern suffragists especially relied on photographs of themselves that stressed attractiveness, youth, and demur simplicity. Ida Clyde Clarke's *Suffrage in the Southern States*, for example, included photographs of suffragists from every southern state. The women presented were uniformly attractive and feminine and in poses that were always demur and appealing.[26] Wielding the image of the proper southern lady as a "shield against criticism,"[27] southern suffragists knew the value of image and the importance of appearances. While they might long, like Minnie Fisher Cunningham, to wear their "saucy" red dresses and appear in their "true colors,"[28] southern suffrage activists continued to campaign as decorously as possible.

By adhering to the image of the southern lady, southern suffragists may also have shielded themselves against physical attack, since instances of violence against southern suffragists is quite small. In one instance, in Tennessee in 1913, an unknown assailant broke through a skylight and threw a can of noxious chemicals at Pattie Ruffner Jacobs (who was uninjured in the attack). Such a minimal record of violence in a society known for violence as a means of social control can serve as evidence that southern suffragists played the southern lady well.[29]

Women on both sides of the suffrage question recognized the value of image and stereotyping and attempted to control the popular perceptions of themselves as well as of their opponents. Motherhood and femininity constituted the foundation of the imagery that both sets of women desired to capture for themselves. Suffragists attempted to demonstrate that voting in no way af-

Cartoon depicting antisuffragist as powerless little mouse (Courtesy of Tennessee State Library and Archives, Nashville)

fected maternal affection or feminine decorum, while antisuffragists insisted that women could never emerge from the polls unscathed. As Texas suffragist Lena Gardner complained, "our anti-suffrage friends seem to think that after we get the vote there will never be another bed made, another husband loved, another baby born, or another prayer offered."[30]

Many of our own assumptions about who the suffragists and antisuffragists were have been affected by these women's efforts to control image and stereotype. Although the stereotypical suffragist was depicted as youngish, unmarried, perhaps a recent college graduate who had eagerly entered the work force in a nontraditional job, the average southern suffragist fit none of those categories. Instead, the *average* southern suffragist was in her late forties or early fifties, had nearly completed the rearing of her family, had more education than the typical southern white female but probably did not have a four-year college degree, and spent more time in voluntary associations than in paid work.

In contrast, the stereotypical antisuffragist was an outdated matron, still wearing the gowns and gloves of her youth in the nineteenth century, peering down her patrician nose with contempt at those beneath her who insisted on abandoning the separate sphere. In reality, the *average* southern antisuffragist closely mirrored her opponents in age and marital status (although much else did separate them, as will be explained below). The following pages will examine in turn each component of the stereotypical image and compare it to the statistical profile of the real women involved.

Age and Marriage

Suffragists themselves seemed to believe that there was a generation gap between them and their antisuffrage opposition. A Virginia suffrage worker wrote that "few of our ladies over forty are suffragists, but nearly all of the younger generation (of the upper classes) are."[31] As shown in Table A.1, a comparison of the average age (in 1920) of southern prosuffrage and antisuffrage women immediately defies the first stereotypical image. Suffragists were not "thirty somethings." Women from both movements were on average between 45 and 55 years of age. There was no significant age difference between the two groups. More important were the similarities: women in both groups were at a point in their life cycles where child rearing and housework were taking up less and less of their time. Although many women in both groups still had children at home, very few had small children, and even fewer had young babies.[32] Often with adult children living at home, or with live-in servants to help with housework and child care, women in both movements had a great deal of free time to devote to activities other than housework.

The second erroneous stereotype about suffragists is their preference for "single blessedness," in comparison to antisuffragists, who are assumed to have married at a much greater rate. Suffragists were slightly more likely to be unmarried than antisuffrage women, but the differences between marriage rates of the two groups of women is not great (see Table A.3).[33] In fact, a remarkable number of southern antisuffrage women were single. In two states

(Virginia and Tennessee) more than one in five antisuffrage women were unmarried.[34] Caroline Patterson and Mildred Rutherford of Georgia, Molly Elliot Seawell of Virginia, Mary Hilliard Hinton of North Carolina, and Josephine Pearson and Mary Shackelford of Tennessee, all were state leaders who never married. Yet antisuffragists still managed to portray themselves as the wives, mothers, and homemakers content in their separate sphere.[35]

Ironically, it was often the unmarried antisuffrage leaders who were the most vocal about the centrality of motherhood and the sanctity of the home. Molly Elliot Seawell wrote that "it is the law of nature, as well as of custom, that the man should be the bread-winner of the family; and he is, ninety-nine times out of a hundred. . . . How many mothers with young children are capable of self-support?"[36] Seawell herself, however, never married and was an independent woman who supported herself by her writing. In fact, she became a novelist of regional renown. Mildred Lewis Rutherford, antisuffrage leader from Georgia, was also a self-supporting unmarried woman. Rutherford made a career as the principal of Lucy Cobb Institute and considered herself the mother of the many young women under her instruction. "The greatest thing in my life," she believed, "is my influence over the young girls of my precious State of Georgia. To know that I have a hand in molding the fine character of many of the mothers of this Empire State, that brings me my sweetest joy."[37] Despite the maternal flavor, Rutherford was still an unmarried working woman.

The "motherhood" theme appears in the writings of other single antisuffragists as well. In a speech to her state antisuffrage association in 1920, Josephine Pearson of Tennessee told her coworkers that she considered the antisuffrage movement to be a "Holy War, a crusade in memory of my Mother for Southern Motherhood, through which her guiding spirit has led me all the way!" Pearson defined motherhood as "the highest Coronation of Women." Furthermore, the final test of suffrage for women, she asserted, would be whether "it strengthens or weakens Woman's motherhood—physical, intellectual, spiritual!"[38]

Like Mildred Rutherford, Josephine Pearson made her living as a teacher of young women. And like Rutherford, she portrayed her career as a substitute for the mothering role that she could not fulfill in the traditional way: "I have given my life-work for what I felt were the highest educational standards, ideals, progressively for my sex. I do not believe that the object of woman's creation is merely to produce commodities and oddities, or to amass learning. I believe that the highest education for women is, to yet, undergo radical scholastic and vocational changes; that real womanhood and her FAMILY may not perish from the Earth!"[39] Pearson hastened to add, however, that her career

Prosuffrage political cartoon mocking antisuffrage claims that woman suffrage would mean the end of domesticity (Courtesy of Tennessee State Library and Archives, Nashville)

*Josephine Pearson (*left*) and Nina Pinckard of the Anti-Ratification League (Courtesy of Tennessee State Library and Archives, Nashville)*

as a substitute mother could never be as richly rewarding as true motherhood. Sensitive to the fact that her own life contradicted her prescriptions, she dramatically confessed her unhappiness at her unmarried condition: "Do you, women peers of my native state, surmise, that any sacrifices ever made, or ambitions of a professional career ever attained, have recompensed the loss of love and companionship of home for the desolated spinster; no matter if her life-service is given voluntary?"[40]

Just five years after she gave this speech, Pearson received an offer of marriage. Letters from her friends and relatives giving their opinion of the proposed match offer a rare glimpse into the private world of courtship and marriage, and into the values and priorities of one antisuffrage woman. Pearson's friend Emmy Roberts encouraged Pearson to marry the unnamed doctor who had proposed: "I think you are foolish not to accept his offer of marriage. . . . You must not hold his past secrets against him—men are not perfect and all make mistakes, so forgive him."[41] Later, after Pearson had decided to reject the offer of marriage (for reasons which remain unstated in the extant correspondence), a cousin wrote of her approval of the decision: "I am glad you are not going to marry him for unless you love him enough to sacrifice everything for him, I don't believe you would be happy."[42] While the cousin acknowledged that marriage to a doctor might solve Pearson's financial difficulties,[43] she understood that Pearson valued her independence and her chosen career, both of which marriage might curtail. Regardless of her expressed defense of marriage and motherhood, Pearson chose career and independence instead.[44]

In the two important categories of age and marital status, then, the experiences of suffragists and antisuffragists were more similar than different. But the similarities end there. The life experiences of the two groups of women diverge when education, paid work, or voluntary associations are considered. Those differences were very much the product of the social and economic status of their families and of their husbands.

As has been discussed in considerable detail in Chapter 2, antisuffrage women often came from families with economic or political interests that pitted them against the forces supporting woman suffrage. Big agriculture, railroads, and textile manufacturers figure prominently in this antisuffrage equation (see Table A.15). Other notable trends in the professions of the husbands and fathers of antisuffrage women become more prominent when contrasted directly with similar information on the husbands and fathers of suffrage women (see Table A.14).

Although historians have sometimes categorized suffragists as members of the "elite," or from "old and aristocratic" families,[45] in fact the typical suffragist was solidly middle class. While both pro- and antisuffragists were married to lawyers and doctors, suffrage supporters were more often married to men in the newer, urban-oriented professions such as architecture, civil engineering, and educational administration. They were less often the spouses of bankers or doctors than were women in the antisuffrage camp.

In the larger category of commerce and trade, suffrage supporters less often came from families engaged in "general merchandizing" and instead were more often employed in newer commercial fields in positions such as insurance agents or sales agents for the growing national firms like Western Union, Singer, Coca-Cola, or Wells Fargo. Other suffragists came from families running small businesses such as car dealerships, gas stations, bakeries, or construction companies. Not only were these jobs more urban oriented, they were also more integrated into the national commercial economy. Suffragists were products of the growing southern bourgeoisie, which was increasingly linked into national networks of commerce and trade, who made their livings selling goods and services to the residents of urban centers.[46]

Suffragists and antisuffragists alike were daughters of the South's "better" classes, the only southern white females at the turn of the century privileged to pursue postsecondary education. A popular theme of historical literature in recent years is how higher education and voluntary associations have influenced the development of feminism and suffragism. Yet not all college educated women became suffragists, nor did all club women become feminists. Education did not guarantee support for woman suffrage, for educated women disagreed on the subject.[47] A closer examination of volunteerism and higher education helps to determine why some women became suffragists and others did not.

Education and Employment

Women from both ideological positions attended ladies' finishing schools, female institutes, normal colleges, and institutions offering a full four-year degree. The educational backgrounds of 157 prosuffrage women and 75 antisuffrage women are known (see Table A.7). Women who were suffrage supporters were more likely to have attended college and were more likely to have graduated from college. Antisuffrage women were more likely to have attended a female seminary, collegiate institute, or private academy rather than a full four-year college. Similarly, more antisuffrage women are known to have had no postsecondary education at all. It appears that both the level of education reached and the kind of education obtained had much influence on a given woman's position on the suffrage question.

Seminaries, institutes, and "ladies' colleges" differed in important ways from colleges granting baccalaureate degrees. Female seminaries seldom had standard admission policies; students were admitted much earlier than those matriculating at four-year colleges. Girls as young as age ten or twelve could enter some of the female institutes. Once admitted, they studied a much narrower range of subjects and attended for a shorter period of time (usually for a maximum of three years) than those attending other kinds of institutions.[48] Moreover, the mission of the seminaries and institutes had not changed much from their antebellum origins. The goal of these institutions was to produce skilled wives and mothers rather than independent professionals, and the values they reinforced were domesticity and female subordination in place of independence and equality.[49]

The Lucy Cobb Institute in Athens, Georgia, headed by antisuffragist Mildred Lewis Rutherford, was an exclusive and well-respected female seminary especially favored by planters for the education of their daughters. As teacher and principal there for more than forty years, Rutherford influenced the development of two generations of southern women. As one sympathetic contemporary phrased it, "the hundreds of young girls who have passed through this historic institution have been taught not only in the lore of books but in all of those graces which contribute to the making of the highest type of Southern womanhood."[50] A more neutral observer has noted that Rutherford was responsible for continuing Lucy Cobb's antebellum traditions of nurturing "the Old South's principles of gentility and culture in its students."[51]

Wesleyan Female College, in nearby Macon, Georgia, had a similar approach to women's education. One scholar has described the "ideological underpinning" that remained steadfast from Wesleyan's founding in the 1830s all the way through to the first graduating classes of the twentieth century this way: "The Georgia school publicly proclaimed its simple purpose: to educate succeeding generations of southern women to be better Christian wives and mothers."[52] A young woman receiving an education with such a fundamental foundation would likely graduate having traditional views on gender roles and class, which had been reinforced by her schooling.

By way of contrast, suffragists more often attended colleges and universities that stressed educational standards equal to those emphasized by men's institutions. The pioneers in the field—Vassar (established in 1865), Wellesley (1875), Smith (1875), and Bryn Mawr (1884)—had achieved national reputations that attracted the best and the brightest (and the financially able) from throughout the country.[53] Southern women were no exception, and a small but steady stream of southern middle-class women headed northward for their educations in the late nineteenth century.

An education received in one of the above named institutions remained exceptional. But a notable number of women who joined the southern suffrage movement had attended one of those elite, superior colleges. To name a few: Gertrude Weil and Nell Battle Lewis of North Carolina graduated from Smith College; Annette Finnigan of Houston and Angie Perkins of Knoxville graduated from Wellesley; Flora Gifford of Mississippi received her degree from Bryn Mawr; and Zaida Kirby (Ala.), Elizabeth Roden (Ala.), Katherine Warner (Tenn.), and Kate Tuttle (Va.), all received their educations at Vassar. The small number of southern women eligible to join the Southern Association of College Women proudly listed that membership in their biographies. In the two samples of women used in this study, all known members of the SACW were suffrage supporters (see Table A.7).

Just as antisuffrage women's educational background helped to reinforce conservative values, so too did their work experiences. Antisuffragists often claimed that they were from a wide range of classes with a wide range of work experiences. *The Woman's Protest* asserted that the women "who are leading the movement against suffrage are well known for their work in municipal, civic, educational and philanthropic lines. Because of their knowledge of what can be done without the vote they regard the franchise as a non-essential for them, and consider that their efforts for the amelioration of the conditions of women and children can be better accomplished without suffrage."[54] Georgia's antisuffragists claimed that the majority of their members were business women.[55] The Virginia Antisuffrage Association purported to represent "very busy women," wage earners, professional women, volunteer activists, reformers, and church workers. The Virginia antis added that they were adding factory workers and store clerks to their rosters in Richmond.[56]

Such claims notwithstanding, the southern antisuffragist nevertheless had a different work experience than the suffragist. Antisuffragists were actually much less likely to work for pay than were suffragists (see Table A.9). Allowing for much variation between the different states, on average one out of four suffragists was gainfully employed, while only one out of ten antisuffragists took home a paycheck. Furthermore, more prosuffrage women worked for pay after marriage than their antisuffrage counterparts. Using Texas as an example, of the seven antisuffragists (out of fifty-three) who worked in 1920, only one was married at the time; all the others were unmarried or were widowed. In contrast, thirteen of the forty-four suffragists who were gainfully employed in 1920 were married; the remainder were unmarried or widowed.

The differences between the two groups of women did not end there (as demonstrated in Table A.11). Suffragists engaged in a wider range of jobs than did antisuffragists, often entering nontraditional fields like law, medicine, and the clergy. Suffragists had taken other white-collar office positions that only recently had been open to women, such as real estate or insurance sales. Southern suffragists were among the New Women entering nontraditional fields and creating professions for women where none had previously existed, especially in the field of social work. Their college degrees enabled them to pursue professions just beginning to open to women at the turn of the century. Many such careers put suffragists in contact with the full range of urban and industrial problems of the day, problems that antisuffrage women continued to observe only from a distance. By contrast, antisuffrage women tended to cluster in more typical "women's jobs," such as teaching and clerical and literary work.

Although a larger percentage of southern suffragists were gainfully employed, the majority of women on both sides of the suffrage question in the South remained unpaid workers, participating in voluntary associations and various reform movements. Having nearly completed the rearing of their children, these women of the middle and upper classes filled their days with an extraordinary amount of club, church, and civic work. But antisuffragists participated in fewer women's organizations and tended to join a different type of group than did suffragists, and the dissimilarities are significant.

Antisuffrage women joined voluntary associations less often than suffragists (approximately half of the antisuffragists were so listed, compared to nearly 80 percent of the suffragists, as shown in Table A.16). Moreover, antisuffrage women were involved in a much narrower range of voluntary associations. Women's clubs, mothers' clubs, literary clubs, religious associations, and patriotic societies were the mainstays of antisuffrage voluntary activities. The emphasis of such associations was on improving one's self and one's children, not on improving the lives of other women and children.

Women's clubs were extremely popular with women on both sides of the suffrage issue and were often the scenes of civil wars between suffragists and antisuffragists attempting to gain control of their local and state clubs. For example, Richmond suffragist Julia Sully warned her coworker Lila Meade Valentine in 1913 that the antisuffragists were planning a frontal assault on the local woman's club. "The 'Antis' have sent a bunch of literature to Mrs. Mitchell to be distributed at the next meeting of the Woman's club on Tuesday," Sully wrote.[57] Both suffs and antis flocked to the women's clubs, and membership in these organizations did not predict what a woman's position on suffrage would be. However, other voluntary associations had much clearer connotations. Organizations with a more overtly political bent (such as the WCTU) attracted smaller numbers of antisuffrage women, as did reform efforts that demanded extensive contact with the urban working class (such as free kindergartens, settlement houses, the YWCA, or the infant mortality campaign). And although work like that of Lucy Randolph Mason with the Industrial Department of the YWCA (and later with organized labor)[58] was not the most common experience for suffragists, it was extremely rare for antisuffragists. Whenever involved in reform movements, antisuffrage women were more likely instead to aid the needy from a polite distance (such as serving on the board of "lady managers" for local charities and benevolent societies).

Suffragists often had women's club experiences that put them at the forefront of southern racial liberalism. In many communities, the WCTU, the YWCA, and other local women's clubs quietly attempted cross-class and interracial activities. Home missions, work with settlement houses, interracial prohibition campaigns, and other such reforms gave some suffragists a heady dose of interracial sentiment. One recent study has found that nearly one-third of white women leaders of the interracial movement in the 1920s had been active in their state Equal Suffrage League. By contrast, no antisuffragists appeared in the ranks of the women's interracial movement.[59]

Of these organizations, the YWCA emerges again and again as an important training ground for interracialism and cross-class cooperation. YWCA workers were often the most progressive of the progressives in their support for industrial reforms, working-class reform issues, and the need for organized labor. The Y workers often found themselves in conflict with the socially prominent "ladies" of the board.[60] Suffragists were likely to be the Y workers; antisuffragists were likely to be the ladies of the board.

Aside from the women's clubs, the most important voluntary associations for the antisuffragists were the patriotic societies, notably the United Daughters of the Confederacy (UDC). One of the plethora of patriotic organizations formed at the turn of the century, the UDC was one of the few that purposely limited its membership to women from the middle and upper classes.[61] Its function was to celebrate the past, not to reform the present.

Women of the UDC worked hard to stay within their prescribed sphere. The Daughters did not politicize domesticity as much as they reinforced it. As the 1913 president told the UDC convention, "I love the UDC because they have demonstrated that Southern women may organize themselves into a nation-wide body without losing womanly dignity, sweetness or graciousness."[62] While the work of the UDC had a decidedly political agenda (the defense of the Confederate rebellion), it carefully maintained its nonpolitical facade. The organization insisted that the nonpolitical role was the only proper public role available to women.

Although one study has concluded that the UDC was ambivalent toward woman suffrage and another has claimed that in one state it actually worked for woman suffrage,[63] the UDC was in reality quite strongly antisuffrage. In an action that spoke volumes about its views on woman suffrage, the annual UDC meeting in New Orleans in November 1913 refused to receive a welcoming telegram from Kate Gordon's Southern States Woman Suffrage Conference (the one suffrage organization that could not be charged with being soft on states' rights and disfranchisement).[64] The Alabama chapter of the UDC established an antisuffrage department within its ranks. By forming an "anti" association within the UDC, antisuffragists could thereby draw upon the name and reputation of the Daughters without forcing the organization to make antisuffragism its official position.[65] In Virginia, an anonymous Daughter announced firmly in the *Times-Dispatch* that "no daughter of the Confederacy will be a suffragette."[66]

The Daughters had other ways of making their opinion known without establishing antisuffragism as an official policy. The UDC in Richmond consistently avoided woman suffrage and any other progressive issue, remaining concerned only with the preservation of the past. But a substantial number of officers led the opposition to woman suffrage in that state.[67] In Georgia, for example, the leadership of the antisuffrage association was nearly interchangeable with that of the state UDC. So well known was UDC president Mildred Lewis Rutherford that when she spoke against woman suffrage, Georgians heard the voice of the Daughters.[68]

In addition to the patriotic societies and women's clubs, antisuffrage women were drawn to the literary clubs in large numbers. In Montgomery, for example, the antisuffragists Margaret Janney, Elizabeth Sheehan, Elizabeth Hannah, Lucy Andrews, and Daisy Thigpen were all also members of the Ionian Literary Club. Literary clubs, which included art, music, and reading societies, emphasized self-improvement and community benefit. But the kinds of community benefit programs that they supported, such as art shows and operatic concerts, were more likely to benefit and entertain the educated middle class rather than the urban working class. In other words, women in literary clubs often worked to benefit themselves and their families rather than "the community" at large.

Membership in such literary clubs usually was limited to those women living in a small town or urban center, as did the Montgomery women just named. A large number of antisuffrage women lived in rural environments, however, which limited their abilities to engage in club activity. Women like Mary Hilliard Hinton, who lived in Wake County outside of Raleigh, for example, often could join only the patriotic societies (which did not require frequent meetings) and some rural church groups rather than the literary and women's clubs that filled the daily lives of urban women.

Religious Affiliation and Activism

Reinforcing a predisposition for social stasis, southern Protestant churches did much to encourage women in their opposition to woman suffrage. The Episcopal Church, for example, never officially opposed woman suffrage, nor did it ever publicly lobby against the reform. But the southern Episcopal Church had decidedly conservative views about the role of women in both religious and secular life. According to one student, the Episcopal Church expected its women remain in traditional roles. Women were allowed a realm of independent activity in the missionary societies, but they were excluded from any real power within the church.[69]

The impact that Episcopal conservatism had on its female communicants is demonstrated by the consistently large numbers of Episcopal women in the antisuffrage movement. In Texas, more than one-fourth of the antisuffrage women were members of Episcopal churches; in Tennessee, the number was more than one-third. In both cases, Episcopalians were the largest single denomination of the known antisuffrage church members. This fact becomes all the more significant when contrasted with the numbers of Episcopalians in the state as a whole. In both Texas and Tennessee, roughly 1.0 percent of all church members were Episcopalians (see Table A.5).[70]

But Episcopalians did not uniformly oppose woman suffrage. A sizable number in every southern state supported the reform. One study of the nature of the Episcopal organization concluded that the reluctance of local units to accept any more centralization than was absolutely necessary precluded the formation of an official policy for the church as a whole. The result was an institution encompassing a wide range of opinion, with little ability to enforce standardization.[71] On woman suffrage, and nearly every other political issue, the Episcopal churches allowed room for disagreement.

The Episcopal Church was not unique in its internal conflict over woman suffrage. Southern Methodist churches found their memberships divided over the suffrage question as well. Historians have generally given a positive cast to the role of the Methodist church in the development of suffragism because of the strong relationship between Methodism and the WCTU and the high visibility of Methodist women in the suffrage movement.[72] There is considerable evidence to support the contention that Methodist women were indeed drawn to the support of suffrage. A 1914 survey of southern Methodist women active in their churches found that a large majority favored woman suffrage.[73] Many well-known southern Methodist women were prominent in both the laity rights campaign and the suffrage movement.

When it came to institutional support, however, the antisuffragists probably had as much right to claim the Methodist Church as their own as did the suffragists. As an institution, the Methodist Church, South, worked to conserve existing gender relations. The Southern Methodist Church held out against women's laity rights long after Methodist women in the rest of the country were voting in their own conferences. In addition, individual Methodist clergymen exerted powerful influence against the enfranchisement of women. The Georgia Antisuffrage Association proudly advertised the endorsement it received from Warren Candler, bishop of the Southern Methodist Church.[74] Candler, although a supporter of Prohibition, condemned any cooperation with the WCTU because of its position on suffrage.[75] That Candler's opposition carried weight and influence was demonstrated in a letter to the editor of the Atlanta *Constitution* from the state president of the WCTU, Mrs. W. C. Sibley. "The Oxford Women's Christian Temperance Union, of course, from its very environments, has suffered from the effects of Dr. Candler's opposition," Sibley wrote. "The good work of those noble Christian women—women well known in the Methodist church in all good works—has been so crippled till it is now of little worth."[76] Even allowing for some exaggeration on the part of the WCTU leader, it is nevertheless clear that the opposition of powerful clergymen represented a formidable obstacle for southern suffragists.

Moreover, Methodist laymen did not always demonstrate an appreciation for woman suffrage equal to that of Methodist women. In the North Carolina legislative vote on the Nineteenth Amendment, for example, thirty Methodist legislators voted against the suffrage amendment while only nineteen Methodist lawmakers voted for it (see Table A.25). Thus, while it is true that Southern Methodist women drew upon their experiences in the missionary societies and the WCTU in their movement for woman suffrage, it is also true that the Methodist Church as an institution was a powerful source of stasis in the realm of gender relations. Historians have yet to deal adequately with this dichotomy of institutional intransigence and the "theology of liberation."

Other southern denominations were even more reluctant than the Southern Methodists to support changes in women's roles. Few historians or contemporaries would make a claim that Southern Baptists were a positive force in support of woman suffrage, for example. But one study of Southern Baptists and woman suffrage has concluded that the popular conception of Baptists' uniform opposition to the reform is incorrect. Southern Baptists were split on the issue of woman suffrage, particularly since many Baptists felt that women voters could be a vanguard for Prohibition.[77] Although Baptist laymen and clergy could be found on either side of the suffrage contest, even Baptist Prohibitionists were not always swayed by the argument that women voters would support the cause of temperance. Rev. J. B. Hawthorne, pastor of the First Baptist Church of Atlanta, criticized the WCTU for "pressing women into the gospel ministry, as preachers and leaders, contrary to the teachings of the Scriptures." He took this position in spite of the fact that he was a lifelong Prohibitionist.[78]

Like their Methodist and Baptist counterparts, the southern Presbyterian churches split on the issue of woman suffrage. The General Assembly of the Presbyterian Church made no official pronouncements on woman suffrage, either for or against. Nevertheless, it was clear that the denomination opposed it.[79] Of all the southern denominations, Presbyterians held some of the most conservative positions on the acceptable roles for women. The effort to organize women's missionary societies "met stiff resistance" by the General Assembly. When the women persisted, the Assembly conceded their right to organize, but refused to allow the resultant missionary circles to control their own finances. Firmly under the control of the church, the women's missions did not have the level of autonomy even of that of the Southern Baptist women. Historian Wayne Flynt has concluded that no denomination more adamantly resisted the expanding role of women than the southern Presbyterians.[80]

Although southern churches have rightfully been credited with providing women space for personal development, they should not be seen as leading the fight for women's emancipation. Even though a small number of individual ministers might have made their churches agents of change, collectively the clergy did much to hinder the perceived attack on established gender roles. As Dewey Grantham concluded, southern evangelical Protestantism did more to conserve than to undermine the dominant culture of the South. Churches "constituted a sturdy bulwark in support of existing institutions, class relationships, and cultural values."[81]

The Separate Female World

Through their churches and women's associations, many southern women who opposed suffrage developed friendships and relationships that they drew upon when it came time to organize a resistance movement. Whether they had families, neighborhoods, jobs, schools, or voluntary associations in common, antisuffrage women were part of a closely knit network of like-minded women who often had known each other for many years, had worked together on numerous church, school, or civic projects, and had had numerous experiences in creating and maintaining women's organizations.

The preservation of the family was an important part of the antisuffragist's ideology, so many women made the antisuffrage movement a family affair, joining the organization with other women of their immediate family. In Nashville, for example, Josephine Farrell and her two daughters joined the Southern Rejection League together; in Houston, Mrs. Reuben Sloane Yocum and her daughter Laura Yocum, both were active in the antisuffrage association; in Selma, sisters Nellie V. Baker and Grace Baker Evans were both leaders of their state's antisuffrage movement; and in Montgomery, Annie and Ellen Goldthwaite, mother and daughter, joined the local antisuffrage association.

Other antisuffrage women were close neighbors, often residing in some of the finest residential districts in the region. In Richmond, the antisuffrage association roster read like a city directory for Grace Street; in Raleigh, a large number of antisuffragists could easily have walked to a meeting on Hillsborough Street; Nashville antisuffragists drew a large number of recruits from the exclusive West End; and Montgomery's South Court Street was an antisuffrage enclave in that town. The affluent neighborhood provided a physical tie among women of the antisuffrage persuasion in addition to the social, religious, and economic relationships that had already been established. The depth of the relationships among antisuffrage women was demonstrated as they turned to each other in times of need. For example, Adelaide Scott and Amelia Seelye, both of Montgomery, shared a house on South Court Street after they were both widowed. Two blocks away, Annie Bandy and Belle Ross also moved in together during their widowhoods. All four women joined the antisuffrage movement together.

When the time came to organize, the pre-existing network of conservative women made possible the swift organization of those opposed to woman suffrage. In Montgomery, Alabama, Margaret Janney could call upon her old friends of the Ionian Literary Club and overnight could form an antisuffrage association. In Virginia, at least 20 percent of the antisuffragists had known each other through the Association for the Preservation of Virginia Antiquities. (An equal number of Virginia antisuffragists would have had contact with one another through the Colonial Dames.)

The great wave of female activism rising at the turn of the century, which historians have lumped together in the category of voluntary associations, attracted women on both sides of the suffrage issue. The organizations in which antisuffragists participated, however, were less likely to convert them to suffragism. Their days might be filled with club work, volunteer work, and "reform" efforts, but it was work of a nature least likely to stir them to demand the vote. Like their family connections and their churches, the kinds of voluntary associations they joined worked to reinforce their predisposition to oppose woman suffrage.

Mari Jo Buhle, writing about American socialist women, concluded that "through their specialized role and separate institutions, native-born women achieved a collective consciousness that took on an explicitly political dimension." Their common gendered experiences produced feelings of sisterhood, because socialist women "inherited a distinct female culture rich in political potential."[82] Ironically, the identical description can be applied to antisuffrage women, who relished their specialized roles and created support networks through their separate institutions, which they then utilized in the antisuffrage movement.

Historians, searching for the roots of modern feminism, have stressed the role of "the female world of love and ritual" in nurturing feminism. But they have overlooked the ways in which "sisterhood," the "separate sphere," and "women's culture" could serve the needs of conservatism as well as feminism. The UDC, literary clubs, and women's clubs all provided networks for the support of political activism on behalf of antifeminist ideas. The separate sphere might nurture feminism; but it might also bear more conservative fruit.[83] Not all public activities of women are necessarily feminist.[84] Female antisuffragism, with its claim to have "women's interests" or "women's needs" at its heart, was organized, political, and public, and certainly not feminist.

Southern women were important in the dissemination of antisuffrage ideology in the region. Although not as numerous nor as well organized as the prosuffrage forces, antisuffragists had some distinct advantages in the contest over woman suffrage, one of the most important of which was a powerful arsenal of argument and rhetoric. Forged in the white-hot fire of southern race relations at the turn of the century and draped with the emotionally laden bunting of the Lost Cause, the antisuffrage ideology provides important insights into the people involved in the opposition to woman suffrage in the South, as shown in the following chapter.

4

The Ideology of Southern Antisuffragism

You may preach a thousand isms,
You may pass a million laws,
You will never cure an evil
If you fail to treat the cause.
If the coming generation
Would be strong and undefiled—
Then regenerate the mothers—
For the mother trains the child.

There is no regeneration
That will put a stop to sin
Save the righteous sense of humans
Working outward from within;
There is naught in "Votes for women"
Which will lead our steps aright,
But a host of praying mothers
Are colossal in their might.

Florence Goff Schwartz,
from Key Pittman Papers, undated

The Gilded Age was a time of enormous changes in American society. Characterized by an economy with unpredictable periods of prosperity and poverty; an angry agrarian sector seeking solutions to problems originating in the world agricultural markets; frustrated workers experimenting with new forms of organization and collective power; and a political system still attempting to adjust to postwar regional politics, the Gilded Age was marked by experimentation and flux.

Reacting to both the increased immigration of the 1880s and to the newly acquired colonial empire in the wake of the Spanish-American War, racial liberalism faded as Americans struggled with questions of who should vote, who should pay for ever more expensive urban services, and who should govern. Expressed in numerous ways, including increasing expressions of racism and nativism, this conservatism contributed to a rejection of the country's earlier moderate commitment to the protection of the rights of the freedmen in the South.[1]

Veiled in scientific respectability in the literature of doctors, historians, sociologists, and other intellectuals, racial conservatism penetrated every level of American society. When African American mortality rates surpassed birth rates in many cities, biologists saw in this evidence that the "fittest" were surviving. The Dunning school of historians provided "evidence" from the past that the Negro's inferiority resulted from natural proclivities, not from any patterns of oppression inflicted by white Americans. Social Darwinism seeped into American social policy and justified such inequities as the reduction of funding for public schools and the curtailing of public health programs.[2]

In such an intellectual climate, many of the South's long-held views on the nature and the character of the African American gained acceptance by a larger audience. Propagated by writers such as Thomas Nelson Page and Thomas Dixon, the racial ideas of the South had become the ideas of the nation.[3] Validating these social values, in 1896 the Supreme Court emasculated the Civil Rights Act of 1875 and replaced it with the doctrine of "separate but equal." Two years later, in *Williams vs. Mississippi*, the Court gave its blessing to the disfranchisement of black voters. The Court thereby granted tacit permission for white southerners to continue their reconstruction of the South in any way they saw fit, without fear of interference by the federal government.[4]

Out of this conservative intellectual clay, southern antisuffragists molded their ideology. Borrowing from social Darwinism, the Bible, contemporary sociology, and long held racial beliefs, southern antisuffragists crafted a systematic body of thought, which they disseminated with an impressively large stock of arguments. The ideology of southern antisuffragists, used by both men and women, was designed to defend current racial and gender roles and served to preserve class interests as well.[5]

A comparison of antisuffrage literature generated by white southerners or widely disseminated in southern antisuffrage circles to similar literature of northeastern origins reveals a regional rhetoric that reflected southern concerns about race and gender and a relative absence of arguments based on fear of immigrants and radicalism. Northeastern antisuffragism, responding to changing conditions of that region's ethnically diverse cities, evolved to incorporate nativism and antiradicalism into its ideology; southern antisuffragism, with its roots deep in plantation soil, remained firmly grounded in its nineteenth-century worldview. Southern antisuffrage ideology rested solidly on a combination of theological, biological, sociological, racial, and states' rights principles.

Southern Antisuffrage Ideology

Theological arguments against woman suffrage assumed that the separate spheres for men and women had been ordained by God and that biblical support for the subordination of women in the church and in society was the literal will of God. As a committee of "representative ministers" of Nashville wrote, "each and every revealed religion has taken cognizance of this [the inequality of the sexes], and in the economy of the divine creation man and woman have each his or her distinct sphere."[6] A broadside from Alabama warned that "if we degrade [woman] from the high station that God has placed her in to put her at the ballot-box, at political or other elections, we UNMAN ourselves and refuse to do the duties that God has assigned to us."[7] J. C. McQuiddy, editor of the Nashville *Gospel Advocate*, encouraged "every one who believes that the word of God is divinely inspired . . . and would keep women out of politics, should write at once to his Representative in the Tennessee legislature and ask him to use his vote and influence against the ratification of woman suffrage."[8]

Antisuffragists regularly reminded their audiences of the numerous passages of the Bible that implied or directly demanded male superiority. A male antisuffragist from Tennessee quoted Timothy: "Let a woman learn in quietness with all subjection. But I permit not a woman to teach, nor to have dominion over a man, but to be in quietness."[9] Robert C. Walsh, in a preface to his antisuffrage tract, announced his intention "to call your attention to bible [*sic*] references enough to convince you that to be an advocate of 'votes for women' is evidence of disbelief in God,"[10] and then he proceeded to fill several pages with quotations. Isaac Lockhart Peebles, a Mississippi minister, likewise produced several pages of biblical citations and then summarized: "That woman's relation to man is subjection is unmistakable from God's own language to her after her most wilful [*sic*] sin against God."[11] Bishop Warren Candler stated it even more succinctly: "The whole basis of the woman's suffrage movement is unscriptural and sinful."[12]

Suffragists had a difficult task in refuting biblical injunction, especially in the fundamentalist South. Pauline opprobrium in antisuffrage rhetoric had remarkable tenacity in the South.[13] Florida congressman Frank Clark spoke for many who believed that "God has decreed that man is to be the head of the family and woman is to be his 'helpmeet,' and any attempt to change this order of human affairs is an attempt to change and to overthrow one of the solemn decrees of God almighty."[14] An antisuffrage tract published in Raleigh asked, "How can you repudiate St. Paul as an inspired writer and as a biblical authority without knocking the entire structure of the Christian Faith?"[15] Suffragists tried to distinguish between the will of God and the prejudices of the male conduits of his word, as did Elizabeth Cady Stanton, with her now-famous *Woman's Bible*. For the faithful, such exegesis merely proved that the suffrage movement was the work of "infidels."[16] "Marse" Henry Watterson, the nationally known Kentucky editor, accused the suffragists of "rejecting the Religion of Christ and Him Crucified and repudiating the man-made Bible of Moses and the Prophets in favor of Elizabeth Cady Stanton's 'Woman's Bible,' which teaches the religious heresies of Voltaire, Paine and Ingersoll, along with the Free Love theories of Mary Wollstonecraft, Victoria Woodhull and Ellen Key."[17]

Confronted with biblical arguments at every turn, Virginia suffragist Mary Johnston began including "answers to St. Paul" in her suffrage speeches.[18] Most southern suffragists, however, were less willing than Johnston to address biblical arguments so directly and preferred to avoid this line of thought when at all possible. Instead, they stressed the good works and Christian reforms that enfranchised women might enact.[19]

Often closely related to the biblical arguments, the biological arguments against woman suffrage were based on the belief that women were physically unfit for the types of activity that public life required. Even if a woman had more education and more intelligence than a man, Isaac Peebles asserted, "nature will not allow her to vote, arrest a negro if she is sheriff, hold court if she is judge, nor to attend to state business, if governor."[20] Eugene Anderson, president of a woman's college in Georgia, believed that "woman is nervous, sensitive and not physically strong. This is especially true of the higher types of people. Man's mind is strong, calm, cool and collected. His mind is mathematical. It takes the two in combination to carry out God's plan in the world. The woman conserves energy. There are times when she must be secluded from the world, so that posterity may not suffer from shocks or excitements that disturb."[21]

Antisuffrage women in the South relied on biological arguments just as frequently as did men.[22] A Nashville woman wrote that "women's physical nature is not adapted to political life and strains of conventions, meetings and speeches that men have to meet."[23] A Texas woman agreed: "Woman . . . was never created to battle with the stern realities of life. She is unfit for such. She is not qualified to fill the public offices she is to-day seeking."[24] Molly Elliot Seawell enlarged on the biological restrictions placed on women:

> [A voter] must, except in occasional individual instances, be physically able to make his way to the polls, against opposition if necessary; and, second, he must be able to carry out by force the effect of his ballot. Law consists of a series of Thou-shalt-nots, but government does not result until an armed man stands ready to execute the law. . . . The spectacle of one half the electorate unable to execute a single law it has made, or even to deposit its ballots without the assistance of the other half, is a proposition so fantastic that it is difficult to attack it seriously. . . . The trouble would begin with the mere attempt of women to deposit their ballots. A dozen ruffians could prevent a hundred women from depositing a single ballot.[25]

The Virginia Association Opposed to Woman Suffrage announced its belief that "there are mental and emotional differences between men and women that should prevent women from being forced into political strife, or from having additional responsibilities thrust upon them."[26] And a Macon, Georgia, woman firmly tied the biological and biblical arguments together. "[The suffragists'] megaphone voices," she argued, "have rendered inaudible the wise warning that some women are robbing all women of their normal sphere in life and placing the sex in serious jeopardy in their endeavor to change the plan of the Creator."[27] Although antisuffragists did not frame the discussion in terms of "sex" versus "gender," they clearly believed that sex dictated human activities.[28]

Southern antisuffragists also drew upon a rich vein of contemporary intellectual and scientific trends in American thought to support their position. Historian Kemp P. Battle, a professor emeritus at the University of North Carolina, claimed that "women are inferior in physical strength, and must inevitably pass through periods of sickness and weakening of nervous power."[29] John J. Vertrees, a Nashville attorney, produced an antisuffrage pamphlet in 1916 that emphasized that "up to about forty-five years of age a woman's life is one of frequent and regular periods marked by mental and nervous irritability, when oftentimes even her mental equilibrium is disturbed. Students of such matters inform us that these periods lengthen as the race becomes civilized."[30]

The antisuffragists frequently turned to "scientific" evidence to prove that biology rendered women incapable of public life, and if women entered this realm it was to the detriment of themselves and their progeny. Southern antisuffrage literature eagerly adopted statistics produced by Cornell University professor Max Schlapp that purported to prove that "motherhood will become rarer as the cause of suffrage gains." Schlapp explained that, since women were already overburdened by the work within their own sphere, "to further burden the poor things with politics means loss of energy entailing decrease of formative power."[31] Dr. Charles Dana, a neurophysiologist, also berated feminism for putting unbearable strains on overburdened women and predicted that the outcome would be "25 per cent more insanity than they have now. I am not saying that woman suffrage will make women crazy, . . .[but] I do say that woman suffrage would throw into the electorate a mass of voters of delicate nervous stability."[32] Impressed by such arguments, the southern historian Walter Cooper claimed he opposed woman suffrage because "the finest scientists base their objections to female suffrage on physical grounds. They say that women are not physically intended to vote."[33]

Delaware antisuffragist Emily Bissell also cited contemporary scientific thinking in her arguments against woman suffrage: "Science finds the greatest distinction of sex in the highest animals. The nobler and higher the type, the greater the difference in function. Man, as the highest form of animal life, has the widest differences in function. It is natural, it is scientifically right, that woman should be as womanly as possible, and man as manly." Therefore, Bissell concluded, "the suffrage demand for all the rights and duties of men is absurdly unscientific. It would send modern society on the road back to savagery."[34]

The sociological arguments against woman suffrage all derived from the assumption that the family, not the individual, served as the basic unit of society. The danger in woman suffrage, according to the antisuffragists, was that it would allow women to vote as individuals. No longer would men vote as an expression of the needs of the family. Society, even civilization itself, would crumble into chaos if women broke away from the family and established "individualism." Texas antisuffrage leader Ida M. Darden predicted that "if another vote were never cast and another law never passed, we could survive the ordeal, but without home, civilization would wither and die."[35]

The family versus "individualism" constituted a pervasive theme in antisuffrage literature. Georgia's Eugene Anderson wrote that he saw the suffrage movement as "an attempt at individualism and an attack on the home." He remained unwilling to "set up Individualism in America in place of the family unit," since it was the "purpose of the founders of the government to make the family the unit and to encourage family unity, and not to encourage individualism."[36] A Kentucky editor wrote that woman suffrage "means the breaking up of the family which has been the basal institution of human welfare thus far from the very dawn of history. . . . 'Votes for women' means that the individual and not the family is to be the unit of the State."[37]

And, of course, the man was the head of the family. Isaac Peebles argued that "if a woman is elected governor of a state, she becomes the head of all the men in that commonwealth, and if she is elected president of the United States, she becomes the head of all the men who are citizens of the United States and even head of her husband, and thereby changes God's order completely which has fixed man for the headship of the woman."[38] The family as a unit could have only one head. Any other arrangement endangered the survival of the institution. For "in the home, the source of all good to the state, would surely come sooner or later discussions, divisions and dissensions," as Annah Watson of Memphis argued. "There would inevitably be two sides and these in many instances hotly contested. It is an old saying that a man and his wife should not play chess," she reasoned. "Surely, it is a graver question whether they should play at the dangerous game of politics."[39]

Southern antisuffragists refused to relinquish the nineteenth century's ideals of separate spheres and "republican motherhood." According to the doctrine of the separate spheres, women possessed enormous power within the family unit. They even wielded political power, albeit in an indirect form. As wives and mothers, women could influence politics by influencing the men who represented them at the polls. The Jackson, Mississippi, *Clarion-Ledger* warned suffragists that "they had better be at home . . . instructing their sons, future voters, in lessons of good citizenship and in the shaping of them into citizens into whose hands in future years the affairs of State may be safely placed."[40] Congressman Frank Clark of Florida rhapsodized about the power of the "queen of the home": "As the mother, as the wife, as the sister she exercises a broader and deeper and mightier influence than she can ever exercise or hope to on the stump and in the byways of politics in this land."[41] The separate spheres, it was believed, provided women with guarantees of protection, and crossing over the line that divided the spheres could be dangerous. It would produce masculine women and feminine men. Louisville editor Henry Watterson contended that "since this [suffrage] agitation became general, women have been distinctly going down hill in all womanly qualities. As the woman gains in what the he-women call 'opportunity,' she loses in character.

These he-women are themselves essentially masculine. They are, like the male politicians, blatant and self-seeking. In the home life, those of them who have had any home life have been failures. They are no more fit to lead decent and true women than if they were morally bankrupt; for their influence is wholly immoral."[42]

Men were not alone in demanding the continuation of the separate spheres. Female antisuffragists also clung tenaciously to their separate sphere, which they believed assured them one area of power and influence. A world without the separate sphere might just be a world where women had no influence at all.[43] A Tennessee woman explained that she did not chose to vote because she was "so 'old-fashioned' as to believe that woman has a 'sphere' and that in this sphere her influence is more potent than in any other."[44] Annah Watson of Memphis wrote in 1895 that women's power lay "in their influence with husbands, brothers and sons, . . . in their power to direct the votes of those nearest and dearest for the accomplishment of the uplifting of society. This may seem slow in method and practical results but it is safe."[45] In 1919, the Alabama Anti-Ratification League affirmed, "we are home keepers and the mothers of children, and we seek to discharge our duty to our country and to the cause of civilization and right living, not by voting and holding office, but . . . by instilling into our children love of their country and devotion to high ideals."[46] Rosa-Leigh Towers of Birmingham believed that the power of women in their separate sphere represented "a much more powerful field of action than women will ever find in politics."[47] As late as 1940, former Tennessee antisuffrage leader Josephine Pearson still operated under the old rules. When she wished to make a suggestion to presidential candidate Wendell Willkie, Pearson wrote to *Mrs.* Willkie and implored her to "use your high mission and influence your illustrious husband."[48]

This traditional interpretation of the proper relations between the sexes produced another potent antisuffrage argument: women themselves did not wish to vote. An often repeated theme in the suffrage debate, antisuffragists claimed that the vast majority of southern (white) women did not desire to leave their sphere and enter the political realm. Nina Pinckard, Alabama antisuffrage leader, wrote Carrie Chapman Catt in protest of "the campaign of your organization to plunge women into perpetual political turmoil." She asserted that "Southern women abhor political combat for their sex."[49] Virginia novelist Molly Seawell reminded her readers that "the suffragists have consistently and successfully opposed a referendum to women, of whom only 8 per cent. in the United States are on record as favoring suffrage."[50] Representative Frank Clark of Florida felt "absolutely safe in asserting that practically all the women of America who are happily married are opposed to woman suffrage."[51] An anonymous anti "[knew] of no true Southern woman who feels that she has time or inclination to do duty at the polls after she has filled her higher obligations to society, church and family."[52]

Frustrated with combating the entrenched traditional view of woman's place in the world, a local suffrage leader in Hickory, North Carolina, complained to her state president that the opposition in her hometown was "largely sentimental—same old story—Woman and the home—loss of her sweet, high femininity—&c &c—but it is opposition good and hard—and the situation has to be handled mighty carefully."[53] Rebecca Latimer Felton had less patience for women holding such views on gender roles: "To these I can only say if they prefer to hug their chains, I have no sort of objection."[54]

In addition to the theological, biological, and sociological lines of argument, southern white antisuffragists had two additional, far more potent, weapons in their arsenal: states' rights and the "Negro question." Stemming from the same worldview as the other three arguments, states' rights and the black vote became the most important tenets of southern antisuffrage thought.

In spite of the successful suffrage restriction movement at the turn of the century, white southerners continued to fear (or at least claimed to fear) the potential power of black voters. Antisuffragists warned that the black "majority" would dominate the South as it allegedly had done during Reconstruction and any possible good that might come from enfranchising well-born, educated white women would be more than offset by the masses of poor black women entering the electorate. Congressman Edwin Yates Webb of North Carolina claimed that woman suffrage would "enfranchise 110,000 Negro women of North Carolina for the sake of letting a few active agitating white women in spots throughout North Carolina have the right to vote."[55] A Memphis woman believed that black suffrage had already proven itself disastrous. When black men were enfranchised, she claimed, they "were utterly unprepared and unfit for such a gift. . . . Should this unwise gift be doubled in its weight and power and the ballot given to the women of the race[,] untold misfortune would be the result."[56]

In the conservatives' view, the evils of black suffrage knew no limits. James Callaway, editor of the Macon, Georgia, *Telegraph*, linked black suffrage with assaults on white women:

> What was this white woman's problem in the Negro belt? Go ask the farmer's wife as she sat in her home in fear and trembling. The very vine and fig tree in her yard, Bible emblems of peace, tranquility, domestic serenity, were but the crouching places of the lustful Negro awaiting to pounce upon his helpless victim. . . . All those who insist on the Susan B.

> Anthony amendment, giving the ballot to 3,000,000 Negro women of the South, which will also revitalize the fifteenth amendment, and necessarily bring the Negroes back into politics, creating Negro night meetings again on the plantations, are agencies that will again imperil the farmer's wife.[57]

Inextricably intertwined with the race issue was the states' right argument. Many white southerners maintained that woman suffrage, if obtained by amendment to the federal constitution, would be an infringement on the right of the states to control their own electorates. North Carolina congressman John Humphrey Small, for one, insisted that "the regulation of suffrage has always been recognized as a part of the local self-government of every state." This alteration in the federal constitution would "violate one of the fundamentals of our government," he argued.[58] Likewise, Christie Benet of South Carolina told the U.S. Senate that "we believe in my state, and I subscribe to that doctrine, that one of the fundamental rights of the sovereignty of our state is involved in this resolution—the right to prescribe the qualification of our electors."[59]

The enforcement clause of the proposed Nineteenth Amendment alarmed many white southerners because they believed it would establish federal control over elections, which would destroy the Democratic Party, the main agency for the protection of white supremacy. One suffrage opponent from Georgia lauded "the Democratic party, and its policies, and its glorious defense of woman, when Republican bayonets were trying to set black heels on white necks throughout the Southland." Without such protection, he continued, "we would have been the most miserable set of people that ever suffered at the hands of a conquering enemy."[60] Congressman Thomas Heflin of Alabama claimed that during Redemption, "by the exercise of the sovereign power of the State[,] we have purified the ballot and removed a danger that threatened our very civilization."[61] Only the maintenance of states' rights could continue to secure the safety of southern civilization.

To many, the two arguments, "the black peril" and states' rights, were inseparable. Virginia's Molly Seawell, for example, maintained that "the right of a State to create and control its own electorate is the corner-stone of its autonomy, and where there is a race problem involved it is the rock upon which its civilization rests."[62] A widely reproduced broadside also linked black suffrage with the attack on states' rights:

> *Men of the South*: Heed not the song of the suffrage siren! Seal your ears against her vocal wiles. For, no matter how sweetly she may proclaim the advantages of female franchise,—*Remember*, that *Woman Suffrage* means a

> reopening of the entire *Negro* Suffrage question; loss of State rights; and another period of reconstruction horrors, which will introduce a set of female carpetbaggers as bad as their male prototypes of the sixties. *Do Not Jeopardize* the present prosperity of your sovereign States, which was so dearly bought by the blood of your fathers and the tears of your mothers.[63]

The postratification philosophy of the antisuffragists was also based on the notion that woman suffrage equaled black domination. When the Nineteenth Amendment was ratified and finally went into effect, former antisuffragists lined up to register and vote. The Norfolk *Virginian-Pilot* deemed it "the duty of every woman in preserving the safety of Southern institutions to register and vote." The chairman of the state Democratic central committee urged white women to register and vote, "whether they favor equal suffrage or not, to maintain the prestige, the integrity, the traditions and honors of Virginia."[64]

Similarly, North Carolina's Mary Hilliard Hinton announced her intention to vote in the 1920 presidential contest and urged other antisuffragists to do the same. Hinton insisted that voting did not indicate a change of opinion, nor did it mean that antisuffragists were bowing to the inevitable. Rather, she argued, it was necessary for the opponents of woman suffrage, "in the name of duty and patriotism, to make this sacrifice to serve your State, and by so doing preserve Democracy in the Old North State."[65]

In both of these instances, white conservatives revealed they would use any weapon at their disposal to maintain white supremacy and Democratic Party hegemony. Much like the nineteenth-century constitutional conventions that had debated woman suffrage as a tool of white supremacy, white conservatives now tried to use white women voters to buttress the racial settlement. Although suffragists interpreted this turn of events as a flip-flop for antisuffragists, in one sense it was quite consistent with past conservative agendas: the underlying purpose was always white supremacy. As opposing woman suffrage had been a strategy to maintain white supremacy, ironically, so too was supporting the measure. When women were awarded the vote, antisuffragists were able to claim that they *had* to vote and had been forced to do so against their will. Female antisuffragists registered and voted in order to outvote their black neighbors.[66] Antisuffragists—*not* the suffragists—were concerned about outnumbering black women.

Significantly, the five basic categories of southern antisuffrage rhetoric—biblical, biological, sociological, racial, and constitutional—remained unchanged over time. In 1894, the San Antonio *Express* took an opinion poll of sorts, asking local men and women what they thought of the issue of woman suffrage. The opinions expressed by these Texans relatively early in the suffrage struggle in the South conveniently summarize the most widely used arguments against woman suffrage at the end of the nineteenth century: the fear of the loss of chivalry; the belief that men already accurately represented their women; the "negro question"; and the notion of separate spheres as ordained by God.[67] Twenty years later, Mississippi suffragist Nellie Nugent Somerville similarly catalogued what she considered to be the most commonly heard objections to woman suffrage in the South: the fear of enfranchising black women, biblical injunction, apathy toward the ballot by women themselves, and the belief that Mississippi men represented their women at the polls.[68] To a remarkable degree, the arguments remained unchanged. While prosuffrage ideology had undergone significant transformation around the turn of the twentieth century, southern antisuffragism remained based on the same firm foundation as when the movement began. This dichotomy requires some further examination.

As the heirs of the Enlightenment, with its emphasis on natural rights and equality, American suffrage theorists in the nineteenth century insisted that women deserved the vote because they were citizens, and equal citizenship alone entitled them to equal rights. Elizabeth Cady Stanton, Susan B. Anthony, Lucretia Mott, and other early feminists spoke in terms of justice and equal rights.[69] As part of a larger feminist agenda intended to bring women into full and equal partnership with men, nineteenth-century suffragism was indeed a daring and radical position. Accompanied by the demands for divorce reform, equality of pay, a single standard of morality, dress reform, equal access to education and the professions, suffrage was only one part of a wider vision of equality for women.[70]

Yet a number of powerful forces whittled away at the more radical demands of the feminists, eventually leaving suffrage as the only reform upon which all the various women's movements could agree. As discussed in Chapter 1, a series of scandals and public attacks compelled suffragists to prove their respectability while they demanded reform. Controversial issues such as divorce, birth control, the sexual double standard, and equal pay were discarded as they became unacceptable to one faction or another or tainted in the public eye.[71]

A second element in suffragism's retreat from radicalism was the emergence of a southern suffrage movement in the late 1880s and early 1890s. The highly symbolic National American Woman Suffrage Association (NAWSA) convention of 1903, held in New Orleans, testified to the development. With southern women taking a prominent part, the NAWSA delegates at that convention voted to accept a states' rights structure that would allow southern suffrage organizations to work for state amendments, which promised to discriminate by race. For the time being, at least, NAWSA quietly accepted racial discrimination within its organization.[72]

Similarly, national antisuffrage rhetoric and ideology also evolved after the turn of the century. As a product of a palace coup in 1917, the National Association Opposed to Woman Suffrage acquired a new president, Alice Wadsworth, and a new managing editor for its journal, Minnie Bronson. Under this new leadership, the NAOWS took a decided turn toward the right and began to attack suffragists as socialists, Bolsheviks, and unpatriotic German sympathizers.[73] At the national level, antisuffrage ideology thus reached out to target a wide range of enemies from which the home needed protection. Always conservative, northeastern antisuffragism became reactionary hyper-Americanism.

By contrast, southern antisuffrage arguments never wavered from their nineteenth-century origins. Southern antisuffragism could remain so consistent over time because antisuffragists' assumptions about the fundamental structure of society remained unchanged. The region's antis saw the world as an integrated whole: class, gender, and race relations were set in a permanent configuration, each mutually reinforcing the others. This ideal world was one with a traditional patriarchal hierarchy, a triangular structure with white male elites at the top and everyone else in their assigned positions beneath. A blow to any part of the edifice endangered the integrity of the entire structure. As antisuffrage senator Joe Bailey of Texas concluded, "we have our ideals of government, of home and of women."[74] And as Eugene Anderson of Georgia added, "we appreciate the Negro in his proper relationship."[75]

The ideal world created by the antisuffragists institutionalized inequality. Antisuffragists witnessed with horror the trend toward wider participation in the electoral system and fought the implied social equality that came with political equality. As one southern woman put it, "negro women would be placed on the same par with white women."[76] An antisuffrage pamphleteer opposed woman suffrage because he was "uncompromisingly and unalterably opposed to anything approaching social equality between whites and blacks, and any and everything that may lead to, or further, such equality, or may give political power to the negro."[77]

Antisuffragists' adherence to this mythical ideal world explains why they painted a postsuffrage world in such apocalyptic terms. For example, Fernand Mouton, Louisiana's lieutenant governor, claimed that "there is nothing in the form of disaster, yellow fever, cyclones, or earthquakes that could wreak the ruin of the South as effectively as the operation of the Susan B. Anthony amendment." Another Louisiana antisuffragist wrote that woman suffrage "would lead to the end of family life and finally to the end of our civilization."[78] "Pitchfork" Ben Tillman believed that "ultimately politics will destroy [woman] as we know her and love her; and when good women are no longer to be found, and we have lost the breed, the doom of the Republic is near."[79] A Nashville minister foresaw that "woman suffrage, if put into effect, is simply a key that's going to unlock the gates of hell and turn the demons loose upon the human family."[80] This extreme rhetoric appears to have been raving exaggeration, but the antis understood how precariously balanced their world's structure was, and they knew that *they* had the most to lose should it collapse.[81]

In a sense the antisuffragists were right, of course. American society *was* moving from "familialism" to "individualism," but no amount of tinkering with the electorate could stop the trend. For it was being produced by economic and demographic forces that the political process was powerless to halt. The enfranchisement of women did not produce those changes; rather, economic and demographic change produced woman suffrage.

Antisuffragists also knew that woman suffrage meant a refutation of the nineteenth-century doctrine of the separate spheres. They never forgot the arguments of the nineteenth-century suffragists that had struck at the foundations of family structure and gender relations. They remained suspicious of the suffragists' more recent moderation and taunted them unmercifully with examples of past radicalism. Sexual scandals (such as the Victoria Woodhull affair), the "bloomer" dress reform controversy, and discussions of divorce, birth control, and sexuality had permanently tainted the suffrage movement in the eyes of many southerners. In 1918, Isaac Peebles of Mississippi was still using Elizabeth Cady Stanton's *Woman's Bible* as evidence of the "free love" values of suffragists.[82] Henry Watterson, Louisville's prophet of the New South who nonetheless opposed the idea of the New Woman, claimed that "behind this Suffrage agitation stands Feminism. There shall be no such thing as love and marriage; as husband and wife; as a home and a family," if woman suffrage became a reality.[83] The Easley (S.C.) *Democrat* accused suffragists of "bring[ing] Mrs. [Mary Elizabeth] Lease and Mrs. Victoria Woodhull and some of the Yankee female viragoes" to speak on behalf of a suffrage bill.[84] And the Jackson *Clarion-Ledger* prominently featured articles on the militancy of the English "suffragettes," in an effort to tarnish all suffragists.[85]

Southern antisuffragists, therefore, continued to demand separate spheres for the sexes, just as they demanded separate castes for the races. Their dedication to the ideal of white supremacy was unmatched, and their efforts to protect it unfailing. The specter of black woman suffrage provided some of the most powerful arguments against woman suffrage in the minds of many white southerners, and those arguments put suffragists on the defensive.

The Suffragists' Response: The Statistical Argument

In answer to charges that woman suffrage would mean black woman suffrage, southern suffragists frequently produced statistics to show that white women outnumbered black women in the South and would therefore always outvote them. Ironically, the first use of this statistical argument came from the pen of the northern abolitionist Henry B. Blackwell. His pamphlet, written in 1867, entitled "What the South Can Do," encouraged southern legislators to utilize the votes of white women to "make themselves masters of the situation."[86] (Surprising as it might seem, Blackwell presented this argument in an effort to encourage southern whites to accept the Fourteenth Amendment's protection of black male voters. The pamphlet suggested that the enfranchisement of women would dilute the power of black votes. Blackwell continued this argument in a second pamphlet entitled "A Solution to the Southern Question," published by NAWSA in 1890. Again, the timing of the pamphlet's publication does much to explain Blackwell's position: the campaign to disfranchise southern blacks was underway.[87])

Southern suffragists saw the strength of the statistical argument and it proved to be extremely popular. In 1876, the *Memphis Appeal* endorsed white woman suffrage as a tactic for limiting the impact of the black vote.[88] Mississippi senator John Sharp Williams claimed, "[woman suffrage] might be made a bulwark of white supremacy in the State."[89] A broadside by the Equal Suffrage Association of North Carolina stressed that, "IF white domination is threatened in the South, it is, therefore, DOUBLY EXPEDIENT TO ENFRANCHISE THE WOMEN QUICKLY IN ORDER THAT IT BE PRESERVED."[90] Even the progressive North Carolina jurist Walter Clark could ask "from what reserve [other than women] can we draw the votes to offset the 25,000 colored soldiers, or other colored men, who will assuredly vote in this State at the next Presidential Election?"[91]

The frequent use of this statistical argument has led numerous historians to contend that southern antis and suffs, whatever else their differences, were identical in their support for white supremacy.[92] Such an interpretation might seem valid, considering the vigor with which some southern suffragists, like Louisiana's Kate Gordon, endorsed white supremacy. Gordon and others claimed that black disfranchisement, obtained by questionable means and maintained only by constant vigilance, would ultimately be reversed. The disfranchising clauses, based as they were on literacy and property requirements, would eventually "act as a stimulus to the black man to acquire both education and property," making disfranchisement null and void.[93] Gordon argued that southern legislatures should enfranchise women, thus helping to tip the scales in favor of the white majority. Gordon claimed that woman suffrage could legally do what the current state constitutions had illegally done: insure a white supremacy over the electorate.

Gordon's extreme position, however, did not represent that of the majority of southern suffragists. Most southern suffs found the statistical argument so appealing because it allowed them to sidestep the race issue.[94] As the North Carolina Equal Suffrage Association wrote, "it would be impossible to raise the color issue on the equal suffrage amendment, because there is no mention of color, and color cannot be dragged in by the utmost strain on construction."[95] The statistical argument was a moderate means used by women who wanted to calm white southerners' fears of black suffrage without engaging in race baiting.

As popular as this statistical argument proved to be among southern suffragists, it nevertheless could not persuade most southern conservatives. Newspaper editor Hiram Henry, for example, remained unconvinced: "The best brain of Mississippi was employed to disqualify the Negro men as voters, in the Constitutional Convention of 1890, and the work of . . . that notable body will not be set aside at the behest of a few fanatical suffragettes, who do not seem to comprehend that the Susan B. Anthony amendment would make their cooks and washerwomen voters."[96] But suffragists understood full well the implications of their demands. (They could not help but know, since the antis reminded them at every turn.) But as one southern suffragist phrased it, "the time has come to lay, once and for all, this old, old ghost which still stalks, [but] has outlived its time."[97] Suffragists were convinced that white women would outvote black women, and that was enough.

The antisuffragists, on the other hand, were determined to keep *any* blacks from voting in the South. They wanted a white *monopoly* of the franchise and of political power. As the always-outspoken James K. Vardaman put it, "I am opposed to Negro voting; it matters not what his advertised mental and moral qualifications may be. I am just as much opposed to Booker Washington as a voter . . . as I am to the . . . typical little coon, Andy Dotson, who blacks my shoes every morning. Neither is fit to perform the supreme function of citizenship."[98] And as one self-styled "Old Line Democrat" wrote, he "question[ed] the patriotism of any white person who believes that one single negro ought to be allowed to cast a ballot in Alabama."[99] To racial conservatives, allowing even *some* black voters was dangerous because "the colored population is not distributed with exact equality, like the sugar in a pudding," and could result in the election of blacks to office in some districts.[100] Furthermore, according to Louisiana Governor Ruffin Pleasant, woman suffrage was dangerous because it threatened to end an "absolutely white government."[101]

The pervasive term "white supremacy," however, does not correctly describe the antisuffragists' goal. "White monopoly," a term historians may find more accurately descriptive, better identifies the antisuffrage objective.[102] The distinction between the two terms prevents the historian from making the error of stirring the suffragists and the antisuffragists together in one racist stew. Distinguishing between "white supremacy" and "white monopoly" helps to explain why suffragists failed to convince southern legislators to enfranchise them when they claimed to support white supremacy. Laura Clay of Kentucky is a case in point: Clay spoke the language of southern Democracy (meaning white supremacy, states' rights, and Democratic Party loyalty) and worked wholeheartedly for the state amendment approach to enfranchisement, yet she failed to gain the support of the majority of southern legislators.[103] This failure can only be explained by the recognition that "white supremacy" was not an accurate portrayal of the goal of the southern Democratic Party in the early twentieth century.

Implicit in the prosuffrage position was the acknowledgement that some blacks, both male and female, *would* vote. The Kentucky suffragist Madeline McDowell Breckinridge openly admitted that some black women would vote, but she urged southern men to "ask themselves if they were going to deprive intelligent white women forever for that reason."[104] Another Kentucky suffragist wrote in 1920 that she had worked for "more than forty years in vain, to get the People to alter the Constitution of Kentucky in such a way as to make it confer upon white and colored women the same right to vote for state officers that if confers upon white and colored men."[105] A Tennessee congressman maintained that "if the negro women should vote no more numerously in proportion to numbers than do the negro men there is no danger of negro domination even if [the Susan B. Anthony] amendment should be adopted."[106] Harry Stilwell Edwards expressed his views of the inevitability of the black vote in a letter to Georgia suffragist Rebecca Latimer Felton, writing, "Well, it seems we are never to be done with the negro. All my life he has been held up as a bugaboo to scare people into putting small men into office. Now, just as we had almost gotten him buried, here comes the poor old negro 'mammy!' "[107] And Anna Dallas Dudley made clear her opinion of the black vote when she asked rhetorically, "Do you think [a southern woman] would hesitate [to vote] even if her cook should be in front of her?"[108] Dudley and her fellow suffragists saw no reason to fear black voters. Their presence in the polls posed no threat, for they had no chance of "dominating" the South.

Indeed, some southern suffragists took their stance on the black vote even further, exhibiting remarkable racial egalitarianism for their time and place.

The Tennessee suffrage association, for instance, proudly recorded the successful cooperation between black and white women voters in 1920:

> In Nashville [black women] registered about 2,500 and voted almost their full quota. They organized under the direction of the suffrage association, had their own city and ward chairmen and worked with an intelligence, loyalty and dignity that made new friends for their race and for woman suffrage. There was not a single adverse criticism of them from any ward. They kept faith with the white women even when some of their men sold out the night before the election to a notorious political rounder. They proved that they were trying to keep step with the march of progress and with a little patience, trust and vision the universal tie of motherhood and sisterhood can and will overcome the prejudice against them as voters."[109]

In another example of racial moderation, the Birmingham suffrage organization was nearly split in two over a resolution debated in 1913 condemning segregation. In fact, a minority of its members favored the resolution.[110] For many southern whites, the acceptance of a black voting minority, with its underlying admission of political equality of the races, was what was truly at stake in the southern suffrage contest.

The danger of political equality lay in its tacit admission that blacks had the right to vote simply because they were citizens. Political equality might imply social equality to southern blacks, encouraging them to strive for even more changes in the relations between the races. Antisuffragists stressed this possible implication over and over again throughout their campaign. An anonymous broadside entitled "Planks from the Suffrage Platform" stated the antisuffragists' feared notion clearly: suffrage "stands for race equality—social and political."[111] Texas's deposed governor, Jim Ferguson, agreed: "This talk about equal suffrage also means equal nigger."[112] According to three female opponents of the Anthony Amendment, it had four dangerous principles "lurking in it": surrender of state sovereignty; *race equality*; voluntary ratification of the Fourteenth and Fifteenth Amendments; and Negro woman suffrage.[113] Virginia antisuffragists reminded their legislators that "every argument for sexual equality in politics is, and must be, an argument also for racial equality. There is no way around it. If the white woman is entitled to the vote because she bears, has borne, may bear, or might have borne children, the Negro woman is entitled to the same right for the same reason."[114]

In fact, to some it seemed that political equality meant not only racial equality but black supremacy as well. James Callaway, a tireless editorial writer from Georgia, believed that the "Susan B. Anthony Amendment Means

Negro Rule."[115] Having seen a photograph of Carrie Chapman Catt marching between two black women in a suffrage parade, Episcopal bishop Thomas Gailor suggested that Catt "may have been proclaiming the *supremacy* of the negro race."[116] A Mississippi legislator contended that "every vote cast for the adoption of the Anthony amendment is a vote cast for Negro supremacy."[117] And a Texas man insisted that "Negro domination in a few states and several counties in other states would be inevitable."[118]

Even though most southern counties had white majorities, many antisuffragists feared that woman suffrage might still tip the scales toward black domination. For, as a Texas legislator put it, "there would be many thousands of white ladies that would not vote; but all the Negro women would do so."[119] A state senator in North Carolina protested that woman suffrage "would enable every colored woman in the State, who could read and write, to vote. Why, my cook would vote, while my wife would not."[120] Memphis's Annah Watson claimed that "the better women of the section, even the small minority in favor of suffrage, would probably forego the right if it must be exercised in common by the two races, while the colored element, elated by the power put into their hands, would, beyond a question, make use of it."[121] Nancy MacLean's assessment of the Ku Klux Klan is equally applicable to the antisuffragists: their inability to imagine an egalitarian world led them to interpret struggles for black equality as efforts to establish black supremacy.[122]

Antisuffragists warned that the various disfranchisement schemes employed by the South would not hold back the tide of black voters for long. A Mississippi statesman urged that

> the people and especially our legislators should awaken to the fact that the Negroes are rapidly decreasing their percentages of illiteracy, especially among their women, and that in another five years 90 percent of the Negroes, male and female, will be able to comply with the requirements of section 4119 of our code. All of this talk about the Negro of the future not paying his or her poll tax is nothing but "tommy rot." Every student of the situation who understands the Negro knows full well that if the Anthony amendment is adopted that every adult Negro in Mississippi will, if necessary, go barefooted, naked and hungry in order that they may get the money to pay their poll tax and vote.[123]

The Richmond *Evening Journal* expressed a similar view: "It is to be remembered that the literacy test would not work in choking off the colored woman vote. The colored people are decreasing their percentage of illiteracy very fast, especially among their women and girls. The ladies of the suffrage league will hardly come forward with a property test. No safeguard would be left but the poll tax; and if colored women knew they could get votes and rule some very rich and important counties by paying $1.50 apiece, we are inclined to think most of them would be willing to go hungry, if necessary, to do it."[124]

The Virginia Antisuffrage Association informed their legislators that "all who have had practical experience dealing with this problem know it would be ten times as difficult to deal with colored women and keep them from the polls as it ever was with colored men. The woman of the African race has her share of pertinacity too and would be exempt from fear of physical consequences."[125] North Carolina's governor, Thomas Bickett, concurred: "A negro man could be controlled but nothing could frighten a negro woman."[126]

Although both suffragists and antisuffragists used the rhetoric of white supremacy in their debate, they clearly were talking about two different ideas. The term "white supremacy," the definition of which seemed so apparent, actually was open to interpretation.[127]

In his study of the southern progressive movement, Dewey Grantham interpreted southern progressivism as built on a foundation of broad agreement by whites that blacks, both male and female, must be kept out of southern politics. The evidence presented here reveals that there was some room for debate within that broad consensus. Mainstream southern suffragists demonstrated their willingness to allow black women to vote in order to obtain the vote for themselves.[128]

Beneath the five major lines of antisuffrage argument lay a single, albeit complex, worldview. Southern antisuffragists wished to protect as long as possible the last remaining vestiges of "the world the slaveholders made." The patriarchy of the past, with its clearly defined racial, sexual, and class relations, provided a haven of security and stability in a changing and confusing world. Political equality of the races might prove to mean social equality as well, a concept utterly unacceptable to people such as Henry Watterson, whose "belief in an aristocratic form of government," quipped one suffragist, "has continually interfered with [his] attempt to be a Democrat."[129]

This mythical world the antis created, where everyone had a place and knew it, rested upon a systematic ideology.[130] While the arguments the antisuffragists devised might indeed be contradictory at times, the theoretical underpinnings of the antisuffrage position were rock solid. Southern antisuffragists held tightly to the separate spheres and separate castes of a deferential society that was quickly slipping away. In their view, democratization had gone too far. What the electorate needed was refinement, not expansion. And since woman suffrage necessarily meant black woman suffrage, southern antis, both male and female, agreed that it was better to continue the search for methods of disfranchisement rather than discuss any further enlargement of the electorate.

The Ideology of Black Antisuffragism

This discussion of antisuffrage ideology cannot be complete without some consideration of the generally ignored phenomenon of southern *black* antisuffragism. It must be treated separately, however, since its ideological basis was wholly different from that of white antisuffragism.

That southern blacks disagreed among themselves over the issue of woman suffrage should come as no surprise, although the fact remains uninvestigated by scholars of suffrage and of African American history. Southern blacks who advocated the enfranchisement of women did so with two major principles in mind: first, women, as citizens, had the right to vote to protect their interests, and second, black women could use the ballot in order to help their race.[131] Many southern blacks agreed with W. E. B. Du Bois: "First, [woman suffrage] is a great human question. . . . Whatever concerns half mankind concerns us. Secondly, any agitation, discussion or opening of the problem of voting must inevitably be a discussion of the right of black folk to vote in America and Africa. . . . Finally, votes for women means votes for black women."[132] A group of black citizens in Atlanta pledged to "exert our righteous efforts until not only every eligible black man but EVERY ELIGIBLE BLACK WOMAN shall be wielding the ballot proudly in defense of our liberties and our homes."[133]

Black women formed suffrage organizations throughout the South, although their existence has often escaped historians of the suffrage movement, who have generally consulted only white-generated sources. It has been discovered that black woman suffrage existed in Tuskegee, Charleston, and Memphis; and undoubtedly there were many others as yet still hidden from the historical record. Prominent southern black women like Margaret Murray Washington (wife of educator Booker T. Washington), Mary Church Terrell, and Adella Hunt Logan openly worked for woman suffrage in their communities and in the region at large. Christia V. Adair, the Texas civil rights leader, also worked for woman suffrage in her hometown of Brownsville.[134]

However, black woman suffrage carried some potentially explosive baggage for white southerners accustomed to discussing every political issue in terms of "the negro question." Black southerners knew and understood that demands for black woman suffrage might unleash white fury on all southern blacks. The fear of reprisals, in an era when lynchings took place daily and the Ku Klux Klan visited nightly, caused many black southerners to stop and cautiously assess the potential outcome of suffrage advocacy.

In 1913, the Nashville *Tennessean* reported that local blacks were "manifesting interest in a debate . . . between members of their race on the question of woman suffrage." The very fact that such a debate was noted in the white press could only have encouraged even more caution and moderation in the black community. One black woman club leader in Tennessee later insisted that even though woman suffrage was discussed and debated, blacks had not organized for the cause in the state.[135] Mary Johnston reported a debate over woman suffrage that took place among her black servants. Her black gardener, for one, while "intensely interested" in woman suffrage concluded that he must oppose it. Johnston noted that he was "exceedingly anxious" over the dangers the country might suffer if women voted. The dangers were not identified in Johnston's account, however.[136]

Fear of what the white community's reaction might be to black suffragism produced not only caution but outright opposition to the suffrage movement from some quarters. North Carolina's Annie Blackwell, a black temperance leader, is one example. Blackwell reasoned that if the Nineteenth Amendment was ratified, southern states would surely pass "grandmother" clauses designed to prevent black women from voting. Woman suffrage would effectively mean *white* woman suffrage. While woman suffrage might be acceptable if white women could be counted on to vote in the interests of and in support for their black sisters, she asserted, events in the recent past made it doubtful that white women would be the source of sisterly solidarity. White women, after all, had participated in lynchings, had encouraged the Wilmington race riot of 1898, and had campaigned for disfranchisement of blacks in 1900.[137] Blackwell feared that woman suffrage would not benefit the black community, and she opposed it for that reason. Her race came first.[138]

The race also came first for James B. Dudley, president of the black Agricultural and Technical College in Greensboro, N.C. Dudley wrote an open letter to black women in his state encouraging them to stay away from the voting booth, warning "your entrance now in the political field will add fresh fuel to the fires of race prejudice and political hate."[139]

There was a second ideological position taken by southern blacks who opposed woman suffrage, one that closely reflected the traditional values of white antisuffragists. Some southern blacks opposed the reform because of their middle-class philosophies about gender roles. A black newspaper in Augusta editorialized in 1866 that only three groups of citizens could be properly deprived of the vote: foreigners, children, and women, whose "sphere is anywhere but in the arena of politics and government."[140] A religious columnist concurred: "We want supper, our socks darned, buttons sewed on, children dressed, our tired brow and head rubbed. Therefore let us hear, not of sermons she must go and preach, [or] of conventions she must hold."[141] A powerful voice for black antisuffragism was that of Booker T. Washington, who also used the "womanly influence" argument. "It is not clear to me," wrote Washington, "that [woman] would exercise any great or more beneficent influence upon the world than she now does, if the duty of taking an active part in party politics were imposed on her."[142]

As the black middle class in the South grew, its members increasingly accepted middle-class mores, including patriarchal social arrangements. Southern blacks were not immune to the cult of true womanhood and the doctrine of the separate spheres, especially if they judged that their acceptance by the white community depended on their adoption of the values of the white community.[143] The adoption of middle-class values gave the emergent black middle class the opportunity to prove its respectability.[144] And although black men more frequently used the separate spheres imagery in public pronouncements, some black women leaders also opposed any changes in the relations of the spheres. Sarah Pettey, for example, argued that the "home environment" offered higher authority for women than did the world of partisan politics.[145]

Black opposition to woman suffrage in the South stemmed from concerns about both race and gender. As was true for southern whites, southern blacks could not judge woman suffrage merely on its own merits. It could not be treated as a natural right or as simple justice. The potential impact of enfranchisement on all African Americans in the South, not just women, had to be utmost in the minds of southern blacks. For many, the solution was watchful waiting; for others, outright opposition.

It is important to note, however, that these black antisuffragists, male and female, were never included in the organizational efforts to defeat woman suffrage in the southern states. White antisuffragists could not bring themselves to build an interracial movement, even when it would have been dedicated to the protection of prescribed gender roles. An incident in Virginia demonstrated their reluctance to join forces with black antisuffragists. The white antisuffragists held an essay contest through the Richmond *News-Leader*, offering a prize for the best antisuffrage essay. The winner turned out to be a black woman, Mrs. Nannie Goode of Boydton, and the paper refused to publish her photograph.[146] White antisuffragists' racial views prevented them from incorporating black antisuffragists into their movement. Likewise, their philosophies on gender roles played an important part in the way they organized the antisuffrage movement, which is examined in the following chapter.

5

Organizational Strategies and Activities of the Southern Antisuffragists

Way down in Anti-Suffrage country,
Far, far away!
There's where the States refuse to join us,
There's where the fossils stay.
Oh! their world is sad and dreary,
Still as dark as night.
Southern men, you make us mighty weary,
Can't you see the Suffrage light?

from the songsheet
in program of 1920 NAWSA Convention

During the first wave of southern suffragism in the late nineteenth century, opposition to woman suffrage was strong in the South but not organized. But the second wave of the suffrage movement in the 1910s, with its increased numbers, its aggressive publicity, and the possibility of its success, frightened southern antisuffragists into action. Southern antisuffragists were compelled to organize in response, and they utilized many of the techniques of their opponents in their own movement. The antisuffrage organizational movement was no pale imitation of the suffrage movement, however. Factors unique to the antisuffrage ideology, such as class interests, strongly influenced the kinds of organizational activity in which southern antisuffragists engaged. Their movement differed in marked ways from that of their opponents.

Southern antisuffragists looked to the previously existing National Association Opposed to Woman Suffrage for guidance in establishing their own regional movement to halt woman suffrage. But southern antisuffragists nevertheless created organizations that differed from the NAOWS model. In particular, the southern opponents of woman suffrage utilized organizational strategies that were informed by prescribed gender roles, roles that ultimately limited the range of activities in which antisuffrage women could participate.

The relationships between the various antisuffrage groups—national, regional, and state—were complex and occasionally problematic. The southern antisuffrage movement's relationship with its northeastern "sister" movement is a case in point. Southern antisuffrage workers, so resolutely ladylike in word and deed, found many of the northern antisuffrage women too dominating and eager to control the antisuffrage effort in the region. Tensions between the two groups of antisuffrage women simmered just below the surface in the heat of the southern suffrage campaigns. Moreover, southern antisuffrage women found their working relationship with male antisuffragists to be strained, although all of these tensions were carefully hidden from the public eye. These and other dynamics within the movement provide a reminder that, like the suffrage movement itself, the antisuffrage movement was multifaceted. To see the movement as a homogeneous whole is to miss the intricate pattern of relationships that made up the tapestry of the antisuffrage movement.[1]

National Organization

The first organized activity of antisuffragists in the United States occurred in 1868 in Massachusetts, where opponents of woman suffrage conducted a statewide petition drive. Massachusetts also produced the first formal antisuffrage organization, a standing committee that was formed in response to Victoria Woodhull's appearance before a congressional committee. The committee sent petitions to the state legislature every year from 1882 to 1895.[2] In 1895, the same year that the state held a public referendum of the suffrage question, this standing committee formally became the Massachusetts Association Opposed to the Further Extension of Suffrage to Women (MAOFEWS). It subsequently became the largest and most active state association in the country: in 1915, the association claimed nearly 37,000 members from 443 towns in Massachusetts.[3]

Other states were generating antisuffrage associations as well, and in 1911 they joined forces to form the National Association Opposed to Woman Suffrage (NAOWS). Josephine Dodge served as president from 1911 to 1917, traveling the country numerous times over the years, speaking on behalf of her organization.[4] Antisuffrage organizational activity peaked between 1911 and 1916, a period that corresponded with some major setbacks for the suffrage movement: in 1915 alone, suffragists lost important referenda in New York, New Jersey, Pennsylvania, and Massachusetts.[5]

Dodge resigned the presidency of the NAOWS suddenly in July 1917 and was replaced by Alice Wadsworth, wife of the New York senator James Wadsworth Jr. In a few months time, all other officers had also been replaced, and the national headquarters was relocated from Washington to New York. This clean sweep of the founders of the movement, unexplained in the contemporary press, resulted in a visible change in the nature of the NAOWS.[6] Previously a conservative organization devoted solely to opposing woman suffrage and related changes in gender relations, the NAOWS became a reactionary group ferreting out radicalism and pointing accusatory fingers in numerous directions.

Symbolic of this change was the renaming of the official organ of the association from *The Woman's Protest* to *The Woman Patriot*. The new journal's motto was "For Home and National Defense Against Woman Suffrage, Feminism, and Socialism." Its rhetoric became stridently antiradical, as it attempted to associate suffragism with Bolshevism, anarchism, and subversion. Its pages were peppered with stories of socialists who demanded woman suffrage and with character assassinations, which over time grew increasingly shrill.[7]

The national association floundered under Wadsworth's leadership, however. Its public activities dwindled, its organizing drive nearly ceased, and it no longer provided a dynamic focus for the energies of the country's antisuffragists.[8] In January 1919, the NAOWS claimed twenty-six state affiliates and a membership of over 500,000 women. However, the annual convention that year included only seventy-five delegates and was held in the home of the president.[9]

Who were the women who opposed their own enfranchisement? Since membership lists have not survived, there is no evidence on which to assess the backgrounds of the majority of the organization's membership. Only their leaders are generally known to us. One study has concluded that the women who led the national movement were members of the social "aristocracy." Urban, wealthy, native-born, Republican, and Protestant, they were members of "established" families, either by birth or by marriage.[10] It should be reiterated, however, that this description only applied to the national officeholders.

Like the suffragists, opponents of woman suffrage spent much of their time educating both themselves and the general public about the antisuffrage position. The National League for the Civic Education of Women was formed in 1908, with the avowed purpose of studying civic questions "from an antisuffrage point of view." The college committee of the league donated antisuffrage books to college libraries.[11] Similarly, the Guidon Club, founded by nationally known writer Helen Kendrick Johnson, was formed as an antisuffrage study club. It held weekly meetings, where members gave short presentations followed by open discussion.[12]

Financial records are as scarce as membership lists, but there are some suggestions about the source of antisuffrage monies. In Massachusetts, at least, the antisuffragists derived their financial support largely from their own members.[13] If Massachusetts was representative of the national movement, then it would appear that the antisuffragists did less public fund-raising than did the suffragists, who devoted a great deal of their time to such endeavors.

In other organizational activities, the antisuffragists often mirrored the activities of the suffragists. Lobbying, petition drives, and letter writing campaigns were common to both groups. The production and distribution of literature were critical activities for both suffragists and antisuffragists. While the antis usually put an apolitical veneer on their activities, nevertheless they frequently engaged in overtly political actions. For example, they eventually employed professional female lobbyists, such as Massachusetts's Alice George, who not only presented the antisuffrage position before the legislature in her home state but also appeared before Congress.[14]

On the other hand, the antisuffragists could not always use the identical publicity techniques of the suffragists. Female antisuffragism by its very nature confronted an internal contradiction that made its existence difficult: convincing conservative women to act as political creatures so as not to become political creatures required a careful strategy. One approach they advocated was the quiet, "ladylike" campaign, emphasizing traditional female moral suasion methods rather than more aggressive political tactics. The antisuffragists tended to stress educational efforts rather than open-air rallies or street-corner speeches, which the suffragists used more and more as the campaign wore on.[15] Such "spectacles" as hot-air ballooning or car parades, which suffragists used to much advantage, were abhorrent to antisuffrage women.

The disadvantages of the antisuffragists's techniques, however, were counterbalanced by one considerable asset: the status quo. As a movement dedicated to conserving the status quo, the antisuffragists did not need to create a mass movement. The burden of proof lay with the reformers, who found it necessary to prove that large numbers of Americans supported their cause.[16] To that end, antisuffragists liked to cite the National American Woman Suffrage Association's membership totals, pointing out that the relatively small number of women who joined NAWSA provided all the evidence needed to support their contention that the majority of American women did not want the vote.

The national antisuffrage movement had enormous potential, but it ultimately failed to attain its goal. Under the leadership of Josephine Dodge, the NAOWS had maintained a focused vision. Energetic and confident, the movement increased its membership and garnered several significant victories in state referenda. The change of leadership at this critical juncture not only changed the direction of the movement, it also replaced the focused vision of Dodge with the narrow one of Wadsworth. Rather than expressing the opinion of possibly millions of American women, the NAOWS became instead the voice of a hysterical minority.[17] As a conservative movement protecting the status quo, the antisuffrage position was one of significant power. Had the growing and vibrant association that existed before 1917 been able to maintain its organization until after World War I (and the conservative backlash that followed it), it is possible that the antisuffrage movement could have continued to block woman suffrage for several more decades.

Southern States' Organizations

The southern states were also the site of an important antisuffrage movement, one that has not to date received scholarly attention. Although the National Association Opposed to Woman Suffrage did some "missionary" work in the South, several southern states, Virginia, Maryland, Texas, and Tennessee, worked independently of the NAOWS to organize an antisuffrage movement. Virginia and Maryland became affiliated with NAOWS in 1912, but Tennessee's attempt to organize in 1913 was unsuccessful.

Maryland's Association Opposed to Woman Suffrage organized in Baltimore in 1911 because its members perceived that "in the last year or two the suffragists had made such strides that an opposing organization was almost a necessity."[18] By 1914, this state association had grown strong enough to open an office in downtown Baltimore and had begun the work of establishing branches in other cities, starting with Annapolis.[19]

Virginia antisuffragists also organized relatively early (for the southern states), in February 1912. An "impromptu" antisuffrage speech given by the well-known author Molly Seawell while she was visiting relatives in Richmond evidently persuaded many in her audience to organize an association. In what would later prove typical of the southern style of antisuffragism, these Virginia antis, once the organization was established, claimed that they "held no public meetings, and . . . consistently avoided newspaper debates and controversies."[20] Yet, in spite of this conservative approach to activism, the Virginia association claimed a membership of more than 2,000 women just two years later. Nine branch associations had been organized, including a notably active one in Charlottesville, headed by Carrie Preston Davis.[21]

Tennessee's abortive effort at organizing came in the fall of 1913. Annie Riley Hale of Rogersville called a public meeting in Knoxville for the purpose of forming an antisuffrage society. Hale told the audience that the antisuffrage movement was a "silent, invisible force," one that did not lend itself "to the flamboyant methods of the suffragists" but rather found its source "in the primal mother-instinct of the race." Following her address, Hale opened the floor for discussion, but the local press reported that "no steps were taken toward forming an anti-suffrage society."[22]

Perhaps encouraged by these spontaneous efforts, the National Association Opposed to Woman Suffrage undertook some organizing work of its own in the southern states. Then-president Josephine Dodge and chief organizer Minnie Bronson made several southern tours in an effort to increase the number of state affiliates. For example, the two women spent January of 1914 in South Carolina; however, they did not succeed in organizing an affiliate there. A. Elizabeth Taylor has suggested that Dodge failed because, "with both custom and tradition on their side, the 'antis' apparently felt little need" for an organization.[23] Since this line of reasoning does not take into consideration other southern antisuffragists who also had custom and tradition on their side did choose to organize, it inadequately explains their lack of success. It is more probable that South Carolina antisuffragists failed to mobilize at this time because the prosuffrage movement had yet to pose a serious threat in this "most reluctant" state.[24]

In May 1914, the NAOWS was successful in Georgia. Antisuffragists met in Macon and formed their state association.[25] President-elect Caroline Patterson reported three months later that 2,000 women had been enrolled and at least ten branches had been established.[26] Although the Georgia antis made no public acknowledgement comparable to that of the Maryland antisuffragists, it is likely that the impetus for organizing there also came as a result of the increasing visibility of the suffragists. In fact, the Equal Suffrage Party of Georgia had also formed that same year and announced its intent to "undertake more aggressive work in behalf of woman suffrage."[27]

The following year, Texas spawned a spontaneous antisuffrage movement, that is, one not instigated by a visit from the NAOWS. A state woman suffrage amendment in 1915 was fought "almost single-handed" by Pauline K. (Mrs. James B.) Wells. As *The Woman's Protest* exulted,

> there arose one woman with the courage and the spirit of self-sacrifice which was necessary to make a public protest against the effort to thrust man's work and man's duties upon the women of Texas. Supported by the wives, mothers and home-makers from many sections of the State, she went to Austin during the recent session of the Legislature, upon the invitation of that body, and in a modest and becoming manner, voiced the sentiments of a great majority of our women against what they believe to be an effort to lower the standard of womanhood by placing upon her shoulders the degrading and disagreeable work of politics. That woman was Mrs. James B. Wells, of Brownsville.[28]

Wells's appearance before the state legislature appears to have brought other antis out of their parlors, for they began to organize around her immediately, establishing a state association with at least one local affiliate.[29]

NAOWS President Josephine Dodge undertook another organizing tour in 1916, starting out at Tennessee. By this time, the suffragists had recognized the deliberate nature of Dodge's travels and realized that the antisuffragists were attempting to match them in organizational strength. Carrie Chapman Catt warned her cohorts at a suffrage meeting in Memphis about this threat. "They are trying to get an organization in every state, and I think they will succeed," Catt predicted. "Wherever there is a constitutional convention to be held, that is where they go. This is why they are coming to Tennessee."[30] Fulfilling the prophecy, Dodge spoke in Nashville, leaving an antisuffrage society in her wake.[31] The timing of this organizational effort was significant: in 1915, the Tennessee legislature had passed a joint resolution favoring woman suffrage, a necessary first step toward amending the state constitution.[32]

The most active and most important state association was Alabama's. Originally called the Alabama Association Opposed to Woman Suffrage and based in Selma, this organization claimed 1,500 members in 1916. Its motto was "Home Rule, State's Rights, and White Supremacy," and it affiliated with the National Association Opposed to Woman Suffrage. Although the organization was active only in Selma at the time,[33] it became the core of the powerful statewide association that emerged a few years later.

By 1916, state associations had formed in Maryland, Virginia, Alabama, Georgia, Texas, and Tennessee, and all but the latter two had joined the National Association Opposed to Woman Suffrage. Individuals from other southern states had joined the NAOWS but had not formed state branches. All efforts to form antisuffrage organizations had failed in North Carolina and in South Carolina.[34] And no notable antisuffrage activity had occurred in Arkansas, Florida, Kentucky, or Mississippi.

Suffragists had long assumed that antisuffragism was so strong in the southern states as to be nearly insurmountable. The organizational record, up through 1916 at least, indicates that antisuffrage sentiment was present but hardly mobilized. Only three states, Maryland, Virginia, and Georgia, had organizations with memberships large enough to promise future strength. Southerners may have been less inclined than people in other parts of the nation to entertain the thought of women voters, but southern women also seemed less inclined to organize against the reform.

From 1916 to 1919, southern antisuffragists seemed content to keep a low profile. They put forth little new organizational effort, planned almost no public activities, and prompted only occasional individual actions such as writing letters to the editor. While the prosuffrage forces were building their numbers, experimenting with new publicity techniques, and attempting to find a form of woman suffrage that could pass through conservative southern statehouses,[35] the antisuffragists remained quietly on the periphery, watching for the ultimate direction of the suffrage movement.

In response to Congress's adoption of the Susan B. Anthony Amendment in 1919, the southern antisuffrage movement entered a new phase. In June 1919, the Alabama state association reorganized and renamed itself the Southern Women's Anti-Ratification League. Relocating from Selma to the strategically important state capitol, its first meeting was held at the Montgomery home of the new president, Nina Pinckard, who would become the most highly visible antisuffrage woman in the entire region. Headed by a group of women "of wealth and social standing,"[36] this new version of the antisuffrage association immediately went to work to prepare for the upcoming legislative battle over ratification of the proposed Nineteenth Amendment.

Throughout the summer of 1919, Alabama antisuffragists held weekly meetings in anticipation of the ratification contest. These meetings, as well as the public rallies they conducted, received positive coverage by the Montgomery *Advertiser*, whose editor was staunchly antisuffrage.[37] The league announced that it "expects to produce evidence before the legislature that a great majority of the voters and most of the white women of middle Alabama are opposed to ratification [of the Nineteenth Amendment]." Local leaders supported this statement with "a pile of over one thousand letters and telegrams from all sections of the state denoting the concerted movement to defeat the movement before the legislature."[38]

When the state legislature convened in Montgomery in July, the Anti-Ratification League sent a letter to each member, "earnestly beg[ging] that you, as true men of the South, decline to ratify this Amendment which violates the time honored question of *States Rights* and which dishonors the principle for which the Confederate soldier shed his blood." The league claimed that it would support state-regulated enfranchisement, whenever a majority of women desired it, but at present, they asserted, "not more than three women out of every hundred are in favor of the amendment."[39]

As the legislature began its deliberations on the measure, the Anti-Ratification League sent a petition asking that the solons reject the federal amendment. Wedded to the cult of southern womanhood, they felt it inappropriate to appear before the legislature in person. So they asked a sympathetic man to read their petition (which they insisted was a "memorial," a word less overtly political than "petition") for them.[40] The league's 1,200 members, claiming to represent the majority of southern women, reminded the legislators that "adoption would forever forfeit the right of the state to regulate its own election laws, and transfer this power to a government not in sympathy with our social order. The Fifteenth Amendment is not dead. It only sleepeth. Why arouse it from its slumber?"[41]

The combined appeals to chivalry, states' rights, white supremacy, and Democratic hegemony appeared to have made the desired impact. Alabama's legislature soundly defeated the Susan B. Anthony Amendment. Moreover, the successful outcome of the campaign seemed merely to whet the appetites of the Alabama antisuffragists for political activism. The league decided to maintain its offices and organization so as to be ready to fight other manifestations of "feminism" in the event the Nineteenth Amendment was ultimately ratified.[42] Renaming itself the Southern Women's League for the Rejection of the Susan B. Anthony Amendment, Alabama antisuffragists planned a regional organization and began the work of organizing in neighboring states. The new association, generally called the Southern Rejection League, announced that it "will cooperate with anti-suffrage organizations which are in existence, and in states which have no such organizations, the League will take up the fight."[43] Remaining under Nina Pinckard's direction and headquartered in Montgomery, the Southern Rejection League never created the hierarchical organization that its leaders had planned, however. Nor could it truly be called a regional organization, as it never established affiliates in every state, and for the most part its leaders were residents of Alabama.

The Southern Rejection League primarily concerned itself with the federal constitutional amendment, and its major arguments always concerned states' rights, white supremacy, and negro voters, (as opposed to outright opposition to woman suffrage), as its Declaration of Principles demonstrates:

1. State Sovereignty is essential to the Liberty, Happiness, True Progress, and Welfare of the American People.
2. [The Nineteenth Amendment] will force the unrestricted ballot upon unwilling majorities in the Southern States, and will place the control of the electorate outside the Sovereign State.
3. We deny the Justice of the Compulsory Regulation of the Electorate of our States by a combination of other States, who have no sympathetic understanding of our peculiar Social and Racial problems.
4. We oppose any measure that threatens the continuation of Anglo-Saxon domination of Social and Political affairs in each and every State of the Union without strife and bloodshed which would inevitably follow an attempt to overthrow it.[44]

The Southern Rejection League billed itself as a states' rights organization, but some of its members opposed woman suffrage in any form. Claiming that some of its members did not necessarily oppose white women voting, the women of the Southern Rejection League "know that to adopt the Anthony Amendment means bloodshed for their husbands, their brothers and their sons, and perilous days for [the South]."[45] But there is no evidence that the Southern Rejection League ever lobbied *for* a state suffrage bill. Its claim to be a states' rights suffrage organization is suspect at best. It did attract a handful of suffragists, such as Anne Pleasant of Louisiana, who were genuine in their advocacy of a state amendment. But in general, former members of the SSWSC and other prosuffrage women stayed clear of the Southern Rejection League, giving further testament to the true nature of the organization.

The most important organizational function of the Southern Rejection League was the production and distribution of literature. Leaflets, broadsides, and editorials bearing the stamp of the Southern Rejection League can be found in archives throughout the southern states, bearing witness to the breadth of their circulation. (This service proved especially important to some

The Southern Rejection League preparing antisuffrage literature, Nashville, 1920 (Courtesy of Tennessee State Library and Archives, Nashville)

state affiliates, such as North Carolina and South Carolina, who had limited resources for the production of their own propaganda and limited time in which to generate it.) One broadside of the Southern Rejection League bore the title "Negro Women's Resolutions for Enforcement of Federal Suffrage Amendments." Distributed during the Tennessee campaign, the leaflet stressed that black women eagerly awaited their enfranchisement by the federal government. The broadside, which featured a listing of the resolutions passed by the National Association of Colored Women's Clubs in 1920, was intended to highlight the threat of the Fourteenth and Fifteenth Amendments to the federal constitution.[46]

A favorite way to present these campaign broadsides was to quote some of the most radical statements from the feminist, socialist, and suffragist presses and then to suggest that these statements proved the radical nature of suffragism. Quoting Carrie Chapman Catt, a broadside entitled "Planks from the Suffrage Platform" attacked the NAWSA leader as unpatriotic and possibly anarchistic. "If the Constitution stands in the way of what we want, tear it up," Catt allegedly told a House Committee hearing. The broadside also singled out Catt's pacifism for condemnation. "I am myself a pacifist, now and forever," she had written in *The Woman's Journal*.[47]

The Southern Rejection League also reprinted significant antisuffrage editorials and issued them as leaflets and booklets. The Tennessee Division published an editorial by J. C. McQuiddy, editor of the *Gospel Advocate*, entitled "Woman Suffrage—Is it Right for Women to Vote and Hold Office?" McQuiddy based his opposition on biblical injunction, the type of argument the Southern Rejection League apparently found most effective, if the quantity of this kind of publication found in archival collections across the South is an accurate indication.[48]

Even though the institutional structure of the Southern Rejection League was loose, nevertheless the various state organizations could cooperate significantly at critical times. When North Carolina's antisuffragists decided they needed a formal organization to combat the ratification of the Susan B. Anthony Amendment in the summer of 1920, they turned to the Southern Rejection League for assistance. Mary Hilliard Hinton, a longtime opponent of woman suffrage, invited Carrie Preston Davis of Virginia to come to Raleigh to help organize a state branch of the Rejection League. Davis stayed in town throughout the summer, helping to coordinate the opposition forces.[49]

Unlike the prosuffrage associations, for whom institutional records are plentiful, the southern antisuffrage organizations have not left much of a paper trail. Almost no membership lists survive, nor are there minutes of meetings, treasurers' reports, or annual yearbooks, leaving little information about the internal operations of these organizations. There are several hints, however, that their budgets were minimal. An Alabama antisuffragist wrote Josephine Pearson in November 1920 complaining about the "unequal struggle" between suffragists and antis. "The world, the flesh & the Devil against us, & not even the money to buy stamps to carry on the battle from our side," she lamented.[50] If this is not just an exaggeration by a disappointed partisan, it would appear that the "liquor lobby" and other powerful interest groups did not make lavish donations to the Southern Rejection League. It is more likely that the male opponents of woman suffrage used their funds for their own lobbying efforts, while the organized women's groups worked with minimal budgets. Southern antisuffrage organizations never had the kind of financial resources to which Massachusetts, for example, had access.

One leaflet prepared by the antisuffragists in Houston indicates the projected budget and intended activities of the state association during the 1919 state amendment referendum. The Houston organization estimated that the campaign against the state amendment would require $25,000. The money would be used "in organizing clubs opposed to woman suffrage, circulating literature, publicity work and in paying expenses incident to having speakers of National and State prominence present the arguments against the amendment." The association also planned to establish a press service "to keep the activities of the Association constantly before the public."[51]

Membership totals for the Southern Rejection League do not exist, nor did the league ever announce an estimate of the numbers of its members. While the antisuffragists naturally stressed the large body of support they received and claimed that applications for membership were "pouring in,"[52] the bulk of the evidence suggests that membership was actually much smaller than the state suffrage associations. For example, North Carolina antisuffragists, who organized in 1920, appeared to have only twenty active members in their branch of the Southern Rejection League, compared to nearly 1,000 members of the seven-year-old state NAWSA affiliate in the same year.[53] Tennessee's branch of the Southern Rejection League listed approximately sixty members, while Nashville's local prosuffrage association alone had more than 3,000 members.[54] Louisiana, ever contrary, never formed a branch of the Southern Rejection League but organized a separate Anti-Ratification League with approximately 130 members. By contrast, the Woman Suffrage Party of Louisiana (a NAWSA affiliate) claimed 1,000 members as early as 1914 (a year after its formation).[55] Overall, the numbers of women active in the antisuffrage organizations were much smaller than those of the prosuffrage forces, although neither group ever came close to having enrolled a majority of southern women. By way of comparison, the northeastern states had much larger memberships: Massachusetts alone claimed more members than all the southern states combined.

One internal institutional document from the Virginia association, in the form of a set of bylaws, suggests some of the ways the state antisuffrage associations might have operated. Interested women could be enrolled as an associate member by sending their names to the secretary ("Every name is a source of strength.") To become an active member, one was required to pay "very small" annual dues and promise to help in distributing literature, forming new branches of the association, and enrolling new members. A donation of five or more dollars a year made one a "contributing member" of the organization. The bylaws also noted, apparently without recognizing the irony, that dues-paying members of the association became *voting* members of the association.[56]

Newspaper accounts provide further clues to the format and content of organizational meetings. Tennessee antisuffragists held regular meetings in the home of their president, Virginia Vertrees. They read aloud speeches by

Members of the Southern Rejection League, Nashville, 1920 (Courtesy of Tennessee State Library and Archives, Nashville)

prominent antisuffragists, an exercise that not only helped familiarize the members with all current antisuffrage arguments but also provided them with opportunities to practice their public speaking. They announced subjects to be discussed at future meetings, such as "Feminism and Socialism." And then they enrolled any new members who desired to join.[57]

The antisuffragists took seriously their arguments about states' rights. It appears that the National Association Opposed to Woman Suffrage exerted little direct control over the state affiliates, "believing that the women of each community can judge best what is necessary or expedient, but it hopes to cooperate whenever there is a request for assistance."[58] The NAOWS claimed that they "never organize a state until requested to do so by local women. In places where the subject is not already agitated, the anti-suffragists do not organize or urge organization. They believe that women should be free from even anti-suffrage politics, except when it is a duty for them to go into to protect themselves from being forced into the maelstrom of State and National politics."[59] A Tennessee antisuffrage worker confirmed this policy. "The only relation that I know between the states and the national organization in antisuffrage is that we are all working for one great national cause. . . . The policy of the National Organization," she wrote, "is of course to leave to the states the shaping of their own policy according to their own peculiar conditions. . . . They have sent me a tremendous lot of literature free of charge."[60]

The NAOWS did provide local assistance at strategic times. During the state amendment referendum in Texas in 1919, for example, the association provided the local antisuffrage workers with free literature for the campaign.[61] When Tennessee's legislature was considering the ratification of the Nineteenth Amendment, the Southern Rejection League and the NAOWS jointly published advertisements in the Nashville newspaper listing reasons why the amendment should fail and names of prominent people who opposed its passage.[62] The NAOWS also paid for the state antisuffrage headquarters at the Hermitage Hotel in Nashville during the ratification contest.[63]

However, the relationship between the NAOWS and the Southern Rejection League was not without its tensions. Just days after the final ratification of the Anthony Amendment, Louisiana's Anne Pleasant wrote to Josephine Pearson, asserting that "in no case would I ever be in any way affiliated with the National again, and I am sure that you would not."[64] Even without formal institutional power to oversee the local associations, representatives of the NAOWS attempted to take control of the fight away from the local women. As Pearson complained, "the National speaker, Miss [Charlotte] Rowe, considered a wonderful orator in her upholding of anti-suffrage ideals, is militant and has become too much of a factor in directing Tennessee's policies." Pearson, the state leader in Tennessee, felt that the NAOWS agents were "inclined to be too dominant and in a way create confusion and irritation because of their inforced opinions and personalities."[65]

The evidence does not suggest that ideological differences caused the difficulties between the national and the regional organizations. In fact, *The Woman Patriot*, the official newspaper of the national association, fully endorsed states' rights, white supremacy, and other tenets of the southern antisuffrage position. And while the southern antis did not rely on red-baiting rhetoric as did the NAOWS, they did not disagree philosophically with the tactic. The tensions between the two groups appear instead to have been a result of conflict over who would direct the southern campaigns.

Like the southern suffrage movement, the southern antisuffrage movement varied greatly from state to state throughout the region. In Mississippi, for example, antisuffragists never could quite get organized, even with the assistance of Alabama antisuffragists and the editorial support of the *Clarion-Ledger*.[66] Nor did the antis in either Florida or South Carolina ever organize.[67]

On the other hand, the antisuffragists in Texas, Alabama, Virginia, and Tennessee created strong and influential associations, some of which continued their efforts even after the final ratification by Tennessee in August 1920.

The various state organizations demonstrated different approaches to activism, reflecting the personalities of their individual state leaders. Texas, for example, was one of the oldest organizations and perhaps one of the best financed. But apparently the state association, led by Pauline Wells, seldom held public meetings, or any kind of public event.[68] Instead, Texas antisuffragists put their energies into the distribution of antisuffrage literature. During the 1919 state amendment referendum, for example, they scattered over 100,000 pieces of literature throughout the state.[69] By contrast, Alabama antisuffragists actively sought publicity by holding public meetings. Nina Pinckard, the state president there, seemed to enjoy public speaking and therefore was more inclined to use such a forum than her more conservative counterpart in Texas.

Very frequently, the activities of a state association were nothing more than those of its most energetic member, usually the president. For example, Josephine Pearson, president of the Tennessee State Association Opposed to Woman Suffrage, wrote letters at will on the organization's letterhead stationary. What might appear to be impressive organizational activity was little more than the actions of a single dedicated worker.[70] As small organizations with less formal structure at the regional level, the antisuffrage associations were far more individualistic than prosuffrage associations in the South.

Southern antisuffrage organizations never hired female lobbyists (like Alice George of Massachusetts), although they were willing to accept the assistance of NAOWS's professionals when necessary. As was fitting for women who preached the sanctity of the home and separation of the spheres, southern antisuffrage women did much of their lobbying behind the scenes, away from the state capitols, and in the familiar comfort of their parlors. Tennessee state president Pearson recorded in her unpublished memoir how "frequently, members of the Legislatures were entertained in small groups for dinner, at the Vertrees residence, giving ample occasion to discuss—in private" their concerns about upcoming legislation.[71]

Such informal access to the ears of state legislators was greatly facilitated by the close personal relationships that the antisuffrage women had with their representatives. Female antisuffragists had numerous blood and marital ties to those with political power. Texas leader Pauline Wells, for example, had a long-standing relationship with machine boss and state senator Archie Parr. Wells's husband, though he did not hold public office himself, was an important member of the state Democratic Executive Committee as well as the head of a county political machine. Ida M. Darden, through her job as secretary for the Texas Businessmen's League, had developed close friendships with U.S. Senator Joseph Bailey and with state senator Robert Lee Henry. Marie Bankhead Owen came from a prominent political family in Alabama, which included two U.S. senators and a congressman. Mississippi antisuffragist Daisy McLaurin Stevens was the daughter of governor and U.S. Senator Anselm McLaurin.

These important political affiliations did not mean that antisuffragists then relied on political power brokers to conduct their campaigns, however. Antisuffragists in every southern state utilized women speakers, women writers, and women leaders at the forefront of their organizational activities. Antisuffrage activities were often staged in such a way to focus on the women, even when the event was one for male antisuffragists. For example, when men in North Carolina decided to organize formally against woman suffrage, they engaged Mary Hilliard Hinton of the women's association to chair the organizational meeting.[72] The strategy behind highlighting female antisuffragists was to force the suffragists to prove that women really did want the vote despite the fact that prominent women indicated otherwise.

Antisuffragists were always sensitive to the charge that only elite women joined their cause. In response to the suffragists' claims that independent women, working women, and activist women were all suffragists, antis protested that suffragists had no monopoly on reform-minded women, business women, or unmarried wage earners. The Virginia antisuffrage organization asserted that "most of its members are very busy women, many earn their own living, many are at the head of large associations and institutions, many give their time to work among the poor and unfortunate. It is difficult for them to find time for more meetings and added work. But they realize that the day has gone by for arguments alone—facts are before us all."[73] The Virginia association also stressed its success in organizing "among the girls working in department stores and factories."[74] Nevertheless, the popular notion that most antisuffragists were wealthy bluebloods prevailed. And as has already been suggested, the notion was based on at least a grain of truth.

One of the ironies of antisuffrage activism was that it pushed into political activity women who insisted that women were unsuited for politics. Or, as a British antisuffragist put it, antisuffrage women were those "who have emerged in order to retire."[75] Because of their more conservative beliefs about gender roles, female antisuffragists felt obliged to maintain an unbroken image of feminine decorum in their organizational activities. Like the national antisuffrage movement, southern female antisuffragists never copied the publicity stunts—the car parades, the picketing, or the demonstrations—of the prosuffrage activists.[76] A Birmingham woman wrote that the "men opposing the [woman suffrage] movement can lift up their voices against it, while we of the weaker sex who neither want to vote ourselves nor to see other women at the polls can only enter protest through the columns of the press," for, as she believed, "the women who oppose woman suffrage are not the ones who take to the platform."[77]

Men's Antisuffrage Organizations

Male opponents of woman suffrage did indeed lift up their voices, and a few of them organized as well. A handful of men's antisuffrage leagues formed in the South, although for the most part the antisuffragists preferred that women appear to be the source of the opposition. One men's association was formed in Selma, Alabama, in July 1918, although it is not clear whether this organization opposed all woman suffrage proposals or just federal enfranchisement. The organization did little work against suffrage as a group effort, but its individual members, especially Martin L. Calhoun, were highly active in producing and disseminating antisuffrage literature.[78] Another men's organization, which unambiguously opposed all forms of woman suffrage, was formed in May 1919 in Waco, Texas, and led by Robert Lee Henry. In June, they held a mass meeting in Waco, where they pledged "to combat woman suffrage in Texas and to take from women the right they now have . . . to vote in primary elections."[79]

Another men's group, which similarly opposed woman suffrage in any form, organized in Louisiana. The day after a state suffrage amendment passed in the Louisiana legislature in 1918, antisuffragists from the legislature called for a state meeting to form a permanent organization to fight against its ratification. Issued by state senators E. L. Simmons and J. R. Domengeaux, the call to arms warned "against the foolish fallacies and false pretenses of state woman suffrage. State woman suffrage is but the first step toward federal woman suffrage."[80] Meeting at the Istrouma Hotel in Baton Rouge in August, they formed the Men's Anti–Woman Suffrage League and chose Senator Domengeaux, a manufacturer from Lafayette, as president. The league did not release the specifics of its plans to the press, nor is there any record of its subsequent activities. However, it was reported that individual members of the league were prominent in the opposition to the amendment in the public referendum.[81]

In the states where both men's and women's organizations existed, the two groups of antisuffragists usually cooperated extensively.[82] At times it even appeared that the women served as a "front" for the men antisuffragists. For example, although Josephine Pearson of Tennessee was the public leader of the antisuffrage movement of that state, she had been personally selected for the job by John J. Vertrees. Pearson later acknowledged that Vertrees valued her not only because of her "outstanding ability" but also because she was too "tactful" to disobey the directions of the men of the antisuffrage movement.[83] Vertrees obviously considered himself the real power behind the movement, because in a letter to Pearson he indicated that he would provide her with "the idea and the bone-work," and she should rewrite his letters and "put those frills and pleasant[ries] on it which you ladies usually do."[84]

Underneath the public facade of cooperation, serious conflicts occasionally developed between the male and female antisuffragists. Sarah Bradford, an officer in the Tennessee association, complained of the inflexible leadership of Vertrees. "I have been guilty of insubordination in going contrary to the opinion of Mr. Vertrees," she wrote Pearson. "I disobeyed to the extent of going to the Legislature, meeting the Senators, putting the literature on their desks, and writing in the paper. While he may have disapproved," Bradford continued, "I find that the general public did not, but nevertheless it puts me out of the pale of his favor."[85]

After Tennessee had ratified the federal amendment, Josephine Pearson reserved some hard words for her male coworkers in the fight. She wrote to Vertrees, "We had some fine cards which we lost. . . . The fight . . . has been somewhat chaotic in management. All were fine cards, poorly played, for want of some strong dominant mind to clearly direct." Some of Pearson's harshest criticism carried the unmistakable implication that she blamed Vertrees himself. "Worlds of work, money and time have been spent profligatory [*sic*] to little comparative advantage. The men have been earnest and brave," Pearson continued, "but hardly big enough in grasp and vision to marshall the various activities in a direct and forceful way." Using Vertrees's own arguments against him, Pearson reminded him that "you are, and have always been correct that it is the 'man's fight,'—if the men are big or little depends the advantage."[86] The blame for Tennessee's ratification, in other words, rested on his shoulders.

In Texas, by way of contrast, women antisuffragists apparently resented the fact that they were being asked to carry too much of the load of the fight against suffrage. Ida M. Darden, for example, wrote her friend and patron, U.S. Senator Joseph W. Bailey, that the "fight against suffrage is being waged by the women without any material assistance from the men who, it seems,

Headquarters, North Carolina Equal Suffrage League and the State's Rights Defense League of North Carolina, Raleigh, 1920 (Courtesy of North Carolina Division of Archives and History, Raleigh)

are awaiting your opening speech before taking any definite steps. It is such a big burden for women to try to carry alone and we ask you to come to our rescue."[87]

Regardless of the tensions present at times, the men's and women's groups generally found ways to work together. When the States' Rights Defense League organized in Raleigh, it announced few concrete plans other than its intention to work closely with the women's organization.[88] This cooperation undoubtedly was facilitated by the pre-existing personal relationships between men and women in the movement. The members of the various antisuffrage organizations, male and female, were often related by blood, business, and marriage. Frequently a wife would be an officer of the women's association while her husband served on the advisory board or was a member in the men's organization. In North Carolina for example, Episcopal bishop Joseph Blount Cheshire served on the advisory board to the women's organization, while his wife, Elizabeth, held office as a vice president. In Tennessee, Norman Farrell helped to organize the Tennessee Constitutional League (a men's antisuffrage group) while his wife, Josephine, and their two daughters Josephine and Lizinka, joined the Southern Rejection League. And Alabama antisuffrage leader Cola Barr Craig was the mother of William Benjamin Craig, a former congressman who served as a vice president of the Alabama Men's Association Opposed to Woman Suffrage.

Southern antisuffragists usually divided their duties according to prescribed gender roles. Campaign strategy, finances, legislative floor maneuvers, public debates, and development of ideology and rhetoric fell primarily within the male realm. Female antisuffragists wrote private letters, occasionally gave prepared speeches, distributed literature, waved handkerchiefs from legislative galleries, and spent much time distributing red roses (the antisuffrage symbol) to legislative supporters.[89]

In one area, however, antisuffrage strategy demanded that traditional gender roles be transgressed. Although public speaking was still a relatively new role for women, it was the most important vehicle for female antis to demonstrate that women did not want the vote. Antisuffrage women had to be highly visible in the movement. Public speaking, public appearances, and press coverage were absolutely necessary to prevent woman suffrage and thereby preserve true womanhood. And it should not be assumed that the women who became public spokeswomen for the cause were inexperienced, for they were not. These leaders had often had years of work in voluntary associations, women's clubs, and patriotic societies, and had gained valuable experience in public speaking and other such organizational activity. Mary Hilliard Hinton had been a state leader of the North Carolina Daughters of the Revolution for many years. Tennessee's Lizzie Elliott had been a school teacher for twenty years. Her coworker Queenie W. Washington was a state officer in the federation of women's clubs. Ida Fitzpatrick was president of the Georgia state federation of women's clubs and was a member of several patriotic societies. And Laura Montgomery Henderson of Alabama, in addition to serving as president of the state federation of women's clubs and as president of her local Woman's Missionary Auxiliary, was a member of the United Daughters of the Confederacy. Such activities had prepared antisuffrage women for their public roles as speakers for their chosen cause. Their years of work in voluntary organizations also had trained them in parliamentary procedure, lobbying techniques, fund-raising, and other skills necessary for a successful organizational effort.[90]

The necessity for public appearances by antisuffrage women was not without its limits, however. Seldom did antisuffrage women accept the challenge to debate a suffragist in public, although the suffragists issued numerous such challenges. A public debate of the suffrage question was simply too overtly political, and, unlike their lobbying efforts, antisuffragists could not find a way to modify the debate format in order to minimize its political nature.[91]

Antisuffrage women knew the value of systematic organization, and they were able to create state associations virtually out of thin air because of their past involvement in such institutional work. In every southern state, women led the way in organizing an antisuffrage movement. They relied on their own extensive experiences of social activism and drew on their own women's networks for strength and support.

The socially conservative nature of southern antisuffragists, however, restricted the development of the movement. For example, the Georgia association described its president, Miss Caroline Patterson, as "an untiring worker, being a woman of unusual intellect and ability, and having had the advantage of travel both in this country and in Europe, being well acquainted with persons of note and conditions of government in many places, holds unusual qualifications as president. . . . She is a splendid home maker, church worker, and is quiet, efficient, and thorough, not aggressive but persistent in her zeal for good. Thus she embodies all the principles that we as a body wish to preserve as women."[92] Women who espoused such values were unlikely to match the aggressiveness of their northern counterparts, such as those in Massachusetts, who had long before given up many of their earlier inhibitions and openly lobbied legislatures and became paid organizers.[93] As historian William O'Neill put it, the antis were forced to violate their own notions of proper feminine conduct in order to sustain them.[94]

In another transgression of traditional gender roles, it was also necessary for women antisuffragists to lobby legislators individually, a function they performed but found particularly distasteful. In order to make such lobbying seem less political and less confrontational, female antis preferred to bring the legislators into their "sphere." During the ratification contest in Tennessee, for instance, antisuffragists set up a "homey" headquarters in the Hermitage Hotel in Nashville, complete with a display of pertinent literature, and invited the legislators to come and visit them, much as if they were being invited to tea at home. Creating such an environment worked to depoliticize lobbying as much as possible.

Other noticeable trends in southern antisuffragism stem more from the lack of resources at their disposal than from gender roles or women's culture. Unlike their northern counterparts, southern antisuffrage organizations seldom published their own newspapers or journals. Undoubtedly, this was partly because they joined the movement so late: they had little time to devote to such projects, when all available hands were required at the state capitol, lobbying for votes. No southern antisuffrage organization published a newspaper or journal that equaled the *Remonstrance* or the *Woman Patriot*. North Carolina's *State's Defense*, the only antisuffrage journal published in the South, had produced only four issues before the end of the ratification contest.[95]

The State's Defense

A Bulletin Issued by the Southern Rejection League and The State's Rights Defense League

Issued ever so often!

No subscription price or advertising rate!

Issued because we practically have no voice in the press!

THE GOVERNOR'S SUFFRAGE MESSAGE.

Governor Bickett's address to the Legislature was the effort of a man to ride horses going in opposite directions. His opening remarks were expressions from the heart voicing his fear that woman suffrage was not what its friends might expect. He touched upon the race question, and every one could see the labor and strain under which the Governor was proceeding. His real argument for ratification was his belief in yielding to the inevitable. "No question or cause ever got so near the top and failed to go over," was the Governor's summing up of the position taken by him.

From our viewpoint, that position is the position of the weakling; of the man who never rallies in the last ditch; of one who never stems the tide of battle that is setting against him. Charles Martel, who saved Europe from Moorish civilization; Stonewall Jackson at Bull Run; the Greeks at Marathon; Leonidas at Thermopylae; the Belgians at Liege; Joffre at the Marne; John Paul Jones on the deck of the Bon Homme Richard; and on and on without limit in human history, stand refutations of the Governor's argument.

The Governor also enjoys the doubtful distinction of being the first of our Democratic statesmen to announce the death of States' Rights from the speaker's platform in the House of Representatives. The South lost much at Appomattox; and it lost its construction of States' Rights upon the questions then at issue. But it took Bickett to discover that "we are no longer a union of States, but one great nation." Even the Suffs in the audience responded very feebly to that statement! Zeb Vance, Tom Jarvis, Matt Ransom, and a whole host of North Carolinians have gone to their rest with a different belief. When the Governor made the statement, one was tempted to peep out the window to see if Vance's bronze figure was not wobbling on its pedestal!

The Governor knows that death is inevitable, but does he plan to die now? Indeed not; but such would be his conclusions if based upon the logic of his message.

Woman suffrage by the Anthony Amendment is not inevitable. Just as thirty-six can ratify, thirteen may reject it! The people of the country have been awakened to the impending danger, and steps are being taken to rescind the action of those Legislatures, who while a war was on and reconstruction under way, betrayed the people of their States. North Carolina may not only add her voice against the Amendment, Governor, but like the Belgians at Liege, she may hold the line until Texas, West Virginia and other States may recover their lost positions, and come forward expressing the real sentiments of their people. But come what may, if Judas must be the last actor on the scene, let not old North Carolina play the part!

LEST WE FORGET

I am tied to a conviction which I have had all my life, that changes of this sort ought to be brought State by State. It is a deeply matured conviction on my part, and therefore I would be without excuse to my own constitutional principles if I lent my support to this very important movement for an amendment to the Constitution of the United States.

Woodrow Wilson.

—Statement to Suffragists. January 6, 1917.

THE MALADY!

Woman suffrage is the influenza of politics. Beginning with the socialists, it has spread into the camps of all political parties. As a malady, it has attacked its victims as viciously as the microbe of influenza ever did. Men who know it to be detrimental to the best interests of the people have gone down, attacked by its chill and fever; in one breath stating that our Legislature ought to adopt it, and in the next, stating that they do not think it a good thing. The most typical example is Senator Simmons. He knows that the ratification of the Anthony Amendment is not good for North Carolina and the South. He has said this, and tacitly admits his personal opposition to it. Witness his latest statement! In one breath he urges the ratification of the amendment, and in the other, states that he has always opposed woman suffrage, and is still opposed to it. Pitiable indeed, is the situation! Simmons the man; Simmons the politician; which is best to follow? And then there is Governor Bickett. He asks the Legislature to ratify—but deep down in his heart he knows that North Carolina is opposed to it, and that it ought not to be done.

The man who urges a North Carolina Legislature to adopt the Anthony Amendment, is expressing but a minority sentiment of North Carolina opinion. Governor Bickett is bound to know that at the ballot box, the question would be buried so deep in the negative that Pompeian excavators could not find it in thirty years. It was the voice of Bickett the politician, not Bickett the statesman, that asked a North Carolina Legislature to ratify the Anthony Amendment. Could any one imagine Zeb Vance, the staunch defender of States' Rights—he who for fourteen years shouted defiance at force bills and upheld the sacred precepts of his party—asking a North Carolina

The front page of the first issue of The State's Defense, *published by North Carolina antisuffragists, 1920 (Courtesy of North Carolina Division of Archives and History, Raleigh)*

The lack of a regular publication can also be seen as evidence of the limited funds available to the antisuffrage organizations. Southern antisuffragists knew the value of a regular press, as many of them subscribed to the *Woman's Protest/Woman Patriot*, published by the NAOWS, and frequently quoted from that journal in their own writings. At that point in time, however, they were limited to smaller pamphlets and broadsides that could be more cheaply reproduced in large quantities and that could be widely distributed.

Finally, the absence of a regular publication also indicates the relative weakness of the regional organization. As a small association with a narrow base and little institutional structure, the Southern Rejection League was in no position to edit and publish a newspaper. Such an endeavor required staffing, subscribers, and advertisers, all of which the league would have had difficulty in obtaining. Contrary to the contention of the suffragists, the antisuffrage organizations never had the unlimited funds one might have expected from a movement with ties to big business and big agriculture. It seems that the male antisuffragists preferred to spend their funds on their own efforts, giving the women's organizations only minimal financial assistance.

Steven Buechler has noticed a pattern in antisuffrage organization: an "eleventh-hour" mobilization that effectively defeated the sustained organizational efforts of the suffragists.[96] In the South, however, the existence of the regional organization and its generally friendly relationship to the national organization, meant that antisuffragists the southern states had access to a powerful support network on very short notice. For example, North Carolina antisuffragists would undoubtedly have been unable to publish the *State's Defense* without the immediate assistance of the NAOWS. Charlotte Rowe, a speaker and organizer for the NAOWS, appeared in nearly every southern state during critical legislative sessions, providing instant experience, talent, and, of course, literature. While the southern antisuffrage movement remained a loosely organized federation of extremely individual associations, it had the strength of the national network behind it. The fact that the NAOWS was at hand means that "eleventh hour" mobilizations were less ad hoc than they might appear.

Why did southern antisuffragists organize when they did? Why not in the 1890s, when the suffragists first joined together? The answer to these questions is a simple but important one. Antisuffragism was a responsive action, a countermovement. It was essentially defensive in nature. Antisuffragists organized only in response to a perceived threat from the suffrage movement. And the southern suffrage movement had not posed a significant threat until the 1910s.

The presence of an antisuffrage organization in a given state therefore can serve as an indicator of the strength or success of the suffrage movement there. Many of the states that had early antisuffrage associations also had strong suffrage associations: Maryland, Virginia, Texas, Tennessee, Georgia, and Alabama all had some of earliest of the southern suffrage movements. (Kentucky, with one of the earliest suffrage organizations in the South and an almost nonexistent antisuffrage organization, is a notable exception to this generalization.) In states where suffragism had arrived late or never matured, antisuffragism had a more difficult time bearing fruit: Mississippi, South Carolina, and Florida never established antisuffrage associations, and North Carolina waited until 1920 to do so. (Arkansas, with its absence of an antisuffrage organization in the face of a successful suffrage movement, is exceptional.)

The Southern Rejection League maintained its organizational structure through the summer of 1920, but after the ratification of the Nineteenth Amendment in August, the regional association lost its raison d'être and ceased to exist. Several state associations lived on for a few more months. The Tennessee branch, for example, worked to defeat Warren Harding, Governor A. H. Roberts, and state representative Harry Burn in the November elections. Then it too folded.[97] The Virginia Antisuffrage Association appears to have lived a few years longer: in 1926, Nellie Parker Henson, speaking for the association, protested a proposed memorial to suffragist Lila Meade Valentine. The antisuffragists rejected the idea of memorializing woman suffrage when the state had defeated the suffrage amendment.[98] The National Association Opposed to Woman Suffrage continued to operate for nearly a decade more, attempting to dig out radicalism, socialism, and Bolshevism from their hiding places throughout American society. But with the passage of the Nineteenth Amendment, southern antisuffragists no longer had an animating force for their activities. With very few exceptions, antisuffrage women returned to the life of the separate spheres, which they had worked to safeguard through their participation in the antisuffrage movement.[99]

Economic interests, party loyalty, and prescribed gender roles worked to produce a distinctively southern antisuffrage movement. Tied to the plantation past, cherishing the ideals of republican motherhood and separate spheres, dedicated to the Democratic vision of white monopoly, southern antisuffragists created a movement that could cooperate with the National Association Opposed to Woman Suffrage but refused fully to submerge itself in the larger movement. The regional association always made it clear, both to the public and to the NAOWS, that it was an independent organization that controlled its own activities.

But the story of the antisuffrage movement remains incomplete at this point, for in the southern states, the suffrage question was complicated by the issue of states' rights. Only in the South did a separate states' rights suffrage movement emerge, creating a complex, three-sided contest. The following chapter will examine the thorny issue of states' rights suffragism and its role in the antisuffrage movement.

The States' Rights Faction

Kate Gordon's Louisiana

If I didn't know that nothing was impossible, I'd certainly say that Alabama was. It's almost impossible for a person from the North to do anything down here, especially a thing so unpopular as the federal amendment.

"States' rights" is no empty phrase down here, and everything "federal" is shunned. . . . I have talked to all kinds of women—society, professional, club, suffrage, working—and have struck not one ray of encouragement or cooperation.

It's a shame we have to work singly in these Southern States. They're a real battlefield.

Beulah Amidon to Alice Paul, 1917

Although Kate Gordon had worked for woman suffrage for twenty-five years, by 1920 she feared that she was "grouped with the Anti's" by those who did not distinguish between opposition to the federal amendment and opposition to woman suffrage.[1] Gordon's fears were well founded. Suffragists at the time and historians since have had difficulty understanding her position as a "states' rights suffragist." The states' rights faction complicated both the suffrage contest in the southern states and historians' later efforts to analyze those contests.

Throughout the second wave of suffragism in the South, southerners discussed the issue of woman suffrage in terms of states' rights. If instituted by federal amendment, according to the states' rights argument, woman suffrage would be enforced by the federal government, which carried the possibility of a repetition of Reconstruction, or as one antisuffragist put it, "the threat of the carpet-baggers to put black heels on white necks throughout the South."[2] But the states' rights argument was not only used against woman suffrage, it was also used by one faction of southern suffragists in *behalf* of woman suffrage. "States' rights suffragists" demanded that the individual states enfranchise their women by means of amendments to the various state constitutions. In this way, white women could be enfranchised, while the southern states could continue to defy the Fifteenth Amendment in discriminating against black voters.

The states' rights faction created a three-sided debate over woman suffrage in the southern states among those who advocated federal suffrage (the ratificationists), those who demanded state suffrage and opposed the federal amendment (the states' rights suffragists), and those who opposed woman suffrage in any form (the antisuffragists). Victory in any given contest would belong to whomever could arrange an alliance between two of the three factions.[3] Since both the states' rights suffragists and the antisuffragists had adopted the states' rights argument as part of the strategy for their respective movements, they found that it gave them a common ground for cooperation. As a result, in many southern suffrage campaigns the states' rights faction became the critical ally of the antisuffragists. Louisiana, although certainly not typical of the rest of the South, presents the clearest example of this phenomenon and will here serve as a case study of the dynamics of the three-way contest in the South.

Although Americans outside the South frequently discussed woman suffrage in terms of "states' rights" and the control of the electorate, only in the South did such concerns generate separate political organizations. Kate Gordon's "Southern States Woman Suffrage Conference" was the most visible expression of this states' rights philosophy, and Gordon was the most widely known exponent of this position. Therefore an understanding of Gordon's suffrage ideology and her activities are fundamental to an understanding of the states' rights position. The fate of both federal and state suffrage amendments in Louisiana demonstrates the divisive nature of the states' rights issue.

The states' rights suffragists constituted a movement entirely separate from the mainstream southern suffrage movement. The states' rights faction broke away from the mother organization in 1913, when it became clear that NAWSA no longer believed in the state-by-state approach to obtaining the ballot for women. After 1913, the suffrage movement in the South must be seen as two separate movements, occasionally overlapping in membership, frequently working at cross-purposes, and providing an opportunity for antisuffragists to win the close suffrage contests in many southern states. At the center of it all stood Kate Gordon.

Kate Gordon and States' Rights Suffrage

Kate Gordon was an outspoken, nationally recognized southern suffragist. But her extreme and inflexible position on the issues of white supremacy and states' rights set her apart from most of her suffrage associates and caused much conflict and tension within the southern suffrage ranks. Kate Gordon's high visibility has made her a natural subject for historical inquiry, and she is noted regularly in the literature on the suffrage movement.[4]

One of three socially prominent and politically active sisters of a family in New Orleans, Kate Gordon always claimed to have come to her suffrage tendencies "through inheritance"; her parents were converted to woman suffrage before the Civil War. In 1896, Gordon and several other young New Orleans suffragists established the Era Club, whose name carried the well-kept secret meaning of "Equal Rights for All Club."

The suffrage movement in New Orleans was, for the South in the 1890s, unusually large and unusually effective. It was one of the few southern cities that could boast of multiple suffrage clubs. It was also the beneficiary of a unique grant of female tax suffrage: when the state constitutional convention of 1898 included a provision that all taxpaying women should have the right to vote on tax questions, 10,000 women in the city of New Orleans gained partial enfranchisement.[5]

Suffragists in New Orleans had other victories to celebrate too. The Era Club agitated for, and won, admission of women to the Tulane University Medical School. It hosted the 1903 NAWSA annual convention, an event that was testimony to the strength and vitality of the suffrage movement in the city. Suffragists helped push through the state legislature a constitutional amendment allowing women to become factory inspectors (a position to which Kate

*Kate (*left*) and Jean Gordon, New Orleans, undated (Courtesy of Louisiana Collection, Howard-Tilton Library, Tulane University, New Orleans)*

Gordon's sister Jean was subsequently appointed). And suffragists founded and supported a day nursery at Kingsley House, the famous settlement house in the city's Irish Channel.[6]

Through her suffrage activities in the Era Club, which she dominated for twenty years, Gordon came to the attention of the leadership of the National American Woman Suffrage Association (NAWSA). President Carrie Chapman Catt, impressed with Gordon's efforts during a famous water and sewerage tax campaign in New Orleans, promised the southern suffragist the next position to come open on the national board. Catt delivered on her promise. In 1901, Gordon was elected corresponding secretary for NAWSA.[7]

The New Orleans suffragist seemed a likely choice for national leadership. Active in local suffrage activities almost from the beginning of the movement, Gordon was from a socially prominent family, and her connections and status made her an important influence in the suffrage movement. As an unmarried woman with ample financial resources, Gordon was free to devote her considerable skills and talents to the cause. And as a southerner in a state that had much more potential for suffragism than some others in the South, Gordon would be important for the regional success of the suffrage movement. All of these factors, plus her intelligence and lively personality, made Gordon good material for national leadership. Although inexperienced, she soon proved to be an exciting public speaker as well. According to one account, she "set the National Federation of Women's Clubs fairly aflame with Suffrage enthusiasm" in Cincinnati in 1910.[8]

Holding national office for nearly a decade, Gordon plunged into the internal politics of the suffrage movement. Gordon, who seemed to relish dissension, became an important source of tension within the NAWSA leadership. She carried this penchant for factionalism with her whenever she returned home to work for suffrage in her own state. Some of the storms that surged around her were the result of her outspokenness and tendency to play petty personal politics. But much of the friction that Gordon stimulated came from her controversial, and inflexible, ideological position.

Gordon was one of a number of southern suffragists dedicated to obtaining the ballot via state constitutional amendments, rather than by a federal amendment. She maintained that the federal amendment was a trick of the Republican Party to split the Solid South, and she stressed that "the Democratic South is nothing else but a concise way of expressing anti-nigger." She believed that federal action would lead automatically to black suffrage, an unacceptable outcome for those, like her, determined to protect the South's hard-won white supremacy.[9] As Gordon wrote in 1915, "if Louisiana employs an understanding clause to preserve white supremacy and will grant woman suffrage, then I will not have a word to say against it. White supremacy is going to be maintained in the South by fair or foul means."[10]

"Miss Kate" had long been outspoken on the racial issue. As early as 1901, she asserted that "the question of white supremacy is one that will only be decided by giving the right of the ballot to the educated, intelligent white women of the South. Their vote will eliminate the question of the negro vote in politics, and it will be a glad, free day for the South when the ballot is placed in the hands of its intelligent, cultured, pure and noble womanhood."[11] In a similar vein, speaking at the NAWSA annual convention in 1907, Gordon delivered a vitriolic attack on the Reconstruction suffrage policies that had allowed the enfranchisement of "cornfield darkies" but not of "intelligent motherhood."[12]

But rather than turn racial fears into an antisuffrage argument, Gordon attempted to harness racism on behalf of woman suffrage. She emphasized that the enfranchisement of southern white women would serve as a powerful device to insure the continued numerical superiority of the white electorate. She recognized that grandfather clauses and other such subterfuges employed by the southern states could be nullified by the U.S. Supreme Court, but she maintained that white woman suffrage would be a constitutional, irreversible form of permanent white supremacy. She believed that "there are many politicians who, while they would fight to the death the idea of women voting purely on the merits of the question, would gladly welcome us as a measure to insure white supremacy. My old point of choice between nigger or woman, and glad to take the woman, has more truth than poetry in it."[13]

Aileen Kraditor has theorized that the states' rights argument rose to such prominence in the last years of the suffrage struggle "in response to the need for an argument that could still win support."[14] The states' rights argument also might have arisen when it did because the suffrage movement had finally gained strength south of the Mason-Dixon line. The use of the argument increased after 1913, when both antisuffragists and states' rights suffragists adopted the strategy for their separate movements.

Gordon's determination to gain white woman suffrage by state amendment apparently knew no bounds. She even considered blackmail: she threatened that if southern legislatures refused to give white women their due, she would publicize the unconstitutionality of the grandfather clauses, literacy tests, and other questionable techniques used to disfranchise black voters and thereby force the federal government to intervene. This threat, while never acted upon, demonstrated the depth of Miss Kate's commitment to her cause.[15]

Gordon, like many others who advocated black disfranchisement, argued that black voters were a source of corruption in southern politics and that elimination of blacks from the electorate would be a progressive reform. Furthermore, Gordon believed that this corruptibility of black voters served to hurt the suffrage cause. As she explained after Louisiana disfranchised its black males, "those of us who know the situation relative to the negroes' virtual disfranchisement are not regretting it, for it removes a large vote against us whenever the question of votes for women is before the people."[16]

As it became increasingly clear that the energies of NAWSA would be directed toward passage of the federal amendment rather than state campaigns, Gordon grew disenchanted with the National organization. Gordon was convinced that NAWSA was becoming a pawn of the Republican Party.[17] The rise of the Congressional Union, led by Alice Paul and dedicated to forcing the federal amendment through Congress, showed the direction that suffrage sentiment was moving at the national level. Gordon called for her fellow southerners to join her in an effort to secure state-granted suffrage. The result was the formation in 1913 of the Southern States Woman Suffrage Conference (SSWSC), headquartered in New Orleans and dedicated to state-controlled suffrage.[18]

In activities, the SSWSC mirrored the mainstream suffrage organizations: it conducted annual conventions, lobbied state legislatures on behalf of suffrage bills, and disseminated literature. In 1914, the SSWSC began publishing its own journal called the *New Southern Citizen*, with the motto "Make the Southern States White." As its first issue made clear, the SSWSC was determined to obtain the "enfranchisement of women of the Southern States, primarily through the medium of State Legislation."[19]

At first, Gordon defined the new suffrage group as a "flank movement" of the NAWSA. But increasingly she envisioned the SSWSC as the sole suffrage organization in the South. While continuing to expect financial support from NAWSA, Gordon also began to demand that NAWSA keep out of all suffrage activities in the region. She insisted that all southern suffragists work only through the SSWSC and warned them to steer clear of the tainted federal amendment philosophy of NAWSA. Privately, Gordon admitted that she was willing to go even further: if the SSWSC proved unable to secure state suffrage, it could serve just as well to organize a filibuster to prevent the adoption of the federal amendment.[20]

Southern suffragists, however, did not generally subscribe to this states' rights suffrage position. Despite some initial enthusiasm, the majority of southern suffrage supporters rejected Gordon's entreaties. Some, like Madeline Breckinridge, never joined the regional organization, although they were courted personally by Gordon.[21] Of those women who did join the SSWSC, it appears that the majority of them were willing to work for both state and federal amendments and did not join the new regional organization because of their rejection of the federal amendment. Indeed, more moderate suffragists halted Gordon's efforts to incorporate the phrase "states' rights" into the name of the SSWSC. The majority of southern suffragists were unwilling to turn their backs on the very promising federal amendment. As Sake Meehan, a suffragist from New Orleans, wrote, "I don't think that 'States Rights' thing will do anybody much good. . . . But 'states rights' catches a lot of these southern women, who do not understand suffrage, anyway."[22]

Some southern suffragists attempted to avoid taking sides by joining *both* the SSWSC and their state NAWSA affiliate. But this was a compromise position that became increasingly difficult to maintain, for Kate Gordon continued to goad and push and antagonize those who joined the regional organization as well as those who did not. Gordon's activities won her an unprecedented record: she was the only suffragist to be formally reprimanded by two different state suffrage associations. Tennessee and Alabama chastised Gordon for her public attacks on national suffrage legislation and for her unsupportable claim to speak for all southern suffragists.[23]

In less than two years after its founding, Gordon had lost much support for the SSWSC. Many supporters quietly left the organization: Mary Johnston resigned as honorary vice president in November 1915, unable to continue

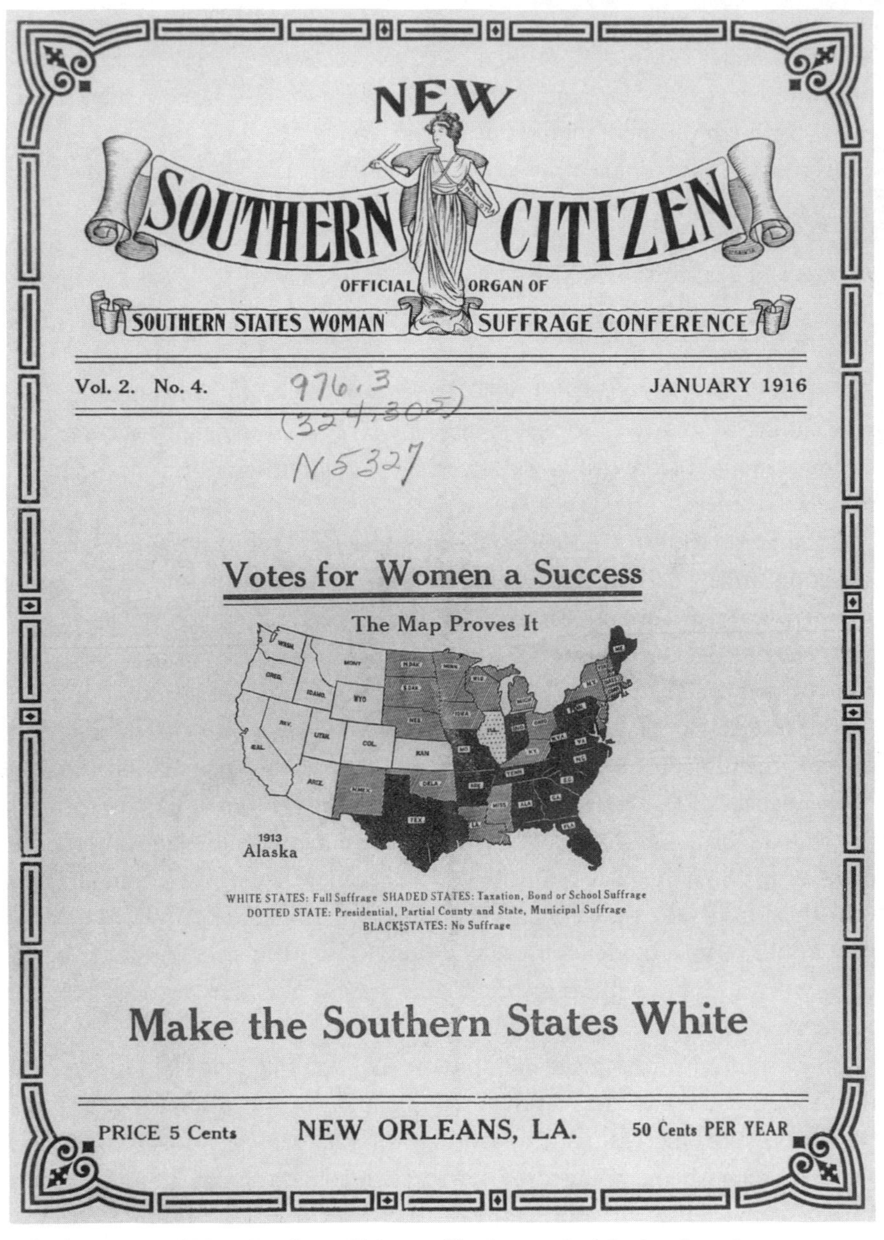
NEW SOUTHERN CITIZEN

OFFICIAL ORGAN OF SOUTHERN STATES WOMAN SUFFRAGE CONFERENCE

Vol. 2. No. 4. JANUARY 1916

Votes for Women a Success

The Map Proves It

WHITE STATES: Full Suffrage SHADED STATES: Taxation, Bond or School Suffrage
DOTTED STATE: Presidential, Partial County and State, Municipal Suffrage
BLACK STATES: No Suffrage

Make the Southern States White

PRICE 5 Cents NEW ORLEANS, LA. 50 Cents PER YEAR

The front page of New Southern Citizen, *official journal of the Southern States Woman Suffrage Conference (Courtesy of Louisiana Collection, Howard-Tilton Library, Tulane University, New Orleans)* her association with the outspoken Negrophobe. Nellie Nugent Somerville, although less liberal in her racial views than Johnston, also found the SSWSC an increasingly inhospitable environment. Somerville severed her ties to the organization when she discovered that representatives of the SSWSC in Washington were actually lobbying *against* the federal amendment.[24] Most southern suffrage activists had rejected Gordon's states' rights strategy and her leadership by 1915.[25]

Back in Gordon's home state, the conflict between the SSWSC and the NAWSA (or better said, the disagreement between federal and state amendment supporters) threatened to undermine or even completely destroy the suffrage movement in Louisiana. In April 1913, Sake Meehan of New Orleans and Lydia Holmes of Baton Rouge led a minirevolt against Gordon and the SSWSC. They formed a separate organization, the Woman Suffrage Party of Louisiana (WSP). Denouncing Gordon's narrow states' rights position, the WSP announced its intention to work for the federal amendment. In a year's time, the WSP claimed a membership of over one thousand.[26]

The women of the WSP apparently resented Gordon's heavy-handed leadership as much as they disagreed with her political position. A few weeks after the formation of the WSP, Meehan philosophized: "We seem to have started something that fills one of those long felt wants you read about, that is, a movement for suffrage only, free of all personalities, jealousies, antagonisms, etc., that naturally grow up in a single club or organization dominated for a long time by a small number of persons."[27] But creating two separate suffrage organizations did not end the conflicts. A few months later, Meehan complained, "If Miss Kate could be silenced or eliminated some way, the cause of suffrage in La. would certainly benefit. . . . In plain words—she is a d—— nuisance."[28]

Gordon, in turn, assailed the formation of the WSP as being nothing more than a personal attack on her and an effort to dethrone the leader of the suffrage movement in Louisiana. When the WSP applied for affiliation to NAWSA, it was granted over Gordon's strenuous objections. NAWSA's recognition of the new organization was a challenge to Gordon's preeminence in her home state.[29]

For a short time the two groups managed to keep their differences quiet, but soon the acrimony between the them surfaced in the press. The New Orleans *Item* condemned Gordon's Era Club for trying to expel any member who joined the WSP and warned that "the suffragist everywhere should cease to regard herself as the petty dictator of a personal clique, and suffrage as a fad to be pursued under her personal supervision."[30] Dr. Anna Howard Shaw, then president of NAWSA, was dismayed that the factionalism had become public knowledge. Attempting to squelch any further fighting, Shaw wrote the WSP that "it is a very bad thing to go into print and discuss our personal differences in the press. . . . My one hope for the year that is to come is that there will be no more personalities on either side, but that each society, which can do excellent work in its own way, will go ahead and do that work without reference to the other."[31] Shaw's mollifying words made little difference; the feuding continued.

In the summer of 1918, the Louisiana legislature took up a bill that would send a state suffrage amendment to the public for ratification. During the session, the WSP suffragists offered to bury their differences and join forces with the Gordon-dominated Era Club in order to lobby for the bill, upon which, as a state measure, both organizations could agree. Less than gracious in reply, Gordon announced curtly that "we do not as a Club affiliate with any organization that does not stand for States' Rights."[32] The two groups of suffragists worked independently for the proposal throughout the campaign.

The state amendment passed the Senate by a vote of twenty-nine to eleven, and the House by eighty to twenty-two (see Table A.17). Yet even in victory, Gordon stubbornly refused to mend the rift in the suffrage ranks. In fact, at the public ceremony in which Governor Ruffin Pleasant signed the state amendment just passed by the legislature, the Gordon sisters managed to keep Lydia Holmes and other representatives of the WSP out of the building.[33] This "coup d'état," well publicized in the press, only further added to the already lengthy list of grievances of the federal suffrage supporters in Louisiana.

Gordon had little time to savor her victory, however, as the newly minted state suffrage amendment now had to be ratified by public referendum, in a contest that all knew would be bitterly fought. The amendment won some influential endorsements. The governor, both the state's U.S. senators, and all but one of the state's congressmen publicly pledged their support. The state's largest newspapers also endorsed the amendment. In the announcement of his support, Governor Pleasant stressed that "equal suffrage, at bottom, is right and just, and it is bound to come." The New Orleans *States*, a suffrage opponent for twenty-five years, bowed to the "expediency" argument and endorsed the measure, conceding that state suffrage was infinitely more acceptable than federal suffrage.[34]

Such powerful support notwithstanding, on 5 November 1918, Louisianans rejected the amendment by 3,500 votes, with Gordon's hometown of New Orleans providing the necessary margin to defeat it.[35] The New Orleans *States* reported that "Mayor [Martin] Behrman was jubilant over the result of the election." His city machine had "returned a handsome majority against the amendment."[36] Ethel Hutson, of the WSP, was also firmly convinced of Behrman's central role in defeating the amendment, claiming he had over 14,000

Martin Behrman, mayor of New Orleans and head of the Choctaw political machine (Courtesy of Louisiana Collection, Howard-Tilton Library, Tulane University, New Orleans)

votes at his disposal.[37] The Behrman machine, operating as the Choctaw Club, had dominated New Orleans politics for more than twenty years and had regularly fought reform efforts attempted by various progressive groups in the state.[38]

With the state amendment lost, Gordon turned her attention to the federal amendment, then under consideration in the U.S. Senate. Gordon wrote Louisiana's Senator Joseph Ransdell, well known to be a suffrage supporter, asking that he vote against the federal amendment anyway on states' rights grounds. The amendment finally passed the Senate in June 1919 and was sent to the states for ratification.[39] Kate Gordon, loath to accept such a possibility, warned the public that a federal law endangered southern interests: "By a federal amendment negro women would be placed on the same par with white women, and . . . while white men would be willing to club negro men away from the polls they would not use the club upon black women."[40] Apparently she believed that southern chivalry would outweigh southern racial prejudice and consign white supremacy to oblivion.

Very quickly, the states ratified the Anthony Amendment. In February 1920, when Mississippi's legislature met to consider the amendment, Gordon traveled to Jackson to fight ratification. She was there at the invitation of the Jackson *Clarion-Ledger*, a longtime opponent of woman suffrage in any form. Gordon realized that her presence in Mississippi made her position even more difficult for many southern suffragists to understand. As she told Laura Clay, "I think [the ratificationists] were disappointed that I did not declare against suffrage, but as I do not believe they are able to differentiate between our points of view I suppose I will be grouped with the Anti's."[41]

When Mississippi's legislature rejected the Anthony Amendment, Gordon returned home to fight the same battle in Baton Rouge. The Louisiana legislature took up the question in June 1920, considering both a federal and a state amendment. Governor Ruffin Pleasant sent a message to the legislators urging them to defeat the federal amendment but pass the state measure instead. "I am strongly in favor of women being enfranchised by the State Constitution just as we men were," he asserted.[42]

As has been noted, in Louisiana, as in most other southern states, the debate over ratification of the Susan B. Anthony amendment was three-sided. As Governor Ruffin Pleasant told the states' rights suffragists in May 1920: "There are three views of the suffrage question, and there are supporters for each. There are those who favor woman suffrage by federal amendment, there are those who favor it by state amendment, and there are those who are in all ways opposed to it. But now the important matter is the fight against the first class and the difference between the others must be forgotten or the required opposing strength will be wanting."[43]

Printing presses worked overtime, churning out literature pro and con, as each of the three camps tried to find allies in the other two. The ratificationists' position was summed up in a widely circulated speech by U.S. Senator Joseph Ransdell: "Some of our Southern friends insist that there is grave danger in giving Negro women the right to vote and for that reason they oppose the Federal Amendment, while willing for women to vote under state laws. . . . In my judgement, the situation can be handled as has been done with negro men for the past twenty-five years. Negroes in the South are prosperous, happy, and contented. . . . As a rule they do not attempt to vote in States where there are a great many negroes like South Carolina, Mississippi, Alabama, and Louisiana, but are satisfied with their lot."[44] Responding to Senator Ransdell, New Orleans attorney Harry Gamble presented the states' rights position.

The Civil War, he wrote, "did not settle 'States' Rights'; 'States' Rights' did not go down in ignominious defeat at that time, as I have somewhere seen it stated." The southern states, to protect their interests, he continued, "should immediately give the ballot to women; delay is unwise."[45] State senator E. L. Simmons of Breaux Bridge presented a common antisuffrage argument: "It is most certain that we shall have woman suffrage by federal action if the states, including Louisiana, vote to give woman suffrage by state action." He claimed that a state amendment would create a body of women voters who would then ratify the federal amendment. Simmons criticized politicians who felt they could control black female voters in the same way they controlled black male voters: "History fails to record where a man has really ever controlled any woman yet, regardless of her race."[46]

Campaigning against Ratification

In Baton Rouge in May 1920, forty men and women organized a new group to fight the ratification of the federal amendment, calling themselves the Anti-Federal League. The group selected Anne Pleasant (wife of the governor) as their president and advocated the passage of a state suffrage amendment.[47] Their numbers soon swelled to include more than 130 members, almost all of whom were women.[48] Although the new states' rights group never formally affiliated with the Southern Women's League for the Rejection of the Susan B. Anthony Amendment, the two groups shared much common philosophical ground.[49] Kate Gordon, however, never joined the new group, claiming she still represented the SSWSC (which at that time existed on paper only).[50]

That a states' rights organization emerged from East Baton Rouge Parish is not surprising. Baton Rouge, the "river capital" of Louisiana, was still a small city in 1920, but it was undergoing significant changes. The discovery of oil in Louisiana at the turn of the century led to the establishment of Standard Oil's major refinery in Baton Rouge, and by 1920, Standard Oil was the largest employer in the capital city, with a payroll of one million dollars a month.[51] Baton Rouge became "a thoroughly Bourbon community in the 1880s," and its conservatism and business-oriented attitudes often set it apart from, and in opposition to, New Orleans.[52] If New Orleans served as the center of federal suffragism in the state (despite Kate Gordon's presence), then Baton Rouge served as the center of the states' rights position.

The formal organization of the states' rights faction led to much maneuvering and shifting of alliances behind the scenes. As Ethel Hutson, of the Woman Suffrage Party, recounted, "Immediately on reaching Baton Rouge, [we] saw the 'anti' forces lining up with the 'states' rights' advocates, and witnessed the curious spectacle of women who had worked and talked for woman suffrage for a generation allying themselves with the paid organizers of the National Association Opposed to Woman Suffrage."[53] Hutson referred in particular to Kate Gordon, who often shared a platform with the outright antisuffragists.[54]

At first, it appeared that the state amendment had the best chance of success, as it passed the House on June 2 by a resounding 93 to 17. But then the Senate acted, defeating both state and federal amendments in quick succession (see Tables A.18 and A.19).[55] Louisiana was not among the growing number of woman suffrage states.

When it was all over and the suffragists had had a chance to survey the damage, they found many people and many interests to blame for their defeat. The WSP singled out the new governor, John J. Parker, a progressive who nevertheless did not support woman suffrage. They believed that Parker was in firm control of both houses of the legislature, and "when he went after anything with all his force he did not fail to get it."[56] The WSP also blamed the states' rights suffragists for the defeat, accusing them of sacrificing the state bill for their overwhelming desire to defeat the federal bill.[57]

The states' rights suffragists, on the other hand, blamed the ratificationists for the outcome. They pointed out that thirteen members of the Senate who voted against the state amendment were supporters of the federal amendment.[58] Some suffragists suggested that lawmakers who were alleged suffrage supporters were actually against the reform altogether, merely professing to support one form or another in order to defeat them both. These legislators, the angry suffragists asserted, saw the factionalism as a means of preventing any bill from passing, while allowing them to "keep right with the folks at home" on the suffrage question. Prosuffrage senator N. C. Williamson openly charged that many of the state amendment supporters were actually antisuffragists in disguise.[59] The New Orleans *States* declared that New Orleans mayor Martin Behrman must be held accountable, since members of his Democratic machine contributed to the failure of the measures.[60] Still others pointed to certain business interests in the state, such as the sugar producers or the liquor lobby, who equated woman suffrage with stricter labor regulations or Prohibition and maintained consistent opposition to the reform. In fact, as far back as 1914, Louisiana suffragists had claimed that their strongest opposition came from "the liquor and vice interests and corrupt political rings."[61]

A comparison of the legislative votes on the 1918 state amendment, the 1920 state amendment, and the 1920 federal amendment offers some further insight into the motivations of the state's legislators. (See tables A.17–A.19.) That a solid core of antisuffrage legislators could be counted on to vote against woman suffrage, no matter what form it took, is the first fact that emerges. Thirty-three votes were cast against the state suffrage amendment each time it was considered. Breaking down the overall vote by percentage of blacks within the population represented, reveals that legislators from Black Belt parishes gave less support to woman suffrage with each successive vote on the question. In 1918, more than half of the prosuffrage votes came from parishes with black populations of 40 percent or more. Two years later, in the second round of voting on the state constitutional amendment, support from those counties had declined to 48 percent of the 116 votes cast in favor of woman suffrage. And in the vote on the federal amendment in 1920, the number of the prosuffrage votes from those same parishes dwindled to 44 percent of the 63 votes cast in support of the Nineteenth Amendment.

The three votes also provide further evidence about the fear of federal control of the electorate. In the parishes with black populations of less than 20 percent, legislators seemed quite secure in supporting a state suffrage amendment, and they did not cast a single vote against it in either 1918 or 1920. But when the federal amendment was under consideration, they reversed their positions, casting all but one vote against the amendment. In the next quintile of parishes (black populations 20–39.9 percent), a similar shift of sentiments appears: where legislators had supported the state amendments by more than a two to one ratio, they opposed the federal amendment 37 to 34.

The outcomes of the three roll call votes support the contention that a sizable number of southerners who supported the right of white women to vote would oppose woman suffrage if it appeared it would include black women voters. The antisuffrage and prosuffrage camps both could count on a fixed block of votes in favor of their respective causes. In the middle lay the states' rights suffragists, who provided the swing votes and effectively controlled the outcome of a given bill. Their support of white woman suffrage allowed the passage of the 1918 state constitutional amendment. Their fear of black voters caused the defeat of the Susan B. Anthony Amendment.

And what of the 1920 state amendment, which also was defeated? Why would this proposal be defeated, when it had seemed acceptable to the legislature just two years before? The evidence is scanty, but suggestive. At the time of the 1918 state amendment vote, the Susan B. Anthony Amendment had not yet passed Congress, and federal suffrage did not seem a tangible threat. Moreover, it also appears that the degree of support for the state suffrage amendment caught the antisuffragists by surprise, since they waited until after it passed the legislature to organize against it. By 1920, after two years of organized antisuffrage activity, the adoption of the federal amendment by Congress and its ratification by more than thirty states made the threat of federal suffrage seem very real indeed. A small but critical number of states' rights supporters appeared to accept Senator Simmons's argument that even state-granted suffrage was dangerous since it would create more sentiment for ratification of the federal amendment.

It is clear that there were powerful interests at work behind the antisuffragism in Louisiana, including the Behrman machine of New Orleans. But these forces, powerful as they were, could not have succeeded in defeating woman suffrage in the state without the help of the suffragists themselves. Their own factionalism and jealous rivalries weakened and divided them, enabling their opponents to join forces and defeat them. Similarly, united behind one bill, the two groups of suffragists had the strength to pass one or the other measure. But the suffragists, battling over ideology, were powerless to hold their legislative supporters in line.

No evaluation of the causes of the defeat can ignore the crucial role of Kate Gordon throughout the whole drama. Gordon antagonized and alienated the leadership of NAWSA, which could have offered her effective support had she chosen to accept it. As early as 1896 she created an atmosphere of competition and acrimony among suffragists, which later escalated into open warfare. She proved incapable of setting aside personal grievances in order to work for the common goal to which she had dedicated the better part of her adult life. Finally, Kate Gordon's views on race and states' rights, while by no means atypical of southerners of her day, proved to be the insurmountable barriers that prohibited her from compromising on her policies, loyalties, or strategies. Gordon's travel to other states to campaign against the amendment, clearly indicates that she saw the issue in terms of a united South against the rest of the country rather than in terms of the right of the individual state to control its internal affairs. She saw no contradiction in arguing for states' rights in her own state and then entering the fracas in another. Similarly, she expressed no resentment at out-of-state interference during the Louisiana campaigns, as long as it came from states opposed to federal enfranchisement.[62] So in a sense, even though she phrased her arguments in states' rights language, what Gordon actually demanded was the *South's* right to control its electorate free from outside intervention.[63]

Although Gordon became a voter and was active in local Democratic politics, she never quite accepted the fact that the South had let her down and ratified the Anthony Amendment. In 1923, she wrote her old friend Laura Clay about her disappointment: "It was months before I could allow myself to even think of the whole horrible experience. . . . I felt then as I do now that if a southern state had not been the medium of ratification no northern or western state would have put it over. I also feel that ratification by Tenn. was as fraudulent as the spirit that put over the 15th. Amendment." Time had not erased Gordon's personal hostilities. "I have had a great contempt for many years for Mrs. Catt and her integrity of purpose," Gordon wrote. "She has no reason to resent our opposition to the Federal Amendment. By conviction and tradition," she continued, "I believe in the State's Right Principle of our Government as a safety valve as well as a guarantee of liberty."[64] Gordon had not forgiven the "betrayal" of the Woman Suffrage Party of Louisiana either. When writing her chapter for the *History of Woman Suffrage*, Gordon omitted the efforts of her competitors whenever possible and belittled the activities she could not ignore. In fact, she began her article with these words: "The history of woman suffrage in Louisiana is unique inasmuch as it records largely the activity of one club [the Era Club]."[65]

The story of Kate Gordon and the Nineteenth Amendment is also the story of the very complicated nature of southern suffragism. In the South, the "woman question" could never be considered separately from the "negro question."[66] Louisiana suffragists, attempting to respond to the delicate nature of race relations in the South, found themselves divided over tactics and philosophy. And for Louisiana suffragists, divided meant conquered. Kate Gordon was both a part and a symbol of the three-sided contest over woman suffrage in the South. She deserves credit for much of the strength of suffrage sentiment in the region, having spent more than two decades working for the cause. Yet she—and those who shared her states' rights philosophy—very nearly prevented the ultimate ratification of the Nineteenth Amendment. Even though the states' rights suffragists were fewer in number, relative to the mainstream suffrage movement, they were the critical factor in the suffrage contest in the South. Louisiana presents the clearest example of how the states' rights issue hurt the suffrage cause in each of the southern states.

The States' Rights Constituency

Who supported the states' rights position? No study has yet addressed the constituency of the states' rights advocates. No membership lists are extant for the regional organization (the SSWSC), and only a handful of its leaders are known (such as Nellie Nugent Somerville of Mississippi and Laura Clay of Kentucky).[67] But the states' rights group that organized in Baton Rouge in 1920 did publish its membership rosters in the local newspaper. An examination of the backgrounds of these 131 women provides some insights into the states' rights agenda and will point out some suggestive differences between states' rights suffragists and NAWSA-affiliated, mainstream suffragists.[68] (Since no women's antisuffrage organization ever formed in Louisiana, antisuffragists could not be included in the following comparative analysis.)

The rates of marriage for women in the states' rights association and the NAWSA-affiliated suffragists differed very little. In 1920, approximately one out of five women in both groups had never been married. These figures are consistent with data examined from other states, as discussed in Chapter 3. Mainstream suffragists in Louisiana married at nearly the same rate as states' rights suffragists (as shown in Table A.4).

Information on the age of the women involved in these two movements is less easily obtained than marital status. Of the 131 states' rights advocates, age (in 1920) could be found for 41. The same information was found for 34 of the 88 NAWSA-affiliated suffragists. (See Table A.2.) Women who supported the ratification of the Nineteenth Amendment in Louisiana were, on average, fifty years old, while state amendment advocates were in their early forties. More important than the difference in their ages, however, was the similarity in the two age groups in one respect: women in both groups had completed or were nearing the completion of their child-rearing years and had reached a stage in their lives where home and family occupied less of their time than ever before.

Religious affiliation could be documented for 32 of 131 states' rights supporters and for 22 of the 88 federal amendment advocates. The numbers are too small to be representative, but they do suggest some interpretations that concur with those gleaned from the larger demographic studies cited in Chapter 3. As was true throughout the South, the majority of women involved in any of the three sides of the suffrage contest appear, based on their religious affiliations, to be from a wide range of socioeconomic levels, with a concentration in the middle- and upper-middle classes (as shown in Table A.6). The only significant difference in the two groups is the prominence of Jewish women in the NAWSA ranks and their complete absence from the states' rights organization.[69]

Information on the careers of women in these two groups was somewhat easier to locate than religious affiliation, since the federal census does track employment (see Table A.10). Federal suffrage supporters worked for wages more often than states' rights women, but not by much (20 percent versus 15 percent). In general, women from both samples worked at the same periods of their life cycle: several of these working women took employment after their husbands died; several others were unmarried women who had to work to support themselves.

A notable difference in the two groups of women was the relationship between marital status and employment. Of the twenty states' rights supporters who worked, only two were married and neither had children.[70] Of the eighteen ratificationists who worked, six were married and two of those had children. For several of these married working women who supported the federal amendment, it appears that their families needed their wages to make ends meet. Their husbands were auto mechanics or office managers or in other jobs for which they were not well paid. These working-class and lower-middle-class families were dependent on the wages of working wives, as they aspired to live a middle-class lifestyle. Marriage, and occasionally even children, were not reason enough for these women to withdraw from the work force. (See Table A.13.)

Another notable trend in the employment patterns of the two groups of women is the larger percentage of NAWSA-affiliated suffragists who worked in professional capacities. Although the numbers in the samples are very small, they do follow the trend established by the larger numbers in the samples referred to in Chapter 3. Mainstream suffragists had more experience in the professions than did the states' rights women. As women doctors, college professors, and journalists, they were more likely to be competing with men in higher paying, higher status positions. The result was arguably greater confidence in their abilities to compete in a man's world, and greater frustration at the impediments they faced throughout their careers.

It has been established that there were subtle differences in the work experiences of states' rights advocates and federal amendment supporters. It does not appear that states' rights women held extremely conservative views on women and work: a large number of them did work for pay, and a small number of them worked in professional, nontraditional jobs. But the experiences of the majority of them were more traditional than those of their NAWSA opponents.

Information on educational attainments was the most difficult to obtain, and the data available is insufficient for quantification. Eleven women in each group are known to have attended or graduated from a four-year college, while two women in each group are known to have attended a female seminary or female institute. Based on this limited information, it would appear that these women had similar educational experiences, an impression that can only be confirmed when additional sources of information become available.

Statistical analysis suggests that the states' rights and federal amendment factions differed little from one another in age or marital status. In religious affiliation and employment patterns, the differences were greater but still not dramatically so. Their life experiences, including perhaps education, were similar, and there is little here to explain why they parted ways on the question of state versus federal amendments. An examination of their husbands' activities, however, does illuminate some important differences in the two groups that may help to explain their differing attitudes toward the federal amendment.

Perhaps the most significant difference in the two groups of men is the large number of government officeholders in the states' rights faction (see Tables A.12 and A.13).[71] At all three levels (federal, state, and local), such jobs were highly dependent upon political patronage or electoral politics. Men dependent upon the will of the electorate for their livelihoods had reason to fear the addition of a large number of voters to the electorate (and men dependent upon control over state government had extra reason to fear federal control over the electorate). New voters introduced an unknown element into the equation: would they vote for politics-as-usual, or would they sweep out all the old and place all elective and appointive jobs at risk? Given the prosuffrage rhetoric about the incorruptibility of women voters, no doubt many men feared that the enfranchisement of women would be the end of their own jobs in the various levels of government. Fear that black women would vote Republicans into office added to the determination of politicians to protect Democratic hegemony by opposing the federal amendment. Like Martin Behrman and his machine, officeholders in Baton Rouge found much potential for political upheaval if women were enfranchised, especially by federal action.

Another significant trend in the employment backgrounds of the two groups of men was influenced by the presence of Standard Oil. Oil had been of growing importance to Louisiana's economy since just after the turn of the century. In 1909, Standard Oil had begun building a refinery just outside of Baton Rouge, which soon was the largest single oil refinery in the world and the largest single industry in Baton Rouge.[72] By 1920, Standard Oil employed more than 3,000 workers, and its financial impact on the city of Baton Rouge was immeasurable.[73] Standard Oil was a powerful national corporation whose interests were tied to other powerful national industries such as railroads and steel. At least seven of the men whose wives joined the states' rights association worked directly for Standard Oil (and one of the women worked as a stenographer for the company); and it is possible that even more were indirectly dependent upon Standard Oil for their livelihoods.[74] In addition, husbands of three other states' rights advocates worked for the Yazoo and Mississippi Valley Railroad, which ran a line directly to the Standard Oil refinery.[75]

The statistical profile of the states' rights faction in Louisiana is suggestive, but it needs further development. A few biographical sketches of the participants in the Baton Rouge organization will help to clarify this picture. One of the most well known women in the Baton Rouge area was Hannah Warren Barnes of the states' rights association. Barnes's husband, William P. (Sr.), the son of a successful Arkansas planter, was president of Holmes and Barnes, one of the largest wholesale grocery outlets in the state, and a banker. The Holmes and Barnes building was a familiar landmark in the city, its image appearing in many "city booster" books and advertisements by the Chamber of Commerce. Barnes had married Hannah Warren in 1917 after the death of his first wife, and she moved into the family mansion on Florida Street. Hannah Barnes's Florida Street neighbor, Lucy Kendall Favrot, was also a member of the association. Favrot's husband, Joseph St. Clair Favrot, was a member of a prominent Baton Rouge family, and in 1920 was secretary of the State Board of Affairs. Lucy Favrot's father was a judge, and in 1921, during John Parker's administration, her husband was appointed to the Louisiana Tax Commission.

Competing with the Favrots for name recognition in Baton Rouge was the prominent states' rights advocate Laura Matta Fuqua. Her husband, Henry Fuqua, owned Fuqua Hardware and was vice president of the State Bank of Baton Rouge. Henry also was a sugar planter who served as manager of the state penitentiary. In 1924, he was elected governor of the state in a race against Huey Long.

The wife of another political officeholder was Loula Bryan. Loula had graduated from normal college and taught school until her marriage to Alexander Bryan, a local merchant. By 1920, when Loula joined the states' rights association, her husband had turned over the management of his general merchandise store to his partner and was himself serving as the warden of the state penitentiary. The Jastremskis, a family long prominent in Baton Rouge politics and business affairs, contributed a member to the states' rights association as well. Frances Holloway Jastremski was married to Henry, the state railroad commissioner. Henry's father, Leon Jastremski, had been mayor of the city for several terms and was the editor of the *Daily Advocate*, which he used as a voice for "the familiar Bourbon dogmas of Democratic solidarity, white supremacy, and suspicion of Yankees (unless they came to town with money to spend or invest)."[76] One such "Yankee" was Frank Clark, a New Jersey native who had arrived in Baton Rouge in 1909 with Standard Oil. By 1920, Clark was the General Superintendent for Standard Oil, Louisiana, and had married a local woman, Daisy Kidd, the daughter of an ice merchant in the city.

Finally, several members of the states' rights faction were products of the sugar industry. Margaret Hill Carruth was married to Frank H. Carruth Sr., a local doctor who was heir to a sugar plantation and the Catherine Sugar Company (a sugar manufacturing concern). Their son, Frank Jr., became the fourth generation of the family to run the Catherine Sugar Company. Annabelle Smith Jones, wife of Phillip H. Jones, had been born on her family's sugar plantation in West Feliciana Parish and had married a doctor, the son of another sugar planting family. Julia Gayden had married Edward Woodside, the tax assessor for the parish, who owned his family plantation of more than 800 acres.

The sugar planters in Louisiana had reason to feel besieged on all sides in 1920 and to fear any tampering with the electorate. Since 1912, a series of economic setbacks (including the removal of tariff protection in 1916) had hit sugar planters hard, and they had not been allowed to make up lost profits during World War I because of strict federal price controls. Perhaps most dangerous to their future, however, was a continuing labor shortage that threatened to destroy the industry. Their mostly black labor force had found higher paying jobs elsewhere and were leaving the sugar parishes in significant numbers.[77] Long able to control state and local politics,[78] Louisiana's sugar planters soon felt their economic and political power waning, and they feared that federally regulated woman suffrage might hurt them as much as federally regulated tariff policies.

The women who joined the states' rights association had more in common than just their husbands' economic position. They also shared a social life in Baton Rouge, and they drew upon a network of women's clubs, church associations, kinship ties, and friendships to build their political organization. Many of these women knew one another from years of activities in voluntary associations.[79] Several of them worked together,[80] a large number of them were related to one another,[81] and an even larger number were neighbors in the residential district of downtown Baton Rouge.[82] Like antisuffragists and federal ratificationists, those women who organized on behalf of states' rights drew upon a web of preexisting relationships and used those networks to find like-minded women to join their political movement.

In social and economic background, the states' rights suffragists most closely resemble the profile of antisuffragists presented in Chapter 2. But there was a distinct difference between the rhetoric of the states' rights forces and that of the antisuffragists. States' rights advocates seldom argued against women voters as such. Fear of feminism or changing gender roles did not dominate their discourse as it did the antisuffragists' rhetoric. While the antis warned of "mannish women and womanish men" as a result of woman suffrage, states' rights supporters feared black voters and the end of Democratic supremacy. At its organizational meeting, for example, the Baton Rouge states' rights association passed four resolutions against the federal amendment, all of which were grounded in racial fears rather than gender concerns.[83]

The race-based ideology of the states' rights position was frequently disseminated by individual members of the Baton Rouge association in the local paper. Sallie Lee, wife of a Louisiana State University professor and daughter of an Alabama planter, for example, wrote that she opposed the Nineteenth

Amendment because "all matters of suffrage should be vested in the state." Vallie Seitz, an unmarried stenographer for the First National Bank, believed that "ratification will give Congress control of our state suffrage" and it would force "political equality between black and white." And Virginia Tucker, wife of a local doctor, saw the ratification of the Nineteenth Amendment as a "ratification and approval of the fifteenth amendment and will mean the adoption of political equality of the white people and negroes of the south."[84]

Mainstream suffragists battling against the powerful states' rights argument pointed out that the southern states were not "shackled to the old States Rights' ideas," as demonstrated by their votes in favor of the Eighteenth Amendment.[85] NAWSA suffragists believed the states' rights position to be "inconsistent and insincere." Chief Justice Walter Clark of North Carolina pointed out the incongruity of senators voting against woman suffrage on states' rights grounds yet voting for Prohibition, which "was largely an invasion of the police power of the several states."[86] Federal amendment supporters likewise could not understand the inconsistency of men like South Carolina governor Richard Manning, who urged the state legislature to ratify the Prohibition amendment and provide "means for its rigid enforcement in the state" but then opposed the Nineteenth Amendment as a violation of states' rights.[87]

As Kentucky suffragist Sophonisba Breckinridge wrote in 1921, "the question of 'states' rights' in the decade 1910–1920, as in 1861, was really a question of the negro."[88] The evidence to support this contention is ample, and it can be found in the states' rights literature. Louisiana's Harry Gamble unabashedly called "Federal Suffrage a Racial Question in the South."[89] John H. Wallace, of Alabama, opposed both the Eighteenth and the Nineteenth Amendments on states' rights grounds but admitted his real fear was that "should the National Suffrage Amendment prevail, black women will be enfranchised along with the white women and become their equal at the ballot boxes."[90] Moreover, the very groups that demanded states' rights when it was a means of securing white supremacy, opposed the same doctrine if its use became a threat to racial segregation, the New South's peculiar institution. For example, the Georgia Federation of Women's Clubs, in an effort to prevent the admission of black women into the General Federation in 1902, opposed the states' rights principle for local admissions policies. The Massachusetts Federation had suggested that the states be left to determine membership restrictions, but the Georgia Federation demanded that an absolute color bar be instituted nationwide.[91]

Regardless of these inconsistencies, states' rights suffragists continued to use the same rhetoric in their opposition to the enfranchisement of black southerners, male or female. Although they were sincere in their desire to enfranchise white women, who they felt could be entrusted with the ballot, their fear of black voters made them cautious about the form that suffrage might take. Female states' rights suffragists shared the views of their male counterparts. As middle-class, educated, urban working women, or professionals, states' rights women would benefit from enfranchisement. As the wives and daughters of planters, officeholders, and big businessmen, the benefit of enfranchisement would be offset by the threat of the black vote.

The understanding of the states' rights prosuffrage position has been clouded by the presence of antisuffragists who espoused the same idea that each state should determine its own destiny. As a result, contemporaries and historians alike have inferred that any use of the states' rights argument meant fundamental opposition to all women voting. As Kate Gordon herself feared, she and others of her ideological bent have been "grouped with the Anti's." When we distinguish between the use of states' rights language against all woman suffrage and its use on behalf of white woman suffrage, the clouds begin to dissipate, and the three-sided woman suffrage contest in the South becomes a more understandable phenomenon. Kate Gordon's high visibility in the suffrage movement and in historical literature on the subject works to obscure the lines of demarcation between the two groups of suffragists. Gordon has often been portrayed as representative of the southern suffrage movement, and her ideological position assumed typical of southern suffragists. But despite her claims to the contrary, Kate Gordon spoke for only one suffrage movement in the South. The majority of southern suffrage supporters rejected both her racism and her states' rights tactics.

7

The State Suffrage Campaigns

Virginia As a Case Study

I agree with you that as far as the present work in Virginia is concerned questions of Federal amendments are largely academic. I don't, however, believe that it is always going to be so. Its a pity to see any division among our workers—and yet, as suffragists grow more numerous, some division along lines of temperament and judgement is bound to occur.

Revolutions have to trot along with all kinds of revolutionaries—with bodies within bodies.

Mary Johnston to
Lila Meade Valentine, 10 May 1915

Virginia's suffragists lamented the conservatism of their home state regularly and publicly. And Virginia had earned its reputation for conservatism, particularly in the area of women's rights. The Old Dominion was the last state in the Union to grant married women the right to own property in their own names and had a similarly lackluster record in supporting higher education for women.[1] Orie Latham Hatcher, a teacher who had seen something of the world outside of the South, complained that Virginia, especially Virginia's men, still held tenaciously to old social ideals: "Nowhere else in the South except in Charleston, after all a small world to itself, has a certain conception of what a woman should be and do persisted so fervently as in Virginia."[2] Novelist Mary Johnston made a similar assessment: "Virginia, if the dearest of states, is also the most conservative. Her men are chivalric, her women domestic; since the eighteenth century no heavy wave of immigration has touched her shores. She has no large cities, she has a lovely country, wood and field and flood, she has great memories. She makes progress, too, but her eyes are apt to turn to the past."[3]

Virginians did indeed regard woman suffrage skeptically. In fact, opponents of the reform had organized earlier and more effectively than those in most other southern states. Consequently, the state's suffragists moved cautiously. As a case study of suffragism in the South, then, Virginia is ripe with opportunities. Narrowing the scope of the story of suffragism and antisuffragism to one state provides the chance to reassemble the disparate pieces discussed in previous chapters. And Virginia provides a good example of what a contest between a notably large suffrage movement, and a notably strong antisuffrage movement entailed. It also permits the close examination of the divisions between suffragists regarding ideology and tactics and how those divisions shaped the suffrage contest in the South.

Virginia: The Early Years

Since at least the 1840s, Virginia's elite women had been practicing partisanship in politics. Although excluded from voting and from officeholding, Virginia women had closely followed party politics and expressed political opinions, generally of the Whiggish variety. Openly partisan sentiments by Whig women appeared in Virginia's newspapers beginning in the 1840s, and women regularly attended political gatherings as well. The state's Whig Party welcomed the support of women and appropriated the image of female nonpartisanship to its political advantage.[4]

In a parallel (but entirely separate) trend, black women in Virginia also found ways to express their political opinions in the years before their enfranchisement. African American women in Richmond, for example, organized political "secret societies" such as the Rising Daughters of Liberty. Part of the vast network of social organizations that undergirded black social life in the postbellum South, these organizations helped to raise money, organize political rallies, and urge blacks to register and vote. Black women also participated in political meetings and rallies, such as the mass meeting held in March 1867 in Richmond to oppose the reelection of the incumbent mayor of the city. And in 1880 women in one of the most important black churches in the city petitioned the deacons to grant them the right to vote in church affairs. The event was so tumultuous that city police intervened to quiet the disorder.[5] Not surprisingly, black women's political activities generally supported Republican or Independent candidates and agendas.

For black and white women alike, political partisanship was steeped in reform politics. Reform-minded women in the late nineteenth century had often been trained or reared in this Whiggish political culture. Partisanship and reformism united under the banner of the Whig Party and then later under that of the Republican Party (although by the twentieth century it would move again, to the Democratic Party). Women were drawn to the Whigs because the party advocated many policies that middle-class women reformers supported: moral reform, public education, and support for benevolent societies. Two of the state's best known suffragists of the late nineteenth century, Elizabeth Van Lew and Orra Langhorne, both came from Whig/Republican families.[6]

Indeed, Virginia's nineteenth-century suffrage movement was very much linked to the Whig/Republican reform effort. Like other such early efforts, the nineteenth-century suffrage movement in Richmond revolved around a single dedicated leader: Anna Whitehead Bodeker. Anna Whitehead was the daughter of a factory superintendent in Richmond who had moved his family from New Jersey in the 1830s. She married a local druggist, Augustus Bodeker, a German immigrant and successful businessman who also served in the House of Delegates during Reconstruction.[7] Although it remains unknown just how and when Anna Bodeker came to support woman suffrage, by 1870 she had committed herself to suffrage activism. Her first action was to bring Paulina Wright Davis, the nationally known suffrage leader, to Richmond to speak to a small group of local civic leaders at her home on 26 January 1870. The meeting apparently fueled an impassioned discussion. At the end of the parlor meeting, Bodeker announced that she planned to form a suffrage organization in the city.[8]

Paulina Davis, greatly pleased with her initial foray into the former capital of the Confederacy, returned home convinced that she had found a southern woman capable of leading the suffrage movement in the South. Davis praised Bodeker's abilities in the pages of the *Revolution*, asserting that Bodeker "might reach the whole south." An indicator of the national leadership's early interest in harnessing the South, other national suffrage leaders soon answered Bodeker's call for assistance. Matilda Joslyn Gage, an organizer for the National Woman Suffrage Association (NWSA), traveled to Richmond several months later to help put together a state suffrage association.[9]

After a public meeting at Bosher's Hall on 5 May 1870, a small group of Richmonders declared themselves the Virginia State Woman Suffrage Association and elected Anna Bodeker as president. Among its leading members were prominent Republicans such as Judge John C. Underwood, Ralza M. Manly, the Freedmen's Bureau's superintendent of education, and Elizabeth Van Lew, the "notorious" Reconstruction postmistress who had been a Union sympathizer and suspected Union spy. (Van Lew was also known for paying her taxes every year under protest, pointing out that as a citizen who could not vote, she was effectively taxed without the right of representation.[10]) The same year it officially organized, the new suffrage association affiliated with the National Woman Suffrage Association, sent delegates to the 1870 national convention, and requested further assistance from the national leadership.[11]

Still feeling optimistic about the opportunities for suffrage activity in Richmond, the NWSA sent some of its most powerful speakers to the city in the next several months to help bolster the fledging state association. Susan B. Anthony, calling Bodeker's request for assistance the "first call from the South for missionaries," personally appeared in Richmond in December 1870. Anthony attempted to appeal to the southern audience with an argument grounded in Reconstruction realities: it was unfair for the government to allow black males to vote but not allow women to do so. Anthony's visit was followed by Lillie Devereaux Blake's, in January 1871. In March, while the state assembly was in session, the Virginia Woman Suffrage Association brought Paulina Wright Davis, Isabella Beecher Hooker, and Josephine S. Griffing to town for several public appearances.[12]

These meetings, and the newspaper coverage that they generated, spurred a great deal of discussion in Richmond about the "woman question." Letters to the local newspapers indicated that people were thinking and talking about woman suffrage, many perhaps for the first time. The opposition appeared in greater numbers, of course, like "Daughter of Virginia" who protested that woman's rights threatened the "overthrow of our political fabric." [13] But comments like this one failed to put an end to the debate. Undoubtedly Anna

Bodeker's unsuccessful attempt to vote in an 1871 election set tongues wagging again all over Richmond.[14]

However, all this activism and attention did not result in the rapid growth of a suffrage movement. Nor did the Virginia Woman Suffrage Association gain any legislative victories. The association appears to have been firmly linked with carpetbaggers and black Republicans in the public mind, and thus it had difficulty gaining support from most whites in Richmond. Anna Bodeker, discouraged by the meager results that had come from all her efforts, ceased her activism after 1872. The Virginia State Woman Suffrage Association disappeared soon thereafter.[15]

It would be nearly twenty years before Lynchburg's Orra Langhorne, an avid suffragist, stepped in to fill the void left by Bodeker's retirement. Langhorne, the daughter of a Unionist and slaveholding "abolitionist," held liberal views on race and spoke them freely, despite the disapproval of her neighbors. She supported the Republican Party, called herself a radical, and was a longtime supporter of the Hampton Institute.[16]

For several years, Orra Langhorne acted alone: she petitioned the Virginia legislature for voting rights for women,[17] and she regularly attended the National American Woman Suffrage Association (NAWSA) conventions as the sole "delegate" from Virginia.[18] Finally, in 1893, she attempted to revive the suffrage movement by establishing a second state suffrage association, centered in her home in Lynchburg. Its activities were quite limited, geographically and otherwise.[19] Perhaps the two most notable events from these years were the appearances of celebrated national suffrage leaders, both undoubtedly as a result of Langhorne's involvement in the NAWSA. The first of these occurred in 1895, when Susan B. Anthony spoke at the opera house in Culpeper, on her way home from the Atlanta NAWSA convention.[20] The state constitutional convention of 1901 was the setting for the second of these "celebrity" appearances. Carrie Chapman Catt appeared before the convention during its meeting to draft the "disfranchisement" constitution. She asked that woman suffrage be included in the new document.[21] Orra Langhorne's death in 1904, however, put another temporary halt to suffrage activity in the state. Langhorne's work was notable, but Virginia was completely dependent upon her personal efforts alone. The suffrage movement would not be revived again in Virginia until 1909.[22]

In the time between the founding of the first suffrage organization in 1870 and the permanent one to emerge in 1909, Virginia experienced two "revolutions": a political coup d'état and an economic transformation. The state's conservative Democrats, challenged by the agendas of Republicans, Populists,

Readjusters, and other shades of Independents, responded with election "reforms" that restored their control of the state government. A secret ballot law helped effectively to disfranchise illiterates (who tended to vote with the opposition); the electorate thus reduced, the Democrats felt confident enough to call a constitutional convention to restrict the electorate more permanently. The convention produced a constitution so controversial that rather than subject it to a public referendum, it was "proclaimed" in effect instead.[23]

At the same time that the Conservatives were reshaping the electorate in their own image, their economic policies were helping to remake urban Virginia as well. Cities were booming, railroads were expanding, factories were appearing. The cities of Norfolk, Portsmouth, and Petersburg experienced real estate booms so intense that the tax assessors were having difficulty figuring tax bills.[24] Norfolk's city boosters formed the "200,000 League," whose goal was to increase the city's population to 200,000 by promoting manufacturing. While the city did not reach the 200,000 mark until World War II, manufacturing did employ 30 percent of the city's residents in 1910 and transportation and trade employed another 30 percent.[25] Richmond, the state's largest city, reached the 100,000 mark by the turn of the century. Its population and its prosperity relied greatly on manufacturing and extensive commercial trade.[26]

These tremendous strides in industrial development were facilitated by the governing elite's belief in unregulated business development as the best solution for the state's economic backwardness. Railroads, real estate developers, and industrialists were allowed free reign in Conservative/Democratic administrations. The state did create a virtually powerless railroad commission in 1877, but that would be the extent of state regulation for decades.[27]

The New Virginia produced great profits for those who survived the competition and the unpredictable economic cycles. Men like Lewis Ginter, James Dooley, and Jed Hotchkiss made their fortunes in various concerns and joined the state's economic elite. Their businesses hired thousands, who joined the state's industrial proletariat. In the mushrooming cities and towns, an urban middle class appeared to provide goods and services to workers who now seldom grew their own food or built their own homes.

Virginia's urban and industrial growth sparked both the rise of trade unionism and the birth of progressive reform groups, two parallel responses to the successes and failures of the New South. In 1900, an estimated 3,900 workers in Virginia were members of trade unions; by 1910 the number had grown to 8,500, and the figures reached a high of nearly 47,000 at the end of World War I.[28] Industrial unrest erupted periodically, such as a large coal miners' strike in 1895, as the newly conscious classes of the New South learned to interact in new ways.[29] Similarly, urban reform associations began to agitate for numerous improvements in the quality of life in Virginia. Although the beginning of the progressive reform movement in Virginia has been dated as late as 1902,[30] in fact, progressive reform organizations had been active in the late 1870s and early 1880s. The state's first local chapter of the Woman's Christian Temperance Union (WCTU) formed in Lincoln in May 1878; the Richmond chapter was organized in 1882. And by 1883, eight unions joined together to form the state WCTU, with Mrs. R. D. Wilson of Loudoun County as the state president.[31] Other manifestations of the emergent progressive sentiment included the establishment of the YWCA in Richmond in 1887; the founding of the Hampton, Virginia, Locust Street Social Settlement in October 1890, by Janie Porter Barrett; the founding of the Richmond Neighborhood Association in 1912, by Ora Brown Stokes; and the opening of the Nurses' Settlement, a visiting nursing service and settlement house in 1901.[32] As progressive reformers elsewhere, those in Virginia began demanding legislative action on behalf of change. The state's first child labor law was passed in 1890, under the sponsorship of Mary-Cooke Branch Munford.[33]

The women, both black and white, involved in "social work" confronted the poverty, disease, illiteracy, and unemployment of Virginia's growing cities. As women of the middle class, with leisure time and extra resources at their disposal, they were able to join reform groups. As religious women, steeped in the language of "mission" and "service," they felt that they had an obligation to do so. When they gained experience in these reform endeavors, they often came to see the need for woman suffrage, out of a desire to serve others or to secure their own equality.

Veterans of the white women's voluntary associations and progressive reform movement were responsible for the reestablishment of the suffrage movement in Virginia. The movement stirred back to life in the spring of 1909, when the Richmond Woman's Club hosted a visit from Kentucky suffragist Laura Clay. Her appearance there helped to spur the establishment of yet another suffrage organization. Despite the skepticism of the local newspaper, which predicted that this, as had all previous efforts, would fail,[34] Ellen Glasgow and twenty other members of the Woman's Club established the Equal Suffrage League of Virginia (ESL) in the fall of 1909. The founders included white women of great standing in the community, such as Lila Meade Valentine, women of distinguished southern lineage, such as Lucy Randolph Mason, women of current fame, such as artist Adele Clark, and women leaders of progressive reforms, such as Kate Waller Barrett.[35]

Selected as president at the very first meeting, Lila Meade Valentine dominated the Virginia suffrage movement for the next decade. Valentine had come from Richmond's social and economic elite and had married well.[36] By the time of her election as president of the ESL, Valentine was a seasoned veteran of women's voluntary associations with connections to the many Progressive Era reform movements then making their way into Richmond. She had spoken before city councils, served on state committees for various causes, including education reform and public health, and helped organize fund-raising drives. Although Valentine's impeccable credentials benefited the suffrage movement by giving her access to leaders of government, business, and education, her conservatism hampered the movement. She ruled the ESL with an iron will, stamping out dissent and purging opposition within its ranks. From the outset, the new league disavowed militancy and radicalism. One of its first press announcements rejected the suggestion that the suffragists would bring militant "suffragettes" like the Pankhursts to Richmond and emphasized the group's patience and willingness to proceed slowly, if surely, toward its goal.[37]

Although Valentine would leave her mark on the ESL, hers was not a one-woman movement. Many other important local leaders emerged both to assist and to challenge Valentine's leadership in the drive for enfranchisement. In Norfolk, Jessie Townsend and Pauline Adams were outspoken and dedicated motivators who helped to build one of the largest city associations in the state. Townsend, the wife of a realtor, was a local suffrage leader who also held state offices occasionally. Pauline Adams, who was born in Ireland, was an attorney (the first woman attorney in the city of Norfolk) and had been a city suffrage leader since the ESL's inception. However, both Townsend and Adams grew restless and frustrated with the ESL and Valentine's conservative leadership; Townsend joined the Congressional Union for a time, and Adams ultimately joined the National Woman's Party, a group with which she was jailed for picketing the White House.

For these local leaders and others, such as Elizabeth Langhorne Lewis of Lynchburg and Louise Taylor Letcher of Lexington, the goal of the first years of organization was recruitment; and they converted women, one by one, to the cause. Mary Johnston recorded in her diary in 1910 that she was "doing a deal of suffrage propaganda. There is here little opposition, a great deal of curiosity, a vague unrest, a few already over, others trembling on the verge. At any rate and at last woman is in the pulpit."[38]

Recruitment could be slow going, as a set of documents from 1912 illustrates. First, Lila Valentine wrote to Merrie Sugg of Guinea, Virginia, who was known for her local mission work. She inquired after Sugg's opinion about suffrage, sent some literature, asked her to forward names of anyone she knew who might be interested, and then asked if Sugg could make arrangements for a public talk by Mary Johnston. Sugg responded with caution, though not with outright hostility. "I have not given this subject serious attention," Sugg wrote, but she did acknowledge that she had once talked to her local legislator about it. He informed her of his opposition to woman suffrage because "the women of the county are opposed to it, and he did not like to vote against their wishes in the matter. I told him I was not opposed to it, but I did not like to offer advice in the matter. He asked me to talk with some of the leading women about it, as in my mission work among the Baptist women of the county, I am acquainted with all parts of the county." And as to Mary Johnston's speaking, Sugg advised, "There is no hall in this immediate neighborhood. I believe there is a small hall at Guinea, our post office. . . . Bowling Green, the county seat would be the best place for it, and I refer you to Mrs. O. P. Smoot, Bowling Green." She added, "P.S. Since writing this letter, I have been looking over some of the woman suffrage literature sent me, and I am favorably impressed."[39] The end result: one possible convert, another name to contact in another small town, and more work to be done.

Suffragists knew instinctively to tap the network of women's voluntary associations to garner new members. In 1916, local leader Elizabeth L. Lewis recommended that organizers focus on securing members "from all the Church associations for women, from all civic and temperance associations, educational bodies and industrials plants."[40] Surprisingly, the women's colleges in the Lynchburg area proved more difficult to reach than Lewis anticipated. Sweet Briar's president, although herself a suffrage supporter, refused to allow Mary Johnston to give a suffrage speech to her students in 1911, permitting her to speak to the faculty only. And Randolph-Macon Woman's College very nearly canceled a scheduled suffrage talk, but it ultimately allowed the event to go on.[41] (Randolph-Macon eventually produced a large college suffrage league; Sweet Briar students remained unorganized.)[42]

Despite the need to recruit as many members as possible, the white suffrage league never reached out to the black middle-class women who might have been their "natural allies." By the early twentieth century, cities like Richmond were populated by a vigorous and substantial black middle class, with women who were the equals to Lila Valentine in voluntary association activity, club work, and progressive reform experiences. Ora Brown Stokes had gleaned organizational expertise from her many years of work with the Negro Organizational Society of Virginia, the Virginia Federation of Colored Women's Clubs, and Baptist missionary societies. (And unlike Lila Valentine, Stokes had also received graduate education from the University of Chicago.) Maggie Lena Walker, now widely known as the first black woman bank president in the United States, also had done years of volunteer work for the National Association of Colored Women, the Virginia Federation of Colored Women's Clubs, the Richmond Council of Colored Women, the National Association for the Advancement of Colored People (NAACP), and the International Council of Women of the Darker Races. But the racial code kept black and white urban middle-class women from joining forces behind a movement that they all supported.

And it does appear that many African American men and women in Virginia supported woman suffrage. As early as 1871, the Richmond press noted the attendance of "three colored men" at a local woman suffrage meeting.[43] Although black women in Virginia did not organize a separate suffrage organization and speak openly or often of their suffragism, when women were finally given the vote in 1920, they marched to the local courthouses to register; they voted when allowed to do so; and they organized the Virginia Negro Woman's League of Voters.

For white suffragists in Virginia, reaching women outside of the biggest cities was critical to the success of the movement, but it was also one of the most difficult tasks confronting the endeavor. Suffragists had little hope for, and expended little energy on, recruiting rural women. Even in small towns, suffragists occasionally found it difficult to compete for the attention of the public. For example, Elizabeth Lewis complained that the low turnout for her suffrage meeting at Drake's Branch in 1916 was "owing to the absence of a number of the representative people who had gone that day to Richmond to see 'The Birth of a Nation.'"[44]

But the diligent and exhaustive work of Mary Johnston, Elizabeth Lewis, and Lila Valentine began to pay off.[45] In 1916, Virginia had 115 local leagues, including 23 organized in that year alone.[46] The Randolph-Macon Woman's College ESL, led by the daughter of Nellie Nugent Somerville, state suffrage leader from Mississippi, had 150 members in 1914.[47] And by 1919, membership had reached 30,000, making it most likely the largest state association in the South. The ESL also had secured endorsements of suffrage from the State Teachers' Association, the State Federation of Women's Clubs, and a number of other women's groups.[48]

In addition to recruiting new members, Virginia suffragists believed that their most important task was to educate the public on enfranchisement issues. As Elizabeth Langhorne Lewis lamented, "it seems that for a few years to come this educational work must proceed in the South before the movement will be sufficiently general to promise legislative action."[49] And in order to educate properly the public, they needed positive publicity. The league sent more than 6,000 press releases a year to the state's newspapers (although few editors supported suffrage and therefore seldom used them).[50] In October 1914, the league began publishing *Virginia Suffrage News*, financed personally by Alice O. Taylor, a local suffragist in Richmond.[51] The ESL also made the usual appearances at county and state fairs, gave talks at conventions, and held public meetings with prominent state and national speakers.

Many of those suffrage talks were accompanied by fund-raising. Both the state and the local suffrage leagues were chronically short of funds and had to use creative measures at times to come up with extra cash. The comments of Jessie Townsend, local leader of the large and active Norfolk league, on fund-raising are telling. "Well," she wrote, "I believe we went about it in a truly feminine way, the way women have raised things since time immemorial, a little here and a little there, everlastingly at it. A member who had a vacuum cleaner rented it out to other members so much a day, the proceeds going into the treasury of the league." Other members sold cakes and breads. And of course, she added, "we passed the hat at most of our evening gatherings."[52]

The message that Virginia suffragists wished to convey was two-fold: women ought to be the legal equals of men and women with the ballot would be catalysts of reform. In 1912, the state convention of the ESL adopted a set of resolutions that effectively defined the Virginia suffragists' agenda. Notably, there was no mention of race or the desire to increase the white electorate. Several items demonstrated their interest in women outside their own class, including a call for an eight-hour work day, the abolishment of child labor, and equal pay for equal work. Several other resolutions, including support for women's equal guardianship rights over their children, advocacy of a single standard of morality, and demand for equal educational opportunities for women "from the kindergarten through the university," revealed their larger feminist vision. Their final plank called for international arbitration, making clear that these women believed that diplomacy and international politics were appropriate areas of interest for women. The domestication of politics included international affairs.[53]

The ESL's resolutions affirm that Virginia suffragists, like the progressive movement itself, accepted the premise that solving modern social problems required the government's intervention. Most of their demands for reform, such as education for all children and a public health initiative, called for legislative actions. As Lucy Randolph Mason wrote, "a divine discontent [had] opened their eyes to the cruel wrong, injustice and human waste of our present social system, to the responsibilities of the individual to society, and to the powerlessness of a class debarred from participation in government."[54] Suffragism was part of a larger agenda that responded to "the changed social and economic order of the present."[55]

Considering the comfortable middle-class lives they lived, a remarkable number of Virginia's suffragists worked to reach organized labor in the state.

As early as February 1911, Mary Johnston and Lila Valentine spoke to the Richmond Central Trade Union Council. Johnston's speech linked the causes of organized labor and woman suffrage: women and working people have been the "under dogs" for ages, she argued, and they are rising together now. "We helped you at the Capitol a year ago [in a fight against proposed labor legislation]," she continued. "Could we not have helped you more effectively with the ballot?" The council officially endorsed woman suffrage at the meeting, and several members spoke in favor of the reform.[56] Valentine eventually backed away from her association with labor unions, but Johnston continued to see women's causes and labor's causes as kindred.[57]

Johnston was not alone in her interest in labor. For example, in a letter to Johnston, a local suffrage activist wrote, "I hope very soon now to be able to report you some progress in affiliation between our League and the Labor people. . . . Indeed, we can best forward our work, by never losing sight of its main purpose for a moment, and at the same time, by aiding as far as we possibly can in the educational and social reform work going on around us."[58] And a Richmond suffragist wrote to Jessie Townsend in 1915 that "we have been speaking before labor unions and are glad to see that you are planning the same thing. The labor people are our friends and their names to the petition would help us greatly."[59] Perhaps most dedicated of all in linking the suffrage and labor questions, however, was Lucy Randolph Mason. In a widely quoted address to Virginia's middle-class women, the future labor organizer chided women of leisure: "We have no right to stand idly by and profit by the underpaid and overdriven labor of people bound with the chains of economic bondage."[60] Such a statement makes it difficult to see that Mason's support for woman suffrage and other progressive reforms actually stemmed from her desire to exert middle-class control over the new industrial proletariat. Female "paternalism" was not apparent in her later career with the CIO either.[61]

Nor can this interest in reaching the South's new industrial labor force be dismissed as just rhetoric, for actions often followed the words. In fact, members of the Hampton local suffrage league reported that they personally attended a meeting of the local Carpenter's Union "where new members and signatures to our petition were obtained."[62] Roanoke suffragist Lillie Barbour arranged for Lila Valentine to speak to the Garment Workers in Danville, because she was "confident the Garment Workers there will adopt Equal Suffrage."[63] And in Lynchburg, the suffragists' interest in labor was reciprocated: seventeen garment workers joined the local ESL in 1914.[64]

Lila Valentine, fearful of the taint of radicalism, soon began to work to limit the amount of contact the ESL made with labor unions. When Alice Taylor and Jessie Townsend tried to recruit a labor union official to be an officer in the Norfolk league, Valentine moved quickly to prevent it. "I am inclined to think it far better to keep entirely clear of other organizations," she asserted. We of course want their endorsement, and we can assist them from time to time by backing up certain welfare measures espoused by them at the Legislature, but we must maintain a strictly non-partisan attitude toward them as towards political parties."[65] Valentine grew even more worried about the great sympathy for socialism shown by some leading suffragists such as Alice Tyler, an active suffragist from Richmond who believed that "if we really love our fellow humans, all of us, you and I and all—are socialists at heart, dont you think so? And some day what is in the heart will become manifest in words and actions. The world's way is towards socialism I think, and we are in the way I know."[66] A socialist speaker had appeared at a Richmond ESL meeting in 1912, giving a talk entitled "Why I am a Socialist,"[67] and Valentine began to fear that the public would associate suffragism with socialism. She warned Jessie Townsend that "our very good friend, Mr. Clinedinst, Factory Inspector, said that he noticed in the Suffrage Shop window in Norfolk Socialist literature and that he would strongly advise that it should not be in the shop, as it savors of partisanship and as Socialism itself is a most unpopular policy amongst the rank and file."[68]

Likewise, Valentine went after her old friend, Mary Johnston. Johnston had never hidden her affinity for socialism from her friends, although she did try to keep it from becoming a hindrance to the suffrage cause.[69] In 1911, Johnston had agreed to be guest of honor at a dinner in Baltimore in honor of socialist leader Max Eastman. In that same year, she had attended her "first socialist meeting" in Richmond, where Eugene Debs was speaking.[70] She regularly attended socialist meetings and speeches in the city. Valentine grew increasingly nervous about Johnston's politics, and in 1912 she asked Johnston point blank if she was a socialist. Johnston replied, "I have never become an enrolled member of the Socialist Party. (You have in that party, you know, to sign your card and pay your dues.) I may never actually join it as an organization. But I call myself a socialist, and to all practical purposes I am one."[71]

Valentine had concluded that the only route to enfranchisement was a moderate one, and she worked diligently to stamp out dangerous radicalism from her ranks. "The more I study the situation in Virginia, the more convinced I am of the necessity of quiet, educational propaganda with an entire elimination of the spectacular for the present at least. The latter method simply shocks the sensibilities of most people without convincing them of the truth of our movement."[72] She made it clear to all that militancy, radicalism, and socialism were to be avoided because they endangered woman suffrage. To that end, Johnston never joined the Socialist Party and kept her political views to herself.

Valentine also worked to keep the racial politics of the New South out of the suffrage movement. Southern reformers had used racism successfully as a strategy in support of other programs, such as Prohibition, and suffragists easily could have used that example in their own crusade.[73] But Virginia's suffragists believed that the racial settlement of 1901 was final and the question therefore moot.

The first hearing of the woman suffrage question took place at the 1912 meeting of the state legislature. The local press acknowledged "the seriousness of the occasion, [that] the feeling that here might be an hour to make history for the commonwealth and to mark the beginning of an era, was in the air." It reported, "Women who work, women who write, women who keep house, women who have nothing else to do, and women who have everything else to do, pleaded for the ballot. Men who believe their cause is just stood with them. . . . Ministers of the gospel and representatives of laboring organizations helped."[74] Kate Bosher, Elizabeth Lewis, and Lila Valentine addressed the legislature, but it was Mary Johnston's speech that received the most attention. She pointed out that thousands of Virginia women work for pay, thousands are self-supporting and supporters of others. "Virginia women are in the economic world to stay," yet, Johnston continued, "the gentleman will rub his hands, smile and say, 'My dear ladies, if you'd just consent to stay where your great-grandmothers were.' To which, Johnston wished to reply, 'When you, gentlemen, come to committee properly bepowdered, pigtailed and snuff-boxed, when you again discuss embargo and whether or no we shall purchase Louisiana, then will we, too, return to where our great-grandmothers were.' "[75] Although the Committee on Privileges and Elections issued an open invitation for response, no one rose to speak in opposition to the amendment. The House voted 88 to 12 against the state amendment. The Senate, the *Times-Dispatch* reported, laughed at the announcement by a Richmond senator that he wished to submit suffrage petitions for consideration, and it did not vote on the question during this session.[76]

The Antisuffragists Organize

The 1912 legislative debate over woman suffrage stirred its opponents to action. Antisuffragists announced their intention to organize that February, denouncing the "atheistic impulse of suffrage" which denied that "women's place has been appointed by God as the mother of the family and the mistress of the home."[77] Mary Johnston noted in her diary: "This week sees the announcement of the long looked for Anti-Suffrage Association. A battle royal's coming."[78] The suffragists tried to take the announcement in stride. In fact, Kate Wise decided that "the organization of the opposition in Richmond is a good sign, they can no longer stigmatize the suffragists because of public work, and with opposition comes greater endeavor on the part of adherents to the Cause."[79]

In one of the first southern states to organize, the antisuffragists set up headquarters in Richmond and began to recruit members. The Virginia Association Opposed to Woman Suffrage soon claimed a membership of more than 2,000 women; and several branch associations developed throughout the state.[80] The organization set rules for voting and membership and published their constitution and bylaws.[81] They set out to write and distribute antisuffrage literature, to publicize the fact that prominent women opposed woman suffrage, and to secure names on petitions opposing suffrage. The first state president, Jane Meade Rutherfoord, was a club woman and mainstay of the women's patriotic societies in Richmond. Quite advanced in age, Rutherfoord retired to an honorary presidency by 1916 and was succeeded by Mary Mason Anderson Williams. Williams came from the wealthy Tredegar Ironworks family of Richmond. Other state leaders also came from Richmond's most prestigious families, such as Mary Miller Cary, whose husband's family had been sending members to the legislature since the seventeenth century. Although these leaders were well known in the state, only one was renowned outside of Virginia: the writer Molly Elliot Seawell. Best known for her novel *Throckmorton*, the prolific Seawell published more than forty books and articles before her death in 1916. Her antisuffrage polemic, *The Ladies' Battle*, published the year before the state antisuffrage organization had formed, won her acclaim and instant leadership in the new movement.[82]

The association held its first open meeting in March 1912. Mary Johnston and other interested suffragists attended. Johnston recounted a few details of the event in her diary: "This evening to the Jefferson [for] the first antisuffrage open meeting. Miss [Minnie] Bronson, Miss [Emily] Bissell speaking. We all went. A crowd. Mr. [Edward] Valentine, John Rutherford [*sic*], Eugene Massie on the platform. Judge [George L.] Christian introducing speakers. Poor speaking, but a curious dramatic evening."[83] As the *Times-Dispatch* reported, it was "the first time in the history of the Commonwealth a band of Virginia women gathered in public meeting to denounce to the world a movement which has infolded five sovereign States and is knocking at the legislative doors of as many more." Emily Bissell, a nationally known antisuffrage speaker, claimed that only one in ten women actually desired the right to vote, while the rest were either opposed or ambivalent. As the voice of all antisuffragists, she challenged suffragists to prove that more than a tiny fraction of American women desired such a momentous change in the polity.[84]

In general, the antisuffragists in Virginia operated in the same fashion as other antisuffragists did: they used the same publicity techniques, utilized the same arguments and evidence, and relied on the weight of their names to impress the public with the gravity of their opinions. They rented a booth at the state fair and distributed literature to the crowds.[85] However, the state's antisuffragists did come up with one unique innovation: they arranged for the free distribution of antisuffrage literature at several bookstores in Richmond.[86] And at least one anti in Virginia was willing to debate the suffrage question in public; Caroline Preston Davis, the field secretary for the VAOWS, challenged the ESL to a debate before the Sweet Briar College Current Events Club. Most antisuffragists avoided this kind of activism, however, because of its overtly political nature and its "unseemliness" for women who were attempting to uphold traditional womanly influence.[87]

Virginia's antisuffragists, much like antisuffragists everywhere, preferred to let women take the lead in the movement, while men organized as a support group. Some of Richmond's most prominent men were members of the state's support group, the "Men's Advisory Committee." James D. Crump was arguably the leading banker in the city; Eppa Hunton Jr. came from a family of politicians and had served as a delegate to the state convention that voted to secede from the Union; Dr. Stuart McGuire, son of famed Confederate surgeon Hunter McGuire, was a leading doctor in the community. Other men on the advisory committee bore names that evoked images of plantations, the Confederate States of America, and the First Families of Virginia: Cabell, Valentine, Pinckney, Rutherfoord, and Anderson. Like other such advisory groups, the male antisuffragists generally stayed in the background, lending their names to letterheads, chairing meetings, and writing literature, but women remained the cornerstone of the antisuffrage organizational effort.

Unlike Virginia suffragists, the VAOWS took advantage of the race issue as the debate grew heated. The idea of the black vote seemed to produce a knee-jerk reaction from white Virginians. Antisuffrage literature began to pound hard at the threat of "negro domination." The antisuffragists injected race into the debate, and it eventually moved to the forefront. By the time the state legislature debated another state suffrage amendment in 1916, white supremacy was a prominent part of the discussion.[88] For example, antisuffragists produced and widely circulated a broadside entitled "Virginia Warns Her People Against Woman Suffrage," which cited 1910 census figures to demonstrate that "the colored people would have absolute and immediate control of" twenty-nine counties.[89]

Meanwhile, the suffragists insisted that white supremacy was not, and could not be, at stake. Lila Meade Valentine defended their position: "A bogey—a mere bogey this. This is not such danger. The state constitutions provide amply for restricting the shiftless, illiterate vote. To assume that only the women of the negro race would be sufficiently interested in citizenship to register and vote is to gratuitously insult the white women of the South. To assume that white women would be less interested than white men in maintaining white supremacy is equally wide of the mark."[90] Although they did not disavow white supremacy, mainstream white suffragists in Virginia did not use it as a weapon. Their strategy of denying that white supremacy was an issue should be seen as the moderate approach.[91] Even a progressive like Mary Johnston used the statistical argument occasionally. "We are asking for the enfranchisement of women on the same terms with men," she asserted. "That means that just as you have closely restricted the negro male voter, so will the amended Constitution closely restrict the woman vote. A few educated, property owning colored women will vote, but not all the mass of the colored women."[92] In fact, the statistical argument became the foundation of official suffrage response to the threat of the black vote. In 1919, the ESL published a "Brief for the Federal Suffrage Amendment," which provided a comprehensive listing of arguments and evidence to refute the states' rights/black voter position.[93] Lila Valentine reminded Jessie Townsend to keep a copy of the Virginia constitution on hand whenever she lobbied any legislator, so she could "prove our statements."[94]

At the same time that race entered the public debate on woman suffrage, the contest was complicated by the developing factionalism of the suffragists. Virginia's suffragists held opinions ranging across the spectrum on issues of race, class, and gender. The ESL, as the state's NAWSA affiliate, desired to be the only suffrage organization in the state. But the ESL did not represent every viewpoint, and dissenters began to look for more congenial associates. Two new suffrage organizations, the Southern States Woman Suffrage Conference (SSWSC) and the Congressional Union (later the National Woman's Party), appeared in Virginia at almost the same time and began to compete with the ESL for members and support.

As state suffrage leaders, both Lila Valentine and Mary Johnston knew Kate Gordon of Louisiana, and both responded to her call for a regional suffrage organization by joining the SSWSC. Neither Valentine nor Johnston was willing to renounce the federal amendment approach as a possible option, but for the time being, they were still working for a state constitutional amendment and therefore could join the SSWSC without reservation.[95] But the relationship between the SSWSC and the ESL deteriorated rapidly, as Kate Gordon seemed determined to dictate a racial agenda in her organization. Women who were members of both organizations found themselves squeezed and pressured by the opposing forces. The SSWSC was scheduled to meet in Richmond in December 1915, and by October, Virginia suffragists were already growing nervous about Gordon's increasingly reckless use of racial rhetoric. Mary Johnston wrote Lila Valentine, "I, no more than you, like the matter or the tone of Kate Gordon's utterances. [crossed out: Those upon the negro question, for instance, are so opposed to] In many instances they are so opposed to my own moral and mental convictions, silent and expressed, that standing to the outsider as they must do for the opinion of the Conference as a whole, I am coming to feel that I cannot much longer leave my name upon its letter heads. . . . Apparently she sees the universal situation through the window pane of Louisiana politics."[96]

Johnston eventually resigned without fanfare as vice-president of the SSWSC, although she did attend the Richmond convention. As did other mainstream southern suffragists, Johnston disagreed with Gordon on both tactics and ideology. While she never publicly challenged the state's disfranchisement laws, Johnston did argue that "as women we should be most prayerfully careful lest, in the future, that women—whether colored women or white women who are merely poor, should be able to say that we had betrayed their interests and excluded them from freedom."[97] By the time of the SSWSC convention in Richmond, Lila Valentine, in an effort to preserve unity in the suffrage ranks, remained one of the few southern suffragists still in the waning SSWSC.[98]

The SSWSC folded, but a second alternative suffrage group proved more long-lived and ultimately posed more of a challenge to the state's suffrage leadership. A state chapter of the Congressional Union provided a home for suffragists who wanted more emphasis placed on passing the federal amendment and more activism on its behalf. Many members of the ESL had been growing impatient with the cautious leadership of Valentine, including several Virginia women who had participated in the March on Washington in January of 1913.[99] Some had grown restive enough to join the Congressional Union (CU). Sophie Meredith of Richmond, vice president of the state ESL, led the movement to establish a state branch of the CU. (Meredith was an unlikely radical, however. Her husband, Charles V. Meredith, was a prominent Richmond attorney most well known as the legal representative of the Richmond Liquor Dealers Association in its fight against Prohibition.[100] He had also been a member of the state's constitutional convention of 1901.)[101]

Lila Valentine did everything possible to prevent this rival organization from forming. She tried to convince her coworkers that "to organize a new State League in Virginia would be a tactical blunder. It would mean the confusing of the issue in the minds of the newly converted, and of those more numerous thousands to be converted. It would mean the duplication of machinery already existing, which is bad business from a practical point of view." Furthermore, she reminded Virginia's suffragists that the state leaders, "with the exception of Mrs. Charles V. Meredith, all agree that it would be unwise to further the organization of the Congressional Union in Virginia."[102] Despite Valentine's opposition, the Congressional Union successfully organized a Virginia chapter.

Mary Johnston and Lucy Randolph Mason both attempted to mollify the factions. "I don't believe it will really or for long hurt things if Mrs. Meredith does decide to have her League," Johnston wrote to Valentine, "though perhaps she will be content with a Congressional Committee."[103] For her part, Mason encouraged tolerance of the militants, remarking that, while each faction "must work in its own way," there was "no reason why we cannot sympathize with all the workers—even those who smash windows, for great has been their provocation."[104] Nevertheless, the tensions between the two groups of suffragists continued to fester. In May 1915, Lila Valentine exploded in wrath at the discovery that CU members had been using the ESL's office and files without permission: "I find they have used our Headquarters after our office hours to further their propaganda. They made use of our typewriter and our card index of city and State members to send out the call to the Conference. . . . Such a proceeding we consider dishonorable in the extreme and if I had no other reason against the existence of their Union in Virginia, this very unscrupulous method of attaining their ends would constitute a strong one."[105]

After failing to halt the formation of the CU, Valentine then tried to limit the appeal of the new group by making it difficult for women to join both the CU and the ESL. In 1916, the ESL issued a new statement of principles and resolutions: "That in order to make plain our position, no person shall be a member of the Executive Council of the Equal Suffrage League who holds an official position in any suffrage organization which does not endorse the policy of the Equal Suffrage League of Virginia."[106] This effectively served as a purge of the Congressional Union.

Renamed the National Woman's Party (NWP) in 1917, the more militant suffragists began picketing the White House. Lila Valentine continued her counteroffensive against the militant faction, announcing that the ESL "condemns the folly of the fanatical women who are picketing the White House." She pled with the public not to "condemn the suffrage cause as a whole because of the folly of a handful of women."[107] Lucy Mason, on the other hand, urged tolerance of the picketers.

Despite the active hostility of Lila Valentine, other Virginia suffragists supported the CU/NWP, both in philosophy and in actions. While none of the Virginia members were as famous as Sue Shelton White of Tennessee, the CU/NWP did attract a number of Virginia's leading suffragists, including Elizabeth (Mrs. Dexter) Otey of Lynchburg, the daughter of Elizabeth Langhorne Lewis, whose "defection" from the ESL disturbed many in the organization. In December 1915, the CU established a state membership committee, whose directive was to recruit new members. Chaired by a Miss J. S. Jennings of Richmond, the committee made steady progress. In December 1915, the Congressional Union had 127 Virginia members; by the end of 1917, the total was up to 401. The increasing militancy of the CU/NWP did not seem to hurt recruitment: in March 1918, after the picketing of the White House began, 54 more Virginia women joined the National Woman's Party. By the end of the year, the total had risen to 504.[108]

In 1916, perhaps in an effort to prevent further defections by the more militant suffragists, the ESL withdrew its longstanding moratorium on open-air and street meetings, tactics previously considered too radical to be effective in Virginia.[109] In fact, the ESL reported that "street meetings have been held in many of the larger cities of the State with most satisfactory results."[110] Although Valentine would undoubtedly have denied it, the successes of the more radical faction effectively pushed the ESL to accept some of their tactics.

Virginia's NAWSA affiliates also found themselves moving toward support of the NWP's central goal: the federal amendment. In 1916, the state legislature considered and once again rejected a state suffrage amendment. Although the number of legislators voting for the amendment had increased since the 1914 defeat, the 40 to 52 vote in 1916 gave suffragists little hope for the immediate future of suffrage through a state amendment. The Virginia state constitution was extremely difficult to amend. It required approval by two consecutive legislatures and then a public referendum before an amendment became law. Under the circumstances, Virginia suffragists turned to the federal constitutional amendment as the best hope for their enfranchisement.[111] At the state convention in 1917, the Virginia ESL unanimously pledged its support for the federal amendment.[112] The ESL was henceforth committed to the same goal and some of the methods of the NWP.

The Ratification Contest

The turn toward the federal amendment carried a burden, however: the states' rights counteroffensive, the issue of the black vote.[113] And the antisuffragists wasted no time launching an attack, publishing a tract called "The Virginia General Assembly and Woman's Suffrage." The pamphlet concisely summarized the antisuffrage position on the federal amendment:

> We are asked to—
>
> Help trample and destroy the soul and purpose of the principle of State rights;
>
> Disrupt and disturb to confusion and danger our local and State political and social conditions and the peaceful and contented relations of the races;
>
> Double the number of uncertain and dangerous votes and put the balance of political power at the mercy of 165,000 colored women;
>
> And for what?
>
> To gratify the whims or satisfy the pleadings or escape the importunities of a small minority of women.[114]

Still, the suffragists stuck resolutely to their statistical argument. Valentine argued that the federal amendment would not—in fact could not—enfranchise masses of black women, for it "leaves absolutely intact all the other qualifications which the State Constitution provides for a voter." Therefore, even though some black women would vote, "white men and women together" would continue to be in the majority as before.[115]

The Equal Suffrage League decided not to campaign during the 1918 legislative session, since most members of the association were engaged in war work, running Liberty Loan drives, organizing Red Cross benefits, and operating wartime canteens. But equally important, the suffragists were waiting for the outcome of the congressional debate over the Nineteenth Amendment. They felt that it would be a tremendous waste of time and effort to work on a state amendment, dissipating resources needed later for a campaign to ratify the federal amendment.

After Congress sent the Anthony Amendment to the states for ratification, Virginia's legislature considered the measure on two separate occasions. The first time was during the summer of 1919, in a special session called to consider good-roads laws. At the direction of the NAWSA and in keeping with Carrie Chapman Catt's "winning plan," the Virginia ESL agreed to attempt to delay introduction of the federal amendment as long as possible in order to avoid a badly timed rejection vote. Catt and the ESL believed that a federal amendment would have a better chance of ratification in 1920, after more states had agreed to the measure and a new legislature would meet. The ESL obtained the cooperation of Woodrow Wilson and Governor Westmoreland Davis, who agreed not to pressure the legislature to introduce the amendment too soon.[116] NWP activists, however, believed that any opportunity to consider ratification should be taken, and they arranged for the introduction of the amendment. Within days, the House passed a rejection resolution, while supporters of the amendment managed to postpone the issue in the Senate.[117]

With lowered expectations, Virginia's suffragists prepared for the second ratification contest that would be held during the 1920 regular session of the legislature. The ESL appointed a ratification committee in charge of conducting the campaign. Appeals from powerful men outside the state began pouring in, as politicians like Woodrow Wilson and A. Mitchell Palmer pressured the state's legislators to ratify. When the legislature convened in January 1920, an impressive body of suffrage supporters waited for them in Richmond, as both civic and political leaders spoke on behalf of the federal amendment.[118] The stakes were so high, tempers were flaring. Just prior to Carrie Chapman Catt's speech on behalf of ratification in the House of Delegates, "small memoranda" had appeared on the desks of the delegates claiming that Catt believed in "free love" and advocated interracial marriages. Her response that "there was a liar in Virginia," although accurate, served to inflame suffrage opponents.[119]

Two of the federal amendment's strongest opponents, Robert F. Leedy of the Senate and Thomas Ozlin of the House introduced a joint resolution rejecting it. The rejection resolution was adopted in the Senate by 24 to 10 and in the House by 62 to 22. One week later Senator J. E. West introduced a resolution to submit to the voters a state amendment. This passed the Senate by 28 to 11. A similar bill, submitting a state amendment to the voters, passed the House by 67 to 10. However, because of the peculiarities of the Virginia constitution, the state amendment would have to pass again in the assembly of 1921 before its submission to the public for approval. Thus "this vote was merely an empty compliment."[120]

Finally, the legislature voted on a third suffrage measure, which had been introduced by Senator Mapp. In order to avoid holding an emergency session later, Mapp's Qualifications Bill set up the machinery for enrolling women in the electorate should the federal amendment be ratified after the legislative session ended. It would go into effect only in the event the federal amendment received the necessary 36 ratifications. The Mapp bill passed the Senate 30 to 6, and the House 64 to 17.[121]

Resounding as the defeat of the federal amendment was, the roll call votes warrant closer scrutiny, for the question of motivation remains. Did the Virginia legislature register opposition to women voting, or to black women voting? Should the defeat of the Nineteenth Amendment be credited to the power of conservative views on gender, or to the force of white supremacy? Why did some legislators vote for one form of woman suffrage, but against another? It is not always easy to determine just exactly what moves a given representative to cast a specific vote. In the case of a single vote, it may not be possible to interpret motive. For example, John C. Blair's lone vote against the Nineteenth Amendment could have been an expression of antisuffragism, or it could have been a vote for states' rights and white supremacy. But when a delegate votes more than once, motivations can be determined more easily.

Twenty-five senators and delegates can be considered with some certainty to be antisuffragists. They voted solidly against any form of woman suffrage. They voted against both the federal and the state suffrage amendments, or they voted against both the federal amendment and the Mapp Qualifications Bill.[122] Senator Leedy, archenemy of woman suffrage in any form, believed that even the Qualifications Bill was a mistake, for "it will go out over the country that Virginia has receded from her position in this matter."[123] Another seven legislators voted against both state and federal amendments, but then approved of the Mapp bill. At the other end of the spectrum, fifteen legislators recorded their support for woman suffrage in whatever form it might take, by voting for both the federal and state amendments and then for the Mapp Qualifications Bill as well.[124] In the middle of these two positions, another group of legislators took the states' rights stance. At least sixteen men voted to reject the federal amendment but then voted in favor of the largely meaningless state suffrage amendment.[125] The Equal Suffrage League believed that these men were really antisuffragists in disguise and condemned those who insisted on a state amendment in 1920 because they supposedly had long opposed any form of woman suffrage: "The very people who are now clamoring for state action fought this state amendment publicly. . . . Those who urge state rights are frequently insincere. *They do not want suffrage at all*! The Association Opposed to Woman Suffrage is now demanding a state amendment, yet for eight years they *have been blocking that identical program*."[126]

The suffragists' assessment may have been correct in general, but in a few cases, their judgment may have been too harsh. While it could be argued that some of these men were actually antisuffragists who voted for a worthless state amendment in order to woo future women voters, at least two of them had records of supporting state amendment in the past. R. O. Norris, representing Lancaster and Richmond Counties, had voted in favor of the state amendment in 1914 and in 1916; and Robert A. Russell, of Campbell County and Lynchburg, had voted for the state amendment in 1916.

In the votes that took place from 1912 to 1920, there was always present a small core of prosuffrage legislators. In 1912, 12 men voted for woman suffrage; in 1916 the number rose to 40; and by 1920, 95 legislators supported the (moot) state amendment. When the federal amendment was considered, however, the number dropped to 32. Conversely, there was also always present a substantial number of men who opposed woman suffrage in any form. In 1912, 88 votes were cast against the state amendment; in 1916, there were still 52 opponents; and in 1920, 21 legislators continued to oppose the state amendment, even in the nonbinding vote.

Virginia's suffragists, like their coworkers in the rest of the country, blamed the ubiquitous liquor lobby for their defeat. Lila Valentine wrote that "the only possible explanation behind the action of the house is liquor money. . . . The speaker himself was noticeably under the partial influence of liquor. Ozlin and Hudgins are partners of a Richmond German lawyer. Boschen, another bitter opponent, is notably German. Stuart, the other patron of the anti resolution, is the ex-governor's nephew, and I cannot account yet for his action."[127] But, as in other states, the suffragists' conviction that the "liquor lobby" stood behind the antisuffrage movement was only partially true. Virginia had passed a state Prohibition bill in 1914 and had ratified the federal Prohibition amendment in January 1918, both of which occurred before a single woman could vote in the state.[128] Opposition to woman suffrage based on fear of women supporting Prohibition, then, was no longer a viable argument. By 1920, the liquor question was not a central issue, even if liquor interests continued to oppose woman suffrage.

More important to most legislators were the fear of the black vote and the fear of the reform vote. Antisuffragists had pounded away on the "negro domination" theme repeatedly, knowing how well it had worked in past political campaigns. Democrats had used the race issue against William Mahone and the Readjusters in the 1880s. Conservatives had raised the "old spectre of Negro supremacy" against the Populists in 1893, despite the fact that there were no blacks in the Assembly at the time. The technique had worked again in 1900, when Democrats successfully used "negro domination" as a reason to call a constitutional convention and then as an excuse not to put the resultant constitution up for a referendum of approval.[129] This time-honored "racial strategy" worked in 1920 as well. The Democratic Party, which had spent a generation working to reduce the electorate to a manageably predictable size, had established an effective monopoly of public offices in Virginia.[130] The party saw woman suffrage as a threat to its past handiwork. As the agent of railroads and planters, industrialists and business groups, the Democratic Party acted as conservators of the economic and political status quo. Together, the planters and the industrialists had directed the economic development of the state in the postbellum period, and together they had benefited from the policies of the Democratic Party and the state government.[131] Admitting women, black or white, into the electorate threatened to increase the reform vote, and Virginia's political and economic elites would have none of it.

Woman suffrage sentiment had grown sufficiently strong in Virginia to produce a large and vigorous suffrage association. Other progressive reform movements, such as child labor restriction, had attracted support from a large number of the state's urban middle classes. But woman suffrage and other reforms failed in Virginia because of the power of the Democratic Party, which was backed by the money and assistance of planters, railroads, and industrialists. Thanks to the disfranchisement of poor Virginians, both black and white, the Democratic Party generally got what it wanted in the Progressive Era. The opposition could rarely mount a serious political challenge under these circumstances.

Epilogue

In 1920, Puralee Sampson, a fifty-eight-year-old black housewife in Richmond, was a suffragist. Her name never appeared in the newspaper, she never spoke at any suffrage rallies, she never joined a suffrage club. She is unknown to suffrage historians and has been historically invisible. Yet Puralee Sampson was so eager to vote that she went immediately to city hall to register when given the chance. She registered successfully on September 4, 1920, the first black woman to do so in the First Precinct of Madison Ward—and perhaps the first black woman to register in the entire city.[132]

Others followed: Blanch H. Wines, a thirty-year-old domestic worker, Katie D. Pratt, a fifty-three-year-old nurse, Rosa Y. DeWitt, a forty-three-year-old teacher, and others like them all registered and paid their poll taxes the first week the registration books were opened. Black leaders in Richmond did what they could to encourage women to take advantage of their new privilege: large public meetings were held at the Elks Home and St. Lukes Hall to give black women instruction on how to register. Maggie Lena Walker visited city hall several times, demanding that more officials be employed to speed up the registration process and reduce the time black women had to stand in line.[133] Ora Brown Stokes, utilizing the organizational strength of the Richmond Neighborhood Association, petitioned the registrar of voters to appoint black deputies to assist in registering the large numbers of black women desiring to vote.[134] Largely silent in the long debate over woman suffrage, these black women nevertheless expressed their opinions quite firmly at registration time. By the time the books closed, 2,410 black women had successfully registered in Richmond alone.[135]

Not surprisingly, white women registered in larger numbers. And the state suffrage association, no longer needing to agitate for ratification, converted itself into the Virginia League of Women Voters with Adele Clark as president. Like the suffrage association that preceded it, the new league was for whites only. (Clark later recalled that the suffragists "never had the nerve" to enroll black women in the LWV.)[136] Black women therefore formed their own voters league, the Virginia Negro Women's League of Voters, with Ora Brown Stokes as president. Unlike white women, who generally joined the dominant Democratic Party, most black women aligned themselves with the Republicans. Several prominent black women in Richmond joined the National Colored Republican Women.[137]

Yet this initial enthusiasm for political participation dwindled rapidly. Continuing opposition by white conservatives kept the numbers of black voters at a minimal level. Maggie Lena Walker ran for office in 1921 on the "lily-black" Republican ticket, hoping to become the superintendent of public instruction. She and an entire slate of black Republicans lost. While a few white women gained political offices and moved up the ranks of the Democratic Party during the 1920s, the experience of black women in politics was quite different. On election day, 1925, Maggie Walker noted the following in her diary: "Out early today.—and voted an entire Democratic ticket. Why.—no reason.—just voted the ticket.—One party is as good as the other."[138] The promise of change by enfranchisement went unfulfilled.

Yet, even though they were disillusioned by the outcome of the enfranchisement of women, both black and white suffragists continued their respective club work and reform activities. It appeared that women's voluntary associations, and not politics, would continue to be the source of change in the postratification South. Women's clubs and missionary societies continued their efforts to provide services and assistance to the poor of their communities, including the continuing support of the Federation of Colored Women's Clubs for the reformatory for girls in Hampton. Coming together in a coordinating group called the Virginia Women's Council of Legislative Chairmen of State Organizations, women's groups in the state lobbied the legislature on dozens of measures during the 1920s.[139] Moreover, black and white suffragists laid plans for future cooperation. Maggie Walker noted in November 1920 that Adele Clark, "white—political leader" contacted her. Clark wanted to work together with Walker "to plan the study of citizenship."[140] Thus the interracial cooperation movement of the 1920s emerged, with veteran suffragists (black and white) taking the lead.

Conclusion

WOMAN'S RIGHTS

Dame Nature, in her mild [illegible] school,
Has taught her daughters just, how to rule,
Don't think of voting for a single hour,
But through soft words at home
just vote yourself a power.

Wear the "habiliments" with soft and gentle tact
So much, the "lord" will ne'er suspect the fact,
Give love in plenty, but "obey" is sluff,
Each woman's heart knows that fact well enough.

We make the promise, because required to do,
Still all the time "we know a thing or two,"
Tall men can talk, and "lord" as they may,
The little female always gets her way.

Julia Lee Sinks, undated

In August 1920, the thirty-sixth, and final, state ratified the Nineteenth Amendment enfranchising women. And it was Tennessee—a southern state—that provided that final vote. In general, this book has focused on the states where ratification failed. But one must consider the fact that not one but four southern states did ratify the Anthony Amendment. The southern border states of Kentucky, Tennessee, Texas, and Arkansas contributed four of the thirty-six votes required ratifications.

Why would these four states approve a federal amendment, when the rest of the South did not? Why these particular states, and not others? Were there some common features they shared that made them more amenable to a federal amendment? One might reason that all four were "border" states and therefore not completely "southern." But that is an insufficient answer. There is no single, simple explanation.

This study has linked the rise of suffragism in the South to the economic changes maturing at the end of the nineteenth century and to the rise of an urban middle class that economic change helped to produce. But there is no cut-off point, no transition point, after which a state invariably became a suffrage state. The simple formula "urbanization plus industrialization equals suffragism" will not do. For such a formula will not explain why Maryland, with its large urban population and industrial sector, failed to produce sufficient interest in suffragism to ratify the Nineteenth Amendment. (Nor, for that matter, will it explain why states like Utah and Washington, with relatively small urban population, had instituted woman suffrage so early.) The rate of increase or decrease of urban and rural populations does not directly explain suffrage success either. The states with the greatest shift in population from rural to urban from 1900 to 1920 were Florida, Texas, and Maryland (as shown in Table A.28). Of the three, only Texas was notably amenable to woman suffrage.

Racial ratios appear to have some bearing on the ratification question in the South, as the figures in Table A.28 suggest. The four states that did ratify the Anthony Amendment were all ranked quite low in black population as a percentage of the whole. Yet only 3 percentage points separate antisuffrage Virginia and North Carolina from prosuffrage Arkansas. Other factors must have been involved. And, as Suzanne Lebsock has pointed out, southern legislators still rejected woman suffrage in campaigns where race did not appear as an issue, such as the state amendment contests in Virginia in 1912 and 1914. (And they regularly defeated other women's causes where race did not seem to be a factor either, such as the coordinate college plan in Virginia.)[1]

Another possible explanation for the southern record on ratification, suggested by the work of J. Morgan Kousser, is the relationship between two-

party politics and success of suffragism in the state houses. Kousser's analysis of the disfranchisement movement in the South concluded that, after the various suffrage restriction schemes were completed, only a handful of states continued to have anything resembling contested politics. Two of the four ratifying states (Arkansas and Tennessee) each had a vigorous Republican Party.[2] Kousser did not include Kentucky in his analysis, but other scholars attest to the continued strength of the opposition party in that state.[3] And at least one

Political cartoons depicting suffragists and antisuffragists lobbying the Tennessee legislature, 1920 (Courtesy of Tennessee State Library and Archives, Nashville)

historian has suggested that Texas suffragists were able to exploit a factional split within the Democratic Party to gain allies for a state suffrage amendment in 1918.[4]

Of course, two-party politics cannot alone explain suffrage success either. On one hand, North Carolina, whose Republican Party was one of the largest in the South (thanks to continued "mountain republicanism"[5]), firmly rejected both state and federal suffrage amendments. On the other hand, in Louisiana, with its crippled Republican Party, thousands of women exercised tax suffrage; and in Georgia, with a similarly disabled opposition party, thousands more women were voting in municipal elections.

So there does not appear to be a single "litmus test" for predicting successful suffragism. A combination of these variables, however, had much to do with its victory: suffragists gained their biggest victories in places where urban populations were larger, where manufacturing and industry were gaining in importance over agriculture, where racial ratios were such that race did not dominate political discussions, and where political dissent still survived. The outcome of the woman suffrage movement, in fact, provides some evidence as to the location and degree of change taking place in various regions in the South at the turn of the century. The constituency of the southern antisuffrage movement reveals that the planter class still exerted a great deal of political power and economic influence well into the 1910s. As James C. Cobb has written, industry was more important in the southern economy than it had been forty years earlier, "but the plantation still towered above the factory, shaping it and most of the rest of southern society in its own image."[6] But, while still powerful enough to halt woman suffrage in most southern state legislatures, the big agriculture/big business coalition was unable to prevent Congress from adopting the Nineteenth Amendment, reminding planters that, as a group, they no longer wielded influence at the national level. More disturbing, from the southern conservatives' perspective, was that they failed to prevent the ratification of the federal amendment in four southern border states.

Planters and industrialists were most successful in defeating woman suffrage when they could combine the racial fears of white southerners with conservative views on gender and family, and wrap it all in the evocative rhetoric of the Lost Cause. The inclusion of gender and family in the equation permitted conservative women to join, and even lead, the organizational effort. Conservative women at the turn of the century would seldom have lobbied to prevent railroad regulation or to reform the state's tax code, but they felt justified in organizing to protect their homes and families from the perceived dangers of suffragism and individualism. Utilizing the imagery of maternalism, antisuffrage women moved into the public realm in defense of their private sphere. The boundary between the two areas was clearly quite permeable.

This will not be the final word on southern suffragism. There remains much yet to learn about the woman suffrage movement in the South—and the United States. Still notably silent are the voices from the factory floor: we know almost nothing about the opinions of the southern working class on the woman suffrage question. We know that working-class women seldom joined the various suffrage organizations; but why? Did they fear that woman suffrage would increase the power the rising middle class wielded over their lives? Or did they hope that with enfranchisement they might be given more influence in directing labor policy in the New South? Did working-class men desire to keep their women at home? We have little evidence.

We also know far too little about suffragism in the black community. We know of a handful of black middle-class leaders who expressed their opinions on suffrage, but they may not represent the positions of poorer African Americans in the South. The question of state versus federal amendments, so important to white suffragists, never seems to surface in discussions of black suffragism.

Nor do we fully understand the relationship between local suffrage organizations and the state movements. Few local studies have yet been produced, and much work remains to be done. Future studies also need to address the question of women's political participation before 1920: How did women use their ballots when voting for school boards, municipal officers, and presidential electors? How many women voted when given the chance? Did they eschew partisanship, or did they openly align with a party?

Although woman suffrage has fascinated women's historians for more than a generation, the suffrage movement remains an enigma. This regional approach to the subject answers some questions, but many more remain.

APPENDIX

Unless otherwise indicated, all information in the following tables comes from my own biographical database. Information was obtained from a wide variety of sources, including biographical dictionaries, obituaries, census schedules, and city directories. All information so gathered was then categorized and quantified.

TABLE A.1. *Average Age of Women in Alabama, North Carolina, Tennessee, Texas, and Virginia in 1920*

	Suffragists		Antisuffragists	
Alabama	54.4	(N = 57)	52.3	(N = 50)
North Carolina	47.4	(N = 31)	49.1	(N = 15)
Tennessee	46.9	(N = 33)	54.9	(N = 70)
Texas	49.0	(N = 60)	44.0	(N = 27)
Virginia	53.0	(N = 38)	59.0	(N = 38)
Average age of all	50.56	(N = 219)	53.12	(N = 200)

TABLE A.2. *Average Age of Louisiana Women in 1920*

States' Rights Organization	50.1	(N = 34)
NAWSA Suffragists	42.7	(N = 41)

TABLE A.3. *Marital Status in 1920: Percentage of Women Never Married*

	Suffragists		Antisuffragists	
Alabama	(N = 21)	21.0%	(N = 10)	13.5%
North Carolina	(N = 34)	34.0	(N = 3)	10.0
Tennessee	(N = 26)	26.0	(N = 42)	24.4
Texas	(N = 16)	16.0	(N = 5)	9.4
Virginia	(N = 29)	29.0	(N = 13)	24.5
Average of all	(N = 126)	25.2%	(N = 73)	19.1%

Note: 27.7% of the total adult white female population in the United States in 1920 was unmarried (Bureau of the Census, *Abstract of the Fourteenth Census of the United States* [Washington: Government Printing Office, 1923], 217).

TABLE A.4. *Marital Status of Louisiana Women in 1920*

	States' Rights Suffragists		NAWSA Suffragists	
Married[a]	(N=106)	80.9%	(N=67)	76.1%
Unmarried	(N=25)	19.1	(N=19)	21.6
Unknown	—	—	(N=2[b])	2.3
Total	131	100%	88	100%

Sources: Brown, *History of Who's Who in Louisiana* and *Who's Who in Louisiana and Mississippi*; Moore, *Men of the South*; Baton Rouge city directories for 1906, 1911, 1924, and 1947; Chambers, *History of Louisiana*; obituaries in the *Times-Picayune* (indexed by the New Orleans Public Library); and the 1910 federal census returns

[a]includes widows

[b]One woman was always identified as "Mrs." Nixon, but since her father was also named Nixon, it may be that "Mrs." was a courtesy title or was her professional name (as a newspaper columnist). A second woman was only identified as "Doctor," leaving the question of marital status unanswered.

TABLE A.5. *Religious Affiliations of Women in Alabama, North Carolina, Tennessee, Texas, and Virginia (combined)*

	Suffragists	Antisuffragists
Episcopal	47 (25.5%)	57 (42.2%)
Methodist	40 (21.7%)	20 (14.8%)
Presbyterian	35 (19.0%)	22 (16.3%)
Baptist	25 (13.6%)	17 (12.6%)
Christian	13 (7.1%)	2 (1.5%)
Jewish	10 (5.4%)	5 (3.7%)
Catholic	8 (4.3%)	7 (5.2%)
Other	6 (3.3%)	5 (3.7%)
Total	184 (99.9%)	135 (100%)

TABLE A.6. *Religious Affiliation of Louisiana Women*

	States' Rights Women	E. Baton Rouge Parish[a]	NAWSA Women	Orleans Parish[a]	Statewide Church Membership[a]
Episcopalian	31.3%	1.7%	27.3%	3.4%	1.4%
Catholic	21.8	51.3	27.3	75.5	59.1
Presbyterian	21.8	3.5	13.6	2.0	1.4
Jewish	—	—	18.2	1.4	0.5
Baptist	18.8	26.3	9.1	6.5	24.7
Methodist	6.3	13.3	4.5	4.2	10.3

Sources: See Table A.4.

[a]Statistics are taken from Bureau of the Census, *Religious Bodies, 1916* (Washington: Government Printing Office, 1916). Figures are percentages of total church membership, not of total population. The percentage of states' rights advocates, nearly all of whom were from Baton Rouge, were compared to the percentage in East Baton Rouge Parish. The percentage of NAWSA-affiliated suffragists, the majority of whom were from New Orleans, were compared to the percentage in Orleans Parish, as well as to the percentage in the state at large.

TABLE A.7. *Educational Attainments of Women in Alabama, North Carolina, Tennessee, Texas, and Virginia (combined)*

	Suffragists	Antisuffragists
Known no higher education	9 (5.7%)	17 (22.7%)
"Seminary"/"institute"	21 (13.4%)	21 (28.0%)
Some college	44 (28.0%)	16 (21.3%)
Known college graduate	83 (52.9%)	21 (28.0%)
Total	157 (100%)	75 (100%)

Note: Of the known college graduates in this sample, 22 (14%) of suffragists and 6 (8%) of antisuffragists had some postgraduate education.

TABLE A.8. *Average Age of Suffragists in 1920 Who Were Known College Graduates Compared to All Suffragists in Sample*

	Age of Known College Graduates	Age of All Suffragists in Sample[a]
Alabama	38.91 (N = 11)	54.4 (N = 57)
North Carolina	42.33 (N = 15)	47.4 (N = 31)
Tennessee	48.50 (N = 6)	46.9 (N = 33)
Texas	46.89 (N = 19)	49.0 (N = 60)
Virginia	53.33 (N = 6)	53.0 (N = 38)
Average of all	45.0 (N = 57)	50.56 (N = 219)

[a]Figures are from Table A.1.

TABLE A.9. *Women in Paid Work*[a] *in 1920*

	Suffragists	Antisuffragists	
Alabama	17 (N = 100)	6 (N = 74)	[8.1%]
North Carolina	18 (N = 100)	0 (N = 30)	[0.0%]
Tennessee	24 (N = 100)	18 (N = 172)	[10.5%]
Texas	49 (N = 100)	8 (N = 53)	[9.4%]
Virginia	28 (N = 100)	6 (N = 53)	[11.3%]

[a]Includes those listed as "author," "writer," "artist." Some may not have made their livings in such work, but the information available does not distinguish between amateurs and professionals. Totals also include part-time work and those who worked for most of their adult lives but were retired by 1920. (Women who ceased to work at the time of their marriages are not counted as retired.)

TABLE A.10. *Job Types of Women in Louisiana*

	States' Rights Suffragists	NAWSA Suffragists
Doctor	—	1
Nurse	—	1
College professor	1	3
Secondary school teacher	2	1
Music teacher	2	—
Professional administrative	2[a]	1
Bookkeeper/stenographer	3	4
Librarian	1	—
Journalist	1[b]	7
Merchant	1	—
Store clerk	5	—
Operate boarding house	1	1
	N = 20	N = 19

Sources: See Table A.4.

[a]One woman was vice president of a female orphanage, one was elected dean of women at LSU in 1920.

[b]This woman worked as society page editor for her father's newspaper after her husband's death.

TABLE A.11. *Job Types of Women in Alabama, North Carolina, Tennessee, Texas, and Virginia (combined)*

	Suffragists (N = 500)	Antisuffragists (N = 382)
School teacher/librarian	28	7
Writer/author	19	8
Journalist	14	3
Lawyer	11	—
Doctor	8	—
Social worker	7	—
Bookkeeper/stenographer	6	5
College professor	5	3
Artist	5	1
Nurse	4	2
Principal/administrator	4	—
Music teacher	3	4
College president/dean	3	—
Boarding house/hotel proprietor	3	—
Merchant/sales	2	3
State government official	2	—
Court reporter	2	—
Minister	1	—
Banker	1	—
Officer manager	1	—
Real estate agent	1	—
Miscellaneous	5	2
Total	135	38

TABLE A.12. *Job Types of Louisiana States' Rights Suffragists' Husbands (or Fathers[a])*

"Traditional" Professions		"Newer" Professions		Commerce		Government		Manufacturing		Agriculture		Miscellaneous	
doctor	10	professor	7	merchant[b]	14	federal	3		1	farmer/planter	4	Standard Oil	6
lawyer	6	journalist[c]	1	own business	3	state	20			cotton buyer	2		
banker	4	architect	1	real estate agent	5	local	5						
minister	1	civil engineer	2	railroads	3	military	1						
		accountant[d]	2	salesman	2								
		office manager	2										
Total	21		15		27		29		1		6		6
	(20%)		(14%)		(26%)		(28%)		(1%)		(6%)		(6%)

Sources: See Table A.4.
Note: Percentages are rounded and thus do not total 100%. N = 105.
[a]for unmarried women
[b]refers to general merchants
[c]includes editors, publisher
[d]includes bookkeepers

TABLE A.13. *Job Types of Louisiana NAWSA Affiliates' Husbands (or Fathers[a])*

"Traditional" Professions		"Newer" Professions		Commerce		Government		Manufacturing		Agriculture		Miscellaneous	
doctor	4	professor	—	merchant[b]	4	federal	—		—	farmer/planter	—	Standard Oil	—
lawyer	7	journalist[c]	3	own business	4	state	1			cotton buyer	2	auto mechanic	1
banker	1	architect	1	real estate agent	2	local	—						
		civil engineer	—	railroads	1								
		pilot	1	salesman	1								
		office manager	3										
		travel agent	1										
		teacher[d]	1										
Total	12		10		12		1		—		2		1
	(32%)		(26%)		(32%)		(3%)				(5%)		(3%)

Sources: See Table A.4.
Note: Percentages are rounded and thus do not total 100%. N = 38.
[a]for unmarried women
[b]refers to general merchants
[c]includes editors, publishers
[d]includes principals, administrators

TABLE A.14. *Job Types of Husbands (or Fathers[a]) of Alabama, North Carolina, Tennessee, Texas, and Virginia Suffragists (combined)*

"Traditional" Professions		"Newer" Professions		Commerce		Government		Manufacturing	Agriculture		Miscellaneous
doctor	30	professor	13	merchant[b]	22	federal	1	9	farmer/planter	9	1
lawyer	46	journalist[c]	11	own business	28	state	5		stock	6	
banker	14	architect	2	real estate agent	6	local	2		cotton buyer	2	
minister	4	civil engineer	3	railroads	3	military	1				
		accountant[d]	1	salesman	10						
		court reporter	1	truck driver	1						
		telegrapher	1								
		travel agent	1								
		office manager	5								
		teacher[e]	5								
Total	94		43		70		9	9		17	1
	(39%)		(18%)		(29%)		(4%)	(4%)		(7%)	(0.4%)

Sources: See Table A.4.

Note: Percentages are rounded and thus do not total 100%. N = 243.

[a]for unmarried women

[b]refers to general merchants

[c]includes editors, publisher

[d]includes bookkeepers

[e]includes principals, administrators

TABLE A.15. *Job Types of Alabama, North Carolina, Tennessee, Texas, and Virginia Antisuffragists' Husbands (or Fathers[a]) (combined)*

"Traditional" Professions		"Newer" Professions		Commerce		Government		Manufacturing	Agriculture		Miscellaneous
doctor	25	professor	7	merchant[b]	35	federal	3	13	farmer/planter	16	4
lawyer	49	journalist[c]	10	own business	27	state	2		lumber	7	
banker	26	architect	—	real estate agent	8	local	7		stock	2	
minister	5	civil engineer	1	railroads	19	military	1		cotton buyer	4	
		accountant[d]	4	salesman	6						
		office manager	1								
		teacher[e]	3								
Total	105		26		95		13	13		29	4
	(37%)		(9%)		(33%)		(5%)	(5%)		(10%)	(1%)

Sources: See Table A.4.

Note: Percentages are rounded and thus do not total 100%. N = 285.

[a]for unmarried women

[b]refers to general merchants

[c]includes editors, publishers

[d]includes bookkeepers

[e]includes principals, administrators

TABLE A.16. *Number of Women in Voluntary Associations in Alabama, North Carolina, Tennessee, Texas, and Virginia (combined)*

	Suffragists (N = 500)	Antisuffragists (N = 383)
Women's clubs	92	47
Patriotic	54	68
Literary[a]	39	38
School improvement[b]	36	13
Missionary society[c]	33	14
WCTU	30	3
YWCA	24	4
Professional	21	5
Child welfare/labor	15	1
Civic	9	4
Charity	11	2
SACW	9	—
Free kindergarten	7	1
Settlement work	5	1
Peace organization	3	—
Other[d]	5	—
Total	393	201

Note: Women in both groups joined multiple organizations, and all those organizational affiliations are counted. Membership in organizations prior to and including 1920 are listed here.

[a]includes art, music, history clubs

[b]includes library associations, PTA, Mothers Congress, illiteracy campaign

[c]includes Council of Jewish Women, King's Daughters, etc.

[d]includes prison reform, antilynching, free clinic, Consumers League, protective labor laws

TABLE A.17. *Louisiana Legislature's Vote on State Suffrage Amendment (1918)*[a]

Percentage of Parish Population Black (1910)[b]	Number of Parishes	Votes against	Votes for
0–19.9	3	—	6
20–39.9	24	20	44
40–59.9	21	11	31
60–79.9	11	2	21
80–100	5	—	7
Total	64	33	109

[a]House and Senate votes combined, not including "pairs"

[b]Four parishes were formed after 1910 census; their population figures have therefore been taken from 1920 census.

TABLE A.18. *Louisiana Legislature's Vote on State Suffrage Amendment (1920)*[a]

Percentage of Parish Population Black (1920)	Number of Parishes	Votes against	Votes for
0–19.9	5	—	7
20–39.9	25	17	53
40–59.9	23	11	40
60–79.9	7	3	10
80–100	4	2	6
Total	64	33	116

[a]House and Senate votes combined, not including "pairs"

TABLE A.19. *Louisiana Legislature's Vote on Nineteenth Amendment (1920)*[a]

Percentage of Parish Population Black (1920)	Number of Parishes	Votes against	Votes for
0–19.9	5	7	1
20–39.9	25	37	34
40–59.9	23	33	21
60–79.9	7	7	4
80–100	4	5	3
Total	64	89	63

[a]House and Senate votes combined, not including "pairs"

TABLE A.20. *Alabama Legislature's Vote on State Suffrage Amendment (1915)*[a]

Percentage of County Population Black (1910)	Number of Counties	Votes against	Votes for
0–19.9	17	17	6
20–39.9	19	13	17
40–59.9	17	16	21
60–79.9	7	8	9
80–100	7	8	11
Total	67	62	64

[a]House and Senate votes combined, not including "pairs"

TABLE A.21. *Alabama Legislature's Vote on Nineteenth Amendment (1919)*[a]

Percentage of County Population Black (1920)	Number of Counties	Votes against	Votes for
0–19.9	19	5	13
20–39.9	20	20	11
40–59.9	15	28	9
60–79.9	7	16	4
80–100	6	9	1
Total	67	78	40

[a]House and Senate votes combined, not including "pairs"

TABLE A.22. *Profile of Alabama's "Steering Committee to Defeat the Susan B. Anthony Amendment"*

Name	County	Percentage of County Population Black[a]	Occupation	College education	Religion
Faulk	Geneva	16	merchant	none	Baptist
Fletcher[b]	Madison	40	planter	graduate	Presbyterian
Jones[b]	Montgomery	69	lawyer	graduate	Episcopal
Long[c d]	Butler	53	cotton buyer	none	Episcopal
Matthews	Clarke	56	farmer	none	Baptist
Smith	Green	87	doctor	graduate	Baptist
Truss	Jefferson	40	farmer	graduate	n/a
Tunstall[c d]	Hale	79	lawyer	graduate	Episcopal

[a]black population statistics according to 1920 census
[b]son of disfranchiser
[c]served in 1901 disfranchisement convention
[d]known ties to Louisville and Nashville Railroad

TABLE A.23. *North Carolina Legislature's Vote on State Suffrage Amendment (1915)*[a]

Percentage of County Population Black (1910)[b]	Number of Counties	Votes against	Votes for
0–19.9	36	22	21
20–39.9	28	38	14
40–59.9	33	36	13
60–79.9	3	5	1
80–100	—	—	—
Total	100	102	49

[a]House and Senate votes combined, not including "pairs"

[b]Two counties were formed after the 1910 census, so population figures for those counties have been taken from the 1920 census.

TABLE A.24. *North Carolina Legislature's Vote on Nineteenth Amendment (1920)*[a]

Percentage of County Population Black (1920)	Number of Counties	Votes against	Votes for
0–19.9	39	21	30
20–39.9	30	35	21
40–59.9	29	35	13
60–79.9	2	2	—
80–100	—	—	—
Total	100	93	64

[a]House and Senate votes combined, not including "pairs"

TABLE A.25. *Religious Affiliations of North Carolina Legislators Voting on Nineteenth Amendment in 1920*[a]

	Prosuffrage (N = 80)		Antisuffrage (N = 90)	
Episcopal	10%	(N = 8)	12%	(N = 11)
Baptist	30	(N = 24)	26	(N = 23)
Methodist	24	(N = 19)	33	(N = 30)
Presbyterian	20	(N = 16)	11	(N = 10)
Other	6	(N = 5)	4	(N = 4)
Unknown	10	(N = 8)	13	(N = 12)
Total	(100%)		(100%)	

[a]House and Senate combined

TABLE A.26. *Virginia Legislature's Vote on State Suffrage Amendment (1916)*[a]

Percentage of District Population Black (1910)	Votes against	Votes for
0–19.9	13	12
20–39.9	20	15
40–59.9	14	11
60–79.9	5	2
80–100	—	—
Total	52	40

[a]House and Senate votes combined, not including "pairs"

TABLE A.27. *Virginia Legislature's Vote on Nineteenth Amendment (1920)*[a]

Percentage of District Population Black (1920)	Votes against	Votes for
0–19.9	24	14
20–39.9	36	10
40–59.9	24	6
60–79.9	2	2
80–100	—	—
Total	86	32

[a]House and Senate votes combined, not including "pairs"

TABLE A.28. *Comparative Statistics for the Southern States*

	1900	1920	Rank (in 1920)
Urban Population			
Texas	520,800	1,500,000	1 *
Maryland	591,200	869,400	2
Georgia	346,400	727,900	3
Virginia	372,700	119,400	4
Kentucky	467,700	633,500	5 *
Louisiana	366,300	628,200	6
Tennessee	326,600	611,200	7 *
Alabama	216,700	509,300	8
North Carolina	186,800	490,400	9
Florida	107,000	353,500	10
South Carolina	171,300	294,000	11
Arkansas	111,700	290,500	12 *
Mississippi	120,000	240,100	13
Urban Population as Percentage of Whole			
Maryland	49.8	60.0	1
Florida	20.3	36.5	2
Louisiana	26.5	34.9	3
Texas	17.1	32.4	4 *
Virginia	18.3	28.2	5
Kentucky	21.8	26.2	6 *
Tennessee	16.2	26.1	7 *
Georgia	15.6	25.1	8
Alabama	11.9	21.7	9
North Carolina	9.9	19.2	10
South Carolina	12.8	17.5	11
Arkansas	8.5	16.6	12 *
Mississippi	7.7	13.4	13
Total Value of Manufactures			
Texas	119.4m	1000.0m	1 *
North Carolina	94.9m	943.8m	2
Maryland	242.5m	873.9m	3
Georgia	106.7m	693.2m	4
Louisiana	121.2m	676.2m	5
Virginia	132.2m	643.5	6
Tennessee	108.1m	556.3m	7 *
Alabama	80.7m	492.7m	8
Kentucky	154.2m	395.7m	9 *
South Carolina	58.7m	381.5m	10
Arkansas	45.2m	299.3m	11 *

TABLE A.28. *(Continued)*

	1900	1920	Rank (in 1920)
Florida	36.8m	213.3m	12
Mississippi	40.4m	197.7m	13
Racial Ratios: Black Population as Percentage of Whole			
Mississippi	56.17	52.23	1
South Carolina	55.15	51.36	2
Georgia	45.11	41.66	3
Louisiana	43.10	38.94	4
Alabama	42.48	38.35	5
Florida	41.02	34.02	6
Virginia	32.55	29.88	7
North Carolina	31.63	29.83	8
Arkansas	28.12	26.95	9 *
Tennessee	21.65	19.32	10 *
Maryland	17.93	16.87	11
Texas	17.71	15.90	12 *
Kentucky	11.43	9.76	13 *

* ratified Nineteenth Amendment

Source: Donald B. Dodd and Wynelle S. Dodd, *Historical Statistics of the South, 1790–1970* (University: University of Alabama Press, 1973), 3, 5, 7, 9, 15, 17, 19, 21, 23, 25, 27, 29, 31, 33, 35, 37, 39, 41, 47, 49, 51, 53, 55, 57, 59, 61.

TABLE A.29. *Percentage of Women (Black and White Combined) in Work Force in Cities of 100,000 Inhabitants or More, 1900, 1910, 1920*

	1900	1910	1920
Atlanta	42.1	42.8	41.2
Baltimore	30.6	35.3	33.5
Louisville	29.2	35.7	36.3
Memphis	40.8	40.4	37.7
Nashville	36.7	38.6	38.4
New Orleans	26.2	33.5	33.8
Richmond	36.9	41.6	39.1

Source: Joseph A. Hill, *Women in Gainful Occupations, 1870 to 1920*, Census Monograph no. 9 (Washington: Government Printing Office, 1929), 31.

TABLE A.30. *Percentage of Native-born White Women (Over the Age of 16) in Work Force in Cities of 100,000 Inhabitants or More, 1900, 1910, 1920*

	1900	1910	1920
Atlanta	21.7	24.6	30.4
Baltimore	24.1	28.8	29.6
Birmingham	—	17.1	22.1
Dallas	—	—	32.4
Ft. Worth	—	—	25.2
Houston	—	—	27.1
Louisville	22.6	29.8	31.8
Memphis	18.8	22.5	28.1
Nashville	19.2	22.8	28.8
New Orleans	17.8	24.7	28.9
Norfolk	—	—	24.2
Richmond	21.1	25.8	30.2
San Antonio	16.1	—	26.4

Source: Joseph A. Hill, *Women in Gainful Occupations, 1870 to 1920*, Census Monograph no. 9 (Washington: Government Printing Office, 1929), 271.

TABLE A.31. *Percentage of Black Women (Over the Age of 16) in Work Force in Cities of 100,000 Inhabitants or More, 1900, 1910, 1920*

	1900	1910	1920
Atlanta	68.0	74.4	64.1
Baltimore	62.1	70.2	62.7
Birmingham	—	56.5	45.6
Dallas	—	—	63.1
Ft. Worth	—	—	51.2
Houston	—	—	56.9
Louisville	54.4	68.1	54.4
Memphis	61.4	64.1	53.2
Nashville	61.7	66.7	59.8
New Orleans	49.3	60.8	54.5
Norfolk	—	—	52.7
Richmond	60.7	67.9	59.0
San Antonio	53.6	—	60.1

Source: Joseph A. Hill, *Women in Gainful Occupations, 1870 to 1920*, Census Monograph no. 9 (Washington: Government Printing Office, 1929), 275.

NOTES

ABBREVIATIONS USED IN NOTES

ADAH	Alabama Department of Archives and History, Montgomery
ESL	Equal Suffrage League
HWS	*History of Woman Suffrage*
LC	Library of Congress
LHC	Louisiana Historical Center, New Orleans
NAWSA	National American Woman Suffrage Association
NCDAH	North Carolina Division of Archives and History, Raleigh
SHC	Southern Historical Collection, UNC–Chapel Hill
SL	Schlesinger Library, Radcliffe College, Cambridge, Mass.
TSLA	Tennessee State Library and Archives, Nashville
UVA	University of Virginia, Charlottesville
VCU	Special Collections and Archives, James Cabell Library, Virginia Commonwealth University, Richmond
VHS	Virginia Historical Society, Richmond
VSLA	Virginia State Library and Archives, Richmond

PREFACE

1. Here I follow the argument of Anne Firor Scott: "It is beyond any doubt that southern women wanted the vote primarily because of their concern about the place of women in the world, not because of their concern about the place of Negroes" (*Southern Lady*, 183). Recent scholarship emphasizing the racism of southern suffragists includes Wheeler, *New Women of the New South*; Link, *Paradox of Southern Progressivism*; and Mary Martha Thomas, *New Woman in Alabama*. Historians who deemphasize the racism of southern suffragists (or emphasize the racism of the antisuffragists) include Glenda Gilmore, "Gender and Jim Crow"; Lebsock, "Woman Suffrage and White Supremacy"; and Turner, "White-Gloved Ladies."

2. Again, readers familiar with Anne Scott's *Southern Lady* will note the similarities of our arguments. A suffrage movement was dependent upon the growth of a "constituency of self-confident women" and the presence of large numbers of both leaders and followers who had experiences in church societies and women's clubs (*Southern Lady*, 176).

3. Hall, *Revolt Against Chivalry*, 21.

4. My disagreement with scholars like Wheeler falls in the category of degree rather than kind. Where Wheeler argues that "most [southern suffragists] were willing to use racist arguments" (*New Women of the New South*, 101), I contend that most were not. I would place the majority of southern suffragists in the camp that avoided racism as the major argument in behalf of their enfranchisement.

5. Greenwood, *Bittersweet Legacy*, 128.

6. I am referring to Isaac, "Evangelical Revolt."

7. The term "gender roles" is used in this study to mean the commonly prescribed social and economic roles based on the perceived differences between the sexes. Gender roles reflect current economic and social structures, and they can also serve to reinforce those structures (including the current power relationships within a given society). As "acquired characteristics" or as patterns of learned traits, manifestations of gender can change and be changed. Such changes in themselves give evidence to other contemporary currents in society. See Joan Scott, "Gender: A Useful Category of Historical Analysis."

8. Brian Harrison, writing about the antisuffrage movement in Great Britain, noted that the odds that institutional records for the losing side would survive were understandably smaller than for the winners. He quoted a leading English antisuffragist who, after the campaign ended unsuccessfully, "went through the whole of the sad correspondence that I had accumulated . . . and decided that there was no object in keeping it since it would never interest any one and the cause had been lost" (*Separate Spheres*, 14).

9. Readers interested in the compiled raw data are directed to Appendix B of my dissertation, "Those Opposed."

10. Wheeler's *New Women of the New South* is one of the few works to recognize that the leaders of the suffrage movement were in fact not typical of the rank and file (p. xix).

11. More specifically: Tennessee (upper South; strong antisuffragists; ratified Nineteenth Amendment); Virginia (upper South; strong antisuffragists; rejected Nineteenth Amendment); North Carolina (upper South; weak antisuffragists; rejected Nineteenth Amendment); Texas (lower South; strong antisuffragists; ratified Nineteenth Amendment); Alabama (lower South; strong antisuffragists; rejected Nineteenth Amendment); and Mississippi (lower South; weak antisuffragists; rejected Nineteenth Amendment). However, in the end, Mississippi's antisuffrage "movement" was so weak as to be nearly nonexistent. It did not provide enough numbers to use for comparisons. (Louisiana receives separate treatment in Chapter 6, as an example of the states' rights faction.)

12. Lastly, some notes on terminology: First, defining what is "southern" and what is not is a field of history all to its own. For purposes of this study, "the South" consists of the eleven former Confederate states, plus Kentucky and Maryland. It is both as useful, and as arbitrary, as any other definition. Second, since both the suffrage and antisuffrage organizations were for whites only, the reader should remember that the cast of characters herein is white, except where specifically identified as African American. Third, even though the suffragists themselves called the National American Woman Suffrage Association, "the National" for short, this study will use the abbreviation NAWSA, in order to distinguish between this and other national organizations that also appear in the text (such as the National Association Opposed to Woman Suffrage). And finally, although it should need no mention, "suffragist" is the proper term to refer to those who supported woman suffrage. The word "suffragette," although widely (mis)used, refers only to that faction of British activists known for militant publicity techniques. I feel certain that Laura Clay, for example, would be horrified to see her letters in a collection labeled "Woman Suffragette Papers," as they

are in the Tulane University Library. (See Wheeler, *New Women of the New South*, 76, for Clay's reaction to being identified as a suffragette.)

CHAPTER 1

1. General histories of the woman suffrage movement include: Catt and Shuler, *Woman Suffrage and Politics*; Flexner, *Century of Struggle*; Kraditor, *Ideas of the Woman Suffrage Movement*; Morgan, *Suffragists and Democrats*; Scott and Scott, *One Half the People*; Sinclair, *Better Half*; and Stanton et al., *History of Woman Suffrage*.

2. Ellen Carol DuBois speculates that the woman suffrage movement was the first modern mass political movement, in "Working Women, Class Relations, and Suffrage Militance," 35. According to Jane Hunter, the women's missionary movement should be considered the largest women's movement. See Hunter, *Gospel of Gentility*.

3. Scott and Scott, *One Half the People*, 14.

4. A minor historical debate has developed over the interpretation of the split of 1869. Ellen Carol DuBois sees the split as ultimately strengthening the women's movement, since it helped to create a movement led by women only. Kathleen Barry argues that the division had the effect of narrowing the movement, and reducing its radicalism to reformism. See Barry, *Susan B. Anthony*, and DuBois, *Feminism and Suffrage*.

5. Scott and Scott, *One Half the People*, 16–17.

6. Riegel, "Split of the Feminist Movement in 1869," 493.

7. Reading through the chapters of Stanton et al., *History of Woman Suffrage*, from these years, one is struck by the repetition of the reports: "The usual" congressional hearings were held, Mrs. X gave a thorough report "as usual," "the usual" question and answer session was held. The editors of the *History* themselves appear aware of the monotony of these years.

8. See Flexner, *Century of Struggle*, ch. 16.

9. In 1896, Idaho granted women the right to vote, the last suffrage victory until Washington did so in 1910.

10. Beeton, *Women Vote in the West*, 150.

11. Fuller, *Laura Clay and the Woman's Rights Movement*, 139. Both the Congressional Union and the Southern States Woman Suffrage Conference will be discussed in more detail below.

12. O'Neill, *Everyone Was Brave*, 122. Louisiana's Kate Gordon was one of several dissatisfied suffragists who had begun "conspiring" to end Shaw's presidency. See Gordon to "My Dear Insurgents," 3 July 1911, Schlesinger Library, Radcliff College. Had Shaw not agreed to step down when she did, it is very possible that a civil war within the ranks might have occurred at a critical time in the organization's history.

13. Flexner, *Century of Struggle*, 292.

14. For example, Kate Gordon reported that her mother had attended a woman's rights convention in the 1850s (*Daily Picayune*, 7 July 1901). Elizabeth Meriwether registered her protest against taxation without representation in 1871 and joined the NWSA in 1876 as an individual member from Tennessee (Berkeley, "Elizabeth Avery Meriwether," 402). Priscilla Holmes Drake of Huntsville, Ala., affiliated with the NWSA as early as 1868. *HWS* 3:830.

15. Kearney, *Slaveholder's Daughter*, 119.

16. Jean Friedman, *Enclosed Garden*, is one work that very directly addresses the issue of southern exceptionalism. The following paragraph is a summary of her central argument.

17. See for example, Varon, " 'We Mean to Be Counted.' "

18. The experience of the Grimke sisters of South Carolina highlights the difficulty of being a female abolitionist in the South. See Lerner, *Grimke Sisters from South Carolina*.

19. Degler, *At Odds*, 305.

20. Shadron, "Out of Our Homes," 9.

21. Kilman, "Southern Collegiate Women," 176.

22. Judith Wellman, a recent scholar of "northern" suffragism has discovered a similar relationship between constitution making and suffragism has found that the New York state constitutional conventions of 1821 and 1846 both produced a groundswell of woman suffragism, as the lawmakers discussed just which groups of citizens deserved the right to vote ("Seneca Falls Women's Rights Convention," 19–20).

23. Winegarten and McArthur, eds., *Citizens at Last*, xi; A. Taylor, "Woman Suffrage Movement in North Carolina," 45, and "Woman Suffrage Movement in Arkansas," 18; *HWS* 3:805–6.

24. *HWS* 6:248n; Carol Clare, "Woman Suffrage Movement in Virginia," 2–3. This early suffrage club only lasted two years; Terborg-Penn, "Nineteenth Century Black Women and Woman Suffrage," 16.

25. Anne Scott indirectly made the connection between constitution making and rising suffragism (*Southern Lady*, 172).

26. A. Taylor, *A Short History of the Woman Suffrage Movement in Tennessee*, 15–16.

27. *HWS* 4:678. Marjorie Spruill Wheeler has astutely compared this to the strategy of western conservatives who used woman suffrage as a tool to consolidate their political position. In several western states, woman suffrage was a means to another political end, not an end in itself. Wheeler, *New Women of the New South*, 101.

28. *HWS* 4:678.

29. Ibid., 3:789.

30. Ibid., 830.

31. Ibid., 819.

32. *HWS* 4:964.

33. Ibid., 184.

34. See also Wheeler, *New Women of the New South*, 20–22.

35. Ella Harrison to Dear Pa, 1 March 1897, Harrison Collection, SL.

36. *HWS* 4:222.

37. Fuller, *Laura Clay and the Woman's Rights Movement*, 72.

38. Wheeler, *New Women of the New South*, 43.

39. Suzanne Bynum to Lila Meade Valentine, 10 October 1913, Valentine Papers, VHS.

40. A. Taylor, "Woman Suffrage Movement in Arkansas," 19.

41. Sims, "Woman Suffrage Movement in Texas," 18–20.

42. A. Taylor, "Woman Suffrage Movement in Florida," 42.

43. Hewitt, "Politicizing Domesticity," 24. Many further examples of this trend

exist: Mary Martha Thomas noted that Alberta Taylor established the first suffrage club in Huntsville after having visited the suffrage state of Colorado (*New Woman in Alabama*, 153). And Lila Meade Valentine of Virginia traveled to England, where she was first influenced by suffragism (L. Taylor, "Lila Meade Valentine," 481).

44. *HWS* 4:251.

45. Ibid., 5:59.

46. Wheeler, *New Women of the New South*, 118–19.

47. Ibid., 122–25.

48. Disfranchisement will be discussed in much more detail in Chapter 2.

49. Tipton, " 'It Is My Duty,' " 18. Belle Kearney later claimed that she was responsible for the original suggestion, but I have not been able to substantiate her assertion. Mary Martha Thomas has pointed out that the Mississippi constitutional convention considered woman suffrage as a means of white supremacy "with little or no organized female support" (*New Woman in Alabama*, 124).

50. In 1892, Arkansas added a poll tax and in 1906 added a white primary to complete its disfranchisement scheme (Niswonger, *Arkansas Democratic Politics*, 20–21).

51. Fuller, *Laura Clay and the Woman's Rights Movement* , 62.

52. Lee Allen, "Woman Suffrage Movement in Alabama" (M.A. thesis), 10.

53. The Louisiana convention did permit women taxpayers to vote on tax issues only.

54. The *History of Woman Suffrage* hinted at this relationship in its chapter on Alabama: "Actual work for woman suffrage in Alabama began in 1890, at the time the constitutional convention of Mississippi was in session" (*HWS* 4:465).

55. See Kearney's statement in *HWS* 5:83.

56. Mary Martha Thomas, *New Woman in Alabama*, 130–31.

57. Wheeler, *New Women of the New South*, 121.

58. Ibid., 102.

59. Lee Allen is one of the few historians to note the relationship between final disfranchisement of southern black males and the beginning of the doldrums in the southern suffrage movement ("Woman Suffrage Movement in Alabama," *Alabama Review*, 85).

60. A. Taylor, "Woman Suffrage Movement in Florida," 44.

61. Texas also had an earlier period of decline when its state association split in two over the question of inviting Susan B. Anthony to speak in the state (Gammage, "Quest for Equality," 13).

62. Merideth, "Mississippi Woman's Rights Movement," 43.

63. A. Taylor, "South Carolina . . .: The Later Years," 126.

64. A. Taylor, "Woman Suffrage Movement in Arkansas," 19, 29.

65. Ella Harrison to her father, 7, 27 March 1897, Harrison Collection, SL.

66. For example, unlike the national movement, the southern suffragists had not yet encountered organized opposition. Among the historians who have seen the southern doldrums as a reflection of the national doldrums are Wygant, "A Municipal Broom," 118, and Arendale, "Tennessee and Women's Rights," 63.

67. North Carolina was the last state to organize a state suffrage association, in 1913.

68. A. Taylor, *A Short History of the Woman Suffrage Movement in Tennessee*, 8.

69. *HWS* 6:4.

70. Carol Clare, "Woman Suffrage Movement in Virginia," 31–35.

71. *HWS* 6:580.

72. Ibid., 5:490.

73. See Grimes, *Puritan Ethic and Woman Suffrage*, 125.

74. Kraditor, "Tactical Problems of the Woman Suffrage Movement in the South," 291.

75. See Strom, "Leadership and Tactics in the American Woman Suffrage Movement." Washington enfranchised its women in 1910, breaking the fourteen-year period of the doldrums. In 1911, California became the largest and most important state thus far to institute woman suffrage. And Oregon, Arizona, and Kansas all granted the vote in 1912.

76. Jean Friedman, *Enclosed Garden*, 121.

77. See Sidney R. Bland ("Fighting the Odds," 32) for one of the most succinct statements of the relationship between southern progressive reform movements and the revitalization of the suffrage movement.

78. Doyle, *New Men, New Cities, New South*, 9. See also Woodward, *Origins of the New South*, ch. 5.

79. William Miller, *Memphis During the Progressive Era*, 43; Ayers, *Promise of the New South*, 20.

80. Doyle, *New Men, New Cities, New South*, 11.

81. William Miller, *Memphis During the Progressive Era*, 181.

82. Ibid., 44.

83. Tintagil Club, *Official Guide to the City of Montgomery, Alabama*, 60.

84. Doyle, *New Men, New Cities, New South*, 10.

85. See Gaston, *New South Creed*.

86. For a local study that supports this line of reasoning, see Turner, "White-Gloved Ladies."

87. The literature on the southern progressive movement is voluminous, although most monographs have focused on single states, individual cities, or individual reformers rather than the region as a whole. A recent exception to this generalization is Link, *Paradox of Southern Progressivism*.

88. Hanmer, "Divine Discontent," 27.

89. Quoted by Anne Scott, "After Suffrage: Southern Women in the 1920s," 298.

90. Wheeler, *New Women of the New South*, xx, also suggests that the prime motivation for suffragism was dissatisfaction with the management of the New South.

91. Mayo, *Southern Women in the Recent Educational Movement*, 188.

92. Kilman, "Southern Collegiate Women," 49. Not surprisingly, the one division A rated school in the South, Randolph-Macon, was the home of an impressively large college suffrage club: 150 members in 1914 (Stites, "Inconceivable Revolution in Virginia," 113).

93. Talbot and Rosenberry, *History of the American Association of University Women*, 48.

94. Woody, *History of Women's Education in the United States*, 188.

95. McCandless, "Progressivism and the Higher Education of Southern Women," 303–7.

96. Gordon, *Gender and Higher Education*, 49. The SACW merged with the Association of Collegiate Alumnae in 1921 to form the American Association of University Women. See also McCandless, "Progressivism and the Higher Education of Southern Women," 319–21.

97. This also explains why so many southern women who had the means to do so attended colleges outside the South. Anne Scott pointed out that nearly half of the members of the SACW in 1913 had degrees obtained at northern and western institutions (*Southern Lady*, 115).

98. Newell, "Mary Munford and Higher Education for Women in Virginia," 32.

99. Kilman, "Southern Collegiate Women," 115–20.

100. Doyle, *New Men, New Cities, New South*, 89–93.

101. Quoted by McCandless, "Progressivism and the Higher Education of Southern Women," 311.

102. Fenwick, *Who's Who Among the Women of San Antonio*, 23.

103. Quoted by A. Taylor, "Woman Suffrage Movement in Florida," 50.

104. Kearney, *Slaveholder's Daughter*, 112.

105. Anne Scott, *Southern Lady*, 110.

106. See Tables 29–31 in the Appendix.

107. Joseph Hill, *Gainful Occupations*, 40, 195.

108. Ibid., 41, 193.

109. Ibid., 193. Of course, the vast majority of women who worked for wages worked in factory, agricultural, or domestic work.

110. See Chapter 4 and the Appendix.

111. Mary Martha Thomas, *New Woman in Alabama*, 3, has made this same observation.

112. Lee Allen, "Woman Suffrage Movement in Alabama," *Alabama Review*, 88

113. Shadron, "Out of Our Homes," 9.

114. Quoted by Salmond, *Miss Lucy of the CIO*, 11.

115. Bordin, *Women and Temperance*, 52, 76–78.

116. Baines, *Story of the Texas White Ribboners*, 26.

117. Mary Martha Thomas, "'New Woman' in Alabama," 164–65. In her recent full-length study, Thomas has claimed that the WCTU in Alabama organized first in small towns and rural areas before moving to the larger cities (*New Woman in Alabama*, 5, 14). She does not offer an explanation for this apparent contradiction to the more general patterns of organization.

118. Beard, *W.C.T.U. in the Volunteer State*, 7, 63.

119. Sims, "'Sword of the Spirit,'" 395.

120. Salem, *To Better Our World*, 36–37; Mary Martha Thomas, *New Woman in Alabama*, 17–20.

121. Quoted in Bordin, *Women and Temperance*, 52.

122. Kearney, *Slaveholder's Daughter*, 118.

123. Beard, *W.C.T.U. in the Volunteer State*, 9.

124. Bordin, *Women and Temperance*, 82; Mary Martha Thomas, *New Woman in Alabama*, 15; Jean Friedman, *Enclosed Garden*, 120.

125. Baines, *Story of Texas White Ribboners*, 27.

126. Marchiafava, "Law Enforcement on the Urban Frontier," 92.

127. Glenda Gilmore, "Gender and Jim Crow," 101; Greenwood, *Bittersweet Legacy*, 88–90, 110–13.

128. Beard, *W.C.T.U. in the Volunteer State*, 12.

129. Lee Allen, "Woman Suffrage Movement in Alabama" (M.A. thesis), 17.

130. Ibid., 57. Alabama enacted a dry law in 1915. Professor Thomas has argued that, in Alabama at least, the WCTU was more important than any other organization in developing suffragism in the women of the state (*New Women in Alabama*, 12, 16.) Mary Merideth has concluded that the Mississippi suffrage movement "unquestionably was linked with the temperance crusade" ("Mississippi Woman's Rights Movement," 15). A charter member of the Nashville suffrage league noted that the organizers of the league had belonged to the local WCTU. Sims, " 'Powers that Pray,' " 206.

131. Ella Harrison to Dear Pa, 18 March 1897, Harrison Collection, SL.

132. Gammage, "Quest for Equality," 13–14. On women's clubs in the South, see also Ross, "New Woman as Club Woman."

133. Sims, "Foundation for a Sisterhood," 2.

134. Bowie, *Sunrise in the South*, 49.

135. Price, "Development of Leadership," 130, 135.

136. This model of women's activism has become almost commonplace in the historical literature and is described in much more depth in Anne Scott, "New Woman in the New South," and *Southern Lady*, chs. 6 and 7, and in Lemons, *Woman Citizen*.

137. Fenwick, *Who's Who Among the Women of San Antonio*, 19–20.

138. Ibid., 20.

139. Ibid., 23.

140. Winegarten and McArthur, eds., *Citizens at Last*, 28. Other state federations were slower to endorse the suffrage reform, for example, Alabama in 1918.

141. *HWS* 6:2.

142. William Miller, *Memphis During the Progressive Era*, 110.

143. Janelle Scott, "Local Leadership in the Woman Suffrage Movement," 8.

144. Glenda Gilmore, "Gender and Jim Crow," 402–3.

145. Bowie, *Sunrise in the South*, 156.

146. Lerner, "Early Community Work of Black Club Women," 159; see also Salem, *To Better Our World*, and Neverdon-Morton, *Afro-American Women of the South*.

147. See *The Crisis* 10 (August 1915). Burroughs quote on page 10.

148. Lebsock, "Woman Suffrage and White Supremacy," 80.

149. Salem, *To Better Our World*, 128, 40.

150. Jacquelyn Dowd Hall has noted that in Texas after 1915, the state leaders were women in their early thirties, educated in Texas colleges and experienced in business and professional work outside the home (*Revolt Against Chivalry*, 26.) My research shows the rank-and-file membership of the southern suffrage associations to be a decade older than that (see Chapter 3).

151. Janelle Scott, "Local Leadership in the Woman Suffrage Movement," 12.

152. Rome, Georgia, published an official organ in 1915. Florida, Virginia, and Alabama all published state journals for a short time.

153. Janelle Scott, "Local Leadership in the Woman Suffrage Movement," 8; Wygant, "A Municipal Broom," 124

154. A. Taylor, "South Carolina . . .: The Later Years," 307.

155. *HWS* 6:134.

156. A. Taylor, "South Carolina . . .: The Later Years," 302.

157. See sketch in Powell, ed., *Dictionary of North Carolina Biography*.

158. List of state membership committees, 1915, National Woman's Party Papers, ser. 2, sec. 9, membership department (reel no. 87), LC.

159. Wheeler, *New Women of the New South*, 170.

160. Specifically: 17 members in Alabama, 55 in Arkansas, 28 in Florida, 26 in Georgia, 21 in Kentucky, 38 in Louisiana, 361 in Maryland, 7 in Mississippi, 43 in North Carolina, 27 in South Carolina, 139 in Tennessee, 182 in Texas, and 401 in Virginia. From Annual Report of the Membership Department, 1916–17, National Woman's Party Papers, ser. 2, sec. 9 (reel no. 87), LC.

161. Kate Gordon and the SSWSC will be given fuller treatment in Chapter 6. Only a brief summation will be given here.

162. See Kenneth Johnson, "Kate Gordon and the Woman-Suffrage Movement."

163. Gilley, "Kate Gordon and Louisiana Woman Suffrage," 300.

164. Lee Allen, "Woman Suffrage Movement in Alabama" (M.A. thesis), 62, emphasis mine.

165. See Chapter 7.

166. *HWS* 6:209.

167. Gilley, "Kate Gordon and Louisiana Woman Suffrage," 292–93. According to the 1900 census, there were 74,313 white women age 20 and greater living in New Orleans. This would mean that approximately 13.5 percent of adult white women voted in this election.

168. *HWS* 6:120.

CHAPTER 2

1. Kearney, *Slaveholder's Daughter*, 120.

2. *HWS* 6:641–42.

3. Three recent women's history textbooks, designed for use in college classrooms, are indicative of this tendency: Evans, *Born for Liberty*, does not mention antisuffragists at all; Riley, *Inventing the American Woman*, discusses antisuffragists in terms of immigrants and liquor dealers; and Banner, *Women in Modern America*, devotes a single sentence to female antisuffragists, calling them "socially prominent women." The antisuffragists have received far less attention by historians than the suffragists, and most analyses ignore the differences in southern antisuffragism and that of the rest of the country. When historians do pay attention to the existence of female antisuffragists, they tend to separate the activities of men and women completely. See Thurner, "Better Citizens Without the Ballot"; Mambretti, "Battle Against the Ballot"; and Stevenson, "Women Anti-Suffragists in the 1915 Massachusetts Campaign."

4. The female southern antisuffragists who are analyzed here were identified primarily through membership lists published in various newspapers and journals, and from listings of officers on letterhead stationery. Names of male antisuffragists exam-

ined here came from two sources: membership rosters and legislative roll call votes. On average, approximately 100 female antisuffragists from each state were identified for analysis. In addition, 100 prosuffrage workers from each state were chosen randomly from membership lists in both manuscript collections and in published sources. Especially important here was the six volume *History of Woman Suffrage*, with its reports from each state, and Clarke, *Suffrage in the Southern States*, which listed not only state officers but local suffrage leaders as well. All available information pertaining to the social, economic, and political backgrounds of the people involved in the southern suffrage contest was then collected. The data came from a wide range of sources, primarily biographical dictionaries, newspaper obituaries, city directories, and the manuscript population schedules of the U.S. Census for 1910 and 1920. The information in its raw form can be viewed in the Appendix of my unpublished dissertation. The statistical compilations appear in the Appendix of this book.

5. The long and complicated debate about the hegemony of the planter class began in 1965 with Genovese's *Political Economy of Slavery*, in which Genovese argues that the planter class dominated the southern political economy. Challengers to Genovese's model, including Escott, *After Secession*, and Michael Johnson, *Toward a Patriarchal Republic* generally have focused on manifestations of discontent by nonslaveholders. Much of the complication stems from disagreement over definitions of key concepts such as "class," "hegemony," and "power." In the following discussion, I contend that the "planter class" (those with land, wealth, power, and at one time, slaves) was a class-conscious ruling elite who continued to exert powerful influence over southern politics and the economy throughout the period under discussion. "Exerting influence" does not mean the planter class had a monopoly of power, nor does it mean that non-elites never challenged their rule. (In fact, the outcome of the suffrage movement itself is evidence of the waning power of the planter class during the period.)

6. Cobb, "Beyond Planters and Industrialists."

7. Billings, *Planters and the Making of a "New South,"* 60–61, 65–67; Wood, *Southern Capitalism*, 34.

8. Genovese, *Political Economy of Slavery*, 191. On Pratt, see also Randall Miller, "Daniel Pratt's Industrial Urbanism."

9. These men all became active in the opposition to woman suffrage.

10. Billings, *Planters and the Making of a "New South,"* 77; Rabinowitz, *First New South*, 24, 84.

11. Rabinowitz, *First New South*, 86.

12. Ayers, *Promise of the New South*, 64.

13. Ibid., 37; Escott, *Many Excellent People*, 175–79. See also Hahn, *Roots of Southern Populism.*

14. Niswonger, *Arkansas Democratic Politics*, 17.

15. Hahn, *Roots of Southern Populism*, 283–84.

16. Escott, *Many Excellent People*, 252. On the interracialism of the Populists (and the limitations on their interracialism), see also Woodward, *Origins of the New South*, 255–58. On blacks in the Populist movement, see Gaither, *Blacks and the Populist Revolt.*

17. Niswonger, *Arkansas Democratic Politics*, 17. Escott, *Many Excellent People*, 185–86.

18. Hackney, *Populism to Progressivism*, 43.

19. Franklin and Moss, *From Slavery to Freedom*, 238. On lynching, see Raper, *Tragedy of Lynching*.

20. Hackney, *Populism to Progressivism*, 149. On the historical background and economic conditions of Dallas County, see Barney, "Ambivalence of Change."

21. As discussed in Chapter 1.

22. Kousser, *Shaping of Southern Politics*, 191.

23. Winston, *It's a Far Cry*, 237. Winston's brother George was president of the University of North Carolina and later led the antisuffrage movement in his state. Another brother, Robert, was a law partner to Charles B. Aycock, prominent Democratic demagogue and antisuffragist.

24. Escott, *Many Excellent People*, 254.

25. Grantham, *Hoke Smith*, 161.

26. Hackney, *Populism to Progressivism*, 153. Once started, the pace of disfranchisement was rapid: Tennessee in 1889–90, Mississippi and Florida in 1890, South Carolina in 1895, Louisiana in 1898, North Carolina in 1900, Alabama in 1901, Virginia in 1902, and Georgia in 1908. See Kousser, *Shaping of Southern Politics*, 238–40.

27. The Democratic Party in Alabama, Virginia, North Carolina, and Georgia went on record promising not to disfranchise whites (Lewinson, *Race, Class, and Party*, 86; Cell, *Highest Stage of White Supremacy*, 121, 185).

28. *Advertiser*, 3 March 1913 (editorial).

29. Lockwood, *Woman Suffrage a Menace to the South*, 3.

30. Williamson, *Crucible of Race*, 513.

31. Mathews and De Hart, *Sex, Gender, and the Politics of ERA*, 7.

32. James A. Gray to A. M. Scales, 25 May 1920, Equal Suffrage Collection, NCDAH.

33. Sam B. Cook to Underwood, 13 January 1915, Oscar Underwood Papers, Box 36, ADAH.

34. Advisory Committee Opposed to Woman Suffrage, "The Virginia General Assembly and Woman's Suffrage," undated pamphlet in Southern Pamphlet Collection, Rare Books Division, University of North Carolina-Chapel Hill.

35. Evans Johnson, *Oscar W. Underwood*, 71–73.

36. Mabry, "Disfranchisement of the Negro in Mississippi," 321; *HWS* 6:338.

37. Barr, *Reconstruction to Reform*, 210.

38. William Larsen, *Montague of Virginia*, 3–5, and 83.

39. A complete list of disfranchisers who later became antisuffragists would be lengthy indeed, and such will not be attempted here. A few additional examples will suffice. In addition to those already named, other prominent antisuffragists that were veterans of the disfranchisement movement included U.S. Senator Furnifold Simmons of North Carolina, U.S. Senator Carter Glass of Virginia, and Congressman James Thomas Heflin of Alabama, among many others. Furthermore, a large number of men who opposed the enfranchisement of women were directly related to men earlier active in the black disfranchisement effort. Edward Almon of Tuscumbia, Alabama, was an antisuffragist, while his nephew, D. C. Almon, of Lawrence County was a disfranchiser. John Bankhead Jr. of Alabama wrote the state's disfranchisement clause of the 1901 constitution; his father, John Sr. (a member of the Ku Klux Klan during Reconstruction), worked against the Susan B. Anthony Amendment in the U.S. Sen-

ate. Shelby Fletcher of Huntsville, Alabama, was on the steering committee to defeat woman suffrage in the Alabama House in 1919; his father, A. S. Fletcher, had been an active disfranchiser in the 1901 constitutional convention.

40. Burts, *Richard Irvine Manning*, 21, 25, 188, 214.

41. Haas, *Political Leadership in a Southern City*, 28; Reynolds, *Machine Politics in New Orleans*, 5. Behrman did "recant" his opposition to woman suffrage just prior to the legislative vote on the Nineteenth Amendment, but he did so only after it was certain that the amendment would fail regardless of his change of public position.

42. A remarkable number of suffrage opponents were direct descendants of antebellum legislators, officeholders, and other important political leaders. James Thomas Heflin, a congressman from Montgomery who voted against the federal suffrage amendment, was the son of the largest slaveholder in Randolph County and the grandson of a state legislator from the 1840s. Jeff Davis Clayton, who voted against the federal suffrage amendment as a state representative from Barbour County, Alabama, was the grandson of an 1850s state representative and Confederate general and the great-grandson of an 1830s state legislator. Samuel A. Ashe of the North Carolina States' Rights Defense League was the son of William Ashe, a congressman from the 1850s and member of the secession convention. Richard Dillard, a doctor from Edenton, North Carolina, joined the States' Rights Defense League as well; his father had been a state senator in 1856, a member of the secession convention, and a doctor in the service of the Confederate army. Other examples include Malcolm Graham of Prattville, Alabama, who voted against the Nineteenth Amendment; his father was an antebellum legislator in Texas. Foster K. Hale, an antisuffrage legislator from Mobile, was the son of an antebellum legislator, F. S. Hale, who also was a member of the Confederate Congress. Thomas W. Oliver, who voted against the Anthony Amendment as a state representative from Montgomery, was the son of a planter and the grandson of a state senator from the 1840s. James Edwards, state representative from Pike County, Alabama, voted against the Nineteenth Amendment; his grandfather also had sat in the Alabama House before the Civil War. Harry W. Stubbs, representative from Martin County, North Carolina, voted against woman suffrage amendments in 1915, 1917, 1919, and 1920; his father was an antebellum legislator. Robert Barrett, state representative of Warren County, Mississippi, was the grandson of George Crawford, antebellum governor of Georgia. William S. Barry, representative from Leflore County, Mississippi, was the son of the president of the state's secession convention. Mississippi state senator Clarence E. Morgan, who voted against both state and federal suffrage amendments in 1920, was the grandson of a state representative from 1837. Joseph Rice, state representative from Oktibbeha County, Mississippi, voted against the state suffrage amendment in 1918; his grandfather was an antebellum state senator. Fernand Mouton, lieutenant governor of Louisiana, was the grandnephew of former governor and U.S. senator Alexander Mouton. Adolph D. Starns, a state representative from Livingston, Louisiana, was the grandson of John Kinchen, state legislator in 1840; Starns voted against the Anthony Amendment but for the state woman suffrage amendment of 1918.

Women of the southern antisuffrage movement also shared this antebellum political lineage. Nina Pinckard, president of the Southern Rejection League, was the grandniece of John C. Calhoun. Mildred Lewis Rutherford, an officer in the Georgia antisuffrage association and the Southern Rejection League, was the niece of Howell Cobb, prewar congressman and presidential cabinet member. Mattie Elsberry, who was on the executive committee of the Alabama antisuffrage league, was the daughter of a state senator from 1857 who had also served as personal secretary to Jefferson Davis during the war. Anna Brown Boykin of Richmond, who was on the executive committee of the Virginia antisuffrage association, was the granddaughter of Confederate general and antebellum state senator Francis Boykin. Ellen Goldthwaite of Montgomery, a member of the local antisuffrage league, was the granddaughter of a state supreme court justice from the 1850s and the great-granddaughter of an antebellum congressman. Molly Elliot Seawell, an antisuffrage writer from Virginia, was the grandniece of President John Tyler. Other antisuffrage women from antebellum political families include Nellie Parker Henson of Richmond, whose grandfather was Speaker of the House of Delegates before the war; and Virginia Payne Hunton, whose father was a brigadier general in the Confederate army and whose father-in-law (Eppa Hunton Jr.) served in Virginia's secession convention. Also, James Lyons, husband of Elizabeth Lyons, was a member of the Virginia Constitutional Convention of 1850 and served as an attorney for Jefferson Davis in 1867. Gabrielle Waddell of Wilmington, North Carolina, was married to a former congressman whose ancestors had been in state politics since the Revolution. Mary Stuart McGuire of Richmond was the daughter of Alexander H. H. Stuart, a cabinet member under Millard Fillmore and leader of the redemption effort in Virginia.

43. The farmers/planters were: Alcide Robichaux of Lafourche Parish; Eloi D. Theriot of Terrebonne Parish; Aladin Vincent of Calcasieau Parish; W. J. Zaunbrecher of Acadia Parish. The merchants were: S. S. McCullough of Vernon Parish; L. A. Moresi of Iberia Parish; Robichaux of Lafourche Parish; Theriot of Terrebonne Parish. The lawyers were: L. B. DeBelleue of Acadia Parish; J. Hugh Dore of Evangeline Parish; Judge Gilbert Dupre of St. Landry Parish; W. A. Morrow of Avoyelles Parish. The banker was Zaunbrecher of Acadia Parish. Other members of the league were: Peter Cougot of New Orleans, a railroad president; John C. Davey of New Orleans, an attorney who was a member of the Choctaw Club; Joseph R. Domengeaux of Lafayette, a manufacturer of pharmaceuticals; E. L. Simmons, a newspaper editor from St. Martin Parish; George F. Westfall, a railroad commissioner from St. Martin Parish. (N.B.: three men are listed in more than one occupation.)

44. The constitution of 1901 had preserved the rotten-borough system of apportionment in the legislature, which heavily overrepresented the Black Belt counties (Grantham, *Southern Progressivism*, 46).

45. The vote of Florida's congressional delegation gives further evidence of the relationship between the Black Belt and the antisuffrage vote. In the 1919 House vote, Herbert Drane and William Sears, who represented the central and southern part of the state, voted for the Anthony Amendment; John Smithwich and Frank Clark, who represented the northern and western parts of the state, voted against the amendment (Kenneth Johnson, "Florida Women Get the Vote," 301). The northern part of Florida, which borders Georgia and Alabama, had been the center of Florida's plantation system and had the closest economic ties to the rest of the South. It also contained the highest percentages of the black population. The lower peninsula, on the other hand,

had a more diversified economy, was increasingly populated by immigrants from outside the South, had the smaller black population, and was more dedicated to the New South approach to economic development (Grantham, *Southern Progressivism*, 61).

46. There are hundreds of examples of this "second generation" planter class, but I will limit this to a handful more: Joseph S. Rice, state representative from Oktibbeha Country, Mississippi, was a law school graduate from a long line of planters, and his grandfather had sufficient standing to be elected to the antebellum state senate. Rice voted against the 1918 state amendment. Ida Hester Fitzpatrick of Thomasville, Georgia, was one of the foremost opponents of woman suffrage in the state federation of women's clubs; Fitzpatrick was married to a planter and was herself the daughter of a large landowner who had many slaves. Ella Heyer Stewart, wife of a druggist in Houston, joined the state anti association; her father was a rancher and cotton broker. S. Hubert Dent Jr., congressman from Alabama, was an attorney in Montgomery; his father had been a planter who served in the Confederate army. John S. Graham, state representative from Jackson, Alabama, was a former newspaper editor and merchant who was practicing law when he voted against the Nineteenth Amendment; his father was a planter who had favored secession. His fellow state representative, Acklin U. Hollis of Lamar County, was a merchant and sheriff who served on the steering committee to defeat the Anthony Amendment; Hollis' father was a Confederate army veteran and cotton planter. North Carolina's Samuel Westray Battle, a surgeon and business investor in Asheville, was a member of the executive committee of the States' Rights Defense League; his father was a planter who had served in the state's secession convention.

47. Ayers, *Promise of the New South*, 202.

48. *Advertiser*, 25 June 1919 (editorial).

49. Seawell, *Ladies' Battle*, 115.

50. See the sketch of Hinton in Powell, *Dictionary of North Carolina Biography*.

51. Moss, "Miss Millie Rutherford, Southerner," 57, 61; Fred Bailey, "Mildred Lewis Rutherford," 510, 518–19.

52. See for example the discussion of women's proslavery stance in Fox-Genovese, *Within the Plantation Household*, ch. 7.

53. Emily C. McDougald to Clara Savage, quoted by Grantham, *Southern Progressivism*, 213.

54. Carol Clare, "Woman Suffrage Movement in Virginia," 9, 20.

55. Doyle, *New Men, New Cities, New South*, 11.

56. See Wilkerson-Freeman, "Emerging Political Consciousness of Gertrude Weil," ch. 1.

57. Greenwood, *Bittersweet Legacy*, 128.

58. Flynt, *Montgomery: An Illustrated History*, 58.

59. Lawrence Larsen, *Urban South*, 72; Ida Young et al., *History of Macon, Georgia*, 335–36.

60. Feagin, *Free Enterprise City*, 60.

61. Nell Battle Lewis, suffragist and columnist for the Raleigh *News and Observer*, recognized this point about the suffragists. The phrase "home ground" was hers (*News and Observer*, 10 May 1925).

62. Billings, *Planters and the Making of a "New South,"* 60–67.

63. Many more examples could be given, including North Carolina state representative Edgar Love, a cotton manufacturer who voted against the Nineteenth Amendment. Stakeley W. Slayden of Waco, Texas, was vice president of two cotton mills and a woolen mill; he joined the Men's Anti-Woman Suffrage Association in Texas. Reuben A. Mitchell of Gadsden, Alabama, was president of Dwight Manufacturing Company, which produced cotton cloth; as a member of the executive committee of the state Democratic Party, Mitchell was an important voice against woman suffrage legislation in Alabama.

64. This strong relationship between textiles and antisuffragism was not unique to the South. A study of Massachusetts antisuffragists has pointed out a similar tie. For example, Eben Draper, one of the founders of the Massachusetts Man Suffrage Association (a group of prominent male antisuffragists), belonged to a wealthy textile family that contributed generously to the antisuffrage campaign. Many other antisuffragists in Massachusetts had similar textile interests (Camhi, "Women Against Women," 193). Also, Carol Hoffecker, in her study of the Delaware suffrage movement, noted that the leader of the Delaware antisuffragists was married to a prominent textile mill owner (Hoffecker, "Delaware's Woman Suffrage Campaign," 158). However, Hoffecker does not conclude that this was a widespread trend in that state.

65. Minnie Fisher Cunningham to Alice S. Ellington, 12 July 1917, Minnie Fisher Cunningham Collection, Metropolitan Research Center, Houston Public Library.

66. Virginia Vertrees to Miss Pearson, undated [but before 1917, the year of Pearson's death], Pearson Collection, TSLA.

67. *The State's Defense*, 16 August 1920, 4, copy found in Equal Suffrage Collection, NCDAH.

68. *Clarion-Ledger*, 8 January 1920. No such list was ever published. Even Carrie Chapman Catt herself, responsible for so many of the accusations against the liquor industry, provided some evidence that she may have overstated her case. In the New York state amendment campaign of 1915, Catt wrote to the campaign committee urging caution in the attack on the alleged liquor conspiracy. "Do not state that the liquor interests are fighting us," she warned. "We have seen no sign of it" (quoted by Camhi, "Women Against Women," 343). For Catt's frequent denunciations of the liquor industry, see Catt and Shuler, *Woman Suffrage and Politics*.

69. Yet there have been a few voices urging caution in too broad a condemnation of the liquor interests. One of the few challenges to what he termed the "liquor lobby myth" came from Thomas James Jablonsky, who berated historians for accepting this idea on the basis of so little evidence. The documentation about the relationship between the antisuffragists and the liquor interests, Jablonsky complained, "is nothing more than a collection of rumors, suspicions, and circumstantial evidence." Jablonsky concluded that the evidence demonstrates no authentic connection between the two groups, certainly not on the scale claimed by the suffragists, who were responsible for the charge originally (Jablonsky, "Duty, Nature, and Stability," 319–23).

70. William Miller, *Memphis During the Progressive Era*, 88; Wedell, *Elite Women and the Reform Impulse in Memphis*, 70. Dewey Grantham also singles out these three states for having strong liquor lobbies during the Prohibition contests (*Southern Progressivism*, 167–71).

71. Paul Isaac, *Prohibition and Politics*, 46.

72. But in 1907, 825 out of the 994 counties of the South were dry by local option (Woodward, *Origins of the New South*, 390).

73. I am indebted to Professor Wayne Flynt for suggesting to me the strength of this area of research. His casual mention of the Louisville and Nashville railroad as being behind the antisuffrage movement in Alabama led me into a whole new line of thought. A recent article by Anastatia Sims also pays careful attention to the role of railroads in the Tennessee suffrage campaign. (See Sims, " 'Powers that Pray' "; Catt and Milton quote is from page 212.)

74. Hackney, *Populism to Progressivism*, 152. Tunstall was on the House steering committee to defeat the Anthony Amendment and was an attorney for the Southern Railroad.

75. Evans Johnson, *Oscar W. Underwood*, 133.

76. Prescott, "Woman Suffrage Movement in Memphis," 102. According to a recent account, Walker resented the charge that "a certain railroad" was behind his opposition to the Nineteenth Amendment, but he never denied it (Sims, " 'Powers that Pray,' " 217).

77. Doster, "Railroad Domination in Alabama," 190. For Jones's later conservatism, see Norrell, *Reaping the Whirlwind*, 57.

78. Kousser, *Shaping of Southern Politics*, 189.

79. Simmons pledged that Democrats would not raise corporation taxes if returned to power (Escott, *Many Excellent People*, 258).

80. Escott, *Many Excellent People*, 247.

81. There are numerous additional examples of the ties between railroads and antisuffragists, including Augustus Benners, an attorney for the Illinois Central and Birmingham Southern Railroads, who voted against the Nineteenth Amendment in 1919 as a state representative from Birmingham. Fred L. Blackmon, congressman from Alabama, was known as a friend of the L&N and voted against the Anthony Amendment in 1919. Robert Lee Huddleston, state senator from Speigner, Alabama, was a surgeon in the employ of the L&N; he voted against the Anthony Amendment in 1919. Another surgeon, Dr. Isaac E. Clark of Schulenburg, Texas, was employed by the Southern Pacific Railroad; as a state legislator he voted against both the 1918 primary suffrage bill and the federal suffrage amendment in 1919. Edward D. Smith of Birmingham was a member of the Democratic National Committee and an opponent of woman suffrage; he was an attorney for the Alabama Great Southern Railroad, and his father was vice president of the Birmingham Southern Railroad. Romulus A. Nunn of New Bern, N.C., was president of the Atlantic and North Carolina Railroads; he also was a member of the executive committee of the States' Rights Defense League. Lee S. Overman, U.S. senator from Salisbury, N.C., and opponent of woman suffrage, was the former president of the North Carolina Railroad.

82. Harbert Davenport, "Life of James B. Wells" (unpublished typescript, 1933), 13, found in vertical file, "James B. Wells," Barker Texas History Center, University of Texas Library, Austin.

83. Many more examples include the following: John T. Garrison of Houston represented the Southern Pacific Railroad full time; his wife, Minter Hicks Garrison, was an antisuffragist. Sallie D. Wolters of Houston joined the state antisuffrage association immediately after it formed in 1915; her husband, Jake Wolters, represented the Missouri,

Kansas, and Texas Railroad and later was counsel for Texaco. Ellen and Annie Goldthwaite of Montgomery were both members of the antisuffrage association; Richard Goldthwaite (Ellen's uncle and Annie's brother-in-law) was road master for the L&N. Raybelle Gilpin of Montgomery joined the state antisuffrage association; her husband was assistant yard master for the L&N. Salley May Dooley, who was on the executive committee of the Virginia Antisuffrage Association, was married to multimillionaire James Henry Dooley, who had made his first fortune as founder of the Richmond and West Point Railroad. Virginia Payne Hunton, an opponent of woman suffrage from Richmond, was the wife of Eppa Hunton III, attorney for the Richmond, Fredricksburg, and Potomac and the Washington Southern Railroads. Henry Taylor Jr. of Richmond was counsel for the Chesapeake and Ohio Railroad; his wife, Virginia Bagby Taylor, was a member of the executive committee of the state antisuffrage association.

84. B. B. Munford had once been an advocate of railroad regulation, but when his law firm appointed him to represent the Richmond and Danville, his calls for a regulatory commission were silenced (Moger, *Virginia*, 99–100).

85. Schott, "New Orleans Machine and Progressivism," 141–42.

86. Anders, *Boss Rule in South Texas*, 174, 282.

87. Jeanne Howard, "Our Own Worst Enemies," 463.

88. Walter Clark, "Suffrage a Labor Movement," 392.

89. See sketch of David Clark in Powell, *Dictionary of North Carolina Biography*.

90. Flynt, *Montgomery: An Illustrated History*, 77.

91. Lefler and Newsome, *North Carolina*, 509.

92. Ezell, *South Since 1865*, 214–15.

93. Doster, "Railroad Domination in Alabama," 193.

94. Klein, *History of the Louisville and Nashville Railroad*, 387, 378, 393; Sims, " 'Powers that Pray,' " 214.

95. Klein, *History of the Louisville and Nashville Railroad*, 376.

96. Flynt, *Montgomery: An Illustrated History*, 54; Herr, *Louisville and Nashville Railroad*, 171.

97. Gaston, *New South Creed*, 52–53.

98. As was true for the textile industry and antisuffragism, railroad connections have also been found in the northeastern antisuffrage movement. Eleanor Flexner noted that two directors of the National Association Opposed to Woman Suffrage were the wives of railroad directors. The board of directors of the Man Suffrage Association (a group of prominent male antisuffragists) included five railroad directors (Flexner, *Century of Struggle*, 311).

99. Klein, *History of the Louisville and Nashville Railroad*, 368.

100. Herr, *Louisville and Nashville Railroad*, 164.

101. Flynt, *Montgomery: An Illustrated History*, 54. One side story illustrates the wealth and power of the L&N: during the Panic of 1907, when currency of any kind was greatly in demand, the L&N issued more than $1 million in company scrip. Backed by the company, the scrip became the equivalent of legal tender, accepted widely at stores throughout the region (Herr, *Louisville and Nashville Railroad*, 176–77).

102. Klein, *History of the Louisville and Nashville Railroad*, 377.

103. Sims, " 'Powers that Pray,' " 214.

104. Gay, *Alabama*, 203.

105. Parr and Wells quoted by Anders in *Boss Rule*, 256.

106. Anders, *Boss Rule*, 16–17.

107. Rabinowitz, *First New South*, 89.

108. Kousser, *Shaping of Southern Politics*, 263.

109. Mathews and De Hart, *Sex, Gender, and the Politics of ERA*, 14.

CHAPTER 3

1. See for example, *Woman's Protest*, May 1914, 4.

2. The phrase "True Daughters of the Old South" appeared in a letter from Grace B. Evans to Josephine Pearson, 1 November 1920, Pearson Collection, TSLA.

3. In an analysis of the rhetoric of conservative resistance movements, Barbara Warnick has concluded that it successfully appeals to the fear of loss of status (or of personal identity) that would be caused by the undermining of traditional values ("Rhetoric of Conservative Resistance," 257).

4. Rev. S. A. Steel, quoted by Shadron, "Out of Our Homes," 94.

5. E. L. Simmons, in *State Times*, 31 October 1918.

6. *Times-Dispatch*, 16 February 1912.

7. *Constitution*, 3 February 1895.

8. *News and Observer*, 25 April 1914.

9. Charlotte Shelton, "Woman Suffrage and Virginia Politics," 31.

10. Lee Allen, "Woman Suffrage Movement in Alabama," *Alabama Review*, 88.

11. Sims, " 'Powers that Pray,' " 215.

12. Hall, *Revolt Against Chivalry*, 34.

13. See article by that title, *Birmingham News*, 6 June 1914.

14. Memphis *Weekly Public Ledger*, 9 May 1876, and Memphis *Daily Avalanche*, 9 May 1876.

15. *News and Observer*, 19 April 1914.

16. Quoted by Anne Scott in *Southern Lady*, 181.

17. Quoted by Anne Scott, "After Suffrage: Southern Women in the 1920s," 300.

18. So rarely, in fact, that even the militants themselves noted when one of their southern members bobbed her hair. See reference to Maud Jamison of Norfolk, Va., in Linda G. Ford, *Iron-Jawed Angels*, 149.

19. Quoted by Porter, "Madeline McDowell Breckinridge," 363.

20. A. A. Lyon, *Suffragettes and Suffragettism*, 6. For further examples of antisuffragists attacks on the femininity of suffragists, see Patricia Marks, *Bicycles, Bangs, and Bloomers*.

21. Found in Carrie Chapman Catt Papers, TSLA.

22. Ibid.

23. For a national perspective, see Martha Solomon, ed., *In Their Own Voice*.

24. E[lizabeth] D. L. Lewis to Mrs. [Jessie] Townsend, 6 March 1915, ESL Papers, Box 1, Correspondence, VSLA.

25. Fuller, *Laura Clay and the Woman's Rights Movement*, 71.

26. Clarke, *Suffrage in the Southern States*, passim. See also Wheeler, *New Women of the New South*, 75.

27. Anne Scott, "Ever-Widening Circle," 66.

28. Quoted by Gammage, "Quest for Equality," 46.

29. Wheeler, *New Women of the New South*, 49. However, this argument ignores the actual violence committed against southern members of the National Woman's Party who participated in the White House pickets and other protests in Washington.

30. "Equal Suffrage and Common Sense," Fort Worth *Star-Telegram*, 18 May 1919.

31. Annie W. Fox to Lila Meade Valentine, undated, postmarked 2 December 1915, Valentine Papers, VHS.

32. My calculations for Alabama found that in 1920, eighteen suffragists had children at home under the age of 18, and the average age of those children was 10 years. Twenty-one antisuffragists had children under the age of 18 at home, and those children averaged 9 years of age.

33. The most easily obtained information about a woman in this period was her marital status: in print, her name nearly always included the identifying title "Miss" or "Mrs." Marital status at a given time is perhaps the simplest demographic fact to determine for women. Tracing the change in marital status is more difficult: a woman who was single in 1920 may not have remained single after the suffrage contest ended in 1920. For purposes of this study, however, marital status in the year immediately preceding that of the ratification contest is considered the salient point.

34. These nuptuality patterns were not a regional anomaly. Thomas J. Jablonsky's study of "remonstrants" in New England yielded similar data. Of his sample, 29 percent of antisuffrage women were unmarried ("Duty, Nature, and Stability," 282). Likewise, Louise Stevenson, in her monograph on Massachusetts' antisuffragists, calculated that 21 percent of the members of the state association were unmarried ("Women Anti-Suffragists in the 1915 Massachusetts Campaign," 89).

35. I have been unable to compare the fertility rates of the two groups of women as I had originally hoped to do. Because of a change in the questions asked on the 1920 Census, tracking the number of children born to a given woman has become much more difficult. In 1910, the census asked for both the number of children born to each woman and the number of children surviving. In 1920, both of those questions were omitted from the population schedule, so one is able to determine only how many children still lived in a given household the day the census was taken.

36. Seawell, *Ladies' Battle*, 49.

37. Virginia Clare, *Thunder and Stars*, 227.

38. "President's Message," 20 September 1920, Pearson Collection, TSLA.

39. Ibid.

40. Ibid.

41. Emmy Roberts to Pearson, 8 April 1925, Pearson Collection, TSLA.

42. Sid Roscoe to Pearson, 20 June 1925, Pearson Collection, TSLA.

43. Pearson's financial difficulties began in the 1910s, when she began to care for her sick and aging parents. She stopped working for several years in order to care for them, and the loss of income and her high expenses drained all of her resources. She mortgaged her house, sold off many of her assets, and took in boarders to make ends meet. See "My Story!" manuscript and Pearson to Mary G. Kilbreath, 20 January 1921, Pearson Collection, TSLA.

44. Mildred Lewis Rutherford also rejected "numerous" offers of marriage, al-

though her biographer offered no explanation for Rutherford's decisions (Virginia Clare, *Thunder and Stars*, passim).

45. See for example, Link, *Paradox of Southern Progressivism*, 183.

46. Elizabeth Hayes Turner's study of Galveston, Texas, supports this assessment ("White-Gloved Ladies," 142).

47. Barbara Solomon, *In the Company of Educated Women*, 112. On education of southern women, see also Mayo, *Southern Women and the Recent Educational Movement in the South*, and McCandless, "Progressivism and the Higher Education of Southern Women."

48. Woody, *History of Women's Education in the United States*, 165.

49. Jean Friedman, *Enclosed Garden*, 100.

50. Collier, *Biographies of Representative Women of the South*, 1:53.

51. "Mildred Lewis Rutherford," in James et al., eds., *Notable American Women*. See also Fred Bailey, "Mildred Lewis Rutherford," 519–20.

52. Kilman, "Southern Collegiate Women," 174.

53. Barbara Solomon, *In the Company of Educated Women*, 47.

54. *Woman's Protest*, May 1912, 3.

55. Ibid., August 1914, 16.

56. Ibid., March 1913, 13, and January 1916, 18. I have not been able to document the presence of factory workers in the ranks of the antisuffragists. I have, however, found documentation of factory workers joining the suffrage leagues. See Chapter 7.

57. Julia Sully to Lila Meade Valentine, 10 January 1913, Valentine Papers, VHS.

58. See Salmond, *Miss Lucy of the CIO*, ch. 3.

59. Lebsock, "Woman Suffrage and White Supremacy," 88–89.

60. Salmond, *Miss Lucy of the CIO*, 32.

61. Foster, *Ghosts of the Confederacy*, 171–73.

62. Ibid., 174.

63. Ibid.; Anne Scott, *Southern Lady*, 180.

64. Kenneth Johnson, "Woman Suffrage Movement in Florida," 65.

65. I have found only one oblique reference to this organization and have found no institutional records. There is no evidence as to the size, activities, or membership of this "department." It appears that the state president of the UDC, Mrs. Chappel Cory, was prosuffrage (Mary Martha Thomas, *New Woman in Alabama*, 167), which may explain why the antisuffragists had to form a separate department if they were unable to obtain an official position for the entire organization.

66. Quoted by L. Taylor, "Lila Meade Valentine," 482.

67. Parrott, "'Love Makes Memory Eternal,'" 231, 222.

68. Kelly, "Antisuffrage Arguments in Georgia," 50. Rutherford's fame and influence went far beyond the state borders of Georgia. See Fred Bailey, "Mildred Lewis Rutherford," 516–21.

69. Sharber, "Social Attitudes of the Episcopal Church of Tennessee," 134–135.

70. As reported in U.S. Bureau of the Census, *Religious Bodies, 1916*.

71. Sharber, "Social Attitudes of the Episcopal Church of Tennessee," 6–7, 130.

72. Anne Scott emphasized that the Methodist Church, far more than the Baptist or Presbyterian Churches, provided women with space to grow and develop (see *Southern Lady*, ch. 6). Evelyn Kirkley, in her recent article on the religiosity of the southern

suffrage movement, also tends to view the Methodist Church more favorably in terms of its support for woman suffrage ("'This Work is God's Cause,'" 514).

73. Shadron, "Out of Our Homes," 81.

74. *Woman's Protest*, May 1914, 19.

75. Newman, "Role of Women in Atlanta's Churches," 28. Candler had a colorful career in conservative politics. He opposed the reunification of the Methodist churches, north and south, and he was a vocal opponent of evolutionism. See Kenneth Bailey, *Southern White Protestantism*, 57, 91.

76. *Constitution*, 22 August 1894.

77. Sumners, "Southern Baptists and Woman's Right to Vote," 50–51.

78. Newman, "Role of Women in Atlanta's Churches," 28.

79. Nutt, "Robert Lewis Dabney, Presbyterians, and Women's Suffrage," 344, 350.

80. Flynt, "Feeding the Hungry," 119–20.

81. Grantham, *Southern Progressivism*, 16. Jablonsky's study of antisuffrage women in the northeast showed that they were remarkably similar to southern antis in religious affiliations. Among the Protestants in his sample, the majority belonged to three conservative denominations: Presbyterian, Baptist, and Unitarian. The remaining Protestants were members of what Jablonsky termed "more liberal" churches, the Episcopal and the Congregational. "Yet, even in the case of the Episcopalian remonstrants," Jablonsky warned, "the attraction to that particular church may have been more due to its popularity among the wealthy than to its early support of the Social Gospel" ("Duty, Nature, and Stability," 287).

82. Buhle, *Women and American Socialism*, xv, xvi.

83. My understanding of the work of gender in creating conservative women's networks has been informed by two recent works: Blee, *Women of the Klan*, and MacLean, "Behind the Mask of Chivalry."

84. Cott, "What's in a Name?," 826. Claudia Koonz made the same point earlier in her analysis of women's roles in building the Nazi state in Germany. See *Mothers in the Fatherland*, especially ch. 3.

CHAPTER 4

1. Woodward, *Origins of the New South*, 321–26; Smith, *In His Image, But . . .*, 260–64.

2. Fredrickson, *Black Image in the White Mind*, 246–58; Woodward, *Strange Career of Jim Crow*, 74.

3. Fredrickson, *Black Image in the White Mind*, 260–80.

4. Woodward, *Strange Career of Jim Crow*, 69.

5. Aileen Kraditor, the first scholar to examine the arguments employed by the antisuffrage movement, classified them into three major lines of thought: theological, biological, and sociological (*Ideas of the Woman Suffrage Movement*, ch. 2). Other scholars since Kraditor have devised alternative categories for analyzing antisuffrage rhetoric. Susan E. Marshall, for example, found four major categories with twenty-one subcategories ("In Defense of Separate Spheres," 332). Jeanne Howard created ten categories ("Our Own Worst Enemies," 467–72). I prefer Kraditor's model for its simplicity and

its clarity; no doubt these characteristics are part of the reason her work has stood the test of time so well.

In a separate chapter, Kraditor describes two additional categories of arguments used by southerners in opposition to woman suffrage: states' rights and the black vote. The arrangement of her chapters lent itself to the supposition that white southerners did not use the "mainstream" antisuffrage arguments based on theology, biology, and sociology and that this set of regional arguments was perhaps secondary in importance to the dominant strains of thought. In actuality, white southerners opposed to woman suffrage used all three "mainstream" arguments but gave special place to the racial and constitutional theories that held so much sway in the southern states. Southern white antisuffragists successfully incorporated all five types of arguments into the defense of their larger vision of race, class, and gender relations in the South.

6. Undated Nashville *Banner* clipping, in Lizzie Elliott Papers (Collin D. Elliott Collection), TSLA.

7. Undated broadside, signed W. H. Tayloe, Alabama, found in Bennehan Cameron Papers, SHC.

8. "Mrs. Catt and Woman-Suffrage Leaders Repudiate the Bible," broadside printed by Tennessee Division of Southern Rejection League, found in Lizzie Elliott Papers, TSLA.

9. Ibid.

10. Walsh, *Anti-Woman Suffrage and Criticisms*, 5.

11. Peebles, *Is Woman Suffrage Right?*, 12–13.

12. Quoted in Kelly, "Antisuffrage Arguments in Georgia," 17.

13. Kraditor, "Tactical Problems of the Woman-Suffrage Movement in the South," 293.

14. *Congressional Record*, 63rd Cong., 3rd sess., 12 January 1915, 1413.

15. "The Feminist and Our Bible," undated anonymous tract found in the Equal Suffrage Collection, NCDAH.

16. A Methodist minister in Texas denounced Elizabeth Meriwether for preaching "infidel woman's rights doctrines" (Prescott, "Woman Suffrage Movement in Memphis," 90).

17. *Woman Patriot*, 27 April 1918, 4. Although all the biblical arguments quoted here were by men, I have found some by women. While it is quite difficult to quantify, it does appear that women relied on the biblical arguments less often in their antisuffrage rhetoric than did men.

18. Wheeler, "Mary Johnston, Suffragist," 114.

19. For an interpretation that stresses the positive influences of religion in the southern suffrage movement, see Kirkley, " 'This Work is God's Cause.' "

20. Peebles, *Is Woman Suffrage Right?*, 10.

21. Eugene Anderson, *Unchaining the Demons of the Lower World*, 13.

22. Jablonsky, "Duty, Nature, and Stability," 25n, argued that women avoided the biological argument. Marirose Arendale has also argued that female antisuffragists used a different ideological approach than male antis in Tennessee. She claimed that women stressed the violation of southern traditions, while men emphasized states' rights ("Tennessee and Women's Rights," 70). Louise Stevenson also has argued for

"distinctiveness of women's thought" in the construction of antisuffrage ideology ("Women Anti-Suffragists in the 1915 Massachusetts Campaign," 80). My own reading of the evidence does not find such a difference and does not support such a conclusion. I find that men and women used essentially identical arguments, frequently based upon identical literature and shared publications. However, I will argue in Chapter 5 that gender did influence public organizational activities of antisuffragists.

23. Mrs. Nannie Eakin Steger to editor, *Tennessean*, 7 August 1920.

24. Mrs. J. M. Powell of Orange, Tex., letter to the editor, *Dallas Morning News*, 10 January 1895 (quoted by Strawn, "Woman Suffrage," 28).

25. Seawell, *Ladies' Battle*, 27–29.

26. "Why Women Should Oppose Equal Suffrage," undated pamphlet by the Virginia Association Opposed to Woman Suffrage, NAWSA Papers, Antisuffrage Literature, LC.

27. Quoted in Kelly, "Antisuffrage Arguments in Georgia," 22.

28. For a similar distinction in the contest over the Equal Rights Amendment, see Mathews and DeHart, *Sex, Gender, and the Politics of ERA*, xi.

29. *Woman Patriot*, 1 June 1918, 1.

30. John J. Vertrees, *An Address to the Men of Tennessee on Female Suffrage*, 8.

31. Undated newspaper clipping, Pearson Collection, TSLA.

32. Quoted in Camhi, "Women Against Women," 26.

33. Quoted in Kelly, "Antisuffrage Arguments in Georgia," 26. For a discussion of "scientific" and "academic" views of race in the same period, see Williamson, *Crucible of Race*, 119–24.

34. Emily P. Bissell, *A Talk to Women on the Suffrage Question* (New York: National Association Opposed to Woman Suffrage, 1909), 3. Although Bissell was not from the South proper, nor was this pamphlet produced in the South, it was widely circulated in the region, and the Virginia Association Opposed to Woman Suffrage reprinted it for use in their own campaign, giving some testament to its appeal to southern antisuffragists.

35. "Peril of Equal Rights for Women," *Ferguson Forum*, 27 April 1919.

36. Eugene Anderson, *Unchaining the Demons of the Lower World*, 2, 5, 11.

37. Berea (Ky.) *Citizen*, 1 April 1920, quoted in *Woman Patriot*, 24 April 1920.

38. Peebles, *Is Woman Suffrage Right?*, 14.

39. Watson, "Attitudes of Southern Women on the Suffrage Question," 365.

40. *Clarion-Ledger*, 22 January 1914.

41. *Congressional Record*, 63rd Cong., 3rd sess., 12 January 1915, 1413. Nancy MacLean has noted that women of the KKK used the language of republican motherhood as well, a rhetoric they had appropriated from the WCTU ("Behind the Mask of Chivalry," 167). It is also possible that the antisuffrage movement provided a conduit for this philosophy, linking conservative gender ideology of the nineteenth century with that of the twentieth century.

42. Krock, *Editorials of Henry Watterson*, 365 (24 August 1913).

43. Degler, *At Odds*, 342.

44. Mrs. Charles H. Gill, "Why Women Are Opposed to Suffrage," in *Woman Patriot*, 24 July 1920, 3.

45. Watson, "Attitudes of Southern Women on the Suffrage Question," 367.

46. Petition to the Legislature of Alabama [1919], Suffrage Organization Papers, Alabama Equal Suffrage Association Papers, ADAH.

47. *Constitution*, 4 February 1895.

48. Josephine A. Pearson to Mrs. Wendell Willkie, 9 November 1940, Pearson Collection, TSLA.

49. Mrs. James S. Pinckard to Carrie Chapman Catt, 23 July 1920, NAWSA Papers, LC.

50. Seawell, "Two Suffrage Mistakes," 368.

51. *Congressional Record*, 63rd Cong., 3rd sess., 12 January 1915, 1413.

52. Quoted by Watson, "Attitudes of Southern Women on the Suffrage Question," 368.

53. Mrs. E. B. Cline to Mrs. Palmer Jerman, 14 October 1914, Lida T. Rodman Papers, William Blount Rodman Collection, NCDAH.

54. Mrs. William H. Felton, *On the Subjection of Women and the Enfranchisement of Women*, 11.

55. E. Y. Webb to Capt. L. C. West, 22 May 1920, Edwin Yates Webb Papers, SHC.

56. Watson, "Attitudes of Southern Women on the Suffrage Question," 367.

57. Callaway, "The White Woman's Problem," in *Woman Patriot*, 26 June 1920, 8.

58. J. H. Small to Mrs. J. Arthur Taylor, 14 April 1917, John Humphrey Small Papers, Manuscript Department, Duke University Library.

59. Speech of Senator Benet, 28 September 1918, reprinted in *Woman Patriot*, 19 October 1918, 3.

60. Eugene Anderson, *Unchaining the Demons of the Lower World*, 4–5.

61. *Congressional Record*, 63rd Cong., 3rd sess., 12 January 1915, 1464.

62. Seawell, "Two Suffrage Mistakes," 368.

63. Undated broadside found in Romulus A. Nunn Papers, NCDAH.

64. Buni, *Negro in Virginia Politics*, 78.

65. *News and Observer*, 8 October 1920. (The prosuffrage *News and Observer* could not resist running Hinton's announcement on page 1.)

66. Kraditor, *Ideas of the Woman Suffrage Movement*, 38n.

67. *Express*, 22, 29 July 1894.

68. Report of Legislative Work, 1914, Somerville-Howorth Collection, SL.

69. Morgan, *Suffragists and Democrats*, 22; Banner, *Elizabeth Cady Stanton*, 71.

70. DuBois, "Radicalism of the Woman Suffrage Movement."

71. See, for example, O'Neill, *Everyone Was Brave*, 21–47, and Barry, *Susan B. Anthony*, 200–210.

72. Kraditor, *Ideas of the Woman Suffrage Movement*, 114–15.

73. See Chapter 5 for more detail about this transformation.

74. Acheson, *Joe Bailey*, 357.

75. *Woman Patriot*, 9 August 1919, 2.

76. Undated newspaper clipping (ca. January 1918), Era Club Papers, New Orleans Public Library.

77. Lockwood, *Woman Suffrage a Menace to the South*, 7.

78. *Item*, 29 June 1919; E. von Meyrenberg to Miss M. W. Coate, 8 January 1912, Chamberlain Papers, LHC.

79. *Congressional Record*, 18 August 1913, 3461.

80. Quoted by A. Taylor, *Woman Suffrage Movement in Tennessee*, 78.

81. According to Barbara Warnick, conservatives who rely on such traditional values as the primacy of the family, the American heritage, or the Christian religion, feel threatened by efforts of "liberal interest groups who, in their pursuit of social equality, attempt to change the very elements that define the conservatives' belief system." See Warnick, "Rhetoric of Conservative Resistance," 262.

82. Peebles, *Is Woman Suffrage Right?*, 15. Jablonsky noted that the first instance of antisuffrage organizational activity was in response to Woodhull's appearance before a congressional committee hearing on suffrage ("Duty, Nature, and Stability," 31).

83. Henry Watterson, "Feminism," in *Woman Patriot*, 12 October 1918, 4.

84. Quoted by A. Taylor, "South Carolina . . .: The Early Years," 117.

85. See for example, headline of 29 January 1913: "Frenzied Suffragettes Amuse Themselves Breaking Windows in Parliament Hall." It was because of these kinds of attacks on suffrage "radicalism" that Laura Clay insisted suffrage be separated from all other causes. "When we go through the South advocating woman suffrage, without attaching it to dress reform, or bicycling, or anything else, but asking the simple question why the principles of our forefathers should not be applied to women, we shall win. The South is ready for woman suffrage, but it must be woman suffrage and nothing else" (Fuller, *Laura Clay and the Woman's Rights Movement*, 71).

86. This pamphlet is printed in *HWS* 2:929–31 and is reprinted in Kraditor, ed., *Up from the Pedestal*, 253–57.

87. Wheeler, *New Women of the New South*, 113–15.

88. Quoted by Berkeley, "Elizabeth Avery Meriwether," 405.

89. Quoted in *HWS* 6:332.

90. "Woman Suffrage and White Supremacy in the South," broadside found in Gertrude Weil Papers, NCDAH.

91. Quoted by Morgan, *Suffragists and Democrats*, 135.

92. See for example Kraditor, *Ideas of the Woman Suffrage Movement*, 150–51. In the following pages, I hope to revise this commonly held interpretation.

93. From Belle Kearney, "The South and Woman Suffrage," *Woman's Journal*, 7 April 1903, reprinted in Kraditor, *Up from the Pedestal*, 262–65.

94. Lebsock, "Woman Suffrage and White Supremacy," 71–72, 77–79.

95. Undated broadside entitled "Woman Suffrage Amendment Raises No Race Issue," in Gertrude Weil Papers, Suffrage Literature, NCDAH.

96. Quoted in *Woman Patriot*, 20 December 1919, 8.

97. Dudley, *Negro Vote in the South*, n.p.

98. Quoted by Lewinson, *Race, Class, and Party*, 84.

99. "A Protest Against Woman's Suffrage in Alabama," anonymous, Suffrage Organization Records, Alabama Equal Suffrage Association Papers, ADAH.

100. Quoted by Zimmerman, "Alice Paul and the National Woman's Party," 176. Glenda Gilmore has made a similar observation about white responses to the emerging black middle class: "To white Democrats, the important thing was not how many

blacks entered the middle class, but that any did. The black lawyer, doctor, or teacher represented someone out of his or her place. He or she was a living testament to the capabilities of the race and a perpetual affront to whites" ("Gender and Jim Crow," 142).

101. Telegram from R. G. Pleasant to Westmoreland Davis, 26 June 1919, Westmoreland Davis Papers, Box 82, Manuscripts Division, Alderman Library, UVA.

102. Although he did not himself use the term "white monopoly," my interpretation of the distinction between the two concepts derives from my reading of Fuller, *Laura Clay and the Woman's Rights Movement*, 62. This line of reasoning also parallels the point made by Joel Williamson, that different groups of white southerners supported black disfranchisement for different reasons (and by different means), and some were willing to allow token black voting while others wanted a lily-white electorate (*Crucible of Race*, 230–31, passim).

103. See Kenneth Johnson, review of Paul Fuller, *Laura Clay and the Woman's Rights Movement*, in *Journal of Southern History* 42, no. 1 (February 1976): 130.

104. Porter, "Madeline McDowell Breckinridge," 345.

105. Mrs. James Bennett of Richmond, Ky., to Westmoreland Davis, March 10, 1910, Westmoreland Davis Papers, Box 82, Manuscripts Division, Alderman Library, UVA. Ironically, this woman goes on to say that she supported only a state amendment, not the federal suffrage amendment.

106. *Congressional Record*, 63rd Cong., 3rd sess., 12 January 1915, 1445.

107. Harry Stilwell Edwards to Rebecca Latimer Felton, 18 February 1915, quoted by Grantham, *Southern Progressivism*, 215.

108. Quoted by A. Taylor, *Woman Suffrage Movement in Tennessee*, 42.

109. *HWS* 6:606.

110. Ethel Armes to Alice Stone Blackwell, 26 June 1913, Alabama Suffrage Association Papers, NAWSA Papers, LC.

111. Anonymous undated broadside, found in Lizzie Elliott Papers, TSLA.

112. *Ferguson Forum* , 22 May 1919.

113. Mrs. George Washington, Mrs. James Pinckard, and Mrs. Ruffin Pleasant to editor, *Tennessean*, 6 August 1920 (emphasis mine).

114. *Woman Patriot*, 30 August 1919, 2

115. Undated broadside entitled "Elihu Root Warns the South," found in Lizzie Elliott Papers, TSLA.

116. Thomas P. Gailor to Josephine Pearson, 13 September 1920, Pearson Collection, TSLA.

117. A. J. Whitworth, "Disgrace, Dishonor, and Disaster," in *Woman Patriot*, 10 January 1920, 5.

118. Thomas C. Andrews to editor, *Ferguson Forum*, 27 November 1919.

119. E. D. Word, quoted by Strawn, "Woman Suffrage," 36.

120. Willie M. Person of Franklin County, quoted in *News and Observer*, 28 February 1917. Another senator replied that if Person's cook was more patriotic than his wife, then the cook should be allowed to vote.

121. Watson, "Attitudes of Southern Women on the Suffrage Question," 367.

122. MacLean, "Behind the Mask of Chivalry," 200.

123. A. J. Whitworth, "Disgrace, Dishonor, and Disaster," in *Woman Patriot*, 10 January 1920, 5.

124. From the Richmond *Evening Journal*, 4 May 1915, reprinted in *Woman Patriot*, 8 June 1918, 8.

125. From "Virginia Anti-Suffrage Committee Memorializes Assembly," in *Woman Patriot*, 30 August 1919, 2.

126. Quoted in Stone-Erdman, "A Challenge to Southern Politics," 55.

127. John W. Cell has also analyzed the phrase "white supremacy" and concluded that it really meant "Democratic Party power," an interpretation that parallels my own line of thinking (*Highest Stage of White Supremacy*, 121).

128. Of course, the states' rights faction of suffragists, led by Kate Gordon, are the exception and will be discussed at length in Chapter 6.

129. Quoted by Porter, "Madeline McDowell Breckinridge," 351.

130. Kraditor argued otherwise (*Ideas of the Woman Suffrage Movement*, 23).

131. Terborg Penn, "Nineteenth-Century Black Women and Woman Suffrage," 20.

132. Marable, *W. E. B. Du Bois*, 85.

133. Quoted by Harry Gamble, "Federal Suffrage a Racial Question in the South," privately printed pamphlet, 1918, 26. Copy found in NAWSA Papers, Antisuffrage Literature, LC.

134. Terborg-Penn, "Nineteenth-Century Black Women and Woman Suffrage," 19–21. Christia Adair's papers can be found in the Houston Public Library Metropolitan Research Center. Unfortunately the collection does not include much information on her suffrage activities.

135. A. Taylor, *Woman Suffrage Movement in Tennessee*, 55–56. One can only speculate whether Taylor, a white historian doing an interview in the 1950s, might have gotten a different response than a black interviewer doing an interview in the 1970s.

136. Wheeler, *New Women of the New South*, 106.

137. While women's historians have paid much attention to the role of women in opposing the lynch law and vigilantism in the South, only recently have they begun to examine the opposite phenomenon: the role of white women in encouraging and supporting such violence. See especially MacLean, "White Women and Klan Violence in the 1920s," and Blee, *Women of the Klan*.

138. I am indebted to Glenda Elizabeth Gilmore for sharing her research on southern black women and feminism. The information on Annie Blackwell is summarized in Gilmore's paper, "'When Woman Shall Have Entered Every Door of Usefulness,'" 13–14.

139. Charlotte (N.C.) *Observer*, 4 October 1920, quoted by Gilmore, "'When Woman Shall Have Entered Every Door of Usefulness,'" 16.

140. Litwack, *Been in the Storm So Long*, 532.

141. *Star of Zion*, 11 August 1898, 4, quoted by Gilmore, "'When Woman Shall Have Entered Every Door of Usefulness,'" 13.

142. Quoted by Guy-Sheftall, *Daughters of Sorrow*, 127.

143. Gilmore, "Gender and Jim Crow," 193. In a similar vein, Daniel Webster Davis and Giles Jackson wrote in 1908 that "the Negro Race Needs Housekeepers, . . . wives who stay at home, being supported by their husbands, and then they can spend time

in the training of their children" (quoted by Barkley Brown, "Womanist Consciousness," 622).

144. Greenwood, *Bittersweet Legacy*, 87–88. Greenwood points out that in addition to gender roles, the black middle class embraced the Prohibition movement as another avenue to respectability.

145. Salem, *To Better Our World*, 39.

146. Alice O. Taylor to Mrs. [Jessie] Townsend, 6 July 1914, ESL Papers, Box 1, Correspondence, VSLA.

CHAPTER 5

1. Finally, it should be noted that only organizational efforts will be considered here. Interest groups (such as the textile industry) that opposed woman suffrage but never formally organized are necessarily omitted from this chapter. While those interest groups were extremely important to the movement, they cannot be included here in the context of publicly expressed antisuffragism.

2. Jablonsky, "Duty, Nature, and Stability," 8–34.

3. Ibid., 34–41.

4. Ibid., 114.

5. Buechler, *Women's Movements in the United States*, 183.

6. Jablonsky, "Duty, Nature, and Stability," 189. Jablonsky concluded that this turnover in leadership was simply a palace coup, although one that ultimately changed the nature and effectiveness of the movement.

7. Jablonsky, "Duty, Nature, and Stability," 190–94.

8. Ibid., 201–3.

9. *Woman Patriot*, 11 January 1919, 1. The membership figures for the NAOWS are certainly open to question. The organization also claimed to have state affiliates in some states where no organization existed. But there is no outside source from which to obtain membership figures.

10. Camhi, "Women Against Women," 3; Jablonsky, "Duty, Nature, and Stability," 19.

11. Camhi, "Women Against Women," 164

12. Ibid.

13. Ibid., 218.

14. Ibid., 149.

15. Buechler, *Women's Movements in the United States*, 184.

16. Ibid. Or as Barbara Warnick has phrased it, "Agents proposing a change assume the burden of proof for they must clearly demonstrate to the public that the alterations they propose are expedient" ("Rhetoric of Conservative Resistance," 260).

17. The NAOWS continued to exist after the ratification of the Nineteenth Amendment. At first it devoted most of its energies to challenging the amendment in court, attempting to prove that it had been fraudulently ratified and therefore was invalid. Later, the organization worked against reforms such as the Shepherd-Towner Maternal Health Bill and other expressions of what it considered "feminism." It continued

to publish *The Woman Patriot* throughout the 1920s until both the organization and the journal folded in 1928.

18. Quoted by Camhi, "Women Against Women," 151.

19. *Woman's Protest*, April 1914, 16.

20. Ibid., March 1913, 13. At the time that *The Woman's Protest* ran this article, the Virginia antisuffragists had held at least one public meeting.

21. *Woman's Protest*, June 1914, 15.

22. Knoxville *Journal and Tribune*, 24 October 1913. Another abortive organizational effort occurred in North Carolina. A Mrs. E. G. Edwards claimed to be organizing antisuffrage societies there in 1914 (*Woman's Protest*, April 1914, 16). She appears to have been unsuccessful, however, since there was no association extant in 1916, when the Georgia association reported that North Carolina had "sent for help and suggestions" (*Woman's Protest*, July 1916, 13).

23. *Woman's Protest*, March 1914, 12; A. Taylor, "South Carolina . . . : The Later Years," 303.

24. Local newspaper coverage of this effort to organize an antisuffrage organization in Charleston never included the names of the women involved. "Prominent Charlestonians" was the purposely evasive phrase used (Charleston *News and Courier*, 17 January 1914).

25. It is unclear if Dodge or any other representative of the NAOWS prompted the organizational effort in Georgia. It may have been completely indigenous. But since it so promptly affiliated with the NAOWS, it is certainly possible that the NAOWS had some supporting role in the effort.

26. *Woman's Protest*, June 1914, 14, and August 1914, 16. A. Elizabeth Taylor incorrectly reported that the state antisuffrage organization consisted only of the Macon club and had no auxiliaries in other cities ("Last Phase of the Woman Suffrage Movement in Georgia," 16).

27. *HWS* 6:134.

28. *Woman's Protest*, June 1915.

29. Ibid., January 1916, 18. Houston was the home of a local association.

30. Minutes of the National Woman Suffrage Conference, 30 March 1916, Tennessee Suffrage Association Papers, in NAWSA Papers, LC.

31. *Tennessean*, 11 April, 3 May 1916.

32. Sims, "'Powers that Pray,'" 207–8.

33. Lee Allen, "Woman Suffrage Movement in Alabama" (M.A. thesis), 125. See also Lee Allen, "Woman Suffrage Movement in Alabama," *Alabama Review*, 94–95.

34. In December 1918, the NAOWS had claimed seven southern affiliates: Maryland, Virginia, Alabama, Georgia, North Carolina, South Carolina, and Louisiana (*Woman Patriot*, 28 December 1918, 1). But in the case of the last three named, this can be true only if an individual member could constitute a state association. For instance, Mary Hilliard Hinton of North Carolina appears to have joined the NAOWS as an individual member sometime before 1917, but there was no actual organization in the state until 1920.

35. In the years between 1914 and 1919, southern suffragists attempted a number of different enfranchisement methods: presidential suffrage, primary suffrage, municipal

suffrage, etc. After 1919, most of their efforts were directed toward the federal amendment, although in states where the federal approach seemed doomed, suffragists often continued their support for state amendments.

36. *HWS* 6:7n. These women of wealth and standing included Cola Barr Craig, wife of lawyer/politician Benjamin H. Craig; Mattie Hays Elsberry, whose father had once been Jefferson Davis's personal secretary; Laura Montgomery Henderson, wife of former governor Charles Henderson; and Marie Bankhead Owen, of the powerful Bankhead political dynasty.

37. *Advertiser*, 21, 22, 28 June 1919.

38. Newspaper clippings, 24 June 1919, Woman's Anti-Ratification League Scrapbook, Alabama Equal Suffrage Association Papers, ADAH. If it is true that a thousand letters and telegrams were sent, they have not survived or have not been deposited in any archival collection.

39. Woman's Anti-Ratification League of Alabama to the Honorable Members of the State Legislature, 8 July 1919, in Woman Suffrage Organizations Collection, Alabama Equal Suffrage Association Papers, ADAH.

40. Newspaper clippings, 17 July 1919, Woman's Anti-Ratification League Scrapbook, Alabama Equal Suffrage Association Papers, ADAH.

41. Ibid., 25 June 1919.

42. *Advertiser*, 20 July 1919.

43. Newspaper clippings, 15 November 1919, Woman's Anti-Ratification League Scrapbook, Alabama Equal Suffrage Association Papers, ADAH.

44. Broadside entitled "Declaration of Principles of the Southern Women's League for the Rejection of the Proposed Susan B. Anthony Amendment to the Constitution of the United States," found in Pearson Collection, TSLA.

45. *Clarion-Ledger*, 17 January 1920.

46. Broadside in the Lizzie Elliott Papers, TSLA.

47. Ibid.

48. Ibid.

49. A. Taylor, "Woman Suffrage Movement in North Carolina," 184; *News and Observer*, 10 May 1925.

50. Grace B. Evans (Selma, Ala.) to Miss Pearson, 1 November 1920, Pearson Collection, TSLA.

51. "Statement of Proposed Expenditures," undated leaflet found in Joseph S. Cullinam Papers, Metropolitan Research Center, Houston Public Library. It seems unlikely that any of these planned ventures came to fruition. There are no records to indicate the outcome of this proposed fund drive, nor are there records for any subsequent publicity blitz.

52. *News and Observer*, 22 June 1920.

53. While there may have been more women in North Carolina who identified themselves as members of the Southern Rejection League, I have been able to find only twenty names in the press coverage of the organization.

54. There were an additional 110 women who were members of the state antisuffrage association in 1916 and 1917 who may have considered themselves as automatic members of the Rejection League when the state association joined the regional orga-

nization. If they did count themselves as members, however, they never publicly identified themselves as such, and I therefore have left them out of the membership count.

55. Clarke, *Suffrage in the Southern States*, 41.

56. Virginia Association Opposed to Woman Suffrage, *By-Laws*, copy found in VSLA.

57. *Tennessean*, 3 May 1916.

58. *Woman's Protest*, May 1912, 3.

59. Ibid., April 1916.

60. Sarah Bradford to Miss Pearson, 13 February 1917, Pearson Collection, TSLA.

61. "Statement of Proposed Expenditures," undated leaflet found in Joseph S. Cullinam Papers, Metropolitan Research Center, Houston Public Library.

62. *Tennessean*, 10, 18 August 1920.

63. Josephine Pearson to Mr. Vertrees, 19 August 1920, Pearson Collection, TSLA.

64. Anne Pleasant to Miss Pearson, 29 August 1920, Pearson Collection, TSLA.

65. Josephine Pearson to Mr. Vertrees, 19 August 1920, Pearson Collection, TSLA.

66. See for example, *Clarion-Ledger*, 1, 7 January 1920.

67. Lee Allen, "Woman Suffrage Movement in Alabama" (M.A. thesis), 127.

68. Minnie Fisher Cunningham to Alice S. Ellington, 12 July 1917, Cunningham Collection, Metropolitan Research Center, Houston Public Library.

69. Jablonsky, "Duty, Nature, and Stability," 129.

70. See, for example, Pearson to John Sharp Williams, 4 February 1919, John Sharp Williams Papers, LC.

71. "My Story!" manuscript, Pearson Collection, TSLA.

72. *News and Observer*, 22 June 1920.

73. *Woman's Protest*, March 1913, 13.

74. Ibid., January 1916, 18.

75. Harrison, *Separate Spheres*, 111.

76. It is also true that not all southern suffragists condoned some of the more radical activities such as picketing the White House.

77. Rosa-Leigh Towers, *Constitution*, 4 February 1895.

78. *Woman Patriot*, 6 July 1918, 2. Texas suffragists remarked on the large quantity of antisuffrage literature coming from Selma, Alabama, "being disseminated all over the State," although they didn't identify the sender as Calhoun (*Express*, 4 April 1919). I have found Calhoun's letters in archives scattered throughout the South. His distinctively thin, scratchy handwriting helps to identify his work even when he sent literature anonymously in the mail.

79. *Woman Patriot*, 7 June 1919, 8.

80. *State Times*, 19 July 1918.

81. Other officers were John Davey of New Orleans, vice president, and E. L. Simmons of Breaux Bridge, secretary and state organizer. The meeting was engineered by Charles McLean, field representative of the National Association Opposed to Woman Suffrage (*States*, 19 June 1918).

82. The NAOWS originally had avoided close alignment with the various men's antisuffrage organizations. But with the change in presidency in 1917, it began to work more closely with male antisuffragists (Jablonsky, "Duty, Nature, and Stability," 199).

83. Sims, " 'Powers that Pray,' " 208.

84. John J. Vertrees to Miss Pearson, 8 February 1917, Pearson Collection, TSLA.

85. Sarah P. Bradford to Miss Pearson, 6 February 1917, Pearson Collection, TSLA.

86. Josephine Pearson to Mr. Vertrees, 19 August 1920, Pearson Collection, TSLA.

87. Ida M. Darden to Joseph Bailey, 16 April 1919, Darden Scrapbook, Texas State Library, Austin.

88. *News and Observer*, 22 June 1920.

89. My understanding of the relationship between female and male antisuffragists has been informed by Harrison, *Separate Spheres*, 120–48, and by Stevenson, "Women Anti-Suffragists in the 1915 Massachusetts Campaign," 81–83.

90. As discussed in more detail in Chapter 3.

91. I have found one instance where an antisuffragist was willing to debate the issue, but suffragists backed away from the challenge. See Marianne Martin to Lila Meade Valentine, 25 March 1917, Valentine Papers, VHS.

92. *Woman Patriot*, 27 July 1918, 7.

93. Jablonsky, "Duty, Nature, and Stability," 44–45. Contrast them with the Alabama antis, who "demurred" from addressing the state legislature in person as late as 1919.

94. O'Neill, *Everyone Was Brave*, 57.

95. Copies of the newspaper can be found in the Equal Suffrage Collection, NCDAH. The publication did not identify its publishers or contributors. I can only speculate that Mary Hilliard Hinton had a hand in the effort, since she was also an editor for the *North Carolina Booklet*, a publication of the state chapter of the Daughters of the Revolution.

96. Buechler, *Women's Movements in the United States*, 177.

97. "Following the Verdun 1920," manuscript scribbles by Josephine Pearson, in Pearson Collection, TSLA; Sims, " 'Powers that Pray,' " 220–21. Roberts had endorsed woman suffrage as governor, and Burn had provided the necessary one-vote margin that ratified the Nineteenth Amendment in Tennessee and the nation.

98. Richmond *News Leader*, 27 February 1926. The newspaper article seems to imply that the antisuffrage organization was still intact.

99. In sometimes amazing reversals of position, a handful of antisuffragists continued their very public roles in politics after 1920. Lucille McMillin of Tennessee, for example, as the widow of a former governor, was appointed to federal office by Franklin Roosevelt and entered that privileged circle of Washington women of the New Deal. Ida Fitzpatrick of Georgia, who had done so much to prevent the state Federation of Women's Clubs from endorsing woman suffrage, became a state organizer for the League of Women Voters. Mary Mason Anderson Williams of Virginia became active in the Democratic Party and was nominated as a member of the State Democratic Executive Committee. Marie Bankhead Owen, daughter of a U.S. senator from Alabama, went on to become active in the state Democratic Party. Ida M. Darden of Texas used her experience and contacts from the antisuffrage movement to launch a life-long career in conservative politics, eventually becoming the publisher of a McCarthy-type newspaper, *The Southern Conservative*. But such women are exceptional and should not be seen as having typical post-1920 experiences.

CHAPTER 6

1. Gordon to Laura Clay, 8 February 1920, Laura Clay Papers, University of Kentucky. (Photocopies of some of these papers are found in the artificial collection "Woman Suffragette Papers," Howard-Tilton Library, New Orleans.)

2. Eugene Anderson, in *Woman Patriot*, 9 August 1919, 2.

3. It should be noted that this split over tactics among suffragists was not limited to the South, nor even to the United States. The same phenomenon occurred in the British suffrage contest, as one faction of suffragists favored limitations on the franchise and a second faction opposed limitations of any kind. See Harrison, *Separate Spheres*, 48.

4. Gordon has received attention from Flexner, *Century of Struggle*, Fuller, *Laura Clay and the Woman's Rights Movement*, Kraditor, *Ideas of the Woman's Rights Movement*, and most recently, Wheeler, *New Women of the New South*.

5. Gilley, "Kate Gordon and Louisiana Woman Suffrage," 291–93.

6. Ibid., 294; "Jean Margaret Gordon" in James et al., eds., *Notable American Women*.

7. *Daily Picayune*, 7 July 1901; "Kate M. Gordon" in James et al., eds., *Notable American Women*. An earlier suffrage organization, the Portia Club, was still functioning at the time, but it seems that the younger suffragists in New Orleans wanted a more vigorous group than the staid Portia. Era was also interested in other women's issues, like higher education, while Portia was a single-issue club, working only for suffrage.

8. *Daily Picayune*, 7 July 1901, 6 September 1931; "Kate M. Gordon" in James et al., eds., *Notable American Women*; Clarke, *Suffrage in the Southern States*, 40.

9. Kate Gordon to Laura Clay, 3 December 1908, Clay Papers, "Woman Suffragette Papers," Howard-Tilton Library, New Orleans. See two articles by Kenneth Johnson: "Kate Gordon and the Woman-Suffrage Movement in the South" and "White Racial Attitudes as a Factor in the Arguments Against the Nineteenth Amendment."

10. Kate Gordon to Katherine McCulloch, 19 August 1915, "Woman Suffragette Papers," Howard-Tilton Library, New Orleans (photocopy of the original located in Schlesinger Library, Radcliffe College).

11. *Daily Picayune*, 7 July 1901.

12. Fuller, *Laura Clay and the Woman's Rights Movement*, 107. Although uncomfortable with its more extreme expressions, NAWSA accepted the states' rights rhetoric and the racial prejudices of its southern members during these years. During the final five or six years of the suffrage contest, however, NAWSA grew less tolerant of the more racist statements of its southern affiliates, fearing harm from the negative publicity.

13. Gordon to Laura Clay, 5 December 1907, Clay Papers, "Woman Suffragette Papers," Howard-Tilton Library, New Orleans. See also, Gordon to Clay, 11 October 1907, ibid. Gordon was not the only suffragist to make this claim. Caroline Merrick, one of the founding mothers of the suffrage movement in Louisiana, had expressed much the same sentiments as Gordon: "If Mississippi had then [in the 1890 constitutional convention] settled the race question on the only statesmanlike and just plan—by enfranchising intelligence and disfranchising ignorance—other States would have followed; for the South generally desires a model for a just and legal white supremacy—without the patent subterfuge of 'grandfather clauses' " (*Old Times in Dixieland*, 215).

14. Kraditor, *Ideas of the Woman Suffrage Movement*, 12n.

15. Gilley, "Kate Gordon and Louisiana Woman Suffrage," 297, Kenneth Johnson, "Kate Gordon and the Woman-Suffrage Movement in the South," 376.

16. Kate Gordon to Members of the Official Board, 19 September 1914 [?], "Woman Suffragette Papers," New Orleans (photocopy of original in Schlesinger Library, Radcliffe College).

17. Kraditor, *Ideas of the Woman Suffrage Movement*, 18; Kenneth Johnson, "Kate Gordon and the Woman-Suffrage Movement in the South," 368.

18. *HWS* 5:671–73. Also see Kenneth Johnson, "Kate Gordon and the Woman-Suffrage Movement in the South," passim. Other officers of the SSWSC included Laura Clay of Kentucky, vice president; Hattie (Mrs. John B.) Parker of Louisiana (wife of the future governor), corresponding secretary; and Nellie Nugent Somerville of Mississippi, treasurer.

19. Copies of the journal are in the Louisiana Collection, Howard-Tilton Library, New Orleans. Quote is from *New Southern Citizen* 1, no. 1 (October 1914): 11.

20. *HWS* 5:671; Kenneth Johnson, "Kate Gordon and the Woman-Suffrage Movement in the South," 372; Fuller, *Laura Clay and the Woman's Rights Movement*, 142; Gordon to Clay, 5 July 1913, Clay Papers, "Woman Suffragette Papers," Howard-Tilton Library, New Orleans.

21. Wheeler, *New Women of the New South*, 146.

22. Sake Meehan to Mrs. [Grace] Chamberlain, 10 November 1913, Chamberlain Papers, LHC.

23. Wheeler, *New Women of the New South*, 154–55.

24. Ibid., 155–56.

25. Hall, *Revolt Against Chivalry*, 21.

26. Clarke, *Suffrage in the Southern States*, 41.

27. Meehan to Agnes Ryan, 24 May 1913, "Woman Suffragette Papers,", Howard-Tilton Library, New Orleans (photocopy of original held by Library of Congress).

28. Meehan to Grace Chamberlain, 2 August 1913, Chamberlain Papers, LHC.

29. Kraditor, *Ideas of the Woman Suffrage Movement*, 185; Kenneth Johnson, "Kate Gordon and the Woman-Suffrage Movement in the South," 369n.

30. *Item*, 10 November 1913.

31. Anna Howard Shaw to Grace Chamberlain, 19 December 1913, Chamberlain Papers, LHC.

32. *States*, 30 June 1918; Minutes for 29 June 1918 meeting, ERA Club Papers, New Orleans Public Library. See also Lindig, *Path from the Parlor*, 139–42.

33. *States*, 21 June 1918.

34. Ibid., 27 October 1918; Gilley, "Kate Gordon and Louisiana Woman Suffrage," 303–4.

35. The state vote was 23,077 against and 19,573 for the amendment. New Orleans voted 14,552 against and 5,414 for the amendment.

36. *States*, 6 November 1918.

37. Hutson to *The Woman Citizen*, 11 November 1918, Ethel Hutson Papers, Howard-Tilton Library, New Orleans.

38. Schott, "New Orleans Machine and Progressivism," 142. See also Schott, "Pro-

gressives Against Democracy," and Haas, *Political Leadership in a Southern City*. The defeat of the state amendment in the public referendum suggests the possibility that the legislators approved the measure knowing in advance the outcome of the later referendum (fraud in elections being something of a Louisiana forte during the period). Legislators could then claim to have supported woman suffrage, supported progressivism, and supported reform, without actually making any changes in the electorate.

39. Louisiana's senators split on the amendment, with Gay (a sugar planter) opposed and Ransdell supporting it (despite Gordon's advice to the contrary). In the House, five representatives opposed it, while Garland Dupre abstained.

40. Undated newspaper clipping entitled "Federal Law Called Useless by the Era Club," Era Club Papers, New Orleans Public Library

41. *HWS* 6:338. Gordon to Laura Clay, 8 February 1920, Clay Papers, "Woman Suffragette Papers," Howard-Tilton Library, New Orleans. For details of the suffrage contest in Mississippi, see A. Taylor, "Woman Suffrage Movement in Mississippi."

42. *Official Journal of the House of Representatives*, 23.

43. *State Times*, 5 May 1920.

44. Pamphlet, Ransdell's speech on the federal amendment, 27 June 1918, Ransdell Papers, Louisiana State University Library, Baton Rouge.

45. "An Open Letter to U.S. Senator Ransdell Opposing the Federal Amendment for Woman Suffrage by Harry Gamble, New Orleans, January 26 1918." Copy found in Louisiana Vertical File, Woman Suffrage folder, Manuscripts Department, Louisiana State University Library, Baton Rouge.

46. *State Times*, 31 October 1918.

47. Lindig, *Path from the Parlor*, 162–63. In order to avoid confusion and to distinguish between "antisuffragists" and "anti-federals," I will identify this new organization as "states' rights suffragists" throughout the following discussion.

48. Membership lists published in the newspapers included 131 women and 6 men, all of whom were husbands of female members.

49. Nina Pinckard of the Southern Rejection League was present at the organizational meeting of the Anti-Federal League and pointed out the absence of Louisiana from the Southern Rejection League; but the Rejection League never organized a branch in Louisiana, because the SSWSC and the states' rights association seemed to have adequately organized the sentiment in opposition to the federal amendment.

50. Undoubtedly Gordon did not wish to join an organization not of her making, where she was unlikely to be the leader. There does not seem to be any ideological difference between Gordon and the new association.

51. *Pictorial Review of Baton Rouge*, 4.

52. Mark Carleton, *River Capital*, 120.

53. "Woman Suffrage Party of Louisiana Ratification Campaign, 1920," Ethel Hutson Papers, Howard-Tilton Library, New Orleans.

54. *Daily Picayune*, 3 June 1920.

55. The vote in the Senate on the federal amendment was 19–22. The House defeated the federal amendment 44–67.

56. *HWS* 6:234–35. Parker had been sworn in as governor just as the summer session was beginning. He believed that black disfranchisement was a progressive reform,

and his ambivalence about woman suffrage was the product of his dedication to white supremacy (Perry Howard, *Political Tendencies in Louisiana*, 204).

57. "Woman Suffrage Party of Louisiana Ratification Campaign, 1920," Ethel Hutson Papers, Howard-Tilton Library, New Orleans.

58. *States*, 8 July 1920.

59. *Daily Picayune*, 6, 18 June 1920.

60. *States*, 8 July 1920.

61. Clarke, *Suffrage in the Southern States*, 43.

62. Kate Gordon asked for a woman from each southern state to address the Louisiana Constitutional convention to "show that this movement is not a state movement, but a *Southern* States demand" (emphasis original; Kate Gordon to Members of the SSWSC, July 16, 1915, Mary Johnston Papers, Box 8, Manuscripts Division, Alderman Library, UVA). People from other states, both North and South, were present in every suffrage campaign in every southern state. This frequently became an issue in itself, with the suffragists accusing the antisuffragists of being "Northern" troublemakers, and vice versa.

63. Tennessee antisuffragist Josephine Pearson appeared to have held similar views. Defending the participation of antisuffragists from other states in the Tennessee contest, Pearson claimed that such women were not really outsiders since they had been "invited to this state by united southern sentiment for the preservation of our state constitution and white civilization" (quoted by Sims, " 'Powers that Pray,' " 212).

64. Gordon to Clay, 22 March 1923, Clay Papers, "Woman Suffragette Papers," Howard-Tilton Library, New Orleans.

65. *HWS* 6:216.

66. Gordon's coworker Anne Pleasant also continued her opposition to the expansion of opportunities for blacks. For more than a decade, Pleasant attacked the Mothers' Pension plan in Louisiana because it would offer pensions to black women as well as white women (Dinwiddie, "History of Mothers' Pensions in Louisiana," 55–57, 64).

67. Other known members of the SSWSC include: Edith (Mrs. Wesley Martin) Stoner of Florida; Mrs. Cato Sells of Texas; Mrs. Kate Trenholm Abrahams of South Carolina; Mrs. Kate Waller Barrett of Virginia; Mrs. R. O. Jones of Georgia; and Mrs. E. G. Siggers of Virginia.

68. According to the religious census of 1916, Baton Rouge did not have a Jewish congregation in that year. See U.S. Bureau of the Census, *Religious Bodies, 1916*.

69. For example, Althea Herthum of Baton Rouge: In 1910, she was twenty-seven years old, had been married four years without children, and worked as a clerk in a dry goods store. Lilburne Daspit of Baton Rouge: after graduating from LSU in 1917, she taught mathematics there for the next twenty years. Daspit's father was president of LSU and a math professor himself.

70. The federal employees were a mail carrier, a clerk of court, and an inspector for the Department of Agriculture. The local officials were the parish sheriff, two city health officers, and the commissioner of city streets in Baton Rouge. The state officials included: the state treasurer, a tax commissioner, the manager of the state penitentiary, a state railroad commissioner, a parish tax assessor, a clerk in the state treasurer's

office, a commissioner of state pensions, a livestock inspector, a state dental board examiner, and the governor (Pleasant) himself.

71. Baton Rouge Chamber of Commerce, *Baton Rouge, Louisiana*, n.p.; Carter, *John Law Wasn't So Wrong*.

72. *Pictorial Review of Baton Rouge*, 3.

73. Lee Heroman was an accountant for Standard Oil, Richard Hummel Jr. was a civil engineer in the employ of Standard Oil, Frank Clark was the general superintendent of the plant, and Tom Herthum, C. J. Barrow, and Lazard Blum all worked in some unidentified capacity for the company. In the second category, Alexander Chotin was a steamboat captain, John Dracket built boats for a living, and any number of the attorneys, merchants, and real estate agents (for example) may have derived a considerable portion of their income from business generated by Standard Oil.

74. "Baton Rouge Refinery, 50 Years, 1909–1959," *Esso News* (anniversary edition of newspaper), copy found in Louisiana State Library and Archives, Baton Rouge. The three were James Alley, James H. Kerr, and Kenneth Sale. The Yazoo and Mississippi Valley Railroad later became a part of the Illinois Central railway system.

75. Carleton, *River Capital*, 120.

76. Sitterson, *Sugar Country*, 343–58.

77. Reynolds, *Machine Politics in New Orleans*, 47–48.

78. For example, Cecile Devall, Mary Herget, Thisba Morgan, and Anne Pleasant were all active club women, and Lucy Favrot, Mattie McGrath, Thisba Morgan, and Louisa Duchien were all members of the local patriotic societies.

79. For example, Elvina Benton, Selia Boisvert, Louise Jadot, and Annie Templet all worked together at Farrnbachers Clothing and Dry Goods.

80. For example, Julia Wilkinson was the mother-in-law of Emily Wilkinson. May Taylor was the first cousin to Lulie McKowen's husband, Henry. Betty and Ellen Hummel were married to brothers, and Maud Hummel was married to one of their sons. Margaret and Celeste Carruth were married to brothers. Louisa Duchien was married to Laura Duchien's brother. Several members were mother and daughter: Clothilde Droz and daughters, Cora and Clothilde; May, Catherine, and Agnes McComb; Sallie and Fannie Lee; Mary and Anna Burgess; Ruth and Recha Elgutter; and Louise and Bertha Jadot.

81. A list of those who lived close to one another in downtown Baton Rouge would make up approximately half of the membership of the states' rights association. Two of the most densely packed streets were Florida Street (the Doughterty, Favrot, Jadot, McComb, and Puckett families) and Convention Street (the Alley, Barnes, Blum, Cook, Kerr, Harbour, Thompson, Stroube, and Sachse families).

82. *State Times*, 5 May 1920.

83. Ibid., 26, 28 May 1920.

84. Orville Chamberlain to Belle Kearney, 10 March 1915, Chamberlain Papers, LHC.

85. Walter Clark, "Suffrage a Labor Movement," 392.

86. Burts, *Richard Irvine Manning*, 188.

87. Quoted by Irvin, *Women in Kentucky*, 104.

88. Gamble, "Federal Suffrage a Racial Question in the South."

89. "Let Alabamians Write Their Representatives at Once," pamphlet reprinted from the *Advertiser*, 20 December 1916, NAWSA Papers, Antisuffrage Literature, LC.

90. Karen Blair, *Clubwoman as Feminist*, 109.

CHAPTER 7

1. Lebsock, *"A Share of Honour,"* 100–102.

2. Hatcher, "Virginia Man and the New Era for Women," 650–51. Hatcher had recently resigned her teaching position at Bryn Mawr in order to lead the effort to increase higher educational opportunities for women in her home state of Virginia (Lebsock, *"A Share of Honour,"* 125). On Hatcher see Belinda Friedman, "Orie Latham Hatcher and the Southern Woman's Educational Alliance."

3. Mary Johnston, "Woman's War," 559.

4. See Varon, " 'We Mean to be Counted,' " ch. 3.

5. Rachleff, *Black Labor in the South*, 31, 40, 97.

6. Varon, " 'We Mean to Be Counted,' " epilogue, and " 'Ladies Are Whigs,' " 80–82.

7. Treadway, "A Most Brilliant Woman," 167–68.

8. Ibid., 168–69.

9. Ibid., 169–71.

10. Lebsock, *"A Share of Honour,"* 102. See also the biographical sketch of Van Lew by Hans Trefousse in James et al., eds., *Notable American Women.*

11. Carol Clare, "Woman Suffrage Movement in Virginia," 2; Stites, "Inconceivable Revolution in Virginia," 56; and Treadway, "A Most Brilliant Woman," 171.

12. Carol Clare, "Woman Suffrage Movement in Virginia," 3; Stites, "Inconceivable Revolution in Virginia," 61; Treadway, "A Most Brilliant Woman," 172–75.

13. From the *Richmond Whig*, 1 March 1870, quoted by Varon, " 'We Mean to Be Counted,' " 474.

14. Treadway, "A Most Brilliant Woman," 175.

15. Carol Clare, "Woman Suffrage Movement in Virginia," 5; Wheeler, *New Women of the New South*, 17; Treadway, "A Most Brilliant Woman," 176.

16. See Charles Wynes's sketch in his introduction to Langhorne, *Southern Sketches from Virginia.*

17. Stites, "Inconceivable Revolution in Virginia," 63.

18. *HWS* 3:964.

19. Ibid.

20. Ibid. Langhorne's sister lived in Culpeper.

21. *HWS* 6:669.

22. Carol Clare, "Woman Suffrage Movement in Virginia," 6.

23. Kousser, *Shaping of Southern Politics*, 171–81, and Williamson, *Crucible of Race*, 234–41.

24. Moger, *Virginia*, 131.

25. Carl Abbott, *Evolution of an Urban Neighborhood*, 4–6.

26. Moger, *Virginia*, 129.

27. Pulley, *Old Virginia Restored*, 94–95.

28. Starnes and Hamm, *Some Phases of Labor Relations in Virginia*, 125.

29. Moger, *Virginia*, 155.

30. Pulley, *Old Virginia Restored*, 93.

31. Ironmonger and Phillips, *History of the Woman's Christian Temperance Union of Virginia*, 24–40

32. On the YWCA, see Mrs. Ralph R. Chappell and Mrs. J. W. S. Gilchrist, "A History of the YWCA of Richmond, Virginia, 1887–1937," *Fiftieth Annual Meeting of the Young Women's Christian Association* (Richmond: n.p., 1938). On the Locust Street Social Settlement, see Barrett, *Locust Street Social Settlement*. On Ora Brown Stokes, see sketch in Hine, ed., *Black Women in America*. On the Nurses' Settlement, see Elna C. Green, "Settlement Houses and the Origins of Social Work in the South."

33. Moger, *Virginia*, 155.

34. *Times-Dispatch*, 13 November 1909.

35. Graham, "Woman Suffrage in Virginia," 229–30; Carol Clare, "Woman Suffrage Movement in Virginia," 9–11; Hanmer, "Divine Discontent," 7.

36. L. Taylor, "Lila Meade Valentine," 471–81.

37. Hanmer, "Divine Discontent," 9; *Times-Dispatch*, 14 November 1909. Despite Valentine's record of conservatism and caution, Raymond Pulley called her "the state's most militant suffragette" (*Old Virginia Restored*, 150).

38. Diary entry for 5 July 1910, Mary Johnston Papers, Box 21, typescripts of diaries, Manuscripts Division, Alderman Library, UVA.

39. Merrie Sugg to Lila Valentine, 18 June 1912, Adele Clark Papers, Alice Tyler Correspondence, VCU.

40. 1916 annual report, by Elizabeth L. Lewis, ESL Papers, Box 3, VSLA.

41. Hanmer, "Divine Discontent," 21–22.

42. A search of the Sweet Briar school newspaper and yearbooks found no mention of woman suffrage being discussed openly on campus. The Current Events Club discussed the war, but not woman suffrage.

43. *Richmond Dispatch*, 8 March 1871.

44. Elizabeth D. L. Lewis to Lila Valentine, 11 October 1916, ESL Papers, Box 1, Correspondence, VSLA.

45. In 1913, for example, Valentine reported that she had given 100 public addresses on woman suffrage that year (*HWS* 6:666). Anne Stites speculates that the death of Elizabeth Van Lew in 1900 removed a powerful psychological obstacle to woman suffrage in Virginia ("Inconceivable Revolution in Virginia," 77).

46. Stites, "Inconceivable Revolution in Virginia," 113.

47. 1916 Yearbook (annual report), 14, Adele Clark Papers, VCU.

48. *HWS* 6:668.

49. 1915 annual report of Lynchburg ESL, ESL Papers, Box 3, VSLA.

50. Graham, "Woman Suffrage in Virginia," 232, 242.

51. Carol Clare, "Woman Suffrage Movement in Virginia," 32.

52. Norfolk league annual report (undated), ESL Papers, Box 5 (folder 290), VSLA.

53. Pamphlet entitled "Resolutions adopted by the Equal Suffrage League of Virginia in Convention at Norfolk, Virginia, October 25, 1912," Adele Clark Papers, ESL Correspondence, VCU. Mary Johnston chaired the resolutions committee (Hanmer, "Divine Discontent," 34).

54. Quoted by Hanmer, "Divine Discontent," 7.

55. *Times-Dispatch*, 14 November 1909.

56. Hanmer, "Divine Discontent," 18–19; *Times-Dispatch*, 11 February 1911.

57. Wheeler, *New Women of the New South*, 74.

58. Alice M. Tyler to Mary Johnston, 23 July 1910, Mary Johnston Papers, Box 7, Manuscripts Division, Alderman Library, UVA.

59. Alice O. Taylor to Mrs. Townsend, 23 January 1915, ESL Papers, Box 1, Correspondence, VSLA.

60. "The Divine Discontent," pamphlet by Lucy Randolph Mason, published by the ESL of Virginia, undated, copy found in Box 7, ESL Papers, VSLA.

61. William Link has characterized southern progressive reformers, both male and female, as "paternalistic" (see *Paradox of Southern Progressivism*, 192).

62. Hampton local league, Report, December 1915, ESL Papers, Box 3, Local Leagues, VSLA.

63. Lillie Barbour to Mrs. B. B. Valentine, 7 April 1913, ESL Papers, Box 1, Correspondence, VSLA.

64. See membership list, ESL of Lynchburg, September 1914, ESL Papers, Box 4, VSLA.

65. Lila M. Valentine to Mrs. (Jessie) Townsend, 25 February 1915, ESL Papers, Box 1, Correspondence, VSLA. See also Alice O. Taylor to Mrs. Townsend, 2 February 1915, ibid. Norfolk and Richmond were the two cities with the largest labor organizations in the state during these years. See Starnes and Hamm, *Some Phases of Labor Relations in Virginia*, table 23.

66. Alice M. Tyler to Mary Johnston, 1 July 1910, Mary Johnston Papers, Box 7, Manuscripts Division, Alderman Library, UVA.

67. See Mary Johnston diary entry for 27 February 1912, Mary Johnston Papers, Box 22, Manuscripts Division, Alderman Library, UVA.

68. Lila Valentine to Mrs. C. B. Townsend, 2 July 1915, ESL Papers, Box 1, Correspondence, VSLA.

69. Johnston had once refused a request to declare publicly her support for socialism, saying it "would, I think, be disastrous to my immediate cause without doing much good to yours" (quoted by Wheeler, "Mary Johnston, Suffragist," 107).

70. Hanmer, "Divine Discontent," 19, 25.

71. Mary Johnston to Lila [Valentine], 18 August 1912, Mary Johnston Papers, Box 7, Manuscripts Division, Alderman Library, UVA.

72. 1914 quote from Wheeler, *New Women of the New South*, 74.

73. Mathews and De Hart, *Sex, Gender, and the Politics of ERA*, 15.

74. *Times-Dispatch*, 20 January 1912.

75. Ibid.

76. *Times-Dispatch*, 13 January 1912.

77. Hanmer, "Divine Discontent," 29–30.

78. See diary entry for 29 March 1912, Mary Johnston Papers, Box 22, typescripts of diaries, Manuscripts Division, Alderman Library, UVA.

79. Kate Ellis Wise to Alice M. Tyler, 22 March 1912, ESL Papers, Box 1, Correspondence, VSLA.

80. *Woman's Protest*, June 1914, 15.

81. Virginia Association Opposed to Woman Suffrage, *By-Laws*, copy found in VSLA.

82. On Seawell, see *Woman's Who's Who of America*. For a recent analysis of Seawell's most famous novel, see Long, "Gendered Spaces in Molly Elliot Seawell's *Throckmorton*."

83. See diary entry for 27 Mary 1912, Mary Johnston Papers, Box 22, typescripts of diaries, Manuscripts Division, Alderman Library, UVA.

84. *Times-Dispatch*, 28 March 1912.

85. Interview with Adele Clark, *Times-Dispatch*, 3 July 1949.

86. Copies of several pamphlets in Adele Clark Papers, VCU, contain information on the free distribution of literature at local bookstores.

87. Neither the school newspaper nor the records of the Current Events Club indicate that this debate ever occurred. Since there is no mention in the records, it is impossible to tell whether the suffragists refused the challenge or whether the Sweet Briar administration refused to host the debate.

88. Lebsock, "Woman Suffrage and White Supremacy," 65, 72.

89. This broadside is found in several archives and libraries. One copy is in Governor A. H. Roberts Papers, Box 26, TSLA.

90. Undated pamphlet, "Answer to Anti-Suffragists," Adele Clark Papers, VCU.

91. Lebsock, "Woman Suffrage and White Supremacy," 65. Lebsock used editorials and letters to the editors in the Richmond papers to measure public opinion on white supremacy and woman suffrage. She found that only a small fraction of editorials made explicit mention of race ("Woman Suffrage and White Supremacy," 67).

92. From undated speech quoted by Hanmer, "Divine Discontent," 48.

93. Graham, "Woman Suffrage in Virginia," 247.

94. Lila Valentine to Mrs. (Jessie) Townsend, 10 April 1915, ESL Papers, Box 1, Correspondence, VSLA.

95. Wheeler, *New Women of the New South*, 151–52.

96. Mary Johnston to Lila [Valentine], undated [October 1915?], Mary Johnston Papers, Box 7, Manuscripts Division, Alderman Library, UVA; Hanmer, "Divine Discontent," 47.

97. Quoted by Wheeler, "Mary Johnston, Suffragist," 109.

98. Wheeler, *New Women of the New South*, 156–57.

99. Stites, "Inconceivable Revolution in Virginia," 128. Adams and Townsend of Norfolk marched, as did Mary Johnston. Lila Valentine did not.

100. Pearson and Hendricks, *Liquor and Anti-Liquor in Virginia*, 181n, 276.

101. Meredith went on to become a charter member of the Congressional Union, became local chair of the National Woman's Party, and sponsored Alice Paul's visit to Richmond in 1918 (Stites, "Inconceivable Revolution in Virginia," 130).

102. Lila Meade Valentine to Members of ESL of Va., 1 June 1915, Mary Johnston Papers, Box 1, Manuscripts Division, Alderman Library, UVA; Wheeler, *New Women of the New South*, 152.

103. Mary Johnston to Lila Valentine, 10 May 1915, ESL Papers, Box 1, Correspondence, VSLA.

104. Quoted by Bland, " 'Mad Women of the Cause,' " 86.

105. Quoted by Wheeler, *New Women of the New South*, 244 n. 57.

106. 1916 Yearbook (annual report), 18, Adele Clark Papers, VCU.

107. From copy of Lila Meade Valentine's untitled press release of 2 July 1917, ESL Papers, Box 1, Correspondence, VSLA; Wheeler, *New Women of the New South*, 76.

108. Virginia membership lists and monthly reports, National Woman's Party Papers, ser. 2, sec. 9 (reel no. 87), LC.

109. Charlotte Shelton, "Woman Suffrage and Virginia Politics," 40.

110. 1916 Yearbook (annual report), 14, Adele Clark Papers, VCU.

111. Graham, "Woman Suffrage in Virginia," 240.

112. *HWS* 6:667.

113. Shelton, "Woman Suffrage and Virginia Politics," 47.

114. Advisory Committee Opposed to Woman Suffrage, "The Virginia General Assembly and Woman's Suffrage," undated pamphlet in Southern Pamphlet Collection, Rare Books Division, University of North Carolina–Chapel Hill.

115. Quoted by Graham, "Woman Suffrage in Virginia," 246.

116. Wheeler, *New Women of the New South*, 174; Carol Clare, "Woman Suffrage Movement in Virginia," 45.

117. Wheeler, *New Women of the New South*, 174; *HWS* 6:670. Since only one branch of the legislature voted on this resolution, I have not included it in the roll call vote analysis in Tables 26 and 27.

118. *HWS* 6:671. Speakers included state auditor Roswell Page, U.S. Representatives Thomas Lomax Hunter and Howard Cecil Gilmer, Dr. Lyon G. Tyler, Carrie Chapman Catt, Elizabeth Langhorne Lewis, Kate Waller Barrett, and Lila Valentine.

119. Wheeler, *New Women of the New South*, 32.

120. *HWS* 6:672.

121. Ibid.

122. In this and the following paragraphs, roll call votes were obtained from the journals of the House and Senate for 1920. "Pairs" have not been included in the totals; only votes that were actually cast have been included. The House roll call vote for the state amendment was not recorded, and so those figures are missing from the following discussion. The twenty-five solidly antisuffragist legislators were: M. B. Booker, W. B. Cocke, J. T. Deal, W. H. Jeffreys, R. F. Leedy, W. T. Oliver, E. T. Bondurant, W. H. Buntin, T. C. Commins, J. H. Crockett, P. Dickerson, J. W. Guerrant, W. T. Hicks, J. R. Horsley, J. M. Hurt, C. C. Hyatt, W. M. McNutt, B. E. Owen, W. H. Robertson, W. B. Snidow, J. W. Stephenson, J. W. Stuart, J. B. Beverly, H. J. Taylor, and G. G. Turner.

123. *Times-Dispatch*, 5 March 1920.

124. They are W. C. Corbitt, R. O. Crockett, R. L. Gordon, J. H. Hassinger, G. W. Layman, G. W. Mapp, J. M. Parson, J. Paul, S. G. Proffit, E. L. Trinkle, J. E. West, N. L. Henley, B. F. Noland, F. Williams, and R. H. Willis.

125. The states' rights suffrage voters were: W. L. Andrews, H. F. Byrd, N. B. Early, S. L. Ferguson, W. A. Garrett, C. O. Goolrick, J. Gunn, T. Hening, S. W. Holt, M. R. Mills, J. D. Mitchell, R. O. Norris, G. T. Rison, A. W. Robertson, R. A. Russell, and J. B. Woodson.

126. "Brief for the Federal Suffrage Amendment," Box 4, Legislation Committee Records, ESL Papers, VSLA.

127. Unsigned letter to Carrie Chapman Catt, 5 September 1919, ESL Papers, Box 1, Correspondence, VSLA.

128. See Pearson and Hendricks, *Liquor and Anti-Liquor in Virginia*, ch. 14.

129. Moger, *Virginia*, 64, 110; Pulley, *Old Virginia Restored*, 72–88.

130. Pulley, *Old Virginia Restored*, 111–12.

131. Moger, *Virginia*, 64, 83.

132. Voters Registration Books, "Colored Female," 1st Precinct, Madison Ward, Richmond City Records, Voter Registrations, 1920, VSLA.

133. Maggie Lena Walker diary, entries for 12, 17, 20, 23, 28 September 1920, Maggie Lena Walker National Historic Site, Richmond.

134. Lebsock, "Woman Suffrage and White Supremacy," 84.

135. At the same time, 2,402 black men were registered (compared to 10,645 white women and 28,148 white men). Figures quoted by Lebsock, "Woman Suffrage and White Supremacy," 97 n. 57.

136. Quoted by Lebsock, "Woman Suffrage and White Supremacy," 89.

137. See "List of National Colored Republican Women Arranged According to States," undated (copied from an original in the Nannie Burroughs Papers, LC), in artificial collection labeled "Documents Pertaining to the Public Career of Maggie Lena Walker," Maggie Lena Walker National Historic Site, Richmond. Names on the list from Richmond were: Maggie Lena Walker, Catherine B. Johnson, Emeline Johnson, Margaret R. Johnson, Lillian H. Payne, and Ora B. Stokes.

138. Diary entry for 3 November 1925, Maggie Lena Walker National Historic Site, Richmond.

139. Lebsock, *"A Share of Honour,"* 124.

140. Diary entry for 20 November 1920, Maggie Lena Walker National Historic Site, Richmond.

CONCLUSION

1. Lebsock, "Woman Suffrage and White Supremacy," 74.

2. Kousser, *Shaping of Southern Politics*, 226–27.

3. See Channing, *Kentucky*, 160–63, 176–77; and Fenton, *Politics in the Border States*, 38–41, 78, 209–12.

4. Judith McArthur, "Democrats Divided: Why the Texas Legislature Gave Women Primary Suffrage in 1918," paper delivered at the 1991 Annual Meeting of the Southern Historical Association, cited by Wheeler, *New Women of the New South*, 203 n. 31.

5. North Carolina's western counties had a long history of political opposition to the eastern plantation districts. The western counties had opposed secession, resisted the Confederate draft, and refused to join the postbellum Democratic Party.

6. Cobb, *Industrialization and Southern Society*, 26.

BIBLIOGRAPHY

PRIMARY SOURCES

Manuscripts

Austin, Texas
  Austin History Center, Austin Public Library
    Francis Joseph Hardy Papers
    Jane Y. McCallum Papers
  Barker Texas History Center, University of Texas Library
    Jane McCallum Papers
    Anna Pennybacker Papers
    Julia Lee Sinks Papers
    James B. Wells Papers
  Texas State Library and Archives
    Jessie Daniel Ames Papers
    Ida Darden Scrapbook
    Erminia Thompson Folsom Papers
    Verea Godfrey Papers
    Secretary of State, Election Returns, 1918–1920
Baton Rouge, Louisiana
  Louisiana State University Library
    Joseph E. Ransdell Papers
  Louisiana State Library and Archives
    Vertical Files
Cambridge, Massachusetts
  Schlesinger Library, Radcliffe College
    Ella Harrison Collection (available on microfilm)
    Maryland Suffrage Collection (available on microfilm)
    Somerville-Howorth Collection (available on microfilm)
Chapel Hill, North Carolina
  Southern Historical Collection, University of North Carolina
    Bennehan Cameron Papers
    Cobb Family Papers
    Edwin Yates Webb Papers
Charlottesville, Virginia
  Manuscripts Division, Alderman Library, University of Virginia
    Westmoreland Davis Papers
    Mary Johnston Papers
Durham, North Carolina
  Duke University Library
    John Humphrey Small Papers

Houston, Texas
Houston Public Library, Metropolitan Research Center
Christia Adair Collection
Joseph S. Cullinam Papers
Minnie Fisher Cunningham Collection
Ida M. Darden Collection
Annette Finnigan Collection
Montgomery, Alabama
Alabama Department of Archives and History
Alabama Equal Suffrage Association Papers
John Bankhead Papers
Oscar Underwood Papers
Woman's Anti-Ratification League Papers
Nashville, Tennessee.
Tennessee State Library and Archives
Carrie Chapman Catt Papers
Lizzie Elliott Papers (Collin D. Elliot Collection)
Josephine A. Pearson Collection
A. H. Roberts Papers
New Orleans, Louisiana
Howard-Tilton Library, Manuscripts Department, Tulane University
Ethel Hutson Papers
"Woman Suffragette Papers" [photocopies of manuscripts in other repositories, primarily Laura Clay Papers at University of Kentucky]
Louisiana Historical Center, Louisiana State Museum
Grace Chamberlain Papers
New Orleans Public Library
ERA Club Papers
Raleigh, North Carolina
North Carolina Division of Archives and History
Equal Suffrage Collection
Romulus Nunn Papers
William Blount Rodman Collection (Lida T. Rodman Papers)
Gertrude Weil Papers
Richmond, Virginia
Maggie Lena Walker National Historic Site
"Documents Pertaining to the Public Career of Maggie Lena Walker" Collection
Maggie Lena Walker Diaries
Virginia Commonwealth University, James Cabbell Library Special Collections and Archives
Adele Clark Papers
Virginia Historical Society
Adele Clark Papers
Lila Meade Valentine Papers
Virginia State Library and Archives
Equal Suffrage League Papers (Ida M. Thompson Woman Suffrage Collection)

Richmond City Records, Voter Registration, 1920
Washington, D.C.
Library of Congress, Manuscripts Division
Breckinridge Family Papers
National American Woman Suffrage Association Papers
National Woman's Party Papers (available on microfilm)
Key Pittman Papers
Mary Church Terrell Papers
John Sharp Williams Papers

Published Manuscripts

Brooks, Aubrey Lee, and Hugh Talmage Lefler, eds. *The Papers of Walter Clark*. Chapel Hill: University of North Carolina Press, 1950.
DuBois, Ellen Carol, ed. *Elizabeth Cady Stanton, Susan B. Anthony, Correspondence, Writings, Speeches*. New York: Schocken Books, 1981.
Humphrey, Janet G., ed. *A Texas Suffragist: Diaries and Writings of Jane Y. McCallum*. Austin, Tex.: Ellen Temple Press, 1988.
Krock, Arthur, comp. *The Editorials of Henry Watterson*. New York: George Doran Co., 1923.
Link, Arthur, ed. *The Papers of Woodrow Wilson*. Princeton: Princeton University Press, 1977–90.

Memoirs, Autobiographies

Kearney, Belle. *A Slaveholder's Daughter*. 1900. Reprint. New York: Negro Universities Press, 1969.
Meriwether, Elizabeth A. *Recollections of 92 Years*. Nashville: Tennessee Historical Commission, 1958.
Merrick, Caroline E. *Old Times in Dixieland: A Southern Matron's Memories*. New York: Grafton Press, 1901.
Moore, Alfred Waddell. *Some Memories of My Life*. Raleigh: Edwards & Broughton, 1908.
Park, Maud Wood. *Front Door Lobby*. Boston: Beacon Press, 1960.
Winston, Robert Watson. *It's a Far Cry*. New York: Henry Holt & Co., 1937.

Newspapers and Journals

Advertiser (Montgomery, Ala., 1915–20)
Banner (Nashville, Tenn., 1916–20)
Clarion-Ledger (Jackson, Miss., 1913–20)
Constitution (Atlanta, Ga., 1894–95)
The Crisis (New York, N.Y., 1915)
Daily News (Greensboro, N.C., 1920)
Daily Picayune [*Times-Picayune*] (New Orleans, La., 1903–20)
Express (San Antonio, Tex., 1894, 1919)

The Ferguson Forum (Tyler, Tex., 1917–20)
Item (New Orleans, La., 1914–20)
New Southern Citizen (New Orleans, La., 1914–17)
News and Observer (Raleigh, N.C., 1913–20)
States (New Orleans, La., 1914–20)
State Times (Baton Rouge, La., 1918–20)
Tennessean (Nashville, Tenn., 1916, 1920)
Times-Dispatch (Richmond, Va., 1912–20)
Times (Selma, Ala., 1916–20)
The Woman Patriot (Washington, D.C., 1918–21)
The Woman's Protest (New York, N.Y., 1912–18)

City Directories

Baton Rouge, La., 1906, 1911, 1920, 1924, 1947
Birmingham, Ala., 1919, 1920
Chattanooga, Tenn., 1920
Dallas, Tex., 1918, 1920
El Paso, Tex., 1917
Florence, Ala., 1920
Ft. Worth, Tex., 1910, 1920
Houston, Tex., 1915–20
Knoxville, Tenn., 1918
Memphis, Tenn., 1922
Mobile, Ala., 1920
Montgomery, Ala., 1916, 1920
Nashville, Tenn., 1920
New Orleans, La., 1910, 1920
Norfolk, Va., 1920–21
Petersburg, Va., 1918
Raleigh, N.C., 1915–20
Richmond, Va., 1920
Roanoke, Va., 1919–20
San Antonio, Tex., 1921–22
Selma, Ala., 1916, 1920
Tuscaloosa, Ala., 1917
Waco, Tex., 1911

Pamphlets, Contemporary Periodicals, etc.

Abbott, Lyman. "Answer to the Arguments in Support of Woman Suffrage." *Annals of American Academy of Political and Social Science* 35 (May 1910).
Advisory Committee Opposed to Woman Suffrage. "The Virginia General Assembly and Woman's Suffrage." Undated pamphlet in Southern Pamphlet Collection, Rare Books Division, University of North Carolina, Chapel Hill.
Allen, Joseph Cady. "The South and Suffrage." *New Republic* 13 (5 January 1918).

Allen, William H. *Woman's Part in Government, Whether She Votes or Not*. New York: Dodd, Mead, and Co., 1911.
Anderson, Eugene. *Unchaining the Demons of the Lower World, or A Petition of Ninety-Nine Per Cent. Against Suffrage*. Macon, Ga.: n.p., [1918?].
Arnold, Mrs. George F. *Local Politics and Lessons From Ancient Rome*. [Houston?]: Texas Association Opposed to Woman Suffrage, 1916.
Barrett, Janie Porter. *Locust Street Social Settlement*. Hampton, Va.: n.p., 1912.
Bissell, Emily P. *A Talk to Women on the Suffrage Question*. New York: National Association Opposed to Woman Suffrage, 1909.
Blackwell, Henry B. *A Solution of the Southern Question*. Boston: NAWSA, 1890.
Clark, Walter. "Suffrage a Labor Movement." *American Federationist* 26 (May 1919).
Clarke, Ida Clyde, comp. *Suffrage in the Southern States*. Nashville: Williams Printing, 1914.
Cooper, Anna J. *A Voice from the South*. New York: Negro University Press, 1969.
Dawson, J. W. "Woman Suffrage." *Catholic World* 112 (November 1920).
Dodge, Mrs. Arthur M. "Woman Suffrage Opposed to Woman's Rights." *Annals of American Academy of Political and Social Science* 56 (November 1914).
Du Bois, W. E. B. *Disfranchisement*. New York: NAWSA, 1915.
Dudley, Mrs. Guilford. *The Negro Vote in the South: A Southern Woman's Viewpoint*. New York: NAWSA, 1918.
Felton, Mrs. William H. *On the Subjection of Women and the Enfranchisement of Women*. Cartersville, Ga.: n.p., 1915.
Gamble, Harry. "Federal Suffrage a Racial Question in the South." An Address before the New Orleans Press Club, 11 March 1918. N.C.: n.p., 1918[?]
———. *An Open Letter to U.S. Senator Ransdell Opposing the Federal Amendment for Woman Suffrage*. [New Orleans?]: n.p., 1918.
Goodwin, Grace Duffield. *Anti-Suffrage: Ten Good Reasons*. New York: Duffield and Co., 1912.
Haien, J. A., ed. *Anti-Suffrage Essays by Massachusetts Women*. Boston: Forum, 1916.
Haines, Helen. "Catholic Womanhood and Suffrage." *Catholic World* 102 (October 1915).
Hammond, L[ily] H. "A Southern View of the Negro." *Outlook* 73 (14 March 1903).
Hatcher, Orie Latham, "The Virginia Man and the New Era for Women," *The Nation* 106 (1 June 1918): 650–51
Holland, Robert Afton. "The Suffragette." *Sewanee Review* 17 (June 1909).
Johnston, Mary. "The Woman's War." *Atlantic Monthly* 105 (April 1910).
Jones, Mrs. Gilbert. "Position of the Anti-Suffragists." *American Academy of Political and Social Science Annals*, supplement, 35 (May 1910).
Leatherbee, Mrs. A. T. *Anti-Suffrage Campaign Manual*. Boston: A. T. Bliss, 1915.
Lockwood, George R. *Why I Oppose Woman Suffrage*. [St. Louis?]: n.p., 1912.
———. *Woman Suffrage a Menace to the South*. St. Louis: n.p., 1917.
Lyon, A. A. *Suffragettes and Suffragettism*. Nashville: n.p., 1915.
McKee, Joseph V. "Shall Women Vote?" *Catholic World* 102 (October 1915).
Meyer, Annie N. "The Anti-Suffragist Replies." *The New Republic* 13 (1 December 1917).

———. "Woman's Assumption of Sex Superiority." *North American Review* 178 (January 1904).
National American Woman Suffrage Association. *Objections to the Federal Amendment*. New York: NAWSA, 1917.
———. *Woman Suffrage and the Liquor Interests*. New York: NAWSA, 1916.
Parkman, Francis. *Some of the Reasons Against Woman Suffrage*. 1883. Reprint. Northridge, Calif.: Santa Susana Press, 1977.
Peebles, Isaac Lockhart. *Is Woman Suffrage Right? The Question Answered*. Meridian, Miss.: T. Farmer, 1918.
Seawell, Molly Elliot. *The Ladies' Battle*. New York: McMillan, 1911.
———. "Two Suffrage Mistakes." *North American Review* 199 (March 1914).
The Tintagil Club. *Official Guide to the City of Montgomery, Alabama*. Montgomery: Paragon, 1920.
Vertrees, John J. *An Address to the Men of Tennessee on Female Suffrage*. Nashville: n.p., 1916.
Virginia Association Opposed to Woman Suffrage. *By-Laws*. Richmond: n.p., n.d.
———. *Why Women Should Oppose Equal Suffrage*. Richmond: n.p., n.d.
Walsh, Robert C. *Anti-Woman Suffrage and Criticisms*. St. Louis: Wilson Printing, 1916.
Watson, Annah Robinson. "Attitude of Southern Women on the Suffrage Question." *Arena* 63 (February 1895).
Wells, Mrs. James B. *Why I Am Opposed to Woman Suffrage*. Austin, Tex.: n.p., 1915.

Published Official Records

Congressional Record. Washington: U.S. Government Printing Office, 1885–1919.
Hearings Before House Committee on Woman Suffrage. Washington: U.S. Government Printing Office, 1917, 1919.
Hearings Before Committee on Woman Suffrage of the Senate. Washington: U.S. Government Printing Office, 1917, 1919.
Hill, Joseph A. *Women in Gainful Occupations, 1870 to 1920*. Washington: U.S. Government Printing Office, 1929.
Historical Statistics of the United States. Washington: U.S. Government Printing Office, 1961.
Journal of the House of Delegates of Virginia, 1920. Richmond: n.p., 1920.
Journal of the Senate of the Commonwealth of Virginia, 1920. Richmond: n.p., 1920.
Louisiana Constitutional Convention. *The Convention of '98*. New Orleans: William E. Myers, 1898.
Mississippi Constitutional Convention. *Journal of the Convention*. Jackson, Miss.: n.p., 1890.
Official Journal of the House of Representatives, 1920. Baton Rouge: n.p., 1920.
Official Proceedings of the Constitutional Convention of the State of Alabama May 21st, 1901, to September 3rd, 1901. 4 vols. Wetumpka, Ala.: Wetumpka Printing, 1940.
Report and Hearings of the Judiciary Committee of the Senate, on Brewing and Liquor Interests. Washington: U.S. Government Printing Office, 1918, 1919.

Southern Association of College Women. *Proceedings of the . . . Annual Meeting.* N.p., 1908–17.
U.S. Bureau of the Census. *Negroes in the United States, 1920–1935*. Washington: U.S. Government Printing Office, 1935.
———. *Negro Population, 1790–1915*. Washington: U.S. Government Printing Office, 1918.
———. *Population, 1910*. Washington: U.S. Government Printing Office, 1913.
———. *Religious Bodies, 1916*. Washington: U.S. Government Printing Office, 1919.

Federal Census Population Schedules and Soundex

Thirteenth Census (1910) and Fourteenth Census (1920):
Alabama
Louisiana
Mississippi
North Carolina
Tennessee
Texas
Virginia

SECONDARY SOURCES

Biographical References

Adams, Frank Carter. *Texas Democracy, A Centennial History*. 4 vols. Austin, Tex.: Democratic Historical Association, 1937.
Allison, John. *Notable Men of Tennessee*. Atlanta: Southern Historical Association, 1905.
Andrews, Matthew Page. *Tercentenary History of Maryland*. Vols. 2–4. Chicago: Clarke, 1925.
Ashe, Samuel A., ed. *Biographical History of North Carolina: From Colonial Times to the Present*. 8 vols. Greensboro: Charles Van Noppen, 1905–17.
———. *Cyclopedia of Eminent and Representative Men of the Carolinas of the 19th Century*. 1892. Reprint, Spartanburg, S.C.: Reprint Co., 1972.
Bailey, Emory, ed. *Who's Who in Texas, A Biographical Directory*. Dallas: Who's Who Publishing Co., 1931.
Biographical Souvenir of the States of Georgia and Florida. Chicago: Battey, 1889.
Blair, Ruth. *Georgia Women of 1926*. Atlanta: Georgia Department of Archives and History, 1926.
The Book of Louisiana. New Orleans: New Orleans *Item*, 1916.
Brooks, Elizabeth. *Prominent Women of Texas*. Akron: Werner Co., 1896.
Brown, Dave H. *A History of Who's Who in Louisiana Politics in 1916*. N.p.: *Louisiana Chronicle Democrat*, 1916.
Bruce, Philip. *Virginia, Rebirth of the Old Dominion*. 5 vols. Chicago: Lewis Publishing, 1929.

Carroll, Thomas B. *Historical Sketches of Oktibbeha County, Mississippi*. Gulfport: Dixie Press, 1931.

Chambers, Henry E. *A History of Louisiana*. 3 vols. Chicago: American Historical Society, 1925.

Chapin, George M. *Florida 1513–1913: Past, Present and Future*. Chicago: Clarke Publishing, 1914.

Christian, W. Asbury. *Richmond, Her Past and Present*. Richmond: Jenkins, 1912.

City Directory and History of Montgomery, Alabama. Montgomery: Bingham, 1878.

Clark, Joseph L. *The Texas Gulf Coast, Its History and Development*. Vols. 3–5. New York: Lewis Publishing, 1955.

Collier, Margaret. *Biographies of Representative Women of the South, 1861–1925*. 6 vols. College Park, Ga.,: n.p., 1920–38.

Connor, R. D. W. *Makers of North Carolina History*. Raleigh: Thompson, 1911.

———. *North Carolina, Rebuilding an Ancient Commonwealth*. 4 vols. Chicago: American Historical Society, 1929.

Convention Sketches: Brief Biographies of the Members of the Constitutional Convention, 1877. Atlanta: n.p., 1877.

Cooper, Walter G. *The Story of Georgia*. 4 vols. New York: American Historical Society, 1938.

Cornwall, Ilene J., ed. *Biographical Directory of the Tennessee General Assembly*. Vol. 3 (1901–31). Nashville: Tennessee Historical Commission, 1988.

Crawford, Ann Fears, and Crystal Sasse Ragsdale. *Women in Texas*. Burnet, Tex.: Eakin Press, 1982.

Crawford, Geddings H. *Who's Who in South Carolina*. Columbia: McCaw, 1921.

Crowell, Evelyn. *Men of Achievement*. Dallas: J. Moranz, 1948.

Cruikshank, George. *A History of Birmingham and Its Environs*. 2 vols. Chicago: Lewis Publishing, 1920.

Cutler, Harry G. *History of Florida, Past and Present*. 3 vols. Chicago: Lewis Publishing, 1923.

Daniell, Lewis. *Texas, The Country and Its Men*. Austin, Tex.: n.p., 1924.

Davis, Ellis Arthur. *The Historical Encyclopedia of Louisiana*. N.p.: Louisiana Historical Bureau, [1940?]

Davis, Ellis A., and Edwin H. Grobe, eds. *The New Encyclopedia of Texas*. Dallas: Texas Development Bureau, 1926.

Day, James M. *Women of Texas*. Waco: Texian Press, 1972.

Deacon, William M. *Reference Biography of Louisiana Bench and Bar*. New Orleans: Cox Printing, 1922.

DeCottes, Nina Browne (Mrs. J. M.). *Social Directory of Montgomery, Alabama 1900–1901*. Montgomery: Brown Printing, 1900.

Dowd, Jerome. *Sketches of Prominent Living North Carolinians*. Raleigh: Edwards and Broughton, 1888.

DuBose, Joel C. *Notable Men of Alabama*. Atlanta: Southern Historical Association, 1904.

Fenwick, Marin B., ed. *Who's Who Among the Women of San Antonio and Southwest Texas*. Austin, Tex.: n.p., 1917.

Garlington, J. C. *Men of the Time: Sketches of Living Notables*. Spartanburg, S.C.: Garlington, 1902.
Garrett, Franklin M. *Atlanta and Its Environs*. Vol. 3. New York: Lewis, 1954.
Georgia's General Assembly of 1880–1. Atlanta: Harrison & Co., 1882.
Geraldton, Mrs. William W. *Social Directory, Nashville Tennessee*. Nashville: n.p., 1911.
Gilchrist, Annie Somers. *Some Representative Women of Tennessee*. Nashville: McQuiddy, 1902.
Gillum, James. *Prominent Tennesseans, 1796–1938*. Lewisburg, Tenn.: Who's Who Publishing Co, 1940.
Gilmore, Rose Long. *Davidson County Women in the World War, 1914–1919*. Nashville: Foster & Parks, 1923.
Gresham, John M. *Biographical Cyclopedia of the Commonwealth of Kentucky*. Chicago: Gresham Publishing, 1896.
Hale, William. *A History of Tennessee and Tennesseans*. Chicago: Lewis Publishing, 1913.
Hamer, Philip M., ed. *Tennessee: A History*. 4 vols. New York: American Historical Society, 1933.
Hardy, Dermot. *Historical Review of Southeast Texas*. 2 vols. Chicago: Lewis Publishing, 1910.
Hemphill, James C. *Men of Mark in South Carolina*. Washington, D.C.: Men of Mark Publishing Co., 1907–9.
Hempstead, Fay. *Historical Review of Arkansas*. 3 vols. Chicago: Lewis Publishing, 1911.
Henderson, Archibald. *North Carolina, The Old North State and the New*. 5 vols. Chicago: Lewis Publishing, 1941.
Herndon, Dallas. *Centennial History of Arkansas*. Vols. 2–3. Chicago: Clarke, 1922.
Hine, Darlene Clark, ed. *Black Women in America: An Historical Encyclopedia*. Brooklyn: Carlson, 1993.
History of Texas: Houston and Galveston. Chicago: Lewis Publishing, 1895.
Hoff, N. P. *Alabama Blue Book and Social Register, 1929*. Birmingham: Blue Book Publishing, 1929.
Howell, Clark. *History of Georgia*. 4 vols. Chicago: Clarke Publishing, 1926.
James, Edward T., et al., eds. *Notable American Women: A Biographical Dictionary*. 4 vols. Cambridge, Mass.: Belknap Press, 1971–80.
Johnson, E. Polk. *A History of Kentucky and Kentuckians*. 3 vols. Chicago: Lewis Publishing, 1912.
Johnston, J. Stoddard. *Memorial History of Louisville*. Vol. 2. Chicago: American Biographical Publishers, 1897.
Kelley, Dayton, ed. *The Handbook of Waco and McLennan County, Texas*. Waco: Texian Press, 1972.
Kelley, Sarah F. *West Nashville, Its People and Environs*. Nashville: by author, 1987.
Kerr, Charles. *History of Kentucky*. 5 vols. Chicago: American Historical Society, 1922.
Knight, Lucian L. *Encyclopedia of Georgia Biography*. Atlanta: Cawston, 1931.

———. *A Standard History of Georgia and Georgians*. 6 vols. Chicago: Lewis Publishing, 1917.

LaBree, Benjamin. *Notable Men of Kentucky at the Beginning of the 20th Century*. Louisville: Felter, 1902.

Marks, Henry S. *Who Was Who in Alabama*. Huntsville, Ala.: Strode Publishers, 1972.

———. *Who Was Who in Florida*. Huntsville, Ala.: Strode Publishers, 1973.

Martin, Thomas. *Atlanta and Its Builders*. 2 vols. N.p.: Century Memorial, 1902.

Matlock, Guy A. *Who's Who in Alabama*. Birmingham: DuBose Publishing, 1940.

Mellichamp, Josephine. *Senators from Georgia*. Huntsville, Ala.: Strode Publishers, 1976.

Memoirs of Georgia. 2 vols. Atlanta: Southern Historical Association, 1895.

Moore, A. B. *History of Alabama and Her People*. 3 vols. Chicago: American Historical Society, 1927.

Moore, D. D. *Louisianans and Their State*. New Orleans: n.p., 1919.

Moore, D. D., et al., eds. *Men of the South*. New Orleans: Southern Biographical Association, 1922.

Moore, John T. *Tennessee, The Volunteer State*. Vols. 3–4. Chicago: S. J. Clarke, 1923.

Moreland, Sinclair. *The Texas Women's Hall of Fame*. Austin, Tex.: Biographical Press, 1917.

Moyer, Homer E. *Who's Who and What to See in Florida*. St. Petersburg: n.p., 1935.

Munsell, William P. *Some Notable Americans of the Present Century*. Coral Gables: Munsell, 1936.

Nashville Society Blue Book. New York: Dau Publishing Co., 1900.

Northen, William J. *Men of Mark in Georgia*. 7 vols. Atlanta: Caldwell, 1906–12.

Owen, Marie B. *The Story of Alabama, A History of the State*. 5 vols. Chicago: Lewis Publishing, 1949.

Owen, Thomas M. *History of Alabama and Dictionary of Alabama Biography*. Chicago: Clarke Publishing, 1921.

Owens, W. T. *Who's Who in Louisville*. Louisville: Standard Printing, 1926.

Paddock, B. B. *A History of Central and Western Texas*. Chicago: Lewis Publishing, 1911.

———. *History of Texas: Fort Worth and the Texas Northwest*. 4 vols. Chicago: Lewis Publishing, 1922.

———. *A Twentieth Century History and Biographical Record of North and West Texas*. Chicago: Lewis Publishing, 1906.

Powell, William S., ed. *Dictionary of North Carolina Biography*. 6 vols. Chapel Hill: University of North Carolina Press, 1979–96 .

Rerick, Rowland H. *Memoirs of Florida*. 2 vols. Atlanta: Southern Historical Association, 1902.

Rogers, Lou. *Tar Heel Women*. Raleigh: Warren Publishing, 1949.

Rogers, Mary Beth. *Texas Women: A Celebration of History*. Austin, Tex.: Texas Foundation for Women's Resources, 1981.

Rowland, Dunbar, ed. *History of Mississippi, The Heart of the South*. Chicago: S. J. Clarke, 1925. Reprint, Spartanburg, S.C.: Reprint Co., 1978.

Scharf, J. Thomas. *History of Baltimore City and County*. 2 vols. Philadelphia: Everts, 1881.
Scott, S. S. *The Alabama Legislatures of 1857–8 and 1859–60*. Montgomery: Alabama Historical Society, 1905.
Snowden, Yates. *History of South Carolina*. 5 vols. Chicago: Lewis Publishing, 1920.
Southard, Mary Y. *Who's Who in Kentucky*. Louisville: Standard Publishing, 1936.
Temple, Oliver. *Notable Men of Tennessee 1833–1875*. Nashville: n.p., 1912.
Texas Federation of Women's Clubs. *Who's Who of the Womanhood of Texas*. Ft. Worth: Stafford-London, 1924.
Thomas, D. Y. *Arkansas and Its People*. New York: American Historical Society, 1930.
Tunis, Allyn B. *Press Reference Book of Prominent Virginians*. Richmond: Virginia Newspaper Writers Association, 1916.
Turbeville, Robert. *Eminent Georgians*. Atlanta: n.p., 1937.
Tyler, Lyon G. *Encyclopedia of Virginia Biography*. New York: Lewis Publishing, 1915.
Wallace, David D. *The History of South Carolina*. 3 vols. New York: American Historical Society, 1934.
Who's Who in Louisiana. Chicago: Larkin, Roosevelt and Larkin, 1947.
Who's Who in Louisiana and Mississippi: Biographical Sketches of Prominent Men and Women of Louisiana and Mississippi. New Orleans: *Times-Picayune*, 1918.
Who's Who in Tennessee. Memphis: Paul and Douglas Co., 1911.
Who's Who in the South. Washington, D.C.: Mayflower Publishing, 1927.
Wilks, W. P. *Biographical Dictionary of Alabama Baptists*. Opelika: Post Publishing, 1940.
Woman's Who's Who of America. New York: American Commonwealth Company, 1916.
Woman's Work in Tennessee. Memphis: Tennessee Federation of Woman's Clubs, 1916.
Women of Georgia; A Ready and Accurate Reference Book for Newspapers and Librarians. Atlanta: Georgia Press Reference Association, Byrd Publishing, 1927.
Wooldridge, J., ed. *History of Nashville, Tennessee*. Nashville: n.p., 1890.

Other Books

Abbott, Carl. *The Evolution of an Urban Neighborhood: Colonial Place, Norfolk, Virginia*. Charlottesville: University of Virginia Institute of Government, 1975.
Acheson, Sam Hanna. *Joe Bailey, The Last Democrat*. New York: MacMillan, 1932.
Anders, Evan. *Boss Rule in South Texas: The Progressive Era*. Austin: University of Texas Press, 1982.
Anderson, Nancy Fix. *Woman Against Women in Victorian England, A Life of Eliza Lynn Linton*. Bloomington: Indiana University Press, 1987.
Ansley, Lula. *History of the Georgia Woman's Christian Temperance Union from Its Organization, 1883–1907*. Columbus, Ga.: Gilbert Printing, 1914.
Ayers, Edward L. *The Promise of the New South, Life After Reconstruction*. New York: Oxford University Press, 1992.

Ayers, Edward L., and John Willis, eds. *The Edge of the South: Life in Nineteenth Century Virginia*. Charlottesville: University Press of Virginia, 1991.
Bailey, Hugh. *Liberalism in the New South: Southern Social Reformers and the Progressive Movement*. Coral Gables: University of Miami Press, 1969.
Bailey, Kenneth K. *Southern White Protestantism in the Twentieth Century*. New York: Harper and Row, 1964.
Baines, Mrs. William M. *A Story of the Texas White Ribboners*. N.p., 1935.
Banner, Lois W. *Elizabeth Cady Stanton: A Radical for Woman's Rights*. Boston: Little, Brown and Co., 1980.
———. *Women in Modern America: A Brief History*. New York: Harcourt Brace Jovanovich, 1984
Barr, Alwyn. *Reconstruction to Reform: Texas Politics 1876–1906*. Austin: University of Texas Press, 1971.
Barry, Kathleen. *Susan B. Anthony: A Biography of a Singular Feminist*. New York: New York University Press, 1988.
Bartley, Numan V. *The Creation of Modern Georgia*. Athens, Ga.: University of Georgia Press, 1983.
———. *The Rise of Massive Resistance: Race and Politics in the South During the 1950s*. Baton Rouge: Louisiana State University Press, 1969.
Baton Rouge Chamber of Commerce. *Baton Rouge, Louisiana*. Baton Rouge: Chamber of Commerce, 1929.
Beard, Mattie Carson. *The W.C.T.U. in the Volunteer State*. Kingsport, Tenn.: Kingsport Press, 1962.
Beeton, Beverly. *Women Vote in the West: The Woman Suffrage Movement, 1869–1896*. New York: Garland Publishing, 1986.
Berg, Barbara J. *The Remembered Gate: Origins of American Feminism, The Woman and the City, 1800–1860*. New York: Oxford University Press, 1978.
Billings, Dwight. *Planters and the Making of a "New South": Class, Politics, and Development in North Carolina, 1865–1900*. Chapel Hill: University of North Carolina Press, 1979.
Blair, Karen J. *The Clubwoman as Feminist: True Womanhood Redefined, 1868–1914*. New York: Holmes and Meier, 1980.
Blee, Kathleen. *Women of the Klan: Racism and Gender in the 1920s*. Berkeley: University of California Press, 1991.
Bordin, Ruth. *Women and Temperance: The Quest for Power and Liberty, 1873–1900*. Philadelphia: Temple University Press, 1981.
Bowie, Walter Russell. *Sunrise in the South: The Life of Mary-Cooke Branch Munford*. Richmond: William Byrd Press, 1942.
Buechler, Steven M. *Women's Movements in the United States: Woman Suffrage, Equal Rights, and Beyond*. New Brunswick: Rutgers University Press, 1990.
Buhle, Mari Jo. *Women and American Socialism, 1870–1920*. Urbana: University of Illinois Press, 1981.
Bull, Emily L. *Eulalie*. Aiken, S.C.: n.p., 1973.
Buni, Andrew. *The Negro in Virginia Politics, 1902–1965*. Charlottesville: University Press of Virginia, 1967.

Burts, Robert Milton. *Richard Irvine Manning and the Progessive Movement in South Carolina*. Columbia: University of South Carolina Press, 1974.
Campbell, Barbara Kuhn. *The "Liberated" Woman of 1914: Prominent Women in the Progressive Era*. N.p.: UMI Research Press, 1976, 1979.
Carleton, Don E. *Red Scare! Right-wing Hysteria, Fifties Fanaticism and Their Legacy in Texas*. Austin: Texas Monthly Press, 1984.
Carleton, Mark. *River Capital: An Illustrated History of Baton Rouge*. Baton Rouge: Windsor Press, 1981.
Carter, Hodding. *John Law Wasn't So Wrong*. N.C.: Esso Standard Oil Co., 1952.
Catt, Carrie Chapman, and Nettie Rogers Shuler. *Woman Suffrage and Politics: The Inner Story of the Suffrage Movement*. New York: Charles Scribner, 1923.
Cell, John W. *The Highest Stage of White Supremacy*. New York: Cambridge University Press, 1982.
Channing, Steven. *Kentucky: A Bicentennial History*. New York: Norton, 1977.
Christian, Stella L. *History of the Texas Federation of Women's Clubs*. Houston: Dealey-Adey-Elgin, 1919.
Clare, Virginia. *Thunder and Stars: The Life of Mildred Rutherford*. Oglethorpe, Ga.: Oglethorpe University Press, 1941.
Clayton, Bruce, and John A. Salmond, eds. *The South is Another Land: Essays on the Twentieth-Century South*. Westport, Conn.: Greenwood Press, 1987.
Cobb, James C. *Industrialization and Southern Society, 1877–1984*. Lexington: University Press of Kentucky, 1984.
Cooper, William J. *The Conservative Regime: South Carolina*. Baltimore: The Johns Hopkins University Press, 1968.
Cott, Nancy F. *The Grounding of Modern Feminism*. New Haven: Yale University Press, 1987.
Craighead, Lura. *History of the Alabama Federation of Women's Clubs*. Vol. 1 (1895–1918). Montgomery: n.p., 1936.
Davis, Allen F. *Spearheads for Reform: The Social Settlements and the Progressive Movement, 1890–1914*. New York: Oxford University Press, 1967.
Degler, Carl. *At Odds: Women and the Family in America from the Revolution to the Present*. New York: Oxford University Press, 1980.
Dillman, Caroline Matheny, ed. *Southern Women*. New York: Hemisphere Publishing, 1988.
Dodd, Donald B., and Wynelle S. Dodd. *Historical Statistics of the South, 1790–1970*. University: University of Alabama Press, 1973.
Doster, James F. *Railroads in Alabama Politics, 1875–1914*. University: University of Alabama Press, 1957.
Doyle, Don. *Nashville Since the 1920s*. Knoxville: University of Tennessee Press, 1985.
———. *New Men, New Cities, New South*. Chapel Hill: University of North Carolina Press, 1990.
DuBois, Ellen Carol. *Feminism and Suffrage: The Emergence of an Independent Women's Movement in America*. Ithaca: Cornell University Press, 1978.
Eighmy, John Lee. *Churches in Cultural Captivity: A History of the Social Attitudes of Southern Baptists*. Knoxville: University of Tennessee Press, 1972.

Ellis, John Tracy. *The Life of James Cardinal Gibbons, Archbishop of Baltimore.* Milwaukee: Bruce Publishing, 1952.

Escott, Paul D. *After Secession: Jefferson Davis and the Failure of Confederate Nationalism.* Baton Rouge: Louisiana State University Press, 1978.

———. *Many Excellent People: Power and Privilege in North Carolina, 1850–1900.* Chapel Hill: University of North Carolina Press, 1985.

Evans, Sara M. *Born for Liberty: A History of Women in America.* New York: Free Press, 1989.

Ezell, John Samuel. *The South Since 1865.* Norman: University of Oklahoma Press, 1975.

Feagin, Joe R. *Free Enterprise City: Houston in Political-Economic Perspective.* New Brunswick: Rutgers University Press, 1988.

Fenton, John Harold. *Politics in the Border States: A Study of the Patterns of Political Organization, and Political Changes, Common to the Border States: Maryland, West Virginia, Kentucky, and Missouri.* New Orleans: Hauser Press, 1957.

Filene, Peter. *Him/Her/Self: Sex Roles in Modern America.* Baltimore: The Johns Hopkins University Press, 1974, 1986.

Flexner, Eleanor. *Century of Struggle: The Woman's Rights Movement in the United States.* Rev. ed. Cambridge, Mass.: The Belknap Press of Harvard University Press, 1975.

Flynt, Wayne. *Duncan Upshaw Fletcher: Dixie's Reluctant Progressive.* Tallahassee: Florida State University Press, 1971.

———. *Montgomery: An Illustrated History.* Woodland Hills, Calif.: Windsor Press, 1980.

Foner, Eric. *Reconstruction: America's Unfinished Revolution, 1863–1877.* New York: Harper and Row, 1988.

Ford, Linda. *Iron-Jawed Angels: The Suffrage Militancy of the National Woman's Party.* Lanham, Md.: University Press of America, 1991.

Foster, Gaines M. *Ghosts of the Confederacy: Defeat, The Lost Cause, and the Emergence of the New South 1865 to 1913.* New York: Oxford University Press, 1987.

Fox-Genovese, Elizabeth. *Within the Plantation Household: Black and White Women of the Old South.* Chapel Hill: University of North Carolina Press, 1988.

Frankel, Noralee, and Nancy S. Dye, eds. *Gender, Class, Race, and Reform in the Progressive Era.* Lexington: University Press of Kentucky, 1991.

Franklin, John Hope, and Alfred A. Moss Jr. *From Slavery to Freedom: A History of Negro Americans.* 6th ed. New York: Alfred A. Knopf, 1988.

Fredrickson, George. *The Black Image in the White Mind: The Debate on Afro-American Character and Destiny, 1817–1914.* New York: Harper and Row, 1971.

Friedman, Jean E. *The Enclosed Garden: Women and Community in the Evangelical South, 1830–1930.* Chapel Hill: University of North Carolina Press, 1985.

Fuller, Paul E. *Laura Clay and the Woman's Rights Movement.* Lexington: University Press of Kentucky, 1975.

Gaither, Gerald. *Blacks and the Populist Revolt: Ballots and Bigrotry in the New South.* Tuscaloosa: University of Alabama Press, 1977.

Gaston, Paul M. *The New South Creed: A Study in Southern Mythmaking*. New York: Alfred A. Knopf, 1970.
Gay, Daniel Savage. *Alabama: A Place, A People, A Point of View*. Dubuque, Iowa: Kendall Hunt, 1977.
Genovese, Eugene. *The Political Economy of Slavery: Studies in the Economy and Society of the Slave South*. New York: Pantheon, 1965.
Gordon, Lynn D. *Gender and Higher Education in the Progressive Era*. New Haven: Yale University Press, 1990.
Gould, Lewis. *Progressives and Prohibitionists: Texas Democrats in the Wilson Era*. Austin: University of Texas Press, 1973.
Grantham, Dewey W. *Hoke Smith and the Politics of the New South*. Baton Rouge: Louisiana State University Press, 1958.
———. *Southern Progressivism: The Reconciliation of Progress and Tradition*. Knoxville: University of Tennessee Press, 1983.
Green, James R. *Grass Roots Socialism: Radical Movements in the Southwest, 1895–1943*. Baton Rouge: Louisiana State University Press, 1978.
Greenwood, Janette Thomas. *Bittersweet Legacy: The Black and White "Better Classes" in Charlotte, 1850–1910*. Chapel Hill: University of North Carolina Press, 1994.
Griffith, Elisabeth. *In Her Own Right: The Life of Elizabeth Cady Stanton*. New York: Oxford University Press, 1984.
Grimes, Alan P. *The Puritan Ethic and Woman Suffrage*. New York: Oxford University Press, 1967.
Guy-Sheftall, Beverly. *Daughters of Sorrow: Attitudes Toward Black Women, 1880–1920*. Brooklyn: Carlson, 1990.
Haas, Edward F. *Political Leadership in a Southern City: New Orleans in the Progressive Era, 1896–1902*. Ruston, La.: McGinty Publications, 1988.
Hackney, Sheldon. *Populism to Progressivism in Alabama*. Princeton: Princeton University Press, 1969.
Hahn, Steven. *The Roots of Southern Populism: Yeoman Farmers and the Transformation of the Georgia Upcountry, 1850–1890*. New York: Oxford University Press, 1983.
Hall, Jacquelyn Dowd. *Revolt Against Chivalry: Jessie Daniel Ames and the Women's Campaign Against Lynching*. New York: Columbia University Press, 1974.
Harrison, Brian. *Separate Spheres: The Opposition to Women's Suffrage in Britain*. New York: Holmes and Meier, 1978.
Hart, Roger L. *Redeemers, Bourbons, and Populists: Tennessee, 1870–1896*. Baton Rouge: Louisiana State University Press, 1975.
Hawks, Joanne V., and Sheila L. Skemp, eds. *Sex, Race, and the Role of Women in the South*. Jackson: University Press of Mississippi, 1983.
Herr, Kincaid A. *Louisville and Nashville Railroad, 1850–1963*. Louisville: L&N Co., 1964.
Hill, Samuel S., ed. *Religion in the Southern States*. Macon, Ga.: Mercer University Press, 1983.
Holmes, William F. *The White Chief: James Kimble Vardaman*. Baton Rouge: Louisiana State University Press, 1970.

Howard, Perry H. *Political Tendencies in Louisiana*. Baton Rouge: Louisiana State University Press, 1957, 1971.
Hunter, Jane. *The Gospel of Gentility: American Women Missionaries in Turn-of-the-Century China*. New Haven: Yale University Press, 1984.
Ironmonger, Elizabeth Hogg, and Pauline Landrum Phillips. *History of the Woman's Christian Temperance Union of Virginia and a Glimpse of Seventy-Five Years 1883–1958*. Richmond: Cavalier Press, 1958.
Irvin, Helen Deiss. *Women in Kentucky*. Louisville: University Press of Kentucky, 1979.
Isaac, Paul E. *Prohibition and Politics: Turbulent Decades in Tennessee*. Knoxville: University of Tennessee Press, 1965.
Johnson, Evans C. *Oscar W. Underwood: A Political Biography*. Baton Rouge: Louisiana State University Press, 1980.
Johnson, Michael P. *Toward a Patriarchal Republic: The Secession of Georgia*. Baton Rouge: Louisiana State University Press, 1977.
Kirwan, Albert D. *Revolt of the Rednecks: Mississippi Politics, 1876–1925*. Lexington: University Press of Kentucky, 1951.
Klein, Maury. *History of the Louisville and Nashville Railroad*. New York: MacMillan, 1972.
Koonz, Claudia. *Mothers in the Fatherland: Women, The Family, and Nazi Politics*. New York: St. Martin's Press, 1987.
Kousser, J. Morgan. *The Shaping of Southern Politics: Suffrage Restriction and the Establishment of the One-Party South, 1880–1910*. New Haven: Yale University Press, 1974.
Kraditor, Aileen S. *The Ideas of the Woman Suffrage Movement, 1890–1920*. New York: Columbia University Press, 1965.
Kraditor, Aileen S., ed. *Up from the Pedestal: Selected Writings in the History of American Feminism*. New York: Quadrangle Books, 1968.
Langemann, Ellen C. *A Generation of Women: Education in the Lives of Progressive Reformers*. Cambridge: Harvard University Press, 1979.
Langhorne, Orra. *Southern Sketches from Virginia, 1881–1901*. Edited by Charles E. Wynes. Charlottesville: University of Virginia Press, 1964.
Larsen, Lawrence H. *The Urban South: A History*. Lexington: University Press of Kentucky, 1990.
Larsen, William. *Montague of Virginia: The Making of a Southern Progressive*. Baton Rouge: Louisiana State University Press, 1965.
Lee, David D. *Tennessee in Turmoil: Politics in the Volunteer State, 1920–1932*. Memphis: Memphis State University Press, 1979.
Lebsock, Suzanne. *"A Share of Honour": Virginia Women 1600–1945*. Richmond: Virginia State Library, 1987.
Lefler, Hugh Talmage, and Albert Ray Newsome. *North Carolina: The History of a Southern State*. Chapel Hill: University of North Carolina Press, 1973.
Lemons, J. Stanley. *The Woman Citizen: Social Feminism in the 1920s*. Urbana: University of Illinois Press, 1973.
Lerner, Gerda. *The Grimke Sisters from South Carolina: Rebels Against Slavery*. Boston: Houghton Mifflin, 1967.

Lewinson, Paul. *Race, Class, and Party: A History of Negro Suffrage and White Politics in the South*. London: Oxford University Press, 1932.
Lindig, Carmen. *The Path from the Parlor: Louisiana Women 1879–1920*. Lafayette, La.: Center for Louisiana Studies, 1986.
Link, William A. *The Paradox of Southern Progressivism, 1880–1930*. Chapel Hill: The University of North Carolina Press, 1993.
Little, Priscilla C., ed. *A New Perspective: Southern Women's Cultural History from the Civil War to Civil Rights*. Charlottesville: Virginia Foundation for the Humanities, 1989.
Litwack, Leon F. *Been in the Storm So Long: The Aftermath of Slavery*. New York: Vintage Books, 1979.
London, Lawrence F. *Bishop Joseph Blount Cheshire*. Chapel Hill: University of North Carolina Press, 1941.
London, Lawrence F., and Sarah M. Lemmon, eds. *The Episcopal Church in North Carolina, 1701 1959*. Raleigh: The Episcopal Diocese of North Carolina, 1987.
Mabry, William Alexander. *The Negro in North Carolina Politics since Reconstruction*. Durham, N.C.: Duke University Press, 1940.
Marable, Manning. *W. E. B. Du Bois: Black Radical Democrat*. Boston: Twayne Publishers, 1986.
Marks, Patricia. *Bicycles, Bangs, and Bloomers: The New Woman in the Popular Press*. Lexington: University Press of Kentucky, 1990.
Mathews, Donald G. *Religion in the Old South*. Chicago: University of Chicago Press, 1977.
Mathews, Donald G., and Jane Sherron De Hart. *Sex, Gender, and the Politics of ERA: A State and the Nation*. New York: Oxford University Press, 1990.
Mayo, A. D. *Southern Women in the Recent Educational Movement in the South*. 1892. Reprint, Baton Rouge: Louisiana State University Press, 1978.
McComb, David G. *Houston: The Bayou City*. Austin: University of Texas Press, 1969.
McDanel, Ralph. *The Virginia Constitutional Convention of 1901–02*. Baltimore: The Johns Hopkins University Press, 1928.
McDowell, John P. *The Social Gospel Movement in the South: The Women's Home Mission Movement in the Methodist Episcopal Church, South, 1886–1939*. Baton Rouge: Louisiana State University Press, 1982.
McMillan, Malcolm C. *Constitutional Development in Alabama, 1798–1901: A Study in Politics, the Negro and Sectionalism*. Chapel Hill: University of North Carolina Press, 1955.
Miller, Char, and Heywood T. Sanders, eds. *Urban Texas: Politics and Development*. College Station: Texas A&M University Press, 1990.
Miller, William D. *Memphis During the Progressive Era, 1900–1917*. Memphis: Memphis State University Press, 1957.
———. *Mr. Crump of Memphis*. Baton Rouge: Louisiana State University Press, 1964.
Moger, Allen Wesley. *Virginia: Bourbonism to Byrd, 1870–1925*. Charlottesville: University Press of Virginia, 1968.

Morgan, David. *Suffragists and Democrats: The Politics of Woman Suffrage in America.* East Lansing: Michigan State University Press, 1972.
Morrison, Joseph L. *Governor O. Max Gardner: A Power in North Carolina and New Deal Washington.* Chapel Hill: University of North Carolina Press, 1971.
Neverdon-Morton, Cynthia. *Afro-American Women of the South and the Advancement of the Race, 1895–1925.* Knoxville: University of Tennessee Press, 1989.
Newcomer, Mabel. *A Century of Higher Education for American Women.* New York: Harper & Brothers, 1959.
Niswonger, Richard. *Arkansas Democratic Politics, 1896–1920.* Fayetteville: University of Arkansas Press, 1990.
Nolen, Claude. *The Negro's Image in the South: The Anatomy of White Supremacy.* Lexington: University Press of Kentucky, 1968.
Norrell, Robert J. *Reaping the Whirlwind: The Civil Rights Movement in Tuskegee.* New York: Vintage Books, 1985.
O'Neill, William L. *Everyone Was Brave: The Rise and Fall of Feminism in America.* Chicago: Quadrangle Books, 1969.
Osborn, George Coleman. *John Sharp Williams: Planter-Statesman of the Deep South.* Baton Rouge: Louisiana State University Press, 1943.
Pearson, C. C., and J. Edwin Hendricks. *Liquor and Anti-Liquor in Virginia, 1619–1919.* Durham, N.C.: Duke University Press, 1967.
Pictorial Review of Baton Rouge. Baton Rouge: Sunday Times, 1921.
Potter, Fannie C. *History of the Texas Federation of Women's Clubs, 1918–1938.* Denton, Tex.: n.p., 1941.
Prather, H. Leon, Sr. *We Have Taken a City: Wilmington Racial Massacre and Coup of 1898.* Rutherford, N.J.: Associated University Presses, 1984.
Pulley, Raymond H. *Old Virginia Restored: An Interpretation of the Progressive Impulse, 1870–1930.* Charlottesville: University Press of Virginia, 1968.
Rabinowitz, Howard N. *The First New South, 1865–1920.* Arlington Heights, Ill.: Harlan Davidson, 1992.
Rabkin, Peggy. *Fathers to Daughters: The Legal Foundations of Female Emancipation.* Westport, Conn.: Greenwood Press, 1980.
Rable, George C. *Civil Wars: Women and the Crisis of Southern Nationalism.* Urbana: University of Illinois Press, 1989.
Rachleff, Peter J. *Black Labor in the South: Richmond, Virginia, 1865–1890.* Philadelphia: Temple University Press, 1984.
Raper, Arthur F. *The Tragedy of Lynching.* Chapel Hill: University of North Carolina, 1933.
Reynolds, George M. *Machine Politics in New Orleans, 1897–1926.* New York: Columbia University Press, 1936.
Rice, Lawrence D. *The Negro in Texas, 1874–1900.* Baton Rouge: Louisiana State University Press, 1971.
Richmond, Rebecca. *A Woman of Texas: Mrs. Percy V. Pennybacker.* San Antonio: Naylor, 1941.
Riley, Glenda. *Inventing the American Woman: A Perspective on Women's History.* Arlington Heights, Ill.: Harlan Davidson, 1987.

Rippy, Fred. *F. M. Simmons: Statesman of the New South*. Durham, N.C.: Duke University Press, 1936.

Salem, Dorothy. *To Better Our World: Black Women in Organized Reform, 1890–1920*. Brooklyn: Carlson, 1990.

Salmond, John. *Miss Lucy of the CIO: The Life and Times of Lucy Randolph Mason, 1882–1959*. Athens, Ga.: University of Georgia Press, 1988.

Scott, Anne Firor. *Making the Invisible Woman Visible*. Urbana: University of Illinois Press, 1984.

———. *The Southern Lady: From Pedestal to Politics, 1830–1930*. Chicago: University of Chicago Press, 1970.

Scott, Anne Firor, and Andrew M. Scott. *One Half the People: The Fight for Woman Suffrage*. Philadelphia and New York: Lippincott, 1975.

Shelton, Beth Anne, et al. *Houston: Growth and Decline in a Sunbelt Town*. Philadelphia: Temple University Press, 1989.

Simkins, Francis. *Pitchfork Ben Tillman: South Carolinian*. Baton Rouge: Louisiana State University Press, 1944.

Sinclair, Andrew. *The Better Half: The Emancipation of the American Woman*. New York: Harper and Row, 1965.

Sitterson, J. Carlyle. *Sugar Country: The Cane Sugar Industry in the South, 1753–1950*. Louisville: University of Kentucky Press, 1953.

Smith, H. Shelton. *In His Image, But . . . : Racism in Southern Religion, 1780–1910*. Durham, N.C.: Duke University Press, 1972.

Solomon, Barbara Miller. *In the Company of Educated Women: A History of Women and Higher Education in America*. New Haven: Yale University Press, 1985.

Solomon, Martha, ed. *In Their Own Voice: The Woman Suffrage Press, 1840–1910*. Tuscaloosa: University of Alabama Press, 1991.

Sosna, Morton. *In Search Of the Silent South*. New York: Columbia University Press, 1977.

Stanton, Elizabeth Cady, et al., eds. *History of Woman Suffrage*. 6 vols. Rochester and New York: Fowler and Wells, 1889–1922.

Starnes, George Talmage, and John Edwin Hamm. *Some Phases of Labor Relations in Virginia*. New York: Appleton-Century, 1934.

Talbot, Marion, and Lois Kimball Mathews Rosenberry. *The History of the American Association of University Women, 1881–1931*. Boston: Houghton Mifflin, 1931.

Tatum, Noreen. *A Crown of Service: A Story of Woman's Work in the Methodist Episcopal Church, South from 1878–1940*. Nashville: Parthenon Press, 1960.

Taylor, A. Elizabeth. *A Short History of the Woman Suffrage Movement in Tennessee*. Nashville: Joint University Libraries, 1943.

———. *The Woman Suffrage Movement in Tennessee*. New York: Bookman, 1957.

Thomas, Mary Martha. *The New Woman in Alabama: Social Reforms and Suffrage, 1890–1920*. Tuscaloosa: University of Alabama Press, 1992.

Timberlake, James. *Prohibition and the Progressive Movement*. Cambridge: Harvard University Press, 1963.

Tindall, George. *South Carolina Negroes, 1877–1900*. Columbia: University of South Carolina Press, 1952.

Vance, Linda. *May Mann Jennings: Florida's Genteel Activist*. Tallahassee: University of Florida Press, 1985.
Van Voris, Jacqueline. *Carrie Chapman Catt: A Public Life*. New York: Feminist Press, 1987.
Wall, Joseph Frazier. *Henry Watterson: Reconstructed Rebel*. New York: Oxford University Press, 1956.
Waller, William. *Nashville in the 1890s*. Nashville: Vanderbilt University Press, 1970.
———. *Nashville, 1900–1910*. Nashville: Vanderbilt University Press, 1972.
Wedell, Marsha. *Elite Women and the Reform Impulse in Memphis, 1875–1915*. Knoxville: University of Tennessee Press, 1991.
Wheeler, Marjorie Spruill. *New Women of the New South: The Leaders of the Woman Suffrage Movement in the Southern States*. New York: Oxford University Press, 1993.
Wiener, Jonathan M. *Social Origins of the New South: Alabama, 1860–1885*. Baton Rouge: Louisiana State University Press, 1978.
Williamson, Joel. *The Crucible of Race: Black-White Relations in the American South Since Emancipation*. New York: Oxford University Press, 1984.
Wilson, Charles R. *Baptized in Blood: The Religion of the Lost Cause, 1865–1920*. Athens: University of Georgia Press, 1980.
Winegarten, Ruthe, and Judith N. McArthur, eds. *Citizens at Last: The Woman Suffrage Movement in Texas*. Austin, Tex.: Ellen Temple Press, 1987.
Wood, Phillip J. *Southern Capitalism: The Political Economy of North Carolina, 1880–1980*. Durham, N.C.: Duke University Press, 1986.
Woodward, C. Vann. *Origins of the New South, 1877–1913*. Baton Rouge: Louisiana State University Press, 1951.
———. *The Strange Career of Jim Crow*. 3rd ed. New York: Oxford University Press, 1974.
Woody, Thomas. *A History of Women's Education in the United States*. New York: The Science Press, 1929.
Wynes, Charles E., ed. *Forgotten Voices: Dissenting Southerners in an Age of Conformity*. Baton Rouge: Louisiana State University Press, 1967.
Young, Ida, et al., eds. *History of Macon, Georgia*. Macon: Lyon, Marshall, and Brooks, 1950.

Articles

Allen, Lee N. "The Woman Suffrage Movement in Alabama." *Alabama Review* 11 (April 1958): 83–99.
Arendale, Marirose. "Tennessee and Women's Rights." *Tennessee Historical Quarterly* 39 (Spring 1980): 62–78.
Bailey, Fred Arthur. "Mildred Lewis Rutherford and the Patrician Cult of the Old South." *Georgia Historical Quarterly* 77 (Fall 1994): 509–35.
Barney, William L. "The Ambivalence of Change: From Old South to New in the Alabama Black Belt, 1850–1870." In *From the Old South to the New: Essays on the Transitional South*, edited by Walter J. Fraser Jr. and Winfred B. Moore Jr. Westport, Conn.: Greenwood Press, 1981.

Berkeley, Kathleen Christine. "Elizabeth Avery Meriwether, 'An Advocate for Her Sex': Feminism and Conservatism in the Post-Civil War South." *Tennessee Historical Quarterly* 43 (Winter 1984): 390-407.

Bland, Sidney R. "Fighting the Odds: Militant Suffragists in South Carolina." *South Carolina Historical Magazine* 82 (January 1981): 32-43.

———. " 'Mad Women of the Cause': The National Woman's Party in the South." *Furman Studies* 26 (December 1980): 82-89.

Brown, Elsa Barkley. "Womanist Consciousness: Maggie Lena Walker and the Independent Order of Saint Luke." *Signs* 14 (Spring 1989): 610-33.

Burr, Virginia. "A Woman Made to Suffer and Be Strong: Ella Gertrude Clanton Thomas, 1834-1907." In *In Joy and in Sorrow: Women, Family and Marriage in the Victorian South, 1830-1900*, edited by Carol Bleser. New York: Oxford University Press, 1991.

Cobb, James C. "Beyond Planters and Industrialists: A New Perspective on the New South." *Journal of Southern History* 54 (February 1988): 45-68.

Cott, Nancy F. "What's in a Name? The Limits of 'Social Feminism'; or, Expanding the Vocabulary of Women's History." *Journal of American History* 76 (December 1989): 809-29.

Doster, James F. "Railroad Domination in Alabama, 1885-1905." *Alabama Review* 7 (July 1954): 186-98.

DuBois, Ellen Carol. "The Radicalism of the Woman Suffrage Movement: Notes Toward the Reconstruction of Nineteenth-Century Feminism." *Feminist Studies* 3 (Fall 1975): 63-71.

———. "Working Women, Class Relations, and Suffrage Militance: Harriot Stanton Blatch and the New York Woman Suffrage Movement, 1894-1909." *Journal of American History* 74 (June 1987): 34-58.

DuBois, Ellen Carol, et al. "Politics and Culture in Women's History: A Symposium." *Feminist Studies* 6 (Spring 1980): 26-64.

Effland, Anne W. "Exciting Battle and Dramatic Finish: The West Virginia Woman Suffrage Movement [part 1]." *West Virginia History* 46 (1985-86): 137-58

———. "Exciting Battle and Dramatic Finish: West Virginia's Ratification of the Nineteenth Amendment." *West Virginia History* 48 (1989): 61-92.

———. "A Profile of Political Activists: Women of the West Virginia Woman Suffrage Movement." *West Virginia History* 49 (1990): 103-14.

Eudy, John Carroll. "The Vote and Lone Star Women: Minnie Fisher Cunningham and the Texas Equal Suffrage Association." *East Texas Historical Journal* 14 (1976): 52-59.

Flynt, J. Wayne. "Feeding the Hungry and Ministering to the Broken Hearted: The Presbyterian Church in the United States and the Social Gospel, 1900-1920." In *Religion in the South*, edited by Charles Reagan Wilson. Jackson: University Press of Mississippi, 1985.

Gilley, B. H. "Kate Gordon and Louisiana Woman Suffrage." *Louisiana History* 24 (Summer 1983): 289-306.

Graham, Sara Hunter. "Woman Suffrage in Virginia: The Equal Suffrage League and Pressure-Group Politics, 1909-1920." *Virginia Magazine of History and Biography* 101 (April 1993): 227-51.

Graves, John William. "Negro Disfranchisement in Arkansas." *Arkansas Historical Quarterly* 25 (Autumn 1967): 199–225.
Hawks, Joanne. "Like Mother, Like Daughter: Nellie Nugent Somerville." *Journal of Mississippi History* 45 (May 1983): 116–23.
Hewitt, Nancy A. "Beyond the Search for Sisterhood: American Women's History in the 1980s." *Social History* 10 (October 1985): 299–321.
———. "Politicizing Domesticity: Anglo, Black, and Latin Women in Tampa's Progressive Movements." In *Gender, Class, Race, and Reform in the Progressive Era*, edited by Noralee Frankel and Nancy Dye. Lexington: University Press of Kentucky, 1991.
Hoffecker, Carol. "Delaware's Woman Suffrage Campaign." *Delaware History* 20 (Spring/Summer 1983): 149–67.
Holt, Wythe. "The Virginia Constitutional Convention of 1901–1902: A Reform Movement Which Lacked Substance." *Virginia Magazine of History and Biography* 76 (January 1968): 67–130.
Howard, Jeanne. "Our Own Worst Enemies: Women Opposed to Woman Suffrage." *Journal of Sociology and Social Welfare* 9 (September 1982): 467–72.
Isaac, Rhys. "Evangelical Revolt: The Nature of the Baptists' Challenge to the Traditional Order in Virginia, 1765 to 1775." *William and Mary Quarterly* 31 (July 1974): 345–68.
Jackson, Joy. "Prohibition in New Orleans: The Unlikeliest Crusade." *Louisiana History* 19 (Summer 1978): 261–84.
Jemison, Marie Stokes. "Ladies Become Voters: Pattie Ruffner Jacobs and Woman's Suffrage in Alabama." *Southern Exposure* 6 (Spring 1979): 48–59.
Jensen, Billie Barnes. "'In the Weird and Wooly West': Anti-Suffrage Women, Gender Issues, and Woman Suffrage in the West." *Journal of the West* 32 (July 1993): 41–51.
Johnson, Guion Griffin. "The Ideology of White Supremacy, 1876–1910." In *Essays in Southern History*, edited by Fletcher M. Green. Chapel Hill: University of North Carolina Press, 1949.
Johnson, Kenneth R. "Florida Women Get the Vote." *Florida Historical Quarterly* 48 (January 1970): 299–312.
———. "Kate Gordon and the Woman-Suffrage Movement in the South." *Journal of Southern History* 38 (August 1972): 365–92.
———. "White Racial Attitudes as a Factor in the Arguments Against the Nineteenth Amendment." *Phylon* 31 (Spring 1970): 31–37.
Keeler, Rebecca. "Alma Belmont: Exacting Benefactor for Women's Suffrage." *Alabama Review* 41 (April 1988): 132–45.
Kemp, Kathryn. "Jean and Kate Gordon: New Orleans Social Reformers." *Louisiana History* 24 (Fall 1983): 389–401.
Kenneally, James J. "Catholicism and Woman Suffrage in Massachusetts." *Catholic Historical Review* 53 (April 1967): 43–57.
Kett, Joseph F. "Women and the Progressive Impulse in Southern Education." In *The Web of Southern Social Relations: Women, Family, and Education*, edited by Walter J. Fraser Jr. et al. Athens: University of Georgia Press, 1985.

Kirkley, Evelyn A. " 'This Work is God's Cause': Religion in the Southern Woman Suffrage Movement, 1880–1920." *Church History* 59 (December 1990): 507–22.

Kraditor, Aileen S. "Tactical Problems of the Woman Suffrage Movement in the South." *Louisiana Studies* 5 (Winter 1966): 289–307.

Lebsock, Suzanne. "Woman Suffrage and White Supremacy: A Virginia Case Study." In *Visible Women: New Essays on American Activism*, edited by Nancy A. Hewitt and Suzanne Lebsock. Urbana: University of Illinois Press, 1993.

Lerner, Gerda. "Early Community Work of Black Club Women." *Journal of Negro History* 59 (April 1974): 158–67.

Letsinger, Norman H. "The Status of Women in Southern Baptist Convention History in Historical Perspective." *Baptist History and Heritage* 12 (January 1977): 37–44.

Link, Arthur S. "The Progressive Movement in the South, 1870–1914." *North Carolina Historical Review* 23 (April 1946): 172–95.

Louis, James P. "Sue Shelton White and the Woman Suffrage Movement." *Tennessee Historical Quarterly* 22 (June 1963): 170–90.

Mabry, William Alexander. "Disfranchisement of the Negro in Mississippi." *Journal of Southern History* 4 (August 1938): 318–33.

———. "Louisiana Politics and the Grandfather Clause." *North Carolina Historical Review* 13 (October 1936): 290–310.

McBeth, Henry Leon. "The Role of Women in Southern Baptist History." *Baptist History and Heritage* 12 (January 1977): 3–25.

McCandless, Amy Thompson. "Progressivism and the Higher Education of Southern Women." *North Carolina Historical Review* 70 (July 1993): 302–25.

MacLean, Nancy. "White Women and Klan Violence in the 1920s: Agency, Complicity and the Politics of Women's History." *Gender & History* 3 (Autumn 1991): 285–303.

Mambretti, Catherine Cole. "The Battle Against the Ballot: Illinois Woman Antisuffragists." *Chicago History* 9 (Fall 1980): 168–77.

———. "The Burden of the Ballot: The Woman's Anti-Suffrage Movement." *American Heritage* 30 (December 1978): 24–35.

Marchiafava, Louis J. "Law Enforcement on the Urban Frontier: Houston, 1878–1928." In *Houston: A Twentieth Century Urban Frontier*, edited by Francisco Rosales and Barry J. Kaplan. Port Washington, N.Y.: Associated Faculty Press, Inc., 1983.

Marshall, Susan E. "In Defense of Separate Spheres: Class and Status Politics in the Antisuffrage Movement." *Social Forces* 65 (December 1986): 327–51.

Mayor, Mara. "Fears and Fantasies of the Anti-Suffragists." *Connecticut Review* 5 (April 1972): 64–74.

Miller, Randall. "Daniel Pratt's Industrial Urbanism: The Cotton Mill Town in Antebellum Alabama." *Alabama Historical Quarterly* 34 (Spring 1972): 3–22.

Moss, Margaret Anne. "Miss Millie Rutherford, Southerner." *Georgia Review* 7 (Spring 1953): 57–66.

Newell, Mary Gathright. "Mary Munford and Higher Education for Women in Virginia." In *Stepping Off the Pedestal: Academic Women in the South*, edited by

Patricia A. Stringer and Irene Thompson. New York: Modern Language Association of America, 1982.
Newman, Harvey K. "The Role of Women in Atlanta's Churches." *Atlanta Historical Journal* 23 (Winter 1979–80): 3–30.
Nutt, Rick. "Robert Lewis Dabney, Presbyterians, and Women's Suffrage." *Journal of Presbyterian History* 62 (Winter 1984): 340–51.
Parrott, Angie. " 'Love Makes Memory Eternal': The United Daughters of the Confederacy in Richmond, Virginia, 1897–1920." *In the Edge of the South: Life in Nineteenth-Century Virginia*, edited by Edward L. Ayers and John C. Willis. Charlottesville: University Press of Virginia, 1991.
Porter, Melba. "Madeline McDowell Breckinridge: Her Role in the Kentucky Woman Suffrage Movement, 1908–1920." *Register of the Kentucky Historical Society* 72 (October 1974): 342–63.
Prescott, Grace E. "The Woman Suffrage Movement in Memphis: Its Place in the State, Sectional and National Movements." *West Tennessee Historical Society Papers* 18 (1964): 87–106.
Riegel, Robert. "Split of the Feminist Movement in 1869." *Mississippi Valley Historical Review* 49 (December 1962): 485–96.
Ross, Frances Mitchell. "The New Woman as Club Woman and Social Activist in Turn of the Century Arkansas." *Arkansas Historical Quarterly* 50 (Winter 1991): 317–51.
Schott, Matthew J. "The New Orleans Machine and Progressivism." *Louisiana History* 24 (Spring 1983): 141–54.
———. "Progressives Against Democracy: Electoral Reform in Louisiana, 1894–1921." *Louisiana History* 20 (Summer 1979): 247–60.
Scott, Anne Firor. "After Suffrage: Southern Women in the 1920s." *Journal of Southern History* 30 (August 1964): 298–318.
———. "The Ever-Widening Circle: The Diffusion of Feminist Values from the Troy Female Seminary, 1822–72." In *Making the Invisible Woman Visible*. Urbana: University of Illinois Press, 1984.
———. "Most Invisible of All: Black Women's Voluntary Associations." *Journal of Southern History* 56 (February 1990): 3–22.
———. "The New Woman in the New South." *South Atlantic Quarterly* 61 (Autumn 1962): 417–83.
Scott, Janelle D. "Local Leadership in the Woman Suffrage Movement: Houston's Campaign for the Vote, 1917–1918." *The Houston Review* 12 (1990): 3–22.
Scott, Joan W. "Gender: A Useful Category of Historical Analysis." *American Historical Review* 91 (December 1986): 1053–75.
Sims, Anastatia. " 'Powers that Pray' and 'Powers that Prey': Tennessee and the Fight for Woman Suffrage." *Tennessee Historical Quarterly* 50 (Winter 1991): 203–25.
———. " 'The Sword of the Spirit': The WCTU and Moral Reform in North Carolina, 1883–1933." *North Carolina Historical Review* 64 (October 1987): 395–415.
Smedley, Katherine. "Martha Schofield and the Rights of Women." *South Carolina Historical Magazine* 85 (July 1984): 195–210.

Stevenson, Louise L. "Women Anti-Suffragists in the 1915 Massachusetts Campaign." *New England Quarterly* 52 (March 1979): 80–93.

Strom, Sharon. "Leadership and Tactics in the American Woman Suffrage Movement: A New Perspective from Massachusetts." *Journal of American History* 62 (September 1975): 296–315.

Sumners, Bill. "Southern Baptists and Woman's Right to Vote, 1910–1920." *Baptist History and Heritage* 12 (January 1977): 45–51.

Swenson, Mary E. "The Formative Years of the Alabama League of Women Voters, 1920–1921." *Alabama Historical Quarterly* 32 (Summer 1975): 115–35.

Talmadge, John E. "Rebecca Latimer Felton, Georgian." *Georgia Review* 9 (Spring 1955): 65–73.

Taylor, A. Elizabeth. "The Last Phase of the Woman Suffrage Movement in Georgia." *Georgia Historical Quarterly* 43 (March 1959): 11–28.

———. "The Origins of the Woman Suffrage Movement in Georgia." *Georgia Historical Quarterly* 28 (June 1944): 63–79.

———. "Revival and Development of the Woman Suffrage Movement in Georgia." *Georgia Historical Quarterly* 42 (December 1958): 339–54.

———. "South Carolina and the Enfranchisement of Women: The Early Years." *South Carolina Historical Magazine* 77 (April 1976): 115–26.

———. "South Carolina and the Enfranchisement of Women: The Later Years." *South Carolina Historical Magazine* 80 (October 1979): 298–310.

———. "Woman Suffrage Activities in Atlanta." *Atlanta Historical Journal* 23 (Winter 1979–80): 45–54.

———. "The Woman Suffrage Movement in Arkansas." *Arkansas Historical Quarterly* 15 (Spring 1956): 17–42.

———. "The Woman Suffrage Movement in Florida." *Florida Historical Quarterly* 36 (July 1957): 42–60.

———. "The Woman Suffrage Movement in Mississippi, 1890–1920." *Journal of Mississippi History* 30 (February 1968): 1–34.

———. "The Woman Suffrage Movement in North Carolina." *North Carolina Historical Review* 38 (January 1961): 45–62, 173–89.

———. "The Woman Suffrage Movement in Texas." *Journal of Southern History* 17 (May 1951): 194–215.

Taylor, Lloyd C. "Lila Mead Valentine: The FFV as Reformer." *Virginia Magazine of History and Biography* 70 (October 1962): 471–87.

Terborg-Penn, Rosalyn. "Discontented Black Feminists: Prelude and Postscript to the Passage of the Nineteenth Amendment." In *Decades of Discontent: The Women's Movement, 1920–1940*, edited by Lois Scharf and Joan M. Jensen. Westport, Conn.: Greenwood Press, 1983.

———. "Nineteenth Century Black Women and Woman Suffrage." *Potomac Review* 7 (Spring/Summer 1977): 13–24.

Thomas, Mary Martha."The 'New Woman' in Alabama, 1890 to 1920." *Alabama Review* 43 (July 1990): 163–84.

Thurner, Manuela. " 'Better Citizens Without the Ballot': American Antisuffrage Women and Their Rationale during the Progressive Era." *Journal of Women's History* 5 (Spring 1993): 33–60.

Treadway, Sandra Gioia. "A Most Brilliant Woman: Anna Whitehead Bodeker and the First Woman Suffrage Association in Virginia." *Virginia Cavalcade* 43 (Spring 1994): 166–77.
Turner, Elizabeth Hayes. " 'White-Gloved Ladies' and 'New Women' in the Texas Woman Suffrage Movement." In *Southern Women: Histories and Identities*, edited by Virginia Bernhard, Betty Brandon, Elizabeth Fox-Genovese, and Theda Perdue. Columbia: University of Missouri Press, 1992.
Varon, Elizabeth R. " 'The Ladies Are Whigs': Lucy Barbour, Henry Clay, and Nineteenth-Century Virginia Politics." *Virginia Cavalcade* 42 (Autumn 1992): 72–83.
Warnick, Barbara. "The Rhetoric of Conservative Resistance." *Southern Speech Communication Journal* 42 (Spring 1977): 256–73.
Wellman, Judith. "The Seneca Falls Women's Rights Convention: A Study of Social Networks." *Journal of Women's History* 3 (Spring 1991): 9–37.
Welter, Barbara. "The Cult of True Womanhood, 1820–1860." *American Quarterly* 18 (Summer 1966): 151–74.
Wheeler, Marjorie Spruill. "Mary Johnston, Suffragist." *Virginia Magazine of History and Biography* 100 (January 1992): 99–119.
Wygant, Larry J. " 'A Municipal Broom': The Woman Suffrage Campaign in Galveston Texas." *The Houston Review: History and Culture of the Gulf Coast* 6 (1984): 117–34.
Young, Dina M. "The Silent Search for a Voice: The St. Louis Equal Suffrage League and the Dilemma of Elite Reform." *Gateway Heritage* 8 (Spring 1988): 2–19.

Unpublished Papers, Theses, and Dissertations

Allen, Lee Norcross. "The Woman Suffrage Movement in Alabama." M.A. thesis, Alabama Polytechnic Institute, 1949.
Bachman, Linda S. "Uncompromising Sisters: The Woman's Suffrage Movement in Louisiana, 1900–1921." Honors thesis, Tulane University, 1981.
Bowles, Willie D. "History of the Woman Suffrage Movement in Texas." M.A. thesis, University of Texas, 1939.
Camhi, Jane Jerome. "Women Against Women: American Antisuffragism, 1880–1920." Ph.D. diss., Tufts University, 1973.
Clare, Carol Jean. "The Woman Suffrage Movement in Virginia: Its Nature, Rationale, and Tactics." M.A. thesis, University of Virginia, 1968.
Dinwiddie, Worth. "History of Mothers' Pensions in Louisiana." M.A. thesis, Tulane School of Social Work, 1935.
Drescher, Nuala McGann. "The Opposition to Prohibition, 1900–1919." Ph.D. diss., University of Delaware, 1964.
Friedman, Belinda Bundy. "Orie Latham Hatcher and the Southern Women's Educational Alliance." Ph.D. diss., Duke University, 1981.
Gammage, Judie Karen Walton. "Quest for Equality: An Historical Overview of Woman's Rights Activism in Texas, 1890–1975." Ph.D. diss., North Texas University, 1982.
Gilmore, Glenda Elizabeth. "Gender and Jim Crow: Women and the Politics of

White Supremacy in North Carolina, 1896–1920." Ph.D. diss., University of North Carolina at Chapel Hill, 1992.
———. " 'When Woman Shall Have Entered Every Door of Usefulness': The Double-Edged Feminism of Southern Black Women, 1892–1920." Paper presented to Berkshire Conference, 1990.
Green, Elna C. "Settlement Houses and the Origins of Social Work in the South." Paper presented to the Southern Historical Association, 1994.
———. "Those Opposed: Southern Antisuffragists, 1890–1920." Ph.D. diss., Tulane University, 1992.
Hanmer, Trudy J. "A Divine Discontent: Mary Johnston and Woman Suffrage in Virginia." M.A. thesis, University of Virginia, 1972.
Jablonsky, Thomas James. "Duty, Nature, and Stability: The Female Anti-Suffragists in the United States, 1894–1920." Ph.D. diss., University of Southern California, 1978.
Johnson, Kenneth R. "The Woman Suffrage Movement in Florida." Ph.D. diss., Florida State University, 1966.
Kelly, Mary Kathryn. "Antisuffrage Arguments in Georgia, 1890–1920." M.A. thesis, Emory University, 1973.
Kilman, Gail Apperson. "Southern Collegiate Women, Higher Education at Wesleyan Female College and Randolph-Macon Woman's College, 1893–1907." Ph.D. diss., University of Delaware, 1984.
Knott, Claudia. "The Woman Suffrage Movement in Kentucky, 1879–1920." Ph.D. diss., University of Kentucky, 1989.
Long, Thomas L. "Gendered Spaces in Molly Elliot Seawell's *Throckmorton*." Paper presented at the Virginia Humanities Conference, April 1994.
MacLean, Nancy K. "Behind the Mask of Chivalry: Gender, Race, and Class in the Making of the Ku Klux Klan of the 1920s in Georgia." Ph.D. diss., University of Wisconsin-Madison, 1989.
Merideth, Mary L. "The Mississippi Woman's Rights Movement, 1889–1923: The Leadership Role of Nellie Nugent Somerville." M.A. thesis, Delta State College, Cleveland, Miss., 1974.
Price, Margaret Nell. "The Development of Leadership by Southern Women Through Clubs and Organizations." M.A. thesis, University of North Carolina, 1945.
Roth, Darlene Rebecca. "Matronage: Patterns in Women's Organizations, Atlanta, 1890–1940." Ph.D. diss., George Washington University, 1978.
Shadron, Virginia A. "Out of Our Homes: The Woman's Rights Movement in the Methodist Episcopal Church, South, 1890–1918." M.A. thesis, Emory University, 1976.
Sharber, Patricia F. "The Social Attitudes of the Episcopal Church of Tennessee, 1865–1898." M.A. thesis, Vanderbilt University, 1970.
Shelton, Charlotte Jean. "Woman Suffrage and Virginia Politics, 1909–1920." M.A. thesis, University of Virginia, 1969.
Sims, Anastatia. "Beyond the Ballot: The Radical Vision of the Antisuffragists." Paper presented to Southern Historical Association, November 1990.
———. "The Foundation for a Sisterhood: Origins of Women's Clubs in North

Carolina, 1890–1930." Paper presented to the First Southern Conference on Women's History, Converse College, June 1988.
———. "The Woman Suffrage Movement in Texas." Honors thesis, University of Texas, Austin, 1974.
Spiers, Patricia. "The Woman Suffrage Movement in New Orleans." M.A. thesis, Southeastern Louisiana College, 1965.
Steelman, Joseph F. "The Progressive Era in North Carolina, 1884–1917." Ph.D. diss., University of North Carolina at Chapel Hill, 1955.
Stites, Anne Hamilton. "The Inconceivable Revolution in Virginia, 1870–1920." M.A. thesis, University of Richmond, 1965.
Stone-Erdman, Janet. "A Challenge to Southern Politics: The Woman Suffrage Movement in North Carolina, 1913–1920." M.A. thesis, North Carolina State University, 1986.
Strawn, Sharon. "Woman Suffrage: The Texas Movement, 1868–1920." M.A. thesis, Hardin-Simmons University, 1982.
Tipton, Nancy Carol. " 'It Is My Duty': The Public Career of Belle Kearney." M.A. thesis, University of Mississippi, 1975.
Varon, Elizabeth Regine. " 'We Mean to Be Counted': White Women and Politics in Antebellum Virginia." Ph.D. diss., Yale University, 1993.
Wilkerson-Freeman, Sarah. "The Emerging Political Consciousness of Gertrude Weil: Education and Women's Clubs, 1879–1914." M.A. thesis, University of North Carolina, 1985.
Wooley, Robert Howard. "Race and Politics: The Evolution of the White Supremacy Campaign in 1898 in North Carolina." Ph.D. diss., University of North Carolina, 1977.
Zimmerman, Loretta Ellen. "Alice Paul and the National Woman's Party, 1912–1920." Ph.D. diss., Tulane University, 1964.

INDEX